THE ILLUSTRATED ENCYCLOPEDIA OF

FENg SHUI 風水

THE ILLUSTRATED ENCYCLOPEDIA OF

FENG SHUI

風水

THE COMPLETE GUIDE TO THE ART AND PRACTICE OF FENG SHUI

LILLIAN TOO

ELEMENT

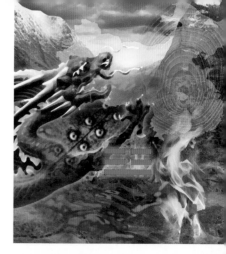

Element
An Imprint of HarperCollins*Publishers*
77–85 Fulham Palace Road
Hammersmith, London W6 8JB

The website address is: www.thorsons.com

First published in Great Britain in 1999 by
Element Books Limited

10 9 8 7 6 5 4 3 2 1

Designed by
THE BRIDGEWATER BOOK COMPANY LIMITED

Illustrations: Peter and Bernard Gudynas,
Ivan Hissey, Nadine Faye James, Ray Martin,
James Neal, Jim Pilston, Stephen Raw

A catalogue record for this book
is available from the British Library

ISBN 1 86204 589 5

Printed and bound in Great Britain by
Butler & Tanner Ltd, Frome and London

CONTENTS

INTRODUCTION

WHAT IS FENG SHUI?

ABOVE *The science of Feng Shui has been practiced in China for at least 3,500 years.*

Feng Shui is an ancient science that goes back at least 3,500 years. The practice of Feng Shui has its roots in the Chinese way of viewing the universe, where all things on the Earth are categorized into the five basic elements (fire, metal, earth, wood, and water) and take on implications of positive or negative energy. This energy is known as Chi, or, more colorfully, the dragon's cosmic breath, which brings good fortune for those who are surrounded by it. The five elements make up a central pillar of Feng Shui analysis and practice and each of these elements can have either Yin or Yang attributes.

Literally translated, Feng Shui means wind and water and refers to the Earth, its mountains, valleys, and waterways, whose shape and size, direction and levels are created by the interaction of these powerful forces. As a technique for living, Feng Shui is best understood as the science of selecting or arranging a living environment where the five elements and the Yin and Yang energies are in complete harmonious balance, thereby bringing the good life to those who reside within that environment.

Feng Shui is also an art – born of experience and common sense – and the skill of correcting disharmony in the environment and of improving one's immediate living and work space to strengthen further this vital balance and harmony.

A certain mysticism continues to surround the practice of Feng Shui. Understanding its many canons and guidelines requires the acceptance of fundamental theories about the universe which may seem alien in the context of modern-day perceptions of the way the world works. Portrayals of perspectives, landscapes, and environments are usually expressed in symbolic representations. Metaphors that embrace classical and mythical Chinese references to animals, elements, and the intangible forces of Yin and Yang energies reflect the ancient roots of this science.

The philosophy and classical techniques of Feng Shui may be studied in those ancient source books that have survived, but the practical usage and the applications of Feng Shui have come down the centuries mostly by word of mouth, passed on from generation to generation, thereby linking it with superstition. As a result, while the theory of Feng Shui

PART ONE
A BACKGROUND TO FENG SHUI

History and concepts of Feng Shui.

PART TWO
THE FUNDAMENTALS OF FENG SHUI

Landscape and Compass Formula Feng Shui. Symbolism, tools, and practical guidelines.

LEFT *The great stele on the summit of Taishan, China, where emperors performed the important "feng" and "shan" sacrifices to the wind and earth. The interaction of the elements has always been fundamental to the practice of Feng Shui.*

PART THREE
FENG SHUI IN THE HOME

Feng Shui for all types of homes, rooms, and interiors.

PART FOUR
PERSONAL FENG SHUI AND FENG SHUI FOR THE FAMILY

Feng Shui for the family, love and marriage, health, careers, and travel.

is not difficult to grasp, the correct application of Feng Shui in a modern context requires at least some basic understanding of its core premises.

The growing popularity of Feng Shui in modern times and at the start of the new millennium may be put down to the fact that it really does work. Feng Shui is indeed a way of living that brings greater happiness and satisfaction into our lives. More than that, Feng Shui is also not difficult to practice. Once you get down to studying it, so much of the practice of Feng Shui seems to be common sense. Many of its basic concepts are very easy to understand: all that is needed is the sheer determination to learn and the confidence to apply it.

This encyclopedia has been written especially for the amateur Feng Shui practitioner who wants to have a comprehensive reference book that covers all aspects of this science. The great promise of Feng Shui is that it will bring wealth, prosperity, and happiness. Its effective practice in today's modern environment – where so many people live in crowded cities and in apartments rather than the open spaces of the countryside – requires patience to learn the fundamentals and the firmness of mind to master the various formulas. Feng Shui practice also improves with experience, and effectiveness improves with an

RIGHT *Feng Shui offers cures and antidotes for all kinds of hostile structures.*

PART FIVE
FENG SHUI IN THE GARDEN

Feng Shui for all types of garden, water features, garden structures, and lighting.

PART SIX
FENG SHUI IN THE BUSINESS WORLD

Tips for entrepreneurs, retail businesses, and corporations.

intelligent approach. Understand the fundamentals but think through the application of theory to your particular environment. Work with what you have.

It is practically impossible to get your Feng Shui completely correct. A place with ideal or perfect Feng Shui is genuinely rare and, even when you do get most of your Feng Shui correct, there is also the "time dimension" to consider. Sometimes, despite excellent spatial Feng Shui, you might well go through intermittent periods of bad luck due to what are referred to as "bad flying stars." Therefore, you need sufficient experience before you can get all the meanings and all the interpretations correct. But if you persevere and really arrange your living space according to the Feng Shui guidelines contained in this encyclopedia, your practice of Feng Shui will improve, and over time you will see your life, your work, and your family begin to benefit enormously. Success will come to each member of the family. If you have your own business, Feng Shui can help you make the most of your office location and improve working relationships among employees. There are Feng Shui tips on methods of significantly improving your profit by creating exciting new business opportunities and attracting new customers. Marriages will get better, families get closer, incomes improve. Health will become more robust and relationships will be enhanced. Feng Shui offers so much and at so little cost.

Once you understand Feng Shui, you will develop an increasing sensitivity to your environment, and with this awareness will come a respect for the environment. By then you will be half way to developing the Feng Shui "eye." As you read this book, be as skeptical as you wish, but consider that the

LEFT *Follow Feng Shui guidelines to ensure health, wealth, success, and happiness for you and your family.*

practice of Feng Shui does not require you to believe in it. You do not have to believe in Feng Shui for it to work. It is neither a religious nor a spiritual practice. It requires no compromise of any of your moral or religious beliefs.

As long as you get your analysis correct according to the theories that underpin the practice you will see Feng Shui working positively for you. If you carry out Feng Shui changes diligently and pay attention to the accuracy and correctness of dimensions and directions, you will definitely benefit from Feng Shui. When reading this encyclopedia, keep an open mind and allow yourself time to understand the way Feng Shui works.

PART SEVEN
FENG SHUI TIPS FOR ALL ENVIRONMENTS

Feng Shui cures and antidotes; dealing with poison arrows.

PART EIGHT
FENG SHUI DICTIONARY

An A–Z reference guide to Feng Shui terms.

木火土金水

PART ONE

A BACKGROUND
TO FENG SHUI

THE ORIGINS OF FENG SHUI

The origins of Feng Shui go back to antiquity. The earliest recorded Feng Shui started in the Tang Dynasty but for centuries, access to authentic Feng Shui knowledge and the classical texts that contained its many secrets was confined to the Imperial family and to China's ruling classes. In this century, however, Feng Shui has become widely accessible to all classes of people, and increasingly popular. It has crossed the wide waters to a great many lands, and in recent years in countries with a strong overseas Chinese population – places such as Taiwan, Hong Kong, and Singapore – Feng Shui has become an essential part of life. And now, it is gaining increasing acceptance in many Western countries as well.

Contemporary Feng Shui talks about harnessing the dragon's cosmic breath in the context of Tien, Ti, and Ren: the trinity of heaven, earth, and mankind luck. This book places Feng Shui in perspective and offers everything needed to bring Feng Shui enticingly within reach of everyone. Thus all the basic concepts, including Yin – Yang cosmology, the five elements' interactions, the compass fundamentals, and the symbolism are covered in fascinating and practical detail. Welcome then to the world of dragons and tigers.

LEFT *Feng Shui originated in ancient China 3,500 years ago. For centuries it remained the exclusive preserve of the Imperial family, and China's ruling classes.*

HISTORY AND BACKGROUND

ABOVE *Early Feng Shui practitioners concerned themselves with the symbolism of the landscape. Later, a more scientific approach emerged, Compass School Feng Shui, which examined specific orientations based on the positions of the eight trigrams around the Pa Kua, and the numbers of the Lo Shu square.*

BELOW *This gently undulating landscape is one of the telltale signs that indicates the presence of the auspicious green dragon.*

Feng Shui has been practiced in China as a formalized technique of selecting auspicious sites since the Tang Dynasty, and probably the most famous Feng Shui master of his day was Yang Yun Sang, who is widely recognized in the old texts as the "founder" of Landscape Feng Shui as we know it today. Master Yang left a legacy of classics that have survived the centuries. As a leading figure at the court of the emperor Hi Tsang (888 B.C.E.), Master Yang's books on the capturing and harnessing of the dragon's breath were required reading in the Imperial exams. He thus exerted tremendous influence at court.

Master Yang's books on what eventually came to be recognized as Feng Shui were also the basis upon which succeeding generations of practitioners set their knowledge. His emphasis was on the shape of the mountains, the direction of water courses, and most of all, on searching for the green dragon's lair hidden in the undulating ridges and valleys of mountain ranges.

Master Yang's theories focused on the way to locate the auspicious dragon in places where dragons do not prominently stand forth. He emphasized the importance of the dragon's breath on the well-being of a household and he went to great lengths to describe places and land formations that enjoyed this breath, which he termed cosmic and central to the core of Feng Shui practice.

Master Yang formulated several important theories that later became the basis of the entire Form and Landscape School of Feng Shui recognized in later centuries as the fundamental texts of Feng Shui. He used the dragon metaphor extensively, and he described landforms, shapes, and weather conditions in terms of the dragon's body parts or the dragon's mood – wrathfulness or frolicking.

Master Yang's theories were also detailed in three famous classics, all of which describe Feng Shui formations in terms of colorful dragon allegories. The first of his great books was *Han Lung Ching*, translated as the "Art of Rousing the Dragon." The second was *Ching Nang Ao Chih*, which explains the methods of locating the dragon's lair. The third book, *I Lung Ching*, "Canons Approximating Dragons," offers detailed instructions on searching for dragons in areas where they are difficult to find.

Many extracts from, and commentaries on, old Feng Shui texts, including the many treatises on Landscape Feng Shui, can be found in Taiwan where Feng Shui practice is widespread. Master Yang's principles came to be regarded as the Form School of Feng Shui, which describes good and bad Feng Shui in terms of the visual appearance of the physical landscape – more specifically hills and mountain ranges.

Hills were described as green dragons and white tigers, and places with good Feng Shui required the presence of the dragon. A corollary of the theory was that wherever there was the dragon there too would be the tiger. Form School Feng Shui practitioners thus began their search for good sites by finding a green dragon. Emphasis was put on landforms, shapes of hills and mountains, and waterways, their orientations and directions. Indeed, how to locate the dragon and its lair made up the greater part of Landscape Feng Shui theory.

Eventually, however, dragon symbolism gave way to the more scientific emphasis of compass orientations. Form School Feng Shui gave way to Compass Formula Feng Shui, which based its analysis on the *I Ching*'s eight trigrams, and the placement of these trigrams

LEFT *Landscape Feng Shui uses the symbolism of the green dragon and white tiger to describe auspicious mountain or hill formations.*

Modern Feng Shui practitioners in Hong Kong and Taiwan today practice a combination of both schools. This book embraces both schools of Feng Shui and indeed assigns much credibility to the importance of the shapes and forms of the topography as well as the levels of the environment. But I also practice Compass Formula Feng Shui extensively, having seen it work with impressive frequency. My approach has been to make certain that the landscape and environment around any abode is harmonious and will benefit from the dragon and its cosmic breath, rather than be hurt by the killing breath of hostile structures.

I look on the practice of landscape Feng Shui as the best form of defensive Feng Shui. It is only after I have ascertained that the dragon's presence around my home brings auspicious breath – the good *Sheng Chi* – that I proceed to energize the various compass formulas I am in possession of, and which have been summarized in this book. Many of the compass formulas are extremely potent, and their application quickly brings positive results.

Astride these two schools of Feng Shui sits the parallel practice of Symbolic Feng Shui: the practice of displaying auspicious good fortune symbols in the home and in the palaces of the emperors goes back to antiquity, as evidenced by the many artifacts dug up since time immemorial. In China, good luck symbols and good luck deities abound, so that homes are said to attract great prosperity and abundance, good health and long life when certain relevant symbols are prominently and correctly displayed. Symbolic Feng Shui is also covered in this book.

ABOVE *Chinese coins, which symbolize the unity of heaven and earth, are auspicious for luck in business and finance.*

around an eight-sided symbol known as the Pa Kua. Compass Feng Shui also used the nine-grid symbol known as the Lo Shu magic square. These symbols, as well as the *Ghanzi* system of the Chinese calendar, the theory of the five elements and maintaining the balance of Yin and Yang, formed the metaphysical speculations that grew up around the practice of Compass Formula Feng Shui.

Compass School Feng Shui stressed the influence and importance of compass directions. Good or bad Feng Shui was defined in terms of the suitability of directions based on a person's date of birth, their sex, as well as the elements that were deemed to be "ruling" at the time of birth. These formulas gave rise to different methods of creating good Feng Shui.

Compass Feng Shui also introduced the concept of time

dimensions into Feng Shui. Using the magic Lo Shu square to provide the basis of numerological calculations, compass methods thus address both time and spatial concepts of Feng Shui. In the early days of the development of Compass Formula Feng Shui, practitioners assigned little importance to the forms and shapes in the environment. The influence of the dragon as postulated by old Master Yang was ignored.

In the end, practitioners realized that the efficacy of the Compass School could not entirely ignore the effect of surrounding hills and water on the well-being of households. In the late nineteenth and early twentieth centuries the two schools of Feng Shui merged. Dragon symbolism reemerged and its appeal widened considerably but Compass Formula applications also continued to gain ground.

SEE ALSO
❖ Landscape Feng Shui *pp.54–65*
❖ Compass Formula Feng Shui *pp.66–79*

CHAPTER ONE: THE ORIGINS OF FENG SHUI

FENG SHUI IN CHINA

ABOVE
Businessmen in China still adhere to the principles of Feng Shui, even if they are not always convinced of its importance in the modern world.

BELOW *The layout of the buildings and water flows in the Forbidden City in Beijing indicates the influence of Feng Shui principles.*

The Chinese have always believed in Feng Shui. Those whose knowledge is based on scholarly works practice it with a reverence, especially the merchant class, traders, and those in business who have benefited enormously from it. Those whose exposure to Feng Shui comes from their parents regard it as superstition. However, they still observe its basic tenets.

In ancient China, only those belonging to the privileged class had access to Feng Shui expertise and knowledge. For centuries, Feng Shui remained the exclusive domain of the Imperial family and the mandarins who managed the emperors' courts. Many of the family homes of the old Manchu courtiers, and the Imperial palaces inside the Forbidden City itself show evidence that Feng Shui has been practiced.

In the old days, Feng Shui enjoyed immense royal patronage. Emperors were particularly concerned about the orientation of Imperial burial grounds. It was firmly believed that the fortunes of the living were largely determined by the quality of ancestral Feng Shui, and China is full of legends and local tales that describe in lyrical terms the graves of the fathers of emperors like Chu Yuan Chuan, who founded the Ming Dynasty, or of Sun Yat Sen, who became the President of China around the turn of the century. Visitors to Beijing can, if they they wish, drive to the northern outskirts of the city to view the historic Ming tombs, which were constructed according to strict Feng Shui guidelines.

More recently, there has been speculation that two of the country's leaders, Mao Tse Tung and Deng Xiao Ping, owed their rise to power in China to the most special orientation of their respective ancestors' graves.

Designing ancestral graves according to Feng Shui is a practice that is still popular in Taiwan, where wealthy families go to great lengths not only to bury their dead in an auspicious orientation, but also to ensure that grave sites are properly maintained and guarded. In particular, they make certain that the drainage and water flows are always auspicious. Living patriarchs of prominent families also select their burial plot in advance to ensure that family fortunes stay intact, and that descendants continue to bring honor to the family name.

In earlier times, Feng Shui also featured strongly in the planning of towns and cities. Canton's prosperity was due to its propitious location on the Pearl River delta, while Shanghai's famous bund was believed to have brought great wealth to this metropolis. At the start of the twentieth century, Hong Kong was no more than a barren rock, but with proper Feng

ABOVE *The good* *helped the lasting*
Feng Shui of Hong *financial success of*
Kong harbor has *the former colony.*

Shui observance by the local population, aided by the excellent orientations of its harbor, the colony has continued to prosper.

In the old days emperors often forbade the practice of Feng Shui and history relates that certain emperors would go out of their way to obscure the old texts, thereby preventing those who might be a threat to the dynasty from practicing Feng Shui and consequently achieving some power. Chinese storybooks describe how the first Ming emperor, Chu Yuan Chuan, had the whole country flooded with fake Feng Shui books that contained ambiguous guidelines on landscape Feng Shui based on incorrect and contradictory theories.

Centuries later, when Mao Tse Tung became the new "emperor" of China, he too was a cunning Feng Shui practitioner. Mao spent a lifetime studying the "Twenty-Four Annals of the Dynasties." Obsessed with the fear of being overthrown, it is said that the "great helmsman" studied books on strategy and politicking in the courts of the old emperors. Like Chu Yuan Chuan,

Mao did not wish anyone to use Feng Shui to loosen his grip on the country, and throughout his time in power Mao banned the practice of Feng Shui in China.

LEFT *Tai chi being practiced on Shanghai's Bund, whose location is believed to be responsible for the city's past prosperity and where it is again growing today.*

CHAPTER ONE: THE ORIGINS OF FENG SHUI

FENG SHUI IN TAIWAN, HONG KONG, AND ELSEWHERE

ABOVE *Master Yap Cheng Hai, the Feng Shui master who has generously revealed some special Feng Shui formulas.*

While the practice of Feng Shui waned in China, Chinese who had fled their homeland and settled in faraway countries continued to keep the practice alive. Feng Shui flourished especially in Taiwan, where many expert Feng Shui masters and practitioners followed Chiang Kai Shek after he was defeated by communists and fled the mainland. The general took with him thousands of old texts on Feng Shui and the masters who followed him continued to put their skills to work – in the process benefiting the Feng Shui of Chiang's regime as well as the island's business community. Today the Feng Shui that is practiced in Taiwan contains some precious Compass School formulas. Two of these formulas have come to see the light of day through the generosity of Master Yap Cheng Hai, who, when he was very young, traveled to Taiwan to study advanced Feng Shui under an old and revered Feng Shui master. Yap Cheng Hai's Feng Shui master was a doyen of Feng Shui practice in Taiwan, consulted by many of the country's leading tycoons. Although he was altogether of another age, many of his disciples continue to practice today. It is

BELOW *The Governor of Hong Kong, C. H. Tung, who reportedly declined to move into the former Governor's mansion due to its bad Feng Shui.*

ABOVE *Hong Kong at night. Good Feng Shui practices have helped to* *make this city one of the most prosperous business centers in the world.*

surely no coincidence that Taiwan is such a prosperous place today!

Feng Shui also flourished in Hong Kong, where many Chinese refugees settled. Today, Hong Kong has become the unofficial capital of Feng Shui and Chinese residents there consider Feng Shui to be a way of life. Indeed, the first post-1997 Chinese Governor of Hong Kong – C. H. Tung – made headlines around the world when he indicated he would not be moving into either the colonial Governor's mansion or the colonial Governor's old office because he believed both locations suffered from inauspicious Feng Shui!

Probably the most exciting development of recent years has been the revival and reemergence of interest in Feng Shui in China. The practice has been brought back by overseas Chinese now investing in business ventures in the new China. Whole townships and property projects spearheaded by Hong Kong Chinese, for instance, now reveal evidence of the Feng Shui man's input.

Another exciting development has been the growing acceptance and popularity of Feng Shui among Western-educated Chinese now

living in the Chinatowns of the United States, Canada, Australia, the United Kingdom, Europe, and Southeastern Asia. In places where there is a significant overseas Chinese population – such as Singapore and Malaysia – Feng Shui is growing in popularity. Many Chinese are eagerly rediscovering the wonderful promise of a practice that is part of their cultural heritage.

In tandem with this growing acceptance of Feng Shui among overseas Chinese has been the increasing awareness and acceptance of Feng Shui by other communities. Feng Shui in the West started as part of the New Age movement that focused on the totality of the mind, body and spirit of mankind. New Age sought out the esoteric teachings of the East, and in the process discovered both the promise and potential of Feng Shui. In recent years Feng Shui has been enjoying growing mainstream appeal – it has now crossed to all corners of the globe.

FENG SHUI GOSSIP FROM HONG KONG

Many Hong Kong residents believe that the famous martial arts superstar Bruce Lee's death was due to bad Feng Shui. The story goes that, in taking the name Hsiao Loong (or Little Dragon), Bruce Lee had offended the nine dragons of Kowloon. They would wait for the right moment to teach the upstart little dragon a lesson. That moment arrived during a typhoon which caused Bruce Lee's protective Pa Kua mirror to fall. Unprotected, the nine dragons had their way and Bruce Lee died prematurely...

Last Governor Chris Patten was believed to have suffered from the bad Feng Shui of the Governor's mansion. There are those who believe that the Hong Kong Governor's mansion had always had excellent Feng Shui, being supported by Victoria Peak and facing the sea – the classical green dragon, white tiger orientation. This excellent Feng Shui had effectively been destroyed with the building of the Bank of China with sharp edges and huge crosses on its façade. One of the edges of the

buildings appeared to slice at the Governor's mansion, affecting Chris Patten's Feng Shui. Residents of Hong Kong were thus not surprised when his Chinese successor, C. H. Tung, politely declined to move into the mansion as expected.

The Hong Kong Bank and its two guardian lions is one of the most famous of Hong Kong's landmarks. Completed in the mid-eighties, several Feng Shui masters worked with the architect to ensure the perfect flow of Chi into the building. The most auspicious Feng Shui feature is the "bright hall" in front of the building. Local gossip has it that in a moment of Feng Shui foresight, one of the bank's taipans in the last century bought the land in front of the building and donated it to the Government, with the condition that nothing was to be built on the land. The bank's entrance thus has an unencumbered view of the sea, and the bright hall allows auspicious Chi to settle for a moment before gently leading into the bank.

BELOW *The Feng Shui of the Hong Kong Governor's mansion was reportedly spoiled by the killing energy of the Bank of China building.*

RIGHT *Bruce Lee, the star of many martial arts movies, who died at an early age – some say because of bad Feng Shui.*

FENG SHUI TRIVIA FROM SINGAPORE

ABOVE *Singapore's prime minister, Lee Kuan Yew, is thought to have used Feng* *Shui in order to aid the republic's stunning economic growth.*

Many people have expressed admiration for Singapore's phenomenal growth and the man who has guided this tiny city state to prosperity – Cambridge-educated Lee Kuan Yew. The gossip among Feng Shui people in Southeastern Asia is that Singapore's good fortune and Mr. Lee's success owe as much to Feng Shui as to his genius.

Mr. Lee apparently enjoyed a close relationship with one of the best Feng Shui masters in the world, a humble monk whose knowledge of Feng Shui is described in reverential terms as being legendary. The story goes that, when Singapore was building its

superb Mass Transit Railroad systems in the early to mid-eighties, the digging had caused the Singapore economy to take a downturn. A worried Mr. Lee apparently turned to his Feng Shui expert for helpful advice. The monk told Mr. Lee that to enable Singapore's fortunes to recover everyone should hang up a Pa Kua – the eight-sided Feng Shui symbol. His Cabinet expressed doubt that, in a multiracial society such as Singapore's, the Government would be able to persuade the population to display a symbol that is so obviously Chinese.

Mr. Lee apparently had his own solution. He introduced the Pa Kua-shaped one dollar coin, which still exists today. Despite this measure, however, Singapore's economy did not recover.

Upon further consultation with the monk, it was suggested that the Pa Kua shape should be more openly displayed, whereupon a novel solution was implemented. The road tax disks on cars took on a Pa Kua shape. This obviously worked since the

economy recovered forthwith. Every car in Singapore now had a Pa Kua shape on its windshield. This practice continues today.

Some years later the monk became ill and it is speculated that when asked, the monk advised that a dragon be placed looking over the mouth of the Singapore River, since this would forever protect Singapore's symbol – the merlion.

Once again another way of safeguarding Singapore's continued prosperity was found. Thus a dragon was to be placed on the top left-hand corner of the country's fifty dollar bill. As the note bore a scene of the Singapore river and harbor, the dragon would be symbolically poised above the merlion, thereby safeguarding its prosperity forever. The next time you go to Singapore you might want to check its fifty dollar bill…

BELOW *To preserve Singapore's prosperity, Mr. Lee even redesigned a* *banknote depicting a dragon guarding Singapore's river and harbor.*

THE PHILOSOPHY OF TIEN TI REN

LEFT *Feng Shui is based on the philosophy of three aspects of luck in our life that affect us: Tien Chai, the heaven luck with which we are born; Ti Chai, the earth luck that is created by our surroundings; and Ren Chai, the mankind luck that we create for ourselves.*

Feng Shui is not a spiritual practice which creates miracles. It does not bring overnight success. It does not change the circumstances of an individual's life immediately. Feng Shui works according to the quality of the energies that surround any domestic or work space. Those who would promise instant wealth, winning the lottery and creating immediate gratification, do not truly understand Feng Shui.

Feng Shui cannot create good fortune on its own but it can create favorable energy around your home or office so that, when bad luck strikes, it tempers the ill-fortune and reduces the loss, making things easier to bear. And when one is going through a time of good fortune according to one's fate or destiny, beneficial Feng Shui enhances the good fortune, bringing greater good luck than if there had been bad Feng Shui. This is based on the philosophy of *Tien, Ti* and *Ren*, the Chinese words for heaven, earth and mankind. This is the trinity of luck. First there is

heaven luck, with which one is born. Heaven luck, or *Tien Chai*, is *not* within anyone's control. No one has dominion over the circumstances of his or her birth, nor of the good and bad periods of one's life. This is why all the great cultures of the world have divination methods that attempt to read one's fate and destiny based on birthcharts and other methods of fortunetelling. This is why prayer is so powerful, and why religion plays such a vital part in life. Divine help from heaven is not within mankind's control and it is not to be confused with Feng Shui.

Earth luck, *Ti Chai*, is within our control. Earth luck is the luck that comes from the environment and this gets strengthened when the Feng Shui of one's surroundings is auspicious.

Viewed within this context, Feng Shui takes on a significant perspective, for if earth luck is within one's control – and, indeed, if we can actively create good Feng Shui in our homes and offices – then doing something to improve

our personal environments must significantly illuminate our life's luck. Feng Shui is a vital component of the circumstances of one's being, for it addresses that part of our destiny over which we can exercise control.

Feng Shui luck brings opportunities, improves chances of success, enhances our living conditions, and creates peace and goodwill in our relationships. Feng Shui luck reaches its maximum potential only when accompanied by equally strong and excellent mankind luck – *Ren Chai* – and this, as the name suggests, is also within our control.

Thus, while having good Feng Shui brings opportunities for advancement and the promise of higher income, if one does not work at complementing one's propitious fortune with good old-fashioned hard work, a positive attitude and a determined outlook (all components of mankind luck), then all your good Feng Shui gets squandered. Mankind luck is the luck you create for yourself.

CHAPTER ONE: THE ORIGINS OF FENG SHUI

FENG SHUI'S APPLICATIONS

Feng Shui practice can be applied to almost every facet of the living and working condition. It has to do with enhancing the energies of the surrounding environment as well as the immediate living and working space. It functions on the premise that if one lives – breathes, sleeps, sits, eats, and works – surrounded by healthy, vibrant energy, then one will be enveloped by an aura of good vibrations that attract excellent good fortune. On the other hand, if one is shrouded by bad energy, dead energy, or killing energy, the environment brings grave misfortunes.

Good luck comes in many different ways and is made up of all your material and spiritual aspirations. Bad luck also manifests itself in different guises: these vary from getting sick, to losing money, to missing opportunities, to being plagued by accidents, constant failure and having everything go wrong with your life. Enjoying good Feng Shui in effect gives you an edge over your competitors. Sustaining bad Feng Shui places you at a very real disadvantage.

Feng Shui principles should be incorporated into the design and layout of homes and offices. If you are in business, Feng Shui can enhance your turnover and your profits. If you are a career professional, Feng Shui will bring you opportunities for profitable recognition. If you are searching for love and happiness, Feng Shui could well bring you a family.

Your home might be a bungalow, a townhouse, an apartment, or a single room, shared with someone or at college. Your home may be rented or owned; it can be temporary or permanent.

ABOVE *Good Feng Shui will ensure happy and successful relationships.*

Any space where you retire to at the end of each day for rest, relaxation, and rejuvenation should offer you the benefits of an auspicious and harmonious flow of energy. When your home enjoys good Feng Shui, you will be wrapped with a vibrant and revitalizing energy.

Every room within the home can benefit from Feng Shui, including more public areas like living rooms and dining rooms, as well as the private areas like family rooms and bedrooms. Layout, orientations, shapes, color schemes, placement of furniture, decorative objects, and paintings all add to the totality of the whole. How to put them together directly to benefit the residents is what Feng Shui application is about.

The best way to benefit from this book is to take a systematic approach. Grasp the basic fundamentals and concepts of Feng Shui before attempting to investigate what is wrong or right about your own Feng Shui. Develop an awareness of the buildings, roads, and structures around you, and try to evolve a sensitivity to the energies around

ABOVE *Bad Feng Shui can lead to many problems at work, leading to stress and possibly illness.*

you. Develop also a solutions-oriented attitude. For everything that you conclude is not according to Feng Shui principles, first satisfy yourself as to why you think it is not right and then test your understanding of the concepts by coming up with solutions that fall within the guidelines.

Remember that there are practical and inexpensive remedies to most Feng Shui problems, and it is seldom necessary to resort to expensive measures. If you cannot do anything about a diagnosed problem, investigate the rest of this book. You may find a solution in the Dictionary section or in the feature boxes scattered throughout.

You can also apply a combination of the various schools of Feng Shui. Do not be surprised by the multitude of Feng Shui guidelines that seem to proliferate in the marketplace today. Different masters offer different recommendations depending on where and how they acquired their knowledge. Remember that among the old masters who live in the East, few would willingly divulge what they rightly regard as their trade secrets. Even among the Chinese, different dialect groups approach the practice differently.

When in doubt, apply a healthy dose of common sense. Do not confuse the set of guidelines that apply to the Form School with those associated with the Compass School. The two schools are very different but both depend on basic concepts for interpretations and correct practice. Focus on developing a working knowledge of the fundamental theories and guidelines. With practice you can use this encyclopedia to do your own Feng Shui.

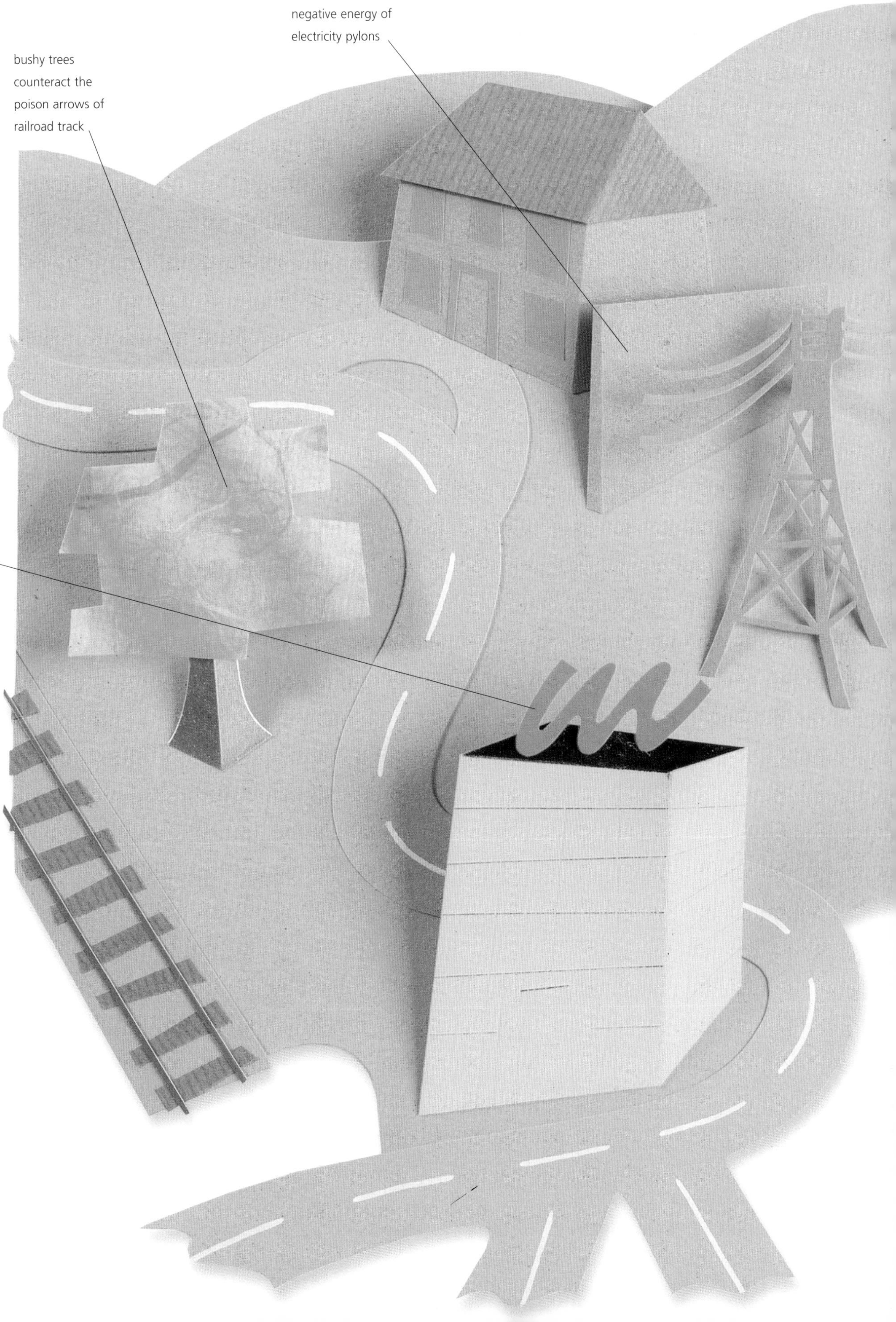

high wall deflects
negative energy of
electricity pylons

bushy trees
counteract the
poison arrows of
railroad track

corporate logo
displayed on top of
office building

RIGHT *The practice
of Feng Shui can be
successfully applied
to your home,
workplace, and the
environment.*

CHAPTER ONE: THE ORIGINS OF FENG SHUI

FENG SHUI TODAY

The practice of Feng Shui in today's world differs substantially from its historical origins. Today Feng Shui is freely available to everyone: it is used by rich and poor alike, as a result of which the practice is applied to individual residences and work places, and by individuals.

Secondly, Feng Shui is today being practiced in a dramatically different world. Because the physical landscape of the world has changed so much, Feng Shui today has greatly adapted old precepts. The growth of cities and the popularity of apartment living in an urban setting have necessitated a reinterpretation of the old texts.

BELOW Modern cities such as Chicago may seem far removed from the ancient laws of Feng Shui, but these are being understood in new ways appropriate to changed conditions.

LEFT The wisdom of the Feng Shui masters that was practiced during the Tang dynasty has been adapted and applied to modern life – skyscrapers are today's mountains and highways are seen as rivers.

New meanings have been attributed to old metaphors.

Thus dragons and tigers, turtles and phoenixes are superimposed onto a cityscape for purposes of interpreting Landscape and Form School Feng Shui in a modern metropolis. In a modern city of high rises, manmade buildings have come to be regarded as mountains; depending on shape, location, and structure, they are likened to the celestial animals of Landscape Feng Shui.

Highways have been described as rivers, while city roads become purveyors of Chi flows. Skyscrapers and large buildings are now regarded as mountains and elevated landforms, and so become symbolic of one of the celestial creatures, with their shapes determining what kind of element they are categorized as. Making this leap in interpretation requires careful application of the theories that make up the basis and the historical context of Feng Shui applications. Once again, therefore, it becomes necessary to refer back to the underlying fundamental concepts upon which all the schools of Feng Shui, and all its compass formulas, are based. Always bear this in mind.

LEFT *Contemporary interiors can still benefit from the fundamental concepts of Feng Shui, even though they were formulated centuries ago.*

CHAPTER ONE: THE ORIGINS OF FENG SHUI

YIN AND YANG FENG SHUI

ABOVE *Yin Feng Shui concerns itself with silence and death and in Taiwan and Malaysia this branch of Feng Shui is still practiced today. An auspicious burial ground ensures that the grave faces an open view backed by a mountain to ensure continued good fortune for the deceased's family.*

In the old days, Feng Shui was extensively applied to Yin dwellings, which are basically ancestral burial grounds. The textbooks on Feng Shui treat Yin Feng Shui as a subject that is separate and different from Yang Feng Shui. Symbols and reference points for the purposes of calculations differ for these two types of dwellings.

The Feng Shui referred to in this book and in all my books is Yang Feng Shui, which is applicable only to Yang dwellings, or houses of the living.

This is not to say that Yin Feng Shui is no longer practiced today. In Taiwan it remains a very important branch of the Feng Shui that is practiced by many of its more prominent families. Ancestral burial grounds for the older generation of families are usually purchased long before their demise, with the grave of the family patriarch or father receiving the most careful attention. This is because the fortunes of the descendants are said to be substantially affected by the Feng Shui of the immediate ancestor's grave. In Malaysia, Yin Feng Shui continues to be studied and practiced by a small group of enthusiastic practitioners. Some of

the more prominent patriarchs of wealthy business families have already selected their graves; they have had them designed according to basic Landscape Feng Shui, with the grave backed by a mountain and facing a view that is not blocked in any way.

Yin Feng Shui is said particularly to affect the male descendants of the family. Female descendants are less affected by ancestral burial grounds. Nevertheless, because one has little control over the actual orientation of most graves in a modern cemetery, I have always advocated that to be on the safe side it might be better not to have a grave at all for one's ancestor. The alternative – cremation – is both respectable and acceptable. According to Feng Shui experts, the effect on descendants' luck is neutral, neither good nor bad, when the patriarch is cremated. This approach allows us peace of mind when we decide how

we should bury our dead. This also puts the focus squarely on Yang dwellings, which is far more meaningful and easy to do.

This book deals only with Yang Feng Shui. This distinction is important since the basic tools used in all the recommendations given are based on the Later Heaven arrangement of trigrams in the Pa Kua, which differs substantially from the Early Heaven arrangement of trigrams. The chapter on the tools of Feng Shui (*see pages 111–121*) gives a detailed explanation of the significance of the arrangement of the trigrams in the Pa Kua.

A second reason for making this distinction is to draw the reader's attention to the intrinsic difference between Yin and Yang energies. Houses of the living are deemed to

ABOVE *If your home is situated next to a cemetery, building a wall in between will help to deflect the Yin energy.*

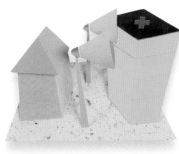

ABOVE *Counteract a Yin energy imbalance from a jail, hospital, or police station with two tall spotlights.*

ABOVE *If you are living in an apartment, position a bright light in the window overlooking a Yin building.*

be Yang because Yang energy represents life, activity, movement, and growth. Yin energy, on the other hand, suggests stillness, silence and death. When applying Feng Shui to Yang dwellings, therefore, it is vital to understand that Yang influences should dominate, though never to the extent that Yin energies are completely absent. The chapter on Feng Shui concepts gives a more thorough explanation (*see pages 31–51*).

Understanding the difference between Yin and Yang Feng

LEFT *A lively home atmosphere, enhanced by the presence of children or pets, is ideal for encouraging essential living Yang energy.*

Shui will enable the amateur practitioner to understand why experts always recommend against siting one's home within the vicinity of buildings that have Yin-dominated energies. Places like hospitals, prisons, cemeteries, abattoirs, and so forth generate too much Yin energy, which creates the kinds of vibrations that are entirely unsuitable for Yang dwellings. They are thus to be avoided.

Experts also warn against living in buildings constructed on land that previously housed such places, believing the Yin energies previously there linger on. Hence, when looking for a suitable new home, always investigate the recent history of the site upon which your new home will be located. Avoid sites where death or killing has taken place (such as an abattoir) in the recent past.

If you already live near Yin-energy dominated places and absolutely cannot move out, the Feng Shui remedy is to introduce features which create Yang energies that effectively balance out the Yin energies. If you live too near a cemetery, paint the side of the wall that faces the cemetery bright red. This will absorb the Yin energy emanating from the cemetery.

If you live next to a hospital, a nursing home, a police station, or even a prison, a very effective way to counter the Yin energy is to erect two tall and bright spotlights between your house and the building. If you live in an apartment next to a hospital place a bright light in any of the windows that open to a view of the hospital or other such buildings.

If your home is built on land which was once a cemetery, or had a hospital or any other Yin dominated structure on it, paint your walls a bright color, keep the radio on for most of the day, and create activity within your home. If your home is empty for most of the day, keep a pet – a dog or a cat, since this is the best way of activating valuable Yang energy.

Even if your home does not suffer from any of the above problems, implementing my suggestions will be auspicious because it represents good Feng Shui to generate Yang energies.

SEE ALSO
❖ The Concept of Balance: Yin and Yang *pp.46–7*
❖ Yin and Yang Energies in Illness *pp.211–13*

FENG SHUI CONCEPTS

The dragon's cosmic breath or Chi is central to the understanding and practice of Feng Shui. Chi is invisible; it is a potent force that circulates in the environment. Good Feng Shui exists when auspicious Chi gathers and accumulates. Such Chi energy brings good fortune. Bad Feng Shui occurs when Chi turns malignant and becomes deadly. The practice of Feng Shui is learning how to tell the difference between good and bad Chi; how to diffuse and overcome bad Chi and how to create and magnify good Chi.

Acquiring these skills requires an appreciation of Feng Shui's basic concepts. Clues are found in the eight trigrams and their arrangements around the eight-sided Pa Kua symbol. It is necessary to develop a deep understanding of the five elements – fire, water, earth, metal, and wood – and their many interactions. Feng Shui also addresses the concept of balance and harmony between the elements, especially in the way they manifest upon the surrounding landscape. Awareness of the environment introduces the symbolism of the four celestial creatures that feature strongly in Landscape Feng Shui. Feng Shui shows you how to activate the essence of these creatures to create great good fortune in your life.

LEFT *It is important for modern practitioners to develop an appreciation and understanding of the age-old concepts behind the art of Feng Shui.*

CHAPTER TWO: FENG SHUI CONCEPTS

THE CONCEPT OF CHI: the dragon's cosmic breath

Feng Shui finds beautiful expression in the flows of invisible energy that gently waft through the earth and the sky, floating on its waters, carried along by gentle breezes, bringing abundant happiness and prosperity wherever it circulates and settles. The Chinese refer to this intrinsic energy as Chi.

Chi is the unseen delicate force that moves through the human body and the environment, invisible and unnoticed, yet always potent. Chi can be compared to radio waves, telephone signals, radar, and magnetic vibrations. Yoga practitioners allude to "Prana," the inner breath that mysteriously energizes the human body, giving a strange sort of strength, an extraordinary kind of vigor. The Chinese regard Chi as the mysterious inner energy, which gives strength and soul to mankind.

BELOW *Chi energy can be manifested in many ways, sometimes subtly, sometimes dramatically, as with this blow by a Kung fu master.*

ABOVE *The literal translation of Feng Shui is "wind and water"; wind for direction, water for wealth.*

Chi is created when, for instance, a monk sits in deep meditation and expertly controls his breathing; each time a kung fu master delivers a well-aimed blow; when the artist calligrapher makes an exquisite brushstroke. In each of these activities a special kind of inner vitality accompanies the movement to create a unique power, a life-force that chaperones the breathing, the action of the blow, and the brushstroke, making each of these actions distinctive and superior. These are manifestations of human Chi.

In Feng Shui, Chi is viewed as an ever-present force that circulates and moves in the environment. Both indoors and out, on land, in water, across mountains… Chi is everywhere. It is the invisible energy that vibrates across the lands of the world, moving, whirling and dispersing, or circulating and settling… and wherever Chi settles it brings with it a special kind of energy that attracts good fortune.

Feng Shui is often described as the art of harnessing "wind and water" to capture and create Chi. The ancients refer to Chi as the dragon's cosmic breath, assigning to it magical connotations that are expressed in lyrical terms. Chinese literature is rich in extraordinary explanations of how balance and harmony in the environment create a wealth of Chi flows. Such explanations attribute the caprices of heaven and earth and their effects on the destinies of mankind to these invisible currents. The Chinese view their fates as being inextricably entwined, with the creative and destructive powers of Nature. The two elements – wind and water – cause the landscape to change and transform, bringing destruction as well as creation. Mankind has always had to exist alongside continuing changes of the landscape brought about by the wind and waters.

In so doing, mankind has inevitably sought explanations about the lie of the land, the way rivers flow and mountain ranges stand, comparing many of Nature's landscapes to the shapes and characteristics of four celestial creatures. Thus the dragon, the tiger, the phoenix, and the turtle came to take on important roles in the basic descriptions of Feng Shui. In particular the celestial dragon came to embody the illustrative aspects of Feng Shui explanations. In addition, much of good or bad Feng Shui came to be expressed as inhaled and exhaled Chi, the vital life-enhancing energy.

It was also believed that Chi was the real power that created the landscapes of the world, its mountains and rivers, hills and valleys. Chi was believed to determine the shapes, forms, and colors of the environment, as well as the health of plants and trees, and all the living creatures within, including and especially man.

In man, Chi is the spirit that governs human behavior and

activity. The excellence of its glow (or lack of it) within the mortal body is what determines the health and vitality of the person. The ancients sought to attain perfection by balancing their internal Chi so that its flow through the body was

smooth and unimpeded, in the process creating a positive aura of vibrancy and energy.

Human Chi differs in quantity and quality from one person to another. Often Chi currents get blocked, causing ailments with negative outcomes. Thus techniques were developed to enhance human Chi, through meditation, kung fu martial arts exercises, or controlled breathing.

Enhancing human Chi alone was deemed insufficient. One also had to live in harmony with the environment. Thus the Chi of the human body had to be in harmony with the Chi of one's surroundings. Household Chi and human Chi had to flow smoothly, the one in rhythm with the other. Feng Shui thus implies living compatibly with one's environment, fitting comfortably into the place we call home, and generally feeling relaxed, happy, and full of the vital life-force.

The entire body of knowledge, techniques, and underlying philosophy of Feng Shui are all about capturing, creating, and accumulating good Sheng Chi (loosely translated as the growth Chi). Feng Shui is also about deflecting, dissolving, and destroying what is termed Shar Chi, or the killing Chi, the kind that brings bad luck.

The techniques of achieving these two goals of Feng Shui are based on interpreting and applying the basic concepts that underpin Feng Shui practice. When one understands these concepts, it becomes easier to appreciate the nuances of Feng Shui. These concepts do not explain how Feng Shui works, but they establish the foundation upon which the practice of Feng Shui is based. They offer explanations into the Chinese view of the universe, an approach that is quite alien to the Western scientific tradition.

LEFT *Meditation is just one of the methods that can be used to improve the flow of vital Chi around the human body.*

BELOW *Chi is the invisible, intrinsic, and potent force circulating in the environment – the dragon's cosmic breath which shapes the landscape.*

SEE ALSO
❖ The Flow of Chi inside the Home *p.150*
❖ Yin, Yang, and Chi *p.249*
❖ Using Lights to lift the Chi , *p.307*

CHAPTER TWO: FENG SHUI CONCEPTS

THE I CHING

ABOVE *A section of a tenth-century copy of the* I Ching, *or Book of Changes, showing the first lines of the Chien hexagram.*

The major source book of Feng Shui is the *I Ching*. The *I Ching* is a text rich with the wisdom of the ancients. Meanings abound, some obvious, some hidden, all derived from the eight mysterious and deceptively simple three-lined trigrams that double up to become the 64 hexagrams of the *Book of Changes*.

Both branches of Chinese philosophy – Confucianism and Taoism – have common roots in the *I Ching* and its origins go back to mythical antiquity. As a book of divination or as a book of wisdom, the *I Ching* has occupied the attention of China's most eminent scholars through the centuries. All that is great and significant in the many centuries of Chinese cultural history has taken its inspiration from the *I Ching*: the philosophy of the Chinese race as well as its science and statecraft have borrowed from the distinctive

ABOVE *An 18th-century Taoist robe decorated with Yin and Yang symbols and the Eight Trigrams.*

prudence of the *I Ching*. The most commonplace practices of everyday life in China are deeply affected by its influence and it is from this singularly great book that many of the cryptic secrets of Feng Shui take their inspiration.

As a result numerous aspects of Feng Shui's many related principles on symbolism, and on its view of the trinity of heaven, earth, and man, take their cue and associations

from the trigrams placed around the eight-sided Pa Kua. The significance of numbers on the Pa Kua comes from the sequence and placement of numbers around the Lo Shu magic grid. Analysis of the quality of the flow of Chi is based on the Pa Kua and compounded by the numbers of the Lo Shu.

Practical applications of the method of Feng Shui then take account of balance and harmony. It is at this stage that the interactions of Yin and Yang, positive and negative, as well as the relationships between the five elements start to add additional layers of meaning to the applications of Feng Shui.

The influence of the *I Ching* on Feng Shui philosophy and procedures is particularly evident in the prominent role played by the eight-sided Pa Kua symbol, with its eight trigrams. Indeed, many of the so-called "Diviners' Formulas" are derived from the special placement and symbolic connotations of these trigrams, which themselves are also the origins of the *I Ching*'s 64 hexagrams. There is thus close interrelationship between Feng

RIGHT *The trigrams positioned around the eight-sided Pa Kua represent the trinity of the Universe: heaven, earth, and man – a principle fundamental to the practice of Feng Shui.*

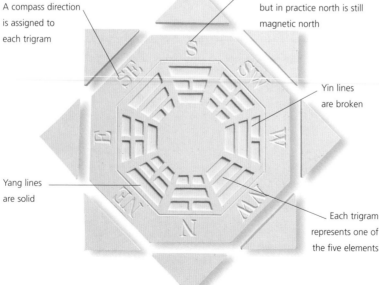

A compass direction is assigned to each trigram

Convention puts south at the top of the compass, but in practice north is still magnetic north

Yin lines are broken

Yang lines are solid

Each trigram represents one of the five elements

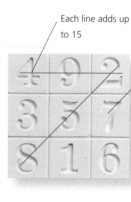

Each line adds up to 15

The Lo Shu grid identifies specific compass sectors

ABOVE *The numbers shown on the Lo Shu square are said to unlock the secrets of the eight-sided Pa Kua.*

Shui formulas and the *I Ching*'s divination aspects.

This is reflected in the similiar philosophical concepts of harmony and balance which both embody. In view of these similarities any attempts to differentiate the blanket of images and symbols from the concepts that represent the whole body of Feng Shui knowledge require a fairly profound knowledge of the classical *I Ching*. This means studying its origins and history, its hexagrams, the eight trigrams, and all derivatives.

The trigrams play a central role in giving the Feng Shui practitioner an understanding of the basis of recommendations offered by a Feng Shui master. Knowledge of the trigrams vastly expands the theoretical basis for Feng Shui's guidelines. Understanding the trigrams lends credence to the practice of Feng Shui and, more importantly, enables the recipient of such advice to consider whether what is being recommended is reasonable, or at least acceptable.

There are not many authentic or reliable translations of the *I Ching*. The earliest translations were published in the late nineteenth century (undertaken by Western academics Wilhelm and James Legge). Probably the most comprehensive and certainly the finest translation of the *I Ching* is the one by Richard Wilhelm who spent more than ten years working on the Texts and related Commentaries of the *I Ching*. Long residence in China, mastery of both the written and spoken language and close association with the cultural leaders of the day made it possible for him to perceive the Chinese classics and understand their profusion of images from the Chinese perspective.

Wilhelm started work on the project in 1911 after the Chinese revolution, when Tsingtao became the residence of several eminent

classical scholars. Among them was Lao Nai-Tsuan, who, in the words of Wilhelm in the Preface of his translation, "...opened my mind to the wonders of the *Book of Changes*." Lao was a scholar of the old school, one of the last of his kind who was thoroughly familiar with the great field of Commentary literature that grew up around the *I Ching* through the centuries. Under Lao's experienced guidance and after much detailed discussion, translation of the Text proceeded. The project was interrupted by the First World War but was later resumed and completed. "These were rare hours of inspiration that I spent with my aged master," says Wilhelm.

Wilhelm's *I Ching* was translated into German, and it was left to another scholar, Cary F. Baynes, to translate it into English, thus making the great wisdom of the *I Ching* available to a wider audience. Overseas Chinese, like the author and many of her contemporaries, whose knowledge of and exposure to so-called "authentic Chinese culture" is at best adapted and juxtaposed from a hodgepodge of secondary literature, superstition, and hearsay from the old folks, owe a debt of gratitude to both Wilhelm and Baynes for making this great work accessible for study.

For implicit in this particular translation of the *I Ching* is the fact that it addresses itself not only to the world of academia, but also, and perhaps more so, to individuals everywhere. It has been especially useful in assisting those of us who are keen to push aside the veil that shrouds much of the Chinese metaphysical sciences.

Four legendary, almost mythical personalities are credited with the authorship and evolution of the

LEFT *The 64 hexagrams of the* I Ching. *The eight trigrams so fundamental to Feng Shui formed the basis for these hexagrams. Each one denotes a specific combination of Yin, Yang, and the elements in order to describe a particular state of being.*

SEE ALSO
❖ The Trigrams *pp.38–9*
❖ The Eight Mansions Formula: Pa-Kua Lo-Shu Formula *p.72–5*

I Ching or *Book of Changes*. These are Fu Hsi, King Wen, the Duke of Chou, and Confucius, the most famous of China's great thinkers.

Fu Hsi is said to have invented the linear signs manifested as the eight three-lined trigrams. These first appeared in two major collections, the *I Ching* of the mythical Hsia Dynasty (around 2205 B.C.E.) called *Lien Shan*, and the *I Ching* of the Shang Dynasty, entitled *Kuei Ts'ang*. These trigrams are the roots of the hexagrams, and are also featured as vital components of the Pa Kua symbol.

King Wen, the progenitor of the Chou Dynasty (1150–249 B.C.E.), took the trigrams further and formulated the 64 hexagrams. These came about by doubling the trigrams from three-line symbols into six-line symbols, done in multiple combinations of the trigrams themselves. Thus there are 8x8 combinations resulting in 64 permutations. King Wen was also said to have appended brief judgments to each hexagram, thereupon laying the groundwork for much of the acknowledged wisdom of *I Ching* philosophy.

The Duke of Chou, the dynamic son of King Wen, authored the Texts

pertaining to each of the individual lines of the hexagrams, assigning meanings to them as and when they changed. His contributions were entitled *The Changes of Chou* and these subsequently came to be used as oracles. These drastically altered the complexion of the *I Ching*, expanding its philosophy to take on colorings of divination.

Confucius came upon the *I Ching* when it had reached the stage described above. Confucius devoted the best part of his life to studying the Texts, Judgments and images of the *I Ching*, and he also expanded the book's scope with a series of Commentaries generally referred to as the "Wings." A great deal of literature grew up around the book during this period, fragments of which continue to be part of the Commentaries of the modern-day *I Ching*. These Commentaries in parts differ greatly in interpretation and content, to the extent that Confucius' role in the evolution of *I Ching* philosophy cannot be overstated. His disciples also did further work.

The *Book of Changes* escaped the fate of other classics in the famous burning of books under the tyrant emperor Chin Shih Huang Ti, but by that time it had already become firmly established as a book of divination and magic.

Around this time (3 B.C.E.), the Yin–Yang doctrine ran riot in connection with popular interpretations of the *I Ching* undertaken by the Han scholars of that period. Their attitudes tended toward magnifying the mysterious and magical aspects of the *I Ching*'s contents. It was not until around 226 C.E. that the *Book of Changes* came to be regarded also as a book of wisdom, and by the time of the Sung period (960–1279 C.E.) the book had evolved further, into a textbook relating to statecraft and the philosophy of life.

In the thirteenth century, successful attempts were made to revive the *I Ching* as a book of oracles and this metaphysical view of the book has continued to the present day. During the last Chinese dynasty, interpretations and commentaries of the book once again tended to be influenced by theories of magic. This view of the *I Ching* has remained and today it is regarded as one of the exalted divination texts of China.

During the K'ang Hsi period, a comprehensive version of the book emerged. This separated the Texts from the Commentaries, the latter fully incorporating extracts that had survived the centuries. The Wilhelm translation is based on this K'ang Hsi edition.

The development of Feng Shui thought and practice occurred alongside that of the *Book of Changes* at least from the Tang period onward. Thus, even as perspectives of the *I Ching* altered from one century to the next, a parallel development also impacted on the practice of, and conceptual approach toward, Feng Shui. The significance of this becomes evident when we begin to question whether Feng Shui really works, and whether the *I Ching* can really foretell outcomes. Both are suggestive of magical connotations; both are based on similiar styles of imagery, particularly the linear trigram symbols. The connections to the forces of Nature and to compass directions appear to exhibit unique manifestations of supernatural, or at least metaphysical forces at work. One must admit that a practice as complex as Feng Shui, and a wisdom as profound as the *I Ching*, could only have survived the vagaries of time because of their perceived potency. That it has kept generation after generation enthralled must suggest that here is something genuinely deserving of study and attention.

BELOW *The philosopher Confucius dedicated most of his lifetime to working on the* I Ching, *despite the fact that it was declared blasphemous by Emperor Chin Shih Huang Ti.*

LEFT *Fu Hsi and the eight trigrams that he is credited with inventing, and which form the basis of the I Ching.*

BELOW *King Wen was responsible for creating the 64 hexagrams of the I Ching.*

ABOVE *The famous and legendary philosopher Confucius, who studied the I Ching extensively and wrote a number of Commentaries on it.*

RIGHT *The Duke of Chou carried on the work of his father (King Wen), assigning meanings to the lines of the hexagrams.*

CHAPTER TWO: FENG SHUI CONCEPTS

THE TRIGRAMS

ABOVE Each hexagram comprises upper and lower trigrams. For example, the combination of the upper trigram "wind" and the lower trigram "mountain" represents steady development. This beautiful Chinese landscape can be seen as a visual interpretation of this hexagram.

Each trigram comprises combinations of three straight lines that are either broken (– –) or unbroken (–). These trigrams collectively represent the trinity of the universe comprising the subject (man), the object having form (earth), and the content (heaven). The lowest place in the trigram is that of the earth; the middle place in the trigram belongs to man; and the top place in the trigram to heaven.

A global concept of the universe is fully expressed by the aggregate meanings of the eight trigrams. Another significant feature is that they intermingle when they become hexagrams. In doing so they create new aspects of their relationships, which create new dimensions of meanings. Some examples of this can be expressed as "heaven and earth determining the directions," such as "mountain and lake uniting" or as "thunder and wind arousing" each other. They can also be expressed as "water and fire not combating."

Every trigram has several sets of meanings, undertones, and associated symbolism. Each trigram is arranged around the eight sides of the Pa Kua in two recognized arrangements – the Early Heaven arrangement and the Later Heaven arrangement. Feng Shui practitioners of the Compass School make extensive references to these trigrams and these two arrangements. This is because the meanings that are associated with each trigram offer significant "clues" to the correct practice of Feng Shui.

ABOVE Trigrams are composed of three lines: the uppermost represents heaven, *the middle represents human-kind and the lower line is the earth.*

As well as having corresponding cardinal points and compass directions, each trigram also has element representations. In addition there is a soft aspect and a hard aspect, a dark side and a bright side, and this is summarized as exhibiting a Yin or a Yang essence. Each trigram also represents a specific member of the family. Herein lie the difficulties of interpretation for Feng Shui implications. Permutations of the various attributes of the trigrams can and do result in multiple interpretations that prove challenging to the amateur Feng Shui practitioner.

Nevertheless, these meanings and interpretations are significant to Feng Shui. They expand the scope of the practice while suggesting clues to what can be "energized." They also suggest how symbolism may be activated, either singly or collectively, to attract prosperity and good fortune in the physical realm. Appreciating the nuances of the eight trigrams is thus an important preliminary in the practice of Feng Shui.

In the *I Ching* there are additional symbols that are connected with each of the trigrams as well as extensive commentaries which offer critiques on the character of the lines themselves. For our purpose, however, the descriptions given above are sufficient for understanding the fundamental derivatives of much Feng Shui practice. These relate mainly (although not exclusively) to their elements, the member of the family indicated, and the basic meanings that are embodied in each trigram.

SUN: the GENTLE. This trigram is made up of two solid Yang lines above one broken Yin line below. The member of the family represented is the eldest daughter and its attribute is the wind – indecisive yet penetrating. The creature symbolized by Sun is the cockerel whose voice pierces the morning air. For Yang Feng Shui analysis, Sun is placed southeast and represents wealth.

LI: the CLINGING. This trigram is made up of a broken Yin line between two Yang lines. It is the trigram of fire and represents the middle daughter of the family. Its character implies strength but is actually weak: exterior Yang lines suggest vigor but inside it is soft and hollow. Li represents fire. Its season is summer and there is potential for great brightness, the kind that illuminates the world.

KUN: the RECEPTIVE. This trigram is made up of three broken lines. This suggests the dark, yielding, primal power of Yin. Kun represents the matriarch, the female maternal. Its image is the entire earth, which remains impartial. Its animal is the cow, which symbolizes fertility. Kun perfectly complements Chien: jointly energizing them creates enormous power. The place of Kun is the southwest and the element is earth.

CHEN: the AROUSING. This trigram is made up of two broken Yin lines above an unbroken Yang line. This is the trigram of the eldest son and meanings attached to it comprise the symbolism of thunder, the dragon rising out from the depths and soaring majestically into stormy skies. This is represented by the single strong Yang line pushing up through two broken Yin lines. The element of Chen is wood.

TUI: the JOYOUS. This trigram is made up of one broken Yin line above two unbroken Yang lines. Tui represents the youngest daughter and its element is small metal. It also symbolizes the lake which rejoices in all things. This is a happy trigram, placed west. It signifies the luck of children.

KEN: the MOUNTAIN keeping still. The main attributes of this trigram are its suggestions of hidden gold and silent strength. Ken is representative of the youngest son. The element of Ken is earth. Ken is placed northeast and it represents wisdom arising.

KAN: the ABYSMAL. This trigram is made up of one unbroken Yang line sandwiched between two broken Yin lines. Kan is the middle son and its element is water. The season suggested is winter when it is wet and cold. Kan is not a happy trigram and it often suggests an approaching dangerous situation.

CHIEN: the CREATIVE. This trigram comprises three unbroken lines. Its nature is Yang and it is often associated with the father, the head of the household. Chien is the male paternal. It also signifies heaven: the sky, immense brightness, energy, and perseverance. The element associated with Chien is big metal; its symbolic animal is the horse. The direction associated with Chien is the northwest.

CHAPTER TWO: FENG SHUI CONCEPTS

THE CONCEPT OF HARMONY: the five elements

Central to Feng Shui's many rules and recommendations is the belief that all physical things, all tangible and intangible energy, all directions and all seasons possess element attributes that relate mutually to each other. Additional to this belief is that everything in the universe is one of five elements and how they relate to each other causes energy near them to become either auspicious or inauspicious.

When the affinity is harmonious, all things move smoothly, bringing happiness. When the relationship is jarring and hostile, the energy causes anger, sadness and frustration. In short, element harmony manifests good or bad Feng Shui. The nature of element interaction is what creates harmony or disharmony in any area. This concept provides the practitioner with the explanation that lies behind many Feng Shui correcting and enhancing

techniques. The reference grid on the right summarizes the relationship between compass directions and the five elements.

The grid offers a simple means of activating correct element energy in the eight direction sectors of any home or room using the concept of the five elements. Superimpose the grid onto the flat layout plan of your home. You can use the same analysis for every level of your home. Divide the area of your house into equal grids. These grids do not need to be square, but they must be of equal size. Use a good compass to get your bearings and then mark out the compass directions of each grid. Then consult the grid below on what to place in the respective corners.

Element harmony also goes beyond activating the respective elements that rule each compass location. Often more significant is the interaction of the five elements. There is a productive and a

SE wood	S fire	SW earth
E wood	center earth	W metal
NE earth	N water	NW metal

ABOVE *The basic reference grid shows the alliance between compass directions and the five elements.*

ABOVE *By placing the reference grid over the floorplan of your home, you will be able to assess the most suitable locations for various features.*

RIGHT *Crucial to the practice of Feng Shui are the five elements (earth, fire, metal, water, and wood) and how they interrelate with each other to create auspicious or inauspicious forces.*

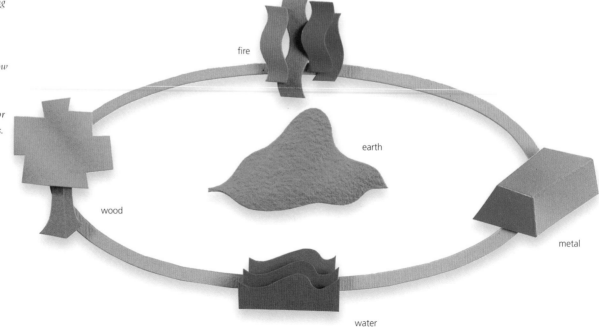

fire

wood

earth

metal

water

destructive interaction between the elements, called the productive cycle and the destructive cycle. These flows are circular, and understanding the nuances of these flows offers added scope for effective Feng Shui enhancement.

In the productive flow, water produces wood, which then produces fire, which produces earth, which produces metal, which produces water…

In the destructive flow, water destroys fire, which in turn destroys metal, which destroys wood, which destroys earth, which destroys water…

To appreciate the subtleties of the circular flow of productive and destructive energies it is useful to understand the attributes of each of the elements.

Fire

Fire is the only element that has to be created. It does not exist naturally and it cannot be stored. Fire burns and destroys many things and in the cycle it is the only element strong enough to destroy metal. Fire is produced by wood and so it is said that fire exhausts wood. At the same time, however, fire also provides the warmth that makes wood grow and flower and come to harvest. Fire is destroyed by water yet this does not make the two elements natural enemies because fire also turns water into steam, in the process transforming it into something powerful and strong.

Fire is associated with the south; when placed in the south corners of rooms and homes it brings soaring energy. Lights in the south part of the garden and in a foyer of the home that is placed south attract upward rising Chi flows that bring success, fame, and recognition to the residents. Fire energy always indicates success associated with public recognition. In addition to fire in the south, wood is also excellent in the south because wood fuels the fire. A little bit of water creates power for the south because water gets turned into steam. The key to what is good or bad is the relative strength of the elements to each other.

The nature of the fire element is always powerful. The Chinese like energizing fire energy because it is so full of the precious Yang essence which magnifies good fortune fast and efficiently. Fire must always be treated with respect. Never overdo the use of fire energy, and do not energize the fire element everywhere. When in doubt it is better to refrain from putting in too many fire element objects. Do not forget the importance of balance. There should never be too much of any single element, so keep the fire under control.

When the moon is full, the fire element becomes extremely strong. The same happens during the summer months. Once fire reaches its maximum potential, as in the cold months, it starts to diminish, and when it does artificially created fire in the form of bright lights and burning candles compensates for the waning fire energy. When working with fire do not forget that the element of wood fans the fire, while the element of water extinguishes it.

People born in the year of this element have a particular affinity with fire because this is their natural element. Snake or horse year people also have an affinity with the fire element simply because fire is the element of these two animals.

ABOVE Fire is a very strong element, and care needs to be taken not to allow it to dominate at the expense of the other elements.

FIREPLACE LOCATION

ABOVE A glowing fire along the south wall balances the Yin and Yang energies. You can recreate the effect with a bright lamp during the summer.

When the fireplace is located along the south wall of your living room, the energy creates perfect Yang energies that counter the excessive Yin energies that have been built up during the winter months. A fireplace in the south also activates great success luck for the whole family.

During the summer months, when the fireplace is not in use, place a bright lamp on the mantelpiece above the fireplace; this will keep the vital Yang energy stimulated.

SEE ALSO

❖ The Feng Shui of Kitchens *pp. 185–6*

RIGHT *The power of water can be very deceptive, but used in the right way will bring good luck to both home and business.*

Water

Water is considered a Yin element. Like fire, water is extremely forceful and at its zenith water can be even more destructive than fire. Indeed, in the *I Ching* water is regarded as a sign of danger. Water above a mountain, i.e. water in a high place, is one of four critically dangerous Feng Shui indications. This is because the symbolism is one of water overflowing its banks. In the cycle, metal is said to produce water because metal can turn into a liquid state. Thus water is said to exhaust metal. In practical terms this means that placing water in a metal corner tends to weaken that corner.

Water is associated with the north. The simple implication of this is that anything which suggests water, when placed in the north, activates the energy of water thereby causing harmony and auspiciousness in the north sector of your home. Water energy moves downward, so a gentle waterfall in the north is very auspicious.

Water is also reminiscent of the new moon, the beginning of a cycle. Dark colors – black or blue – represent this element. Thus, the use of dark colors will energize corners that benefit from the water element. Blue carpets and curtains, as well as upholstery, quilt covers, and cushions, which have dominant blue colors are suitable for this purpose. Household furnishings provide excellent media for activating the elements. Play with colors, and benefit from a Feng Shui-inspired creation of harmony by matching the colors with the correct corners of any room.

Having done all of this, however, do not expect instant and major changes. Always remember that Feng Shui for interiors plays only a small part in the overall Feng Shui of your home. You should never expect interior energizing to lead to big improvements overnight.

Introducing a water feature in the north brings wonderful career luck. Inside the house, the best method of energizing the wonderful essence of the water element is to install an aquarium with bubbling oxygenated water. Keep good luck fish like carp, goldfish, and guppies.

An even better idea is to activate the water element in the garden, if you are lucky enough to have one. Introduce a small fountain where all the water splashes into the center inside and not outside; if you have a big mansion and a big budget, create an artificial waterfall. Place it in the north part of your garden, or somewhere in full view of your main door. Make sure it is on the left-hand side of the garden.

Those born in water element years feel comfortable with this element, as do those born in rat or boar years. Remember that the practice of manipulating energies in the surroundings should be very subtle: less is better than more.

ADVANTAGEOUS WATER FEATURES

Place a waterfall in the north for good luck. An excellent energizer for attracting sustainable wealth and prosperity is a small downward flowing waterfall just a few yards from any doorway around your home. Let the water flow gently and use a pump to recycle the water. Make sure the pump is not too strong; you want a soft, gentle sound of water, not a loud tidal rush. Soft water is auspicious breath; loud gushing water is killing breath. If you wish you can keep fish in the small pond into which the water falls. You can also place gold painted rocks inside the water to symbolize a waterfall bringing gold. The crucial part to get right is the flow of the water, which must appear to be flowing inward and never outward.

LEFT *A small waterfall in the garden will help to generate auspicious Chi to attract wealth luck for your family.*

Wood

Wood symbolizes expansion, epitomized by the happiness and growth of springtime, when plants germinate and start to grow. Of the five elements, wood is the only one with a life of its own. Wood represents the waxing moon, gathering strength and radiance with each passing day. Its energies radiate outward in each and every direction, like the branches of a tree. Wood is therefore an excellent element to energize since all its connotations are associated with positive development.

Wood produces fire and is thus exhausted by it. In winter it is weak, therefore requiring the warmth of fire. In summer, wood is at its strongest. The main danger to wood is the metal element that destroys it. But metal in small quantities transforms wood into implements and objects of value. Furniture is made with implements and tools made of metal. Thus small quantities of metal do not necessarily harm this vibrant growth element.

Wood is placed in the compass direction of the east, the abode of the green dragon, where the element takes on the form of a tall, imposing tree. It is also the element of the southeast, the place of small wood, the place that represents material wealth. Activating the wood corners of the home brings enormous benefits, and especially for those born in wood years or in the years of the tiger or the rabbit, both of which astrological signs also belong to the wood element. Use every kind of plant (even artificial ones work, but not dried plants or flowers) except those with pointed leaves or sharp thorns. All forms of prickly cactus should be avoided inside the home. Bonsai trees, which are artificially stunted, are also unsuitable since they repress the natural growth of wood.

Water features enhance the energy of wood since water

ABOVE *Wood is a living element embodying notions of personal growth and development, and can be auspicious for life and career success.*

produces wood in the productive cycle of the elements.

Set your plants along the east walls of your home to simulate the element of big wood. In the garden, a large tree with spreading branches and good foliage is also effective. The pine tree and the bamboo are effective and they also represent longevity.

Plants are excellent for camouflaging any ugly sights and structures which you may have in the east or southeast of your home or garden. Creepers are also good for softening the hostile energies of sharp edges and protruding corners. If the vines produce beans, place them in the southeast to symbolize a good harvest.

Plants are also excellent energizers for the southeast sector. When plants bloom, they bring wonderful vibrant energy associated with success. The Chinese always describe a successful life as one that has started to blossom. Since the southeast represents wealth, flowers are most suitable here.

SEE ALSO
❖ Yin and Yang Energies in Illness
pp. 211–13

BELOW *As a symbol of longevity, bamboo is an extremely auspicious plant, both in the garden and used as a material for furniture.*

Earth

The earth element epitomizes the core of Feng Shui. Powerful earth energy moves sideways and horizontally, spreading its essence each time the seasons start to change, aiding the transition from summer to fall to winter to spring, and back to summer once again. Earth is produced by fire so those places that lack this vital energy are enhanced by the presence of bright lights. But earth is destroyed by wood to which it gives sustenance. In earth corners, therefore, reduce the presence of wood. It is also a good idea to reduce the presence of metal in earth areas since earth produces metal. This is why metal is said to exhaust earth.

The earth element is associated with the southwest, which represents big earth, and also the northeast, where the element is small earth. The center of a home is also considered to belong to the earth element. In all these sectors of the home, or in the southwest, and northeast, of the garden, strengthening the earth element brings great harmony of energies. Be especially focused on the center because creating harmonious energy in the center brings good fortune to the whole family. It also helps in fostering good relationships between siblings.

Crystals are splendid symbols of the earth element. Both natural crystals and manmade crystals are equally effective. Place them in the southwest corner of your living room to energize romance luck, and in the northeast to help in the attainment of educational success.

Ceramic teapots and vases also make great earth element energizers. Choose those which have good fortune symbols painted on them – these can depict the mou tan flower, or peony, which is excellent for the southwest, or any of the longevity symbols like the crane, pine trees, or bamboo to enhance the energies that bring

ABOVE *Crystals can bring the benefits of the earth element, and if placed correctly in the southwest of the home can benefit relationships.*

ENERGIZING THE EARTH CORNER

Large decorative urns and water vessels make excellent energizers for the earth corners of a home. If you can fill these decorative containers with semiprecious stones and place them on your coffee table, they will create auspicious energies inside your home. They also look very attractive. If you have an altar in your house, you can try placing a large ceramic bowl filled with semiprecious stones on it, where it will create a wonderful earth-energy offering to your deities.

ABOVE *The earth element's energy can be harnessed and used to energize the home by placing ceramic vessels filled with semiprecious stones in strategic positions.*

good health luck into the home. In recent years China's ceramic industry has expanded greatly, and it is not difficult to find some excellent examples. These are best placed in the southwest or northwest of your living room. Do not, however, leave them empty unless the idea is to capture killing energy caused by the presence of secret poison arrows. If these vases are intended to energize the earth corner, fill them with decorative colored stones, or you could even use water or uncooked rice.

BELOW *Sedimentary rock formations, like these in Bryce Canyon, Utah, USA, are dramatic examples of the influence of water over earth.*

Metal

Energies of the metal element are both dense and inward-flowing. Metal is synonymous with gold and silver, and these precious metals have always been the symbols of wealth and prosperity, but this element is also cold and lifeless. Unlike the other elements metal is unbending. It is a manifestation of wealth and energizing its essence in the correct metal corners of the house will be of great benefit to the whole home.

A pot of gold is the best representation of metal. In Feng Shui all things are symbolic, but placing your left-over change – coins – in a metal container and the placing it in the metal directions, the northwest or the west, magnifies the energies of these

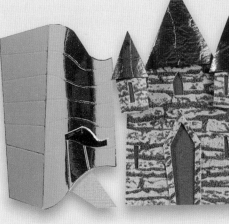

ABOVE *A fake gold ingot – one way of symbolizing the metal element.*

sectors and adds to the harmony and flow of energies moving within the home.

Anything metallic like coins and gold bars is suitable for metal corners. Those born in metal years or in rooster and monkey years have a special affinity with metal. The energies of elements are not static. They interact with each other all the time in either productive or destructive cycles. Understanding the way the energies of the five elements affect each other enables the practitioner to know how to achieve Feng Shui harmony in the living space. Study the cycles of the elements carefully as this will enhance your successful practice of Feng Shui considerably.

BOOSTING METAL ENERGY

The best objects to use for enhancing metal energies are old Chinese coins whose combination of a square hole in a round coin symbolizes the fusion of heaven and earth. Tie three coins together with red thread to energize the coins, and then place them in the metal corner of your living room. This is a very powerful method of enhancing incomes, and there are lots of other ways to use these coins. These other methods are covered in a later section. Remember that the red thread is vital since it causes the energies of the coins to be released.

ABOVE *Copies of Imperial Chinese coins can be used to symbolize the metal element and improve financial prosperity.*

THE FIVE ELEMENTS OF BUILDINGS

Buildings can be identified according to their elements. This categorization is based on the overall shape of the buildings. To find your affinity with buildings check your own element by investigating the heavenly stem of the year you were born. This refers to the element of the year itself

(and it differs from the element of the earthly branch.) Thus, if you were born in a wood year, rectangular shaped buildings would be ideal for you.

In terms of Feng Shui the "safest" type of buildings are the earth and wood buildings since these are generously auspicious and give the fewest Feng Shui problems. Fire

buildings are very aggressive and often attract retaliatory measures from neighbors. Metal buildings are excellent for public buildings but are most unsuitable as residences. Water buildings create the greatest number of problems.

A WATER building

A FIRE building

A WOOD building

An EARTH building

A METAL building

CHAPTER TWO: FENG SHUI CONCEPTS

THE CONCEPT OF BALANCE: Yin and Yang

ABOVE *Feng Shui is concerned with the balance of Yin and Yang energies – the Earth's energies are composed of these two forces and any imbalance can be harmful.*

BELOW *Excessive Yang energy could be created by the large fireplace and ceiling fan in this living room – the occupant will need to introduce some Yin energy for a harmonious effect.*

All the energies of the Earth – which can be regarded as synonymous with the breath of the dragon, the Sheng Chi – are said to be either Yin or Yang in nature.

All the elements of the Earth too are said to have either a Yin essence or a Yang essence. The cosmology of these two opposing yet complementary forces is the conceptual way the Chinese view the universe. Yin and Yang have their own attributes and their own magnetic fields of energy. They are diametrically different but they are nevertheless mutually dependent. Each gives existence to the other; one cannot exist without the other.

Thus, when Feng Shui speaks of balance, what is referred to is the tenuous presence of both types of energy in optimum quantities, relative to each other. There is no known formula to tell us exactly what these optimum quantities are. Feng Shui does advocate more Yang in dwellings of the living and more Yin in dwellings of the dead. This means that in our homes and workplaces there should be a lot more Yang than Yin; however, there should never be so much Yang that Yin completely disappears. Without Yin there can be no Yang.

ABOVE *Yang energy is lively and noisy like this rollercoaster ride in a theme park, but it could not exist without the calm and quiet Yin energy.*

ABOVE *Yin energy contrasts dramatically with Yang in its quietness and tranquillity, but some degree of Yang will be present even in a cemetery.*

The energies around us are deemed to be in a beneficial state of balance when both Yin and Yang are present. The relative strength of each in any given situation has to be finely tuned according to circumstances, but there should never be so much Yin as to completely obliterate Yang, and vice versa. For Yang Feng Shui, Yang energies are of course vital, but never to the extent that Yin is totally diminished, although an excess of Yin energies can cause havoc and sometimes bring illness and death. Similarly, there will be situations when the balance has to be reversed. Exposure to the glare of the western sun causes an excess of Yang energy. Too much noise, too much activity, too much brightness, are all symptoms of an excess of Yang energy.

When there is too much shade and too much stillness, when nights and days are cold and lifeless, the energy is deemed to be excessively

imposing fireplace dominates the room

whirring fan

cluttered coffee table does not necessarily produce bad Feng Shui

heavily patterned furniture

Yin. Such areas lack life, growth and expansion. Yin places are suitable for the dwellings of the dead, not of the living.

Yin and Yang interact continuously, and in the process create change. Thus, summer Yang reaches its zenith and then starts to fade into winter (Yin) before becoming summer once more. Day follows night. The moon gives way to the sun, and darkness becomes light. Everything in the universe contains varying quantities of Yin and Yang energies. In the natural landscape, Yin and Yang are expressed by the contours of the terrain, ground temperatures, and the amounts of sunlight and shade.

Landscapes that are completely flat are too Yin, and require the balance of boulders and plants. Perspectives that have too much exposure to sunlight could be too Yang; plants here will create shade.

A water feature also introduces Yin energies to create good balance. Look at Japanese and Chinese gardens, which are always balanced with Yin and Yang lines. Now think

of the snowcapped polar regions – far too Yin; think also of hot deserts, far too Yang – such places are uninhabitable, never mind the impossibility of good Feng Shui.

ABOVE *This landscape contains both Yin and Yang elements. The flat fields and lake are Yin but receive a great deal of Yang sunlight to grow grapes. They are also surrounded by the Yang energies of the snowcapped mountains in the background.*

LEFT *This Japanese-style garden has been energized with an auspicious balance of water features, boulders, pebbles, and shrubs.*

CHAPTER TWO: FENG SHUI CONCEPTS

THE CONCEPT OF LANDSCAPE:
symbolism of the four celestial creatures

The practice of Feng Shui always starts with location. If the whereabouts of your home are auspicious according to basic Feng Shui tenets, this alone will assure you and your family of a good life. Superb luck will accompany you and all you do will meet with success as long as you live in such a home. The natural environment is extremely powerful; even if the interior of your home might suffer from some negative Feng Shui features, the effect will be insignificant if the location of your home enjoys excellent classical Form School Feng Shui.

Landscape Feng Shui focuses initially on the physical surroundings of your home. If you live in an apartment, use the whole building in which your apartment is situated to determine if your location follows good Feng Shui landscape criteria.

The best location according to classical Feng Shui is represented here. This is defined in lyrical animal metaphors that refer to elevated landforms – these are the four celestial animals.

The black turtle hills are the mountains behind, which are ideally to be placed in the north.

The green dragon hills are on the left, ideally in the east.

The white tiger hills are on the right, which should ideally be in the west; these hills must be lower than the dragon hills on the left and the turtle hills behind.

Finally, there is the red phoenix hillock in front, ideally placed south, with a river hugging the site like a jade belt. The overall shape resembles an armchair, symbolizing a life of comfort.

The locations suggested in the diagram are so auspicious that certain rich Chinese tycoons in the Far East actually have these contours and landforms artificially created around their family mansions to ensure they enjoy excellent Feng Shui. Although in the old days Feng Shui experts went to great trouble to look for natural configurations, nowadays where auspicious landscapes can be artificially simulated and constructed this is being done with great success.

The cardinal rule of Feng Shui is to have the mountain behind and water in front. Contours of the landscape are very significant in Feng Shui, and undulating landscapes are always preferred to flat. But the most vital rule to follow is never to have the mountain in front, blocking your main door. The area in front of your home and your front door should be left empty. The view must not be blocked. If you have water flowing – such as a river – in full view of your home, the Feng Shui is extremely auspicious.

In modern landscapes, this cardinal rule of Feng Shui indicates that if there is a tall or large building near where you live, you make sure it is behind your home, not in front. A tall building behind your home is excellent for you as it simulates the black turtle hills.

Land on the left of your house (from the inside looking out) should be slightly higher than land on the right. This simulates the green dragon and white tiger

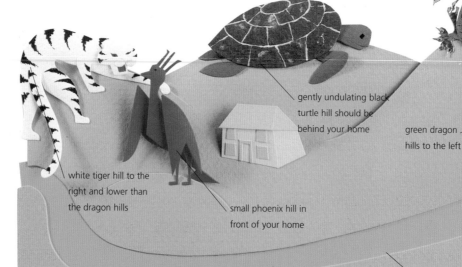

RIGHT *The most auspicious location for your home is determined by the position of the four celestial creatures. This home is surrounded by the four celestial creatures in the correct positions.*

white tiger hill to the right and lower than the dragon hills

gently undulating black turtle hill should be behind your home

green dragon hills to the left

small phoenix hill in front of your home

river flowing past, as if hugging the location

hills. If it is the other way around, the effect is inauspicious because it means the tiger dominates the dragon and can then turn against the residents.

The celestial animals – the turtle, the dragon, the tiger, and the phoenix – are important and powerful symbols of Landscape Feng Shui. Appreciating their significance enables amateur practitioners to correct and enhance their home locations.

The armchair formation is not easy to find in the natural landscape, nor is it within everyone's budget, but it can be ingeniously simulated. This is how it can be done. The celestial animals can also be activated to bring good luck into the home.

First take care of your back. The ground behind should be higher than the land in front; if you can, create a little mound that resembles the back of the turtle. Ideally, the place of the turtle should represent the north part of your home.

If you absolutely cannot create higher ground behind, hang a painting or picture of a turtle in the back part of your home, or better still keep a turtle, or any of its relatives. Tortoises or terrapins are good alternatives. It is not necessary to go overboard. Keep one turtle, not a whole family! The number associated with the turtle is one. The turtle symbolizes support from important people, long life, and continuous protection. Activating the turtle in the home is one of the best possible Feng Shui features. Your home will enjoy Feng Shui protection. If you cannot keep a real turtle, one in ceramic or bronze will do just as well.

The dragon is the ultimate good luck symbol. This mythical creature has a very special place in the hearts and minds of the Chinese people. In Landscape Feng Shui, physical landforms that can house the green dragon are the best indication that a site is auspicious: much authentic

ABOVE If you don't have any higher ground behind your home, an image of a turtle or tortoise can be displayed to energize the north part of your home.

Feng Shui practice involves searching for the hills and mountains where this celestial creature exists. Only undulating land can house dragons. Therefore look for land that is undulating rather than flat, where the grass grows verdant and green, where the soil is fertile, where the air smells good and where the site is relatively sheltered. Avoid mountain tops that are exposed to the elements, and land where even the grass cannot grow. Ensure that there is both sunlight and shade so that Yin blends harmoniously with Yang.

Let the neighbor on your left side be slightly higher than the neighbor on your right. If you live in an apartment apply the same principle to buildings to the left and right of you.

When looking for a place with good Feng Shui, be particularly alert to the contours of the surroundings. When the road is sloping, sites that are halfway between the highest and lowest point are better than those right at the top or at the bottom.

The top of a hill is said to be inauspicious since there is little protection from the elements.

Valleys are less problematic but in general look for sites at midlevel rather than at extremes.

Orient your home so that the left side is higher than the right side. Also try not to live below road level. If you do, let the bedrooms be on the upper level, and if possible orient the home so that the left side of the entrance door is higher than the right side.

Do not let the house stand on exposed stilts since this creates empty space beneath the house, which symbolizes a lack of foundation. Always close up the lower levels and place proper rooms there. Let the house hug the hillside, much like a dragon's lair. This transforms a potentially inauspicious home into a very auspicious home.

The green dragon is said to reside in the east. If you live in an apartment and have little control over the landscape as a whole, it is an excellent idea to activate the dragon within your home by placing a painting of a dragon on any of the east walls of the home.

You can also place a ceramic representation of the dragon on the

ABOVE The black turtle – symbol of mountains behind the home.

ABOVE The green dragon's rolling hills are to the left of the home.

ABOVE The white tiger's hills are on the right, preferably west, side of the house.

ABOVE The crimson phoenix's hillock should be found in front of the house.

BELOW If you cannot obtain a real turtle or tortoise, an ornament is the next best thing and often as effective.

east side of your living room. The dragon is the most popular good fortune symbol used by the Chinese, especially by those in business. If you plan to use the dragon, do not use one with five claws: this is the Imperial dragon and the Yang energies which it symbolizes may be too strong for you. Go for the normal four-clawed dragon. For the same reason, also make sure that your ceramic dragon is not too large.

If you use the dragon as a corporate logo, do not imprison the dragon inside a circle or square, and make sure it looks fat, happy, and prosperous. One of the best examples of the effective use of the dragon as a corporate logo is by the Hong Leong Group of Malaysia. Their dragon is not only fat, but looks pregnant, suggesting plenty of offspring, or successful acquisitions for the Group.

Do not place any representation of the dragon inside the bedroom. The dragon is the ultimate Tang symbol and is not suitable for a place of rest where Yin energies are far more important. It is also useful to note that placing the dragon inside the home may cause some people to become too aggressive. If

ABOVE *The logo of the Hong Leong Group of Malaysia – the fat, happy dragon indicates great wealth and success for the corporation.*

you feel yourself becoming too energetic after placing this creature in your home, it is advisable not to use this method of energizing your home. On the other hand, if you begin to experience better luck, you obviously have an affinity with this creature, and you would do well to continue.

The white tiger is as important as the green dragon and is always found where there is the true dragon. The tiger hills must always be lower than dragon hills. Remember that in Feng Shui references to these celestial animals always refer to hills and landforms. Thus if dragon hills are present, it can be assumed that tiger hills are also present.

The art of Landscape Feng Shui is in determining which are the dragon hills and which the tiger hills. This is not as difficult as it sounds. Looking outward, the hills to the left of your front door are usually dragon hills, those to the right tiger hills. The higher hills must always represent the dragon.

If the higher hills are on your right, then the orientation is said to be inauspicious. The tiger has become dominant and more powerful than the dragon, an extremely dangerous configuration because there is a danger that the tiger could turn against the residents of the home.

Note that, while references are made to hills here, the principle is equally applicable to any land to the left and right of your home. The crimson phoenix symbolizes

the south, or the area that lies in front of your residence. This part of the configuration should be flat, or at least lower than the back, the left or the right of the home, and the view should be uninterrupted. The crimson phoenix is said to represent opportunities that bring material comforts.

If any structure, mountain, or hill blocks the front of your home, it may also block everything you undertake. Success may be hard to come by, and worse, you could suffer severe losses. If, however, you have a small hillock that is lower than the front of the home, this represents the phoenix.

The crimson phoenix is said to represent the footstool upon which you can rest your weary feet. Especially within the home, the presence of this hillock is most auspicious since it allows residents to relax and gather their energies to face the outside world. It is therefore not to be confused with having a "mountain" in front of you. It is possible symbolically to activate the presence of the phoenix by placing a decorative bird in the south. Place a pink marble flamingo in the south corner of your garden to attract opportunities into your life. Alternatively, display a painting or decorative sculpture of a rooster on the south side of your living room.

ABOVE *As an alternative to a phoenix, display a rooster image to generate the same good luck energy.*

QUESTIONS AND ANSWERS

Question: There are so many different books on Feng Shui and so many different consultants, how do I know which are genuine?

Answer: Feng Shui is an ancient practice that has stood the test of time. In the course of its long evolution it has taken many different shapes and forms. Even in China there are different theories and schools of Feng Shui. During the reign of the early Ming emperors, counterfeit Feng Shui books were even published and distributed throughout the land to ensure that few people could lay their hands on the genuine formulas and methods. It is not surprising, therefore, that there are so many texts and treatises on Feng Shui. Today, as the popularity of Feng Shui rises, it is not surprising that there is a blossoming of Feng Shui books and practitioners. My advice is simple. Choose books that are written by authors with credibility and select Feng Shui consultants who already have a number of satisfied clients. Apply a healthy dose of commonsense and skepticism in your investigation of Feng Shui. I myself started out with a great deal of skepticism.

Question: I am so confused by all the different "schools" and formulas. Where do I begin if I want to apply Feng Shui to my home?

Answer: There is no need to be confused if you proceed step by step. In every discipline there is contradictory advice. Go slowly and think things through. Start your practice of Feng Shui in a defensive way. Look around you for things that can hurt you and your home, then slowly start to dismantle the poison arrows around you. Then you can start to energize for all kinds of good luck. Start by using my introductory books on Feng Shui before proceeding to the more advanced formulas. Use this book both as an introduction and as a reference book.

Question: How long does it take for Feng Shui to work?

Answer: Feng Shui can work almost immediately. If you realize that your house is threatened by a poison arrow as a result of reading this book, for instance, and you remedy it, you will instantly feel the effects. Such action is like lifting a load from your shoulders. The effect of withdrawing bad energy can be felt very quickly.

Question: Do I need a Feng Shui consultant?

Answer: Not if you just want to apply Feng Shui to your home. In my opinion you should undertake your own Feng Shui, simply because you tend to be more careful when applying Feng Shui to your own home. Feng Shui consultants should only be used when you have so many homes or offices that you do not have time to do it yourself. The other advantage of carrying out your own Feng Shui is that you know what you want to achieve and you do not then have to invite a perfect stranger into your home and violate your privacy. Treat Feng Shui as a hobby. It will open up a whole new world for you; one that brings its own special brand of magic into your life.

Question: How do I know if a consultant is qualified?

Answer: There is, at present, no official licensing body to establish standards. Indeed, it is hard to do so. I have come across some good Feng Shui masters in my time who are very experienced. Genuine masters are usually very humble and kind. But I am sad to say that in my travels around the world I have come across some charlatans who do not care whose lives they spoil with their nonsensical brand of Feng Shui. I advise you to be careful and not to open up your home too quickly to a stranger claiming to be a Feng Shui consultant. Instead, have the confidence to do your own Feng Shui. If you can make mistakes, so too can the consultant, and if the consultant can get it right, so too can you! Have confidence in youself and enjoy your Feng Shui.

Question: What do I do if I get everything wrong and do not know what to do about it?

Answer: No one can get their Feng Shui 100 percent right. Everyone has a Feng Shui problem or two. If you read this book carefully you will find most of the answers here. If you are in real difficulties, then e-mail me. I answer all my e-mails that do not exceed 50 words in length. My e-mail address is fengshui@lillian-too.com and there is no charge. It is a free service!

木火土金水

PART TWO

THE FUNDAMENTALS
OF FENG SHUI

CHAPTER THREE

LANDSCAPE FENG SHUI

T he Feng Shui of the landscape is classical Feng Shui. Here is where the literal words "wind" and "water" take on expansive meanings – for Landscape Feng Shui is about the environment. It examines the panorama of all the things that have been shaped by the winds and the waters. Shapes take on meanings. Contours and elevations create the undulations of the celestial creatures – the mountains or Shan, hills, and landforms that cause Chi to meander auspiciously or fly maliciously. The flow of water is the same – this can be favorable and friendly or it can be gushing and destructive.

The Feng Shui master smells the ground and breathes the air to diagnose the quality of winds. He traces the shapes of surrounding hills and studies the quality of the vegetation. He appraises the presence of good Chi and looks for harmony in the encircling elements. Wherever poison arrows occur he follows the flight path of hostile Chi created and installs remedies. And where elevations are auspicious he strengthens further. Such is the "magic" of Feng Shui that bad fortune then becomes good fortune and good fortune gets magnified.

LEFT *Feng Shui can help alleviate planning problems in small towns like this one in the US.*

CHAPTER THREE: LANDSCAPE FENG SHUI

FORM SCHOOL FENG SHUI

Feng Shui practice begins with a thorough knowledge of Form, or Landscape School. This has to do with the characteristics and attributes of the land upon which Yang abodes, or houses of the living, are built. Form School Feng Shui, as the name implies, takes account of the lie of the land, its contours, the topography, and the way the levels of the immediate environment relate to the dwelling place.

It then looks at the quality of the winds that blow in the immediate environment. These should always be gentle breezes rather than rushing winds. The air should smell of life and healthy vegetation. It has to be fresh rather than fetid, alive rather than stagnant. Plants should thrive rather than appear weak and

BELOW *Surrounding landscape features have an effect on the Feng Shui of buildings and should never be ignored.*

spindly. Where there is the presence of water the Feng Shui is said to be considerably enhanced. But water, like the wind, should flow gently: fast moving energy is said to be excessively Yang. In Feng Shui anything that moves too fast is considered to be a purveyor of killing energy. Water should thus flow slowly but not to the extent that it appears stagnant. Still water suggests death and is altogether too Yin. Fast water contains the killing breath and is considered too Yang.

It is becoming clear by now that Feng Shui is the science of divining Yin and Yang in one's immediate and surrounding environment. These include all the landforms and landscapes that surround one's homes. Form School Feng Shui also looks at the breadth and flow

of rivers, the traffic on the roads, the height and character of mountains, the shape of hills, surrounding buildings, neighbors' homes, and all sorts of manmade and natural structures. All of these physical structures contain varying amounts of Yin and Yang energies. Some are completely Yang, while others are excessively Yin. To create auspicious Chi that influences one's Feng Shui, the Yin and Yang energies must be at optimum balance. This balance generally depends on the nature of the work being done on the space: places where people live or work should have more Yang than Yin energy. The balance of Yin and Yang is considered on pages 46–7.

Usually, when the Yin and Yang symbols are in balance, the Chi

The orientation of mountains in relation to your home is highly significant

Certain numbers of peaks within view are auspicious, for example, 3, 6, and 8 peaks are thought excellent

Trees help block poison arrows

Hills can protect a home when they are behind it

created is auspicious, bringing prosperity and abundance. When the two become unbalanced, due to excessive amounts of either Yin or Yang, it causes everything to become inauspicious.

The quality of Feng Shui energy can also become exceedingly bad in the presence of fierce and threatening structures. These result in the Chi of the area becoming noxious and poisonous. Hostile, fearsome shapes caused by the peculiar forms of mountains or the edges of large buildings bring into being secret harmful arrows that emit breath so noxious that it poisons the luck of the area (*see pages 317–27 for spotting secret poison arrows and how to deal with them*).

A great deal of landscape and form in Feng Shui is subjective and requires an experienced eye, but there are guidelines that enable the amateur practitioner to read the Feng Shui of a particular landscape and decide whether it is generally good or bad. It is not difficult to tell

if the home and workplace, and even grave sites and burial grounds for one's departed ancestors, are oriented in a beneficial way or not.

These guidelines address the orientations of buildings and suggest various methods for creating auspicious Chi. Correct orientation alone is often sufficient to bring Feng Shui benefits to residents and descendants. It goes further. Feng Shui also offers suggestions for ensuring that the vital and precious Chi circulates and settles, thereby extending the tenure of good fortune for the family, even extending through five generations. In fact, according to the proponents of Form School Feng Shui, its power is said to be so potent that it can more than compensate for ill-fortune caused by incorrect orientations that are based on the Compass Formula schools.

Feng Shui operates on the principle that the landscape is alive with hidden forces caused by the shape, the size, and the color of the

physical structures that make up the landscape. In analyzing the layout of one's home and workplace, these factors must be taken into account. It is also important for the amateur practitioner to understand that everything contained in any Feng Shui guidelines that are based on the old texts of Feng Shui describes a perfect setting.

In the real world, and especially in the context of modern-day living in the city, it is impossible to live in any place where the Feng Shui is perfect. The experienced Feng Shui master accepts this and does the best he can in any given situation, correcting as much as possible. Bad features that cannot be changed, and bad orientations that cannot be demolished and rebuilt, are simply neutralized. This is undertaken in varieties of ways that are dealt with elsewhere under cures and antidote (*see pages 305–15*). Thus, while these often do not present the best solution, they are good enough.

SEE ALSO
❖ History and Background *pp. 16–17*
❖ The Concept of Landscape: symbolism of the four celestial creatures *pp.48–50*

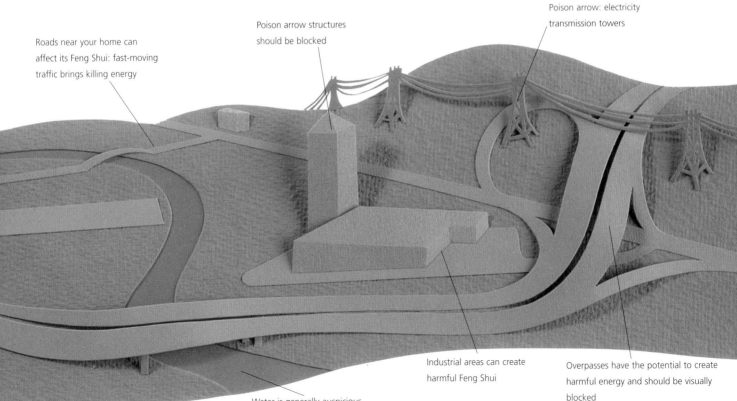

Roads near your home can affect its Feng Shui: fast-moving traffic brings killing energy

Poison arrow structures should be blocked

Poison arrow: electricity transmission towers

Water is generally auspicious
Direction of flow determines whether it will bring you good luck

Industrial areas can create harmful Feng Shui

Overpasses have the potential to create harmful energy and should be visually blocked

CHAPTER THREE: LANDSCAPE FENG SHUI

THE EFFECT OF CONTOURS AND LEVELS

The amateur practitioner is advised to learn how to recognize auspicious and inauspicious shapes, features and orientations, topography, and levels in the environment. Examine the hills and topography behind the home. This is usually defined as the part of the house that is opposite to the main door.

Some texts describe the back of the house as that part which is farthest away from the main road fronting the house, irrespective of where the back door is sited. Others consider the place of the back door to be the back of the house. For practical purposes, I suggest that you use your own judgment to determine which part of your home you consider to be the back. If you are unsure, consider the place of the back door as the back of the house.

If this area behind the home or building is elevated, i.e. it is higher than the front, there is solid support and the Feng Shui is said to be good. Equally, if this elevated land is absent, the Feng Shui of the house is considered inadequate. This happens, for instance, when a house or building is located on a ridge so that behind the home the land falls away and there is no support. The Feng Shui is described as leaving the house completely unprotected against the elements and against bad luck and misfortunes of every kind. A situation like this is corrected by growing very tall trees behind the house symbolically to "raise the energy" of the back. Installing high lights is another method of simulating the protective energy, or you can build a high wall to simulate the presence of a mountain. When applying such cures, select one that is easy and suits your particular circumstances. It is not necessary to do all three.

Next, examine the levels in front of the home or building. To start with, there should never be higher land or, worse, a mountain facing the front of the home and especially facing the main front door. Usually, when the main door of any home is embraced by the surrounding landscape, the house is said to enjoy good Feng Shui. This means that there are protective hills to the back and on the two sides, and the land in front is left reasonably clear of hills save for a tiny hillock that represents a resting place for tired limbs. There should also be nothing threatening the door or the home itself, either from within or without. This is the ideal Feng Shui landscape. In reality, such configurations as described are difficult to come by or to create. The points to remember about Feng Shui are: let land behind you be higher and more solid. You have something to lean on; let land in front of you be level or lower but never higher. Create a bright hall: let land to the left and right of you be higher, seeming to embrace your home; let land to the left of your door (from the inside looking out) be higher than land to the right of the main door.

There is also the question of perspective. When surrounding forms – hills or buildings – seem to be overwhelming because they are too large or too near, the energy of the home becomes stifled. When the main door is being directly hit by poison arrows caused by a sharp ridge of hills, or by the sharp edges of buildings or other structures pointed directly at it, then similarly the home suffers from Shar Chi – killing breath. Shar Chi is the antithesis of auspicious Sheng Chi and is to be avoided at all costs. If this is not possible, the view of offending structures causing the Shar Chi should be blocked off or neutralized by using Feng Shui antidotes. (*See pages 305–15*.)

BELOW *Mountains and hills to the rear of a home are auspicious – but only if they are not so big that they overwhelm it.*

GREEN DRAGON, WHITE TIGER

Feng Shui texts (most written in old Chinese) offer colorful descriptions of perfect sites or locations. These descriptions use symbolic representations that were more easily understood in the old days.

The practicing Feng Shui masters of Hong Kong and elsewhere thus explain good Feng Shui in terms of the four celestial animals. Thus, excellent green dragon, white tiger formations for instance (referred to as Cheng Lung Pak Fu) is a phrase synonymous with the practice of Feng Shui. Locations were always described in terms of the celestial dragon: bad sites were said to be places where dragons were missing, or where dragons were injured.

Form School Feng Shui masters draw conclusions about the significance of specific structures and objects by examining their characteristics. The development of a Feng Shui eye and solid Feng Shui judgment requires not only an appreciation of Yin and Yang forces but also knowledge of the five elements and their productive and destructive cycles.

Many of the old masters also have such deep knowledge of the eight-sided Pa Kua symbol that they are able, simply by looking at hills and smelling the air, to discern nuances in trigrams considered relevant to the Feng Shui of any area. They can assess the intangible forces of how symbolic hill shapes interact to create a balance or imbalance in the atmosphere. To those still unfamiliar with such essentials of Chinese cultural knowledge, the explanations that accompany Feng Shui recommendations may at first seem alien. Once understood, however, the logic that underlies the practice soon becomes clear.

Landscape Feng Shui is not difficult to study and understand, but to be a master practitioner of Form School takes many years of study and a great deal of experience. For our purpose it is sufficient to learn the fundamentals because this should enable us to get our orientations reasonably in line.

The true understanding of Feng Shui requires grasping the true nature of the dragon and the tiger, the two most important of the symbolic celestial animals in Feng Shui and the essence of what physical Feng Shui is about. The green dragon spells the creation of good fortune. The tiger symbolizes the protector of one's good fortune. It is as important to create as it is to maintain. Remember that, once attained, wealth, love, success, and health can also be lost. This is at the core of the *I Ching*: any good fortune can be transformed into bad fortune, hence the need to be vigilant.

Thus the green dragon creates an auspicious life and the tiger helps you to sustain this good life. The dragon on one side of you and the tiger on the other represent the embracing essence of Feng Shui. One without the other is incomplete.

ABOVE *A green dragon on a plate should be placed in the east for good luck.*

LEFT *The green dragon is a highly significant animal in Feng Shui, creating the conditions for good luck in life and at work. The white tiger on the opposite side provides support for the dragon.*

DIFFERENT TYPES OF MOUNTAINS

ABOVE *Mountain landscapes can provide excellent places to live, but it is important to recognize the significance of their individual shapes.*

Since Landscape Feng Shui addresses land contours, the shape and orientation of mountains exert a huge influence on the luck of homes built in their vicinity. The Chinese have always considered mountains (*shan*) as desirable places in which to live. Convinced that celestial dragons nestle in elevated landforms, they shun flat plains, which represent the discarded droppings washed down from the mountains. Undulating mountains epitomize all that is best in Feng Shui.

Keeping in mind the cardinal rule of never allowing the main door to face or confront a mountain, there are methods of analyzing the auspiciousness of surrounding mountains. One method is to learn to discern five different types of mountain, categorized in accordance with the five elements, the shape of the peak determining elemental essence.

The five shapes corresponding to the five elements are *conical, square, round, oblong,* and *ridged.* These match, in the same order, *fire, earth, wood, metal,* and *water.*

Fire

Fire mountains are conical in shape. The peak rises up sharp, bold, and straight, coming to a keenly edged point. These mountains represent triangles and are associated with the planet Mars. Those born during years of the metal element should avoid living near fire mountains. Those born in the years of the earth element benefit enormously, but the mountains should never face your home. They must be behind your home, supporting you.

Earth

Earth mountains are rather stumpy looking. The shape of the peak is square, and thus resembles a plateau with a flat, extensive summit. The associated planet is Saturn. Such mountains are generally excellent for everyone when they stand behind the house, but they are particularly auspicious for those born in metal years and could clash with those born during years ruled by the water element.

Wood

Wood mountains rise up straight but the peaks are rounded. Such mountains look narrow and tall.

The planet associated with these mountain shapes is Jupiter. Fire element people will benefit from living near such mountains while those born during the years of the earth element will be exhausted living close to wood mountains.

Metal

Gold/metal mountains are dome-shaped or softly circular at the peak and have a broader base with gentle slopes. Such mountains are said to be extremely auspicious as they signify a "mountain of gold" nearby. Some texts describe such mountains as oblong in shape. They are suitable for everyone except those born in years dominated by the wood element.

Water

Water mountains are those ranges with a series of ridged peaks. The mountain appears to have several summits that seem alive and undulating, reminiscent of the body of a dragon. The planet identified with such a mountain type is Mercury. Ridged mountains are excellent for those in business since the water element is particularly auspicious for attracting money luck.

COMBINATIONS OF MOUNTAINS

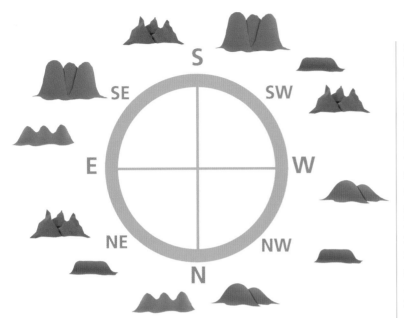

If you live in hilly country, and start to analyze the shape of the peaks and summits that make up the hills around you, make an effort also to analyze the shapes of the hills that are next to each other. Use the productive cycle of the five elements to satisfy yourself that the peaks are in harmony. Thus, tall peaks (wood) are compatible with conical peaks (fire); conical-shaped peaks (fire) are harmonious with square (earth); square peaks are harmonious with round, oblong summits (metal); rounded peaks (metal) harmonize well with ridged hill shapes (water).

To discover peaks that are incompatible with each other, similarly use the destructive cycle of the five elements for your analysis. In undertaking this very judgmental analysis of Form School Feng Shui of the elevated landforms that surround your home, remember to categorize the "shape" according to how the peak appears visually to you from your home. Remember that the shapes of hills and mountains seem to change depending on where you stand looking at the hill. Thus, when you are making a judgment as to the element of the hill, the important rule is to look at it from your house.

To create the best Feng Shui, the elements of the mountain should correspond with the personal year of birth of the father of the family and should also harmonize with the compass direction or the mountain vis-à-vis the house. Thus:

Mountains to the south of your home should be fire or wood mountains for them to create auspicious luck coming from the south toward your home. They should never be water mountains since water destroys the fire Chi coming from the south.

Mountains to the north of your home should be water mountains or gold/metal mountains since this produces auspicious energy from the north. When the mountains here are shaped as earth mountains, the good water Chi becomes afflicted or destroyed.

Mountains that lie to the east or southeast of your home should preferably be wood or water mountains. Such a configuration brings great prosperity because the wood Chi coming from the east and the southeast is then deemed to have been strengthened. If, however, the mountains are shaped like gold/metal mountains, the wood energy is said to have been spoiled or destroyed.

Mountains that lie to the southwest or northeast of your home should be earth or fire mountains for the Chi coming from these directions to be strengthened and to be auspicious. If the mountains are wood-shaped mountains the earth Chi gets exhausted and becomes weakened.

Mountains that lie to the west and northwest of your home will bring enormous good fortune for your family and your descendants if they are gold/metal or earth mountains. Many influential and powerful people will lend you support and help. But if the mountains are fire-shaped, they destroy all the good gold Chi coming from these directions.

LEFT Certain compass locations are more favorable than others for each type of mountain.

BELOW If you live in a mountainous or hilly area, observe the shape of the peaks that surround you to see if they are compatible. Here, a tall, conical-shaped mountain (fire) rises above two square peaks (earth).

CHAPTER THREE: LANDSCAPE FENG SHUI

MOUNTAIN FORMATIONS

Mountains that are visible from your home are also auspicious or inauspicious according to the number of peaks they have. Particular numbers of peaks have certain connotations. (Numbers of peaks not specifically mentioned are neither lucky nor unlucky.)

Mountains behind your home, or on the left of your home

❧ When there are six distinct summits visible, your family will always have the support of the leader and of powerful people in the country. This is very auspicious.

❧ When there are eight distinct summits visible, your family will enjoy great good fortune during the period of eight, i.e. between 2004 and 2023. The good fortune benefits every member of the family.

❧ When there are nine distinct peaks visible, your family will always have wealth and prosperity. Luck reaches its zenith between 2023 and 2043 but overall good fortune stretches through nine generations. If your family home is so placed you should not move out

of the location unless substantial development causes the auspicious summits to be leveled and spoils your Feng Shui.

❧ When there are five peaks visible in the mountains behind, your family will constantly suffer ill-health and the father of the family could die prematurely. This configuration is therefore extremely unlucky. The way to correct this is to create a symbolic sixth peak by hanging a picture of a mountain summit to face the five mountain peaks. This transforms an inauspicious feature into something that is lucky.

❧ When there are two peaks visible, the family will suffer disharmony. Children leave the home and those staying will constantly quarrel and bicker. Mothers-in-law will fight their daughters-in-law. Such homes will have no peace.

❧ When there is one single peak visible at the back of the home this represents the sign of the turtle and is extremely auspicious. The family will enjoy exceptional good protection all through its time in that home. One is also the number

of great success in a career. Luck becomes truly exceptional if the single peak is of the gold/metal element, since this will symbolize great wealth.

Mountains in front of your home

When you have mountains directly in front of your home, and especially blocking the main door, it indicates that every plan you make will fail and there will be complete lack of success in everything you do. Any success you may have will be short-lived. However, when the mountains in front of your home are further away they will not cause this sort of misfortune. The rule of thumb is one li, or about half a mile (1 kilometer), away. According to Feng Shui texts, therefore, mountains that are visible from the front door and are more than one li away are lucky or unlucky, depending on the number of peaks that are clearly visible.

❧ When there are three visible peaks it causes the sons of the family to reach very high positions of power in their careers, and this is further enhanced if the direction of the mountain represents the east. If they go into politics they will rise to the very top. Very auspicious.

❧ When there are two visible peaks, the women will dominate the fortunes of the family. Two peaks in the direction of the southwest brings extreme good fortune in the form of benefits that arise from the perseverance of the matriarch. Very auspicious.

❧ When there are five visible peaks, as for those behind the home, the family will suffer from misfortunes, accidents, and premature loss of the patriarch.

BELOW If you are lucky enough to have six mountain peaks behind your home, it ensures that your family will always enjoy good support.

ORIENTATIONS OF MOUNTAINS

When there is hilly land close to your home, it is vital to ensure that the orientation of your home is designed to tap the luck and protection of the mountain. Orientation means the way the main front door faces. This determines the orientation of the home. The orientation is irrespective of what your personal auspicious directions may be according to the Eight Mansions Pa-Kua Lo-Shu Compass Formula. It is ideal Feng Shui if you can tap both the luck of the mountain and of your personal direction at the same time. The challenge facing a Feng Shui practitioner is to design a home that ingeniously taps both.

The same challenge faces Feng Shui consultants. Just like you, they too need to use their creativity and inventiveness to interpret skillfully Feng Shui guidelines that initially, and on superficial analysis, may appear contradictory.

The guidelines on orientations of the home or building vis-à-vis mountains (or tall structures in the city that can pass for mountains) are summarized as follows:

🍂 Never orientate the home directly facing a mountain. Your front door should not open onto the wall of a mountain. The nearer the mountain is the more dangerous the Feng Shui.

🍂 Never allow the mountain on the left-hand side of the house to be lower than the mountain on the right-hand side. The left and right are taken standing at the front door and looking outward. Put another way, any high land around your home should be higher on the left-hand side and lower on the right-hand side.

🍂 Always make certain that the land behind the house is higher than the land in front of the house. Thus when there are mountains near your house, always ensure that the highest mountain lies behind the building. This effectively taps the power of mountain support. For this Feng Shui feature the best kind of mountain is one that resembles a turtle which, in Feng Shui, is the ultimate symbol of protection and support.

BELOW *Mountains behind the home usually mean good Feng Shui, but certain criteria need to be observed to ensure their auspicious effect.*

GOOD AND BAD SHAPES OF PLOTS, HOUSES AND BUILDINGS

The most auspicious shapes, and the easiest to enhance with Feng Shui energizers, are regular, usually square or rectangular. The square represents "gold" and also signifies "luck from heaven." The rectangle signifies growth and moving upward. The green shapes illustrated (viewed from above) are good, but the last two are not as auspicious. M's missing corner, although not good, does not harm the overall luck of the building. N's small frontage and a large back signifies that residents will retain their wealth. Shapes viewed as frontal elevations should also be regular.

The pink shapes are inauspicious. A and B have a wide front and a narrow back, signifying a good beginning but a bad ending, and poor retentive power of income. C has a sharp point in front which repels all the good Chi flowing into the building. D, E, and F are missing substantial sections, which also constricts the flow of Chi. G is the classical T-shape which spells a serious lack of luck as symbolized by the missing two sides of the front. H is the most damaging, representing complete and total loss.

CHAPTER THREE: LANDSCAPE FENG SHUI

LANDSCAPE FENG SHUI IN A MODERN ENVIRONMENT

ABOVE *Even though the landscape and buildings have changed dramatically since the practice of Feng Shui was developed many years ago, the principles of Feng Shui can be adapted and applied to today's modern environment.*

The old texts also offer variations of perfect configurations, explaining shapes of mountains, river flows, and contours in terms of the five elements and how they interact with each other to generate good or bad Feng Shui.

Many of the suggestions in the old books, however, have over the past hundred years been adapted to the modern practice of Feng Shui. Using their knowledge of fundamental explanations of balance and harmony, and by going back to the source books of Chinese thought, practitioners have successfully penetrated the language of the ancient texts to understand and reveal the symbolism locked within them.

In modern times, buildings are viewed as mountains, roads as rivers. Many of the structures of modern developments – transmission lines, power plant towers, the sharp corners of enormous high-rise buildings, their heights and colors, shapes and orientations – are incorporated into Feng Shui analysis and practice and are seen as different types of hills and mountains.

The occupied and cultivated landscapes of many countries today bear little resemblance to those of ancient times when Feng Shui guidelines were first formulated. So many people now live in cities and urban areas where landscape features have been leveled and roads have taken the place of rivers as conduits of transportation.

Many more people now live in high-rise apartments as well, as opposed to houses. Feng Shui today is being practiced in a world far different from the one in which it originated and thus the application of Feng Shui theory to the modern environment requires new interpretations of ancient precepts. This is especially so in the area of Form School Feng Shui. Thus we see dragons and tigers, turtles and phoenixes – the celestial creatures that symbolize the topography of the land – being artificially superimposed onto a cityscape in order to interpret Form School Feng Shui in a modern metropolis.

In a city of high-rises, man-made buildings have come to be regarded as mountains (or dragons and tigers); depending on their shape, location, and structure they are assigned Yin and Yang characteristics and elemental associations. Highways are described as being similar to rivers while city roads become purveyors of Chi flows.

Skyscrapers and large buildings are regarded as elevated landforms and mountains and so become symbolic of at least one of the celestial creatures.

Most importantly, modern-day practice of Feng Shui reflects its easy availability. Feng Shui books and experts are growing in volume and improving in quality. Where in the past Feng Shui was available only to the rich and powerful, rich and poor alike can today use Feng Shui with equal chances of success.

There are also no rules against applying Feng Shui concepts to one's living space.

RIGHT *The modern cityscape with its tall buildings is regarded in Feng Shui terms as a mountain landscape, incorporating the symbolism of the four celestial animals.*

THE SIGNIFICANCE OF ROADS

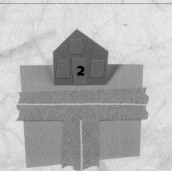

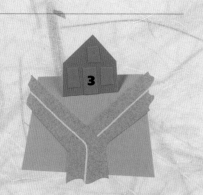

ABOVE *If your house is surrounded by roads, make sure that there is no road passing behind it, or it is vulnerable.*

ABOVE *To have an intersection or T-junction situated directly opposite your home is most inauspicious.*

ABOVE *Y-junctions are equally problematical, and their energy needs to be blocked with trees or mirrors.*

In Feng Shui the effect of roads has been compared with that of rivers in the old days. Roads are said to be purveyors of both good and bad Chi energy. Thus, if your house is located in a busy commercial area, the energy is very Yang, bringing with it a great deal of auspicious energy. If it is too Yang, however, when the road becomes too noisy, crowded, and busy, the energy turns sour. It is like a river that has become polluted from overuse.

Here are some guidelines to look for if you are looking for a new place to live:

🕊 Living in a secondary road is better than living in the main road, where the energy tends to move too fast. The Chi gets dissipated.

🕊 Let the road be at least level with or lower than the house. If you live below road level, the Chi in your house is flawed and you need to build higher and above the road.

🕊 Do not let your house be sandwiched between two roads. If these two roads have two different levels it is bad.

🕊 Make sure the road in front of the house is lower than the land behind the house.

🕊 Better to live along clean roads than dirty roads.

Here are some examples of what not to have in terms of placement of houses in relation to the road:

🕊 If you are surrounded on three sides by roads, make sure the side that does not have the road is behind you. Otherwise you are unprotected.

🕊 Do not directly face a straight road as shown in house 2. This is the classic intersection or T-junction and it is deadly. Block it with trees or hang a Pa Kua mirror above the door in order to counter the straight road.

🕊 Do not directly face a Y-junction. This too is deadly and should be dealt with either by blocking it from view with a clump of trees or by using a Pa Kua mirror.

🕊 In house number 4, the road is like an arrow slicing into the house. This is inauspicious and the orientation of the house should be changed, if possible.

🕊 When the land is triangular in shape as shown in the sketch of house 5, residents of the house will be vulnerable to loss.

🕊 Being located at the corner where the edge of the road is cutting into your house is not as favorable as if the road embraces your house.

BELOW *Roads shaped like arrows, which seem to strike deep at the heart of the house, should be avoided altogether.*

BELOW *Houses erected on triangular plots of land are liable to render their occupants susceptible to loss.*

BELOW *Corner positions are not recommended. It is better Feng Shui if the road curves around your house.*

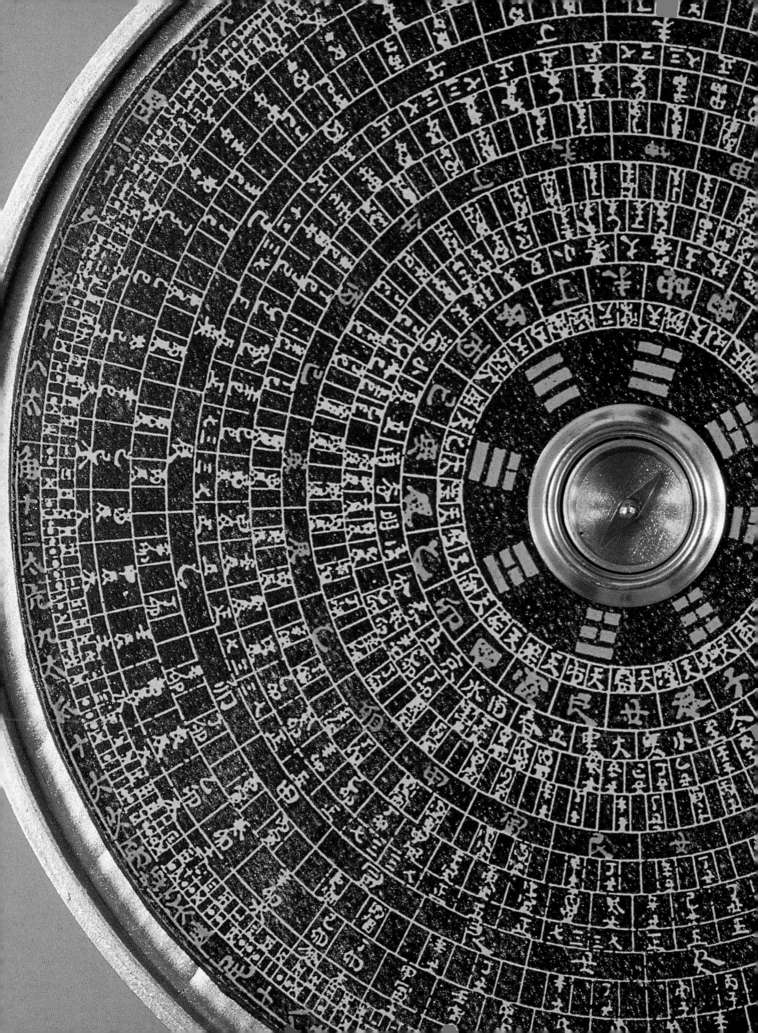

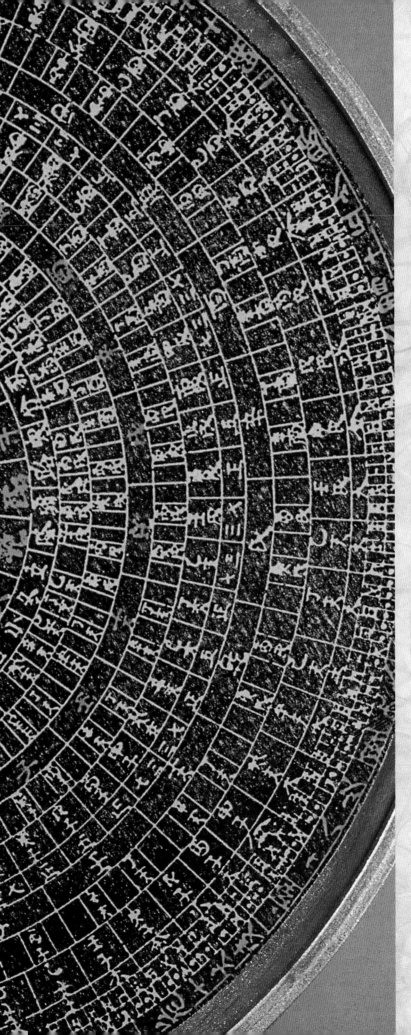

COMPASS FORMULA FENG SHUI

Compass Feng Shui uses special formulas to detect auspicious and bad luck directions (and sectors of the home/office) that are personalized according to gender and date of birth. Compass Feng Shui is an exact science requiring extreme and detailed accuracy, and for a long time, the computation methods of Compass Feng Shui stayed elusively hidden. In recent years however many of the old secrets that unlocked the computation of precious formulas have been released by masters and lineage holders thereby making this vital dimension of Feng Shui available to the world. These formulas have now been made simple, and so they should be.

Getting the formulas right is not difficult, since this requires only that one be accurate in taking compass readings and measurements. Practical difficulties arise when judgments and interpretations are required. There are also controversial issues that reflect differences in the application of Compass formulas. Thus progress in practice comes with experience. Included in this dictionary are many good formulas and techniques, including the powerfully potent Eight Mansions formula and the time dimensional flying star Feng Shui. Read this chapter slowly to understand the formulas. The time invested will bear fruit in real gold!

LEFT *The Feng Shui compass, the Luo Pan, is a complicated instrument, which requires great skill to use, but those engaged in professional Feng Shui consultation must know how to read one.*

CHAPTER FOUR: COMPASS FORMULA FENG SHUI

THE EVOLUTION OF FORMULA FENG SHUI

RIGHT *Form School Feng Shui bases its interpretations on the reading of the landscape, specifically the shapes and locations of mountains and the flow of rivers in the environment. Compass School Feng Shui recognizes the need to align the Chi of the environment with the human Chi of the people existing within it.*

BELOW *Compass School Feng Shui offers formulas that approach Feng Shui from the perspective of orientations based on the date of birth and sex of an individual, the number arrangements of the Lo Shu square, the use of the symbols of the Pa Kua, and compass directions and locations to harmonize the flow of Chi in the environment with the flow of Chi in the human body.*

While Landscape Feng Shui emphasizes the contours and shapes of mountains and the direction of flow of rivers, over the centuries Feng Shui practitioners realized the importance of also aligning the environment's Chi to the human Chi of the people living with the environment. This alignment was considered important to man's destiny and led to the development of specific calculations and techniques that were based on the symbols of the Pa Kua and the number arrangements of the Lo Shu square. The connections between these two main symbols of Feng Shui were the eight directions of the compass, leading Compass School Feng Shui to develop into a distinct and different school from Form School Feng Shui.

Form School, with its colorful animal symbolism, explained landscape in terms of Chi currents, deeming a place to have "good" or "bad" Feng Shui, depending on the way hills were placed relative to each other and how rivers flowed.

Compass School Feng Shui attempted to relate landscape Chi flows with the Chi flows of the human body, making use of the Pa Kua symbols and the Lo Shu square to correlate the individuals' birth dates, characteristics, and elements, with the currents of Chi in the Earth's environment.

These formulations became the basis for designing Yang dwellings (homes and workplaces), the

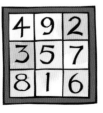

placement of individuals' rooms, the compass orientations of doors and bedrooms, kitchens, and entrances, and even the direction of travel and relocation. Much of the reasoning behind these formulations was based on the way the Lo Shu magic square was superimposed onto the Later Heaven Pa Kua, thereby matching numbers with compass directions.

From the master practitioners of the Compass School came the invention of the Luo Pan, the Chinese geomancer's compass. Interpreting the many rings of the geomancer's compass is a formidable task which incorporates understanding elements, the "star numbers," directions, and trigrams.

ABOVE *One of the Compass School formulations, the Eight Mansions* *formula, divides individuals into east or west group directions.*

A more practical approach toward interpreting Compass School formulations – easier to use and more easily adapted to modern living conditions – is thus recommended. Over the past few years this has led to a step-by-step simplification of various wonderful formulations which have been made available to the public through the generosity of several old masters. They have allowed these formulations, each from a different method, to see the light of day, and thus valuable and precious formulas have been transformed into easy reference tables from which practitioners can determine:

ABOVE *Flying star Feng Shui determines specific* *time periods when "star numbers" will bring good luck.*

◈ Their individual auspicious and inauspicious directions and locations. This is based on the Pa-Kua Lo-Shu theory of Feng Shui which is also known as the Eight Mansions Formula (or *Paht Chay*). This very potent formula divides people into those who should individually use corresponding west or east group directions and locations to enhance and magnify their Feng Shui luck.
◈ The good and bad months and years when auspicious and killing "star numbers" respectively bless or afflict their homes and corners of their homes. This method of Feng Shui is known as flying star (*Fey Sin*) Feng Shui, a formula which

ABOVE *The Feng Shui ruler will help you to calculate the* *most auspicious measurements for your home.*

deals exclusively with time dimension Feng Shui.
◈ The best and most auspicious dimensions to use on home and furniture. This is based on the different good and bad luck measurements on the Feng Shui ruler. This formula also offers specific types of good fortune that can be energized via dimensions therapy; also how to avoid bad luck caused by wrong measurements.
◈ The most auspicious locations for water features and the best directions for water flows, directly using water to attract prosperity and wealth to the dwelling place.

To master each of the above formulas requires a deep understanding of the fundamentals of Feng Shui theory. In the old days apprentices studied for years under

ABOVE *You will be able to recognize specific water* *features that will bring harmony to your life.*

Feng Shui masters. This required deep appreciation of the different nuances of the five element interactions and the Yin and Yang balance of forces.

I am fortunate to have received some of these secret lineages, but I admit that I do not have an in-depth knowledge of all the formulas. I have used the formulas in my books with much success and evidence suggests that they work for others, too. Be relaxed about trying out the formulas in this book. There is no need to believe too intensely in the practice of Feng Shui. Use the formulas as a fun way of decorating your home.

SEE ALSO
❖ The Concept of Chi: the dragon's cosmic breath *pp.32–3*
❖ The Eight Mansions Formula: Pa-Kua Lo-Shu formula *pp.72–5*
❖ Flying Star Feng Shui: the time dimension *pp.76–7*

CHAPTER FOUR: COMPASS FORMULA FENG SHUI

THE IMPORTANCE OF COMPASS DIRECTIONS AND LOCATIONS

ABOVE *Feng Shui masters are experts at using the Luo Pan compass, but today it is possible to use an accurate conventional compass.*

BELOW *If a modern compass is to be used for Feng Shui purposes, it needs to be calibrated in degrees to be used effectively.*

Before embarking on learning the formulas it is fundamental to understand the importance of the compass. In the old days Feng Shui practitioners used the Luo Pan – the ornate and extremely complex master's compass. Today, you can use a good modern compass. Select one that gives you readings in degrees – many of the formulas require very exact readings. These readings are usually related to the direction of the main door. The direction the door faces looking out plays a very big role in determining the suitability of the Feng Shui of the house for particular residents.

The second major input provided by the compass is in determining the different compass locations of the corners or sectors of the house. Many of the formulas, especially those that pertain to the magnification of energy, or Chi, in different parts of the house require different types of symbols to be placed in these corners. How to determine *what* symbol to place *where* depends entirely on the compass sector of the corner being decorated. To delineate these corners accurately you require a compass.

In this context it is useful to point out that not everyone does it this way. The Tibetan Black Hat Sect method of Professor Lin Yun delineates the nine sectors of the house differently, ignoring the real compass direction and using the door as the benchmark for determining the different corners to be activated. The Feng Shui that I have learned thus differs from Professor Lin Yun's method of space demarcation and identification.

Irrespective of the method being taught by different schools, the most important thing is to see what works for you. You should try both methods and then decide for yourself. But you should not try to mix two methods or formulas in the interpretations of specific recommendations. It should, however, be perfectly acceptable to practice different schools in different rooms to activate different aspects and dimensions of Feng Shui.

All this notwithstanding, compass directions and locations matter because of the importance of the five elements. Wuxing, or five elements theory, is so central to the practice of Feng Shui that I have devoted a large section in Part 1 to it (*see pages 40–5*). Without compass bearings in any space it is impossible for anyone to practice Formula Feng Shui.

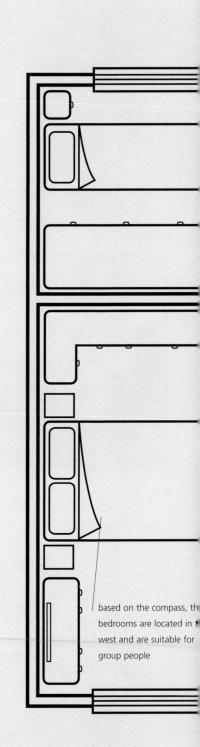

based on the compass, the bedrooms are located in the west and are suitable for group people

ABOVE *A house can be planned to create the best conditions for an auspicious environment using the tenets of Compass Formula Feng Shui.*

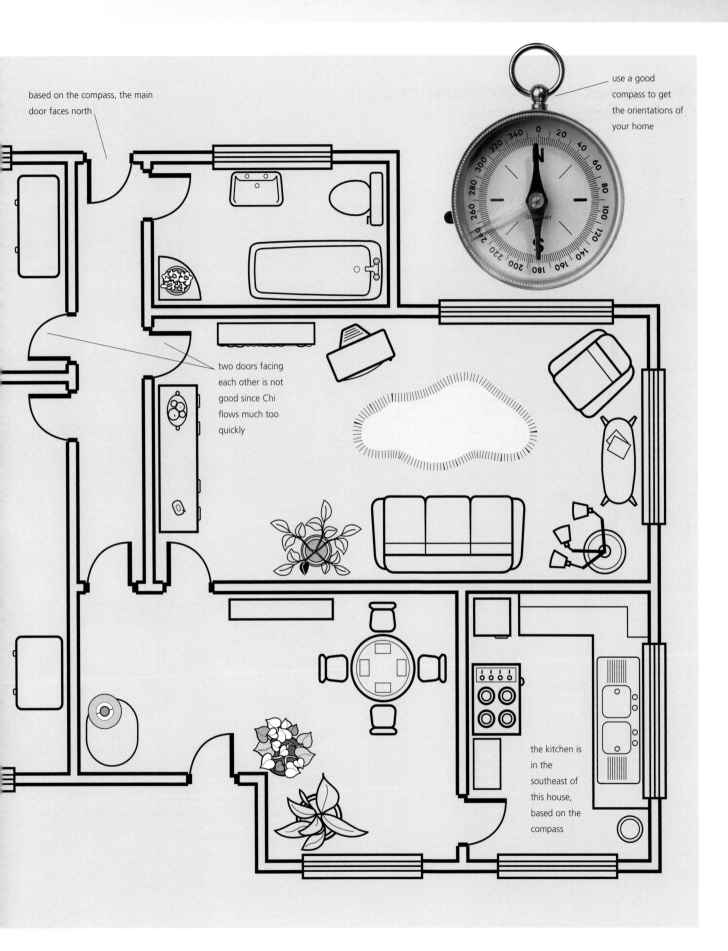

based on the compass, the main
door faces north

use a good
compass to get
the orientations of
your home

two doors facing
each other is not
good since Chi
flows much too
quickly

the kitchen is
in the
southeast of
this house,
based on the
compass

THE EIGHT MANSIONS FORMULA:
Pa-Kua Lo-Shu formula

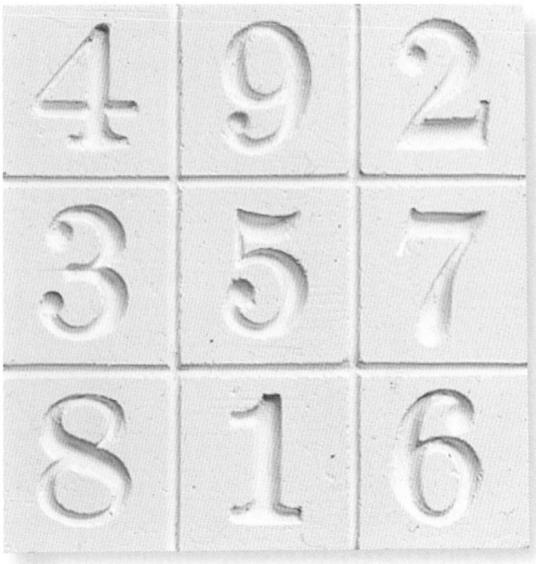

ABOVE *The Lo Shu square is a highly important symbol in Compass Formula Feng Shui and can be used in planning the layout of buildings, towns, and cities.*

I have discovered in more than twenty years of Feng Shui practice that this formula is probably the single most important bearer of excellent Feng Shui luck in our life. The Eight Mansions formula is easy to understand and use. All you need to compute your auspicious and inauspicious directions are:

- Your date of birth.
- Your gender.

This formula is used for identifying lucky locations and for determining auspicious and inauspicious directions. Start by calculating your Kua number. Use the formula here, and then refer to the table opposite for your most auspicious corners and directions. Note that these are your lucky locations as well as your most auspicious directions. The Kua or Eight Mansions formula is based on the premise that every individual is either an east or west group person.

THE FORMULA FOR DETERMINING YOUR KUA NUMBER

First, establish your Chinese calendar year of birth. This means if you were born before the lunar new year each year you must deduct 1 from your year of birth (you need the date of birth to determine this since, generally, this affects those born before February but it is useful to check the lunar calendar to be exact). Once you have done this, add the last two digits together. Keep adding the digits until you get a single digit number. Then:

For men, deduct this number from 10. The result is your Kua number.

For women, add this number to 5. The result is your Kua number.

If you get two digits keep adding until you reduce it to one digit, i.e., if you get the number 10 then 1+0=1; and if you get the number 14 then 1+4=5.

Example: date of birth March 6, 1956
Kua number 5+6=11 and then 1+1=2 and then

For women (add to 5) 2+5=7

For men (deduct from 10) 10−2=8

Example: date of birth January 3, 1962
Because the date of birth is before the lunar new year that year, we need to deduct 1 from the year, so instead of 1962 we will assume that the year of birth is 1961.

Thus Kua number is 6+1=7

For men (deduct from 10) 10−7=3

For women (add to 5) 7+5=9

With your Kua number, refer to the table opposite to determine your auspicious locations.

Note: If you are unable to find a Chinese calendar, this formula generally uses February 4th as the cut-off date to determine the Chinese year.

HOW TO DETERMINE AUSPICIOUS LOCATIONS

YOUR KUA NUMBER	YOUR AUSPICIOUS CORNERS AND LOCATIONS IN DESCENDING ORDER OF LUCK	INDICATING THAT YOU ARE AN EAST OR WEST GROUP PERSON
1	Southeast, East, South, North	East
2	Northeast, West, Northwest, Southwest	West
3	South, North, Southeast, East	East
4	North, South, East, Southeast	East
5	Men: Northeast, West, Northwest, Southwest	West
	Women: Southwest, Northwest, West, Northeast	West
6	West, Northeast, Southwest, Northwest	West
7	Northwest, Southwest, Northeast, West	West
8	Southwest, Northwest, West, Northeast	West
9	East, Southeast, North, South	East

With your Kua number, refer to the table below to determine your auspicious locations.

THE FOUR TYPES OF GOOD AND BAD LUCK

This formula uses the compass points to identify the four auspicious locations which also indicate the four most auspicious directions. But these are generalized good directions. The formula also breaks down the good and bad directions further by identifying exactly what it means by good and bad. Thus there are four types of good luck of which that indicated by the Sheng Chi is supposedly the best. The four types of good and bad luck, together with their meanings, are described below.

Your Kua number	1	2	3	4	5*	6	7	8	9
Auspicious Directions									
Your Sheng Chi, i.e. your success direction	SE	NE	S	N	NE SW	W	NW	SW	E
Your Tien Yi, i.e. health direction	E	W	N	S	W NW	NE	SW	NW	SE
Your Nien Yen, i.e. romance direction	S	NW	SE	E	NW W	SW	NE	W	N
Your Fu Wei, i.e. personal development direction	N	SW	E	SE	SW NE	NW	W	NE	S
Inauspicious Directions	1	2	3	4	5	6	7	8	9
Your Ho Hai, or unlucky direction	W	E	SW	NW	E S	SE	N	S	NE
Your Wu Kwei, or five ghosts direction	NE	SE	NW	SW	SE N	E	S	N	W
Your Lui Sha, or six killings direction	NW	S	NE	W	S E	N	SE	E	SW
Your Chueh Ming, or total loss direction	SW	N	W	NE	N SE	S	E	SE	NW

*Kua number 5, the first directions are for men, and the second are for women.

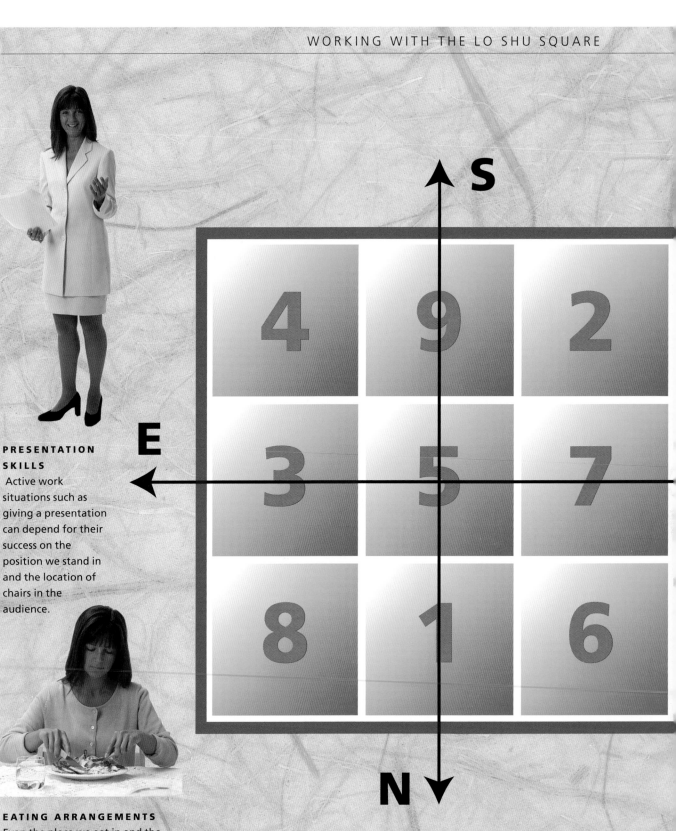

PRESENTATION SKILLS
Active work situations such as giving a presentation can depend for their success on the position we stand in and the location of chairs in the audience.

EATING ARRANGEMENTS
Even the place we eat in and the direction we face when eating can have important implications for the amount of good Feng Shui.

WORK STATION
It is important to face the most auspicious direction for you to ensure success at work.

SLEEPING ARRANGEMENTS
Not everyone can sleep in the ideal location in the house, but make the direction your head is pointing toward the most auspicious possible.

Thus, when orientating your sitting and sleeping directions, you must memorize your personal best (Sheng Chi) direction. Refer to the table (*see page 73*) and memorize the specific direction that is good for you in a particular way. Then always try to sit directly facing the direction you wish to activate. Thus, if wealth and success are what you want, go for the Sheng Chi direction; and if health is important to you, tap the Tien Yi, or doctor from heaven, direction and so forth.

In instances where sitting or sleeping in the desired direction is not physically possible, you should try at least to use one of your other three good directions. It may not be the direction you want but it is infinitely better to sit facing an acceptable direction than to sit facing a direction that is inauspicious and spells total loss for you. The formula describes the specific types of good and bad luck of all the eight directions of the compass.

Sleep with your head pointing in the right direction

If you have a choice of bedrooms, select the one that is in your most auspicious location. This means it should be the bedroom that is located in the corner of the building that corresponds to your best direction, i.e. your Sheng Chi direction. If you want success in your career or business, always try to select your Sheng Chi bedroom. Such a bedroom is located in your personal Sheng Chi direction. If this is north, go to the bedroom that is placed in the north of your house.

If it is not possible for you to have a Sheng Chi bedroom try to get a bedroom which is located in the part of the building that corresponds to one of your four good directions. If this is not possible, try to have a bed that is positioned in such a way that your head is pointing toward your best direction, so that while you sleep

excellent auspicious energy is flowing into you from your Sheng Chi direction. This is a powerful method of enjoying really excellent Feng Shui. If you really cannot tap your Sheng Chi sleeping direction, again try to tap one of your four best directions.

Sit in your best Feng Shui position

Where we sit, and the direction we face when we sit, can have important Feng Shui connotations. Thus, where we sit at work, the direction we face while negotiating, giving a presentation, or making a speech affects our luck. How our chairs are oriented when we eat, gamble, or simply socialize can all have Feng Shui implications.

It is possible consciously to improve our luck merely by using the formula and focusing on our seating arrangement – the placement and orientation of our own chairs and tables. Make certain your office table and chair is positioned to capture your most auspicious directions and placement. When you eat at home do the same thing. I always recommend memorizing one's individual auspicious directions and carrying a compass around so that there is never a time when one does not at least sit facing one of the four good directions.

BELOW *When the chips are down, remember that the direction you face can affect the outcome of your endeavor.*

CHAPTER FOUR: COMPASS FORMULA FENG SHUI

FLYING STAR FENG SHUI: the time dimension

BELOW *Flying star Feng Shui is concerned with time, since auspicious orientations may only last for a specific period. Interpreting the Lo Shu square will enable you to recognize the influence of time on your Feng Shui luck.*

In addition to space considerations, Feng Shui also has a time dimension. This is related to the relevance of time cycles, and the technique of analyzing the Feng Shui of time periods is collectively practiced under what is known as Flying Star Feng Shui. This focuses on the significance of changing forces during different time periods. The process highlights the intangible influences of the numbers and combinations of numbers of the magic Lo Shu square.

This adds vital nuances to "good" and "bad" Feng Shui and explains that good or bad luck in terms of the harmony or disharmony in the environment does not necessarily occur continuously or last forever. Nor do auspicious and inauspicious orientations remain the same throughout one's entire life.

Flying Star Feng Shui allows the practitioner to undertake annual monitoring of changes in the Feng Shui luck of a house by studying the influence of the Earth's intangible forces. This is time dimension Feng Shui which therefore alerts the practitioner to inauspicious forces. Unless dealt with or countered, these intangible

forces are believed to cause serious misfortune to residents. Equally there are auspicious forces, and these too can be enhanced.

Numbers and the Lo Shu grid

Time dimension theory revolves around numbers and reflects the basic fundamentals of Chinese numerology. The main tool in the formulation and understanding of this theory is the original Lo Shu square. In this square, the numbers 1 to 9 are arranged around the nine squares of the Lo Shu grid in such a way that any three numbers read in any direction add up to 15, whether calculated horizontally, vertically, or diagonally. The number 15 expresses the number of days it takes for a new moon to become a full moon.

Even numbers, which carry Yin energy, are placed at each corner of the square. Note the positions of the numbers, 2, 4, 6, and 8.

Odd numbers, which carry Yang energy, appear on the four compass

points. Thus 1, 3, 7, and 9 are placed on north, east, west, and south, while the number 5 is placed in the center.

The numbers move around the grid in a preset sequence that sets the flight path for the way all other numerals should "fly." The numbers have meanings. They signify the elements, and interact with each other and the objects of the compass location in which they are found.

These interactions are dynamic and they create the intangible unseen forces that transform the energy either into bad, killing energy or into good, lucky energy. Flying Star Feng Shui is about diagnosing the relevant combination of numbers in various locations of the home. Flying Star Feng Shui thus requires an understanding of the meanings of these numbers, and the ability to interpret whether or not the numbers in each compass location bring good fortune and, if it turns out they do not, how to counter the effect of bad flying stars.

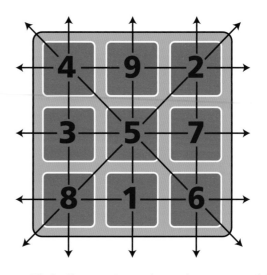

ABOVE *The Lo Shu square is often regarded as having "magical" properties, in part because the arrangement of the numbers means that a line in any direction adds up to 15.*

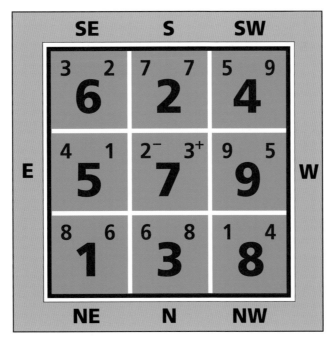

LEFT *An example of a typical Lo Shu flying star natal chart showing the positions of the Siang Sin and Chor Sin stars and their movement around the grid. This is a Period of Seven House natal chart, and the big number 7 is in the center. From this chart I can tell that the house is facing the north direction.*

Hence the name "Fey Sin Feng Shui," or Flying Star Feng Shui. In fact, of course, the stars that are referred to are imaginary stars. In each of the nine grids there is a main star numeral, a mountain star or Chor Sin numeral, and a water star or Siang Sin numeral. These star numerals change (or fly) from one grid to the next. They also fly from period to period.

Look at the example of a typical Lo Shu flying star natal chart. This chart shows a Period of Seven House with its main door located in the north sector and the door facing the first subsection of north direction. The small numbers on the left of the main star numeral are the Siang Sin stars. Note their flight path and also how the numbers change.

The numbers on the right of the main star numeral are the Chor Sin stars. Note also the way they fly around the grid and change numbers as they move from one compass sector to the next.

Flying Star Feng Shui examines these star numerals and draws conclusions about auspicious and inauspicious sectors of a dwelling place during a specific time period, based on these star numbers. This technique, its method of computation, its analyses, and the applications to which it can be put, make up the substance of any book on flying star Feng Shui.

Reigning numbers and time periods

Flying Star usage starts with the knowledge of time periods. The numbers of the Lo Shu square vary from period to period. In each period there is what is referred to as "the reigning Lo Shu number."

At the moment we are in the period of seven. This 20-year period started in 1984 and is scheduled to come to an end in the year 2003. The reigning number is seven, because the applicable Lo Shu arrangement of numbers has seven as the main numeral star situated in the center of the square.

The reigning number for the next 20-year period will be eight, and for the 20-year period following that will be nine. In addition, there are also reigning stars for each year, each month, and each day. These reigning Lo Shu numbers are an integral part of the Chinese Almanac, or Tong Shu, where good and bad days for all sorts of events are worked out each year. These calculations can also be said to be based on flying star Feng Shui. The Almanac is sold throughout the Far East. The Chinese version has a detailed listing of good and bad dates. The English version is more explanatory and is not a reference calendar like the Chinese one.

Natal chart of dwellings

In addition, and more relevant to Feng Shui practice, these reigning numbers also form the basis for casting the natal chart of buildings, homes, and any kind of structure. From the natal chart it is possible to tell whether or not a place or building will enjoy favorable Feng Shui during designated months and years. These periods of good or bad Feng Shui can be as short as a week or as long as a year. The natal chart also reveals the locations within a house that will have excellent luck during that period and the rooms that could cause illness, loss, and serious misfortune.

SEE ALSO

❖ How to Superimpose the Lo Shu Square p.130

❖ How to Apply the Formulas in Your Home p.131

❖ Arrangements of Furniture pp.174–7

CHAPTER FOUR: COMPASS FORMULA FENG SHUI

INTERPRETATION AND MEANINGS OF THE NUMBERS

The interpretation and meanings of the numerals and combinations of numerals are based on two significant symbolic relationships, i.e:

❧ Based on the meanings of the numbers themselves.

❧ Based on the relationship between the numbers and the elements and then on the implied interaction of the five elements as expressed in the form of numbers. This dependence on the five elements, or Wuxing, is the key to really understanding flying star.

understanding Wuxing. The inter-relationship of the two is in fact a lot more complex.

The best Feng Shui master is the one who understands the subtleties and nuances of the way the five elements are said to interact with each other, and such a person will be able to give out the best advice on Feng Shui cures, antidotes, enhancers, or activators.

Each number from 1 to 9 represents an element, but the exact nature of the representation differs from number to number. Thus, for instance, both 3 and 4 represent the wood element, but 3 is big wood and 4 is small wood.

Other meanings of numbers

The numbers also have meanings in accordance with the corresponding trigram. These operate on two different levels:

❧ The symbolic relationship between number and trigram is, at the beginning, based on the placement of the numbers in the original Lo Shu square.

❧ When interpreting natal chart and period Lo Shu flying charts we also have to see the relationship of the numbers in the period flying chart under review. Thus, for example, the number 1 is representative of the trigram Kan in the original Lo Shu square. Then in a flying star chart for, say 1999, the number 1 has *flown* into the center. This means Kan, which represents water, has flown into the center, which is of the earth element; according to conventional analysis, water coming to earth does not harm the earth unless it comes in large amounts. Thus we will need to combine this reading with the actual natal chart of the house. If there is a preponderance of 1s in the center grid, and especially if the water star is also 1 in the center grid, we are then looking at an excess of water in the center. This spells danger.

These symbolic relationships form the basis of Chinese numerology interpretations. It is important to appreciate the subtleties of the five elements. Feng Shui is not usually just about each element or number being bad or good. It is also about the "heaviness" of the occurrence of the number. When there is excess of anything, there ceases to be harmony and balance and the Feng Shui becomes sour.

ABOVE *The relationships between the five elements have an influence on the interactions between numbers.*

The five elements

The impact of Wuxing on flying star interpretation is extremely important. Usually the difference between "good" and "bad" Feng Shui masters is the depth of knowledge they each bring to bear when analyzing and interpreting the element relationships. Only when the understanding is correct can the real remedies or enhancers be recommended. Also, Wuxing is not as simple as it at first appears. Understanding the productive and destructive cycle is only the start of

Furthermore, 3 is arousing wood while 4 is gentle wood. Also, 3 is male and 4 is female and so on. Each of these attributes adds on a layer of meaning. The whole should then be viewed in its entirety so that a coherent and complete picture emerges. It is in implementing the combinations that good Feng Shui is achieved. This is a challenge to the practitioner, but it makes flying star Feng Shui exciting. When you get it right, good fortune comes almost immediately.

MATCHING THE LO SHU SQUARE WITH THE PA KUA

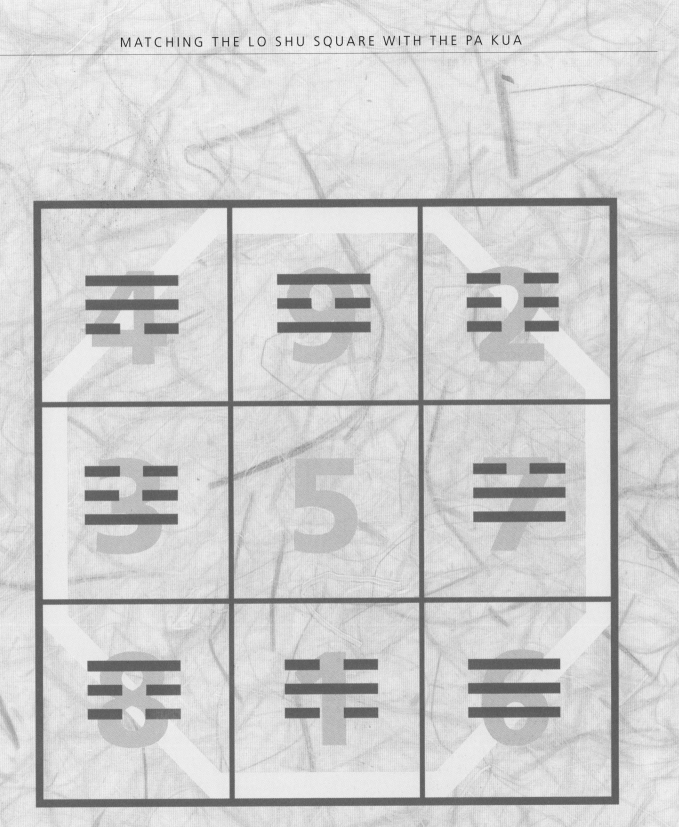

ABOVE *The Lo Shu square, Pa Kua, and trigrams. Each number is related to an element.*

SYMBOLIC FENG SHUI

Symbolism pervades so much of Feng Shui philosophy that understanding its importance is crucial to the correct application of Feng Shui. The origins of symbolic Feng Shui go back as far into Chinese history as the I Ching. Chinese words and writing originated as symbols. The broken and unbroken lines of the trigrams of the Pa Kua are symbols. And symbols pervade all the rituals, beliefs, and folklore of China. In the past, literacy and access to the written sources of Feng Shui were confined to the privileged classes so that among ordinary people symbols became the main way of communicating simple beliefs, particularly in relation to good and bad luck.

The use of symbolic good-fortune motifs, animals, plants, and objects has thus been incorporated into modern-day Feng Shui. When carefully chosen and placed in the personal environment, at work or at home, symbols can quickly bring good fortune. More, they can also be used as effective remedies against bad flying stars and unsuitable directions and locations that are diagnosed under Compass Formula Feng Shui techniques. Understanding symbolism then becomes then an inherent part of Feng Shui practice.

LEFT *The placement of giant-sized Fu dogs outside large buildings is believed to bring great protective luck.*

CHAPTER FIVE: SYMBOLIC FENG SHUI

ORIGINS OF SYMBOLISM

ABOVE *A 19th-century Chinese interior – the application of symbolic Feng Shui has been a part of everyday life in China for centuries.*

ABOVE *The Pa Kua, here in the form of a mirror, is one of the main symbolic elements of protective Feng Shui.*

The symbolism of Feng Shui is rich in the imagery of a people steeped in ancient folklore and legends. This is to be expected since the Chinese have a longer recorded history than that of most other civilizations. The stories and legends associated with China's main symbols of good fortune were handed down by word of mouth. The grand matriarchs of Chinese households ruled their family residences with an iron rod. Feng Shui dictated the allocation of rooms, and the décor of bedchambers, halls, and receiving rooms. Superstition governed the placement of good fortune paintings, urns, and other decorative items. The manuals of placement provided guidance on the flowers to cultivate and the fruit trees to grow. The Tong Shu (the 100-year calendar) gave advice on the most propitious times to organize all kinds of happy occasions – from marriage dates to

dates for travel, for the employment of new servants, and the taking in of new concubines. Old taboos and ancient rituals governed so much of life in China in those days.

Many of these rituals and beliefs came from the ancient practice of Feng Shui. Because China was such a vast country of different groups, literacy was often confined only to

the most privileged classes. It was this more than anything that caused symbols to become so important in the communication of taboos that seemed to veer toward the metaphysical and the superstitious. In the old days, science as we know it today was unknown.

As a result, symbolism came to be the main way of communicating simplistic beliefs of good and bad luck. Objects – animals and plants, domestic and celestial creatures – came to symbolize various life aspirations. Many of these symbols have their roots in the origins of Feng Shui, which include the symbols of the *I Ching*, the symbolism of the Pa Kua, and the numbers of the Lo Shu. The common threads that pulled these three main sets of symbols together were the directions of the compass.

The symbols can protect against bad luck. There are also many good fortune energizers which can be strategically placed in the living space to attract auspicious Chi.

There is great power in the practice of symbolic Feng Shui. When symbols of good fortune are cleverly chosen and strategically placed within the living space, they bring good fortune very quickly. The use of symbolic objects to turn around bad luck also seems to work a lot faster than most people realize.

LEFT *The Chinese have often used animal objects as symbols of good or bad luck. This three-legged toad brings increased prosperity.*

HOW TO USE SYMBOLS AS FENG SHUI ENHANCERS

The best way to activate symbols of good fortune in the living space is first to understand the scope and approach to the branch of symbolic Feng Shui practice. Taoist charms, numerology, environmentalism, deities, fruits, flowers, plants, creatures, animals, and everyday household objects are only some of the categories of lucky symbols that can be harnessed to add to the good fortune of any living space.

The first step is to identify some of the more common powerful symbols and then to learn where to place them to get maximum benefit from their presence in the home or workplace. In this context it is useful to consider some general principles of symbolism.

BELOW *There are many symbolic items for energizing a room. They also look good in their own right.*

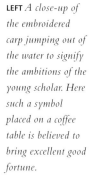

LEFT *A close-up of the embroidered carp jumping out of the water to signify the ambitions of the young scholar. Here such a symbol placed on a coffee table is believed to bring excellent good fortune.*

the Chinese consider orange trees to be auspicious

seven gold elephants bring good fortune

a sailing ship laden with gold encourages wealth and success

peonies enhance love and romance

a pair of goldfish will bring success in abundance

CHAPTER FIVE: SYMBOLIC FENG SHUI

HOW DOES SYMBOLIC FENG SHUI WORK?

ABOVE *Calligraphic symbols for "Feng Shui" echo the fact that symbolism plays a great part in Feng Shui.*

BELOW *Yang energy can be stimulated by nonphysical symbols, such as the smell of burning incense filling a room.*

Symbols impact on the subconscious, which makes up the main part of our mind. The old masters understood this and appreciated the effect of symbols on the general well-being of our living environments. The art and science of symbolism thus play an extremely important role in the practice of Feng Shui.

Symbolism plays an integral part in Chinese culture where everything has a meaning and an effect greater than is realized. This is reflected in the Chinese language itself where every character is a symbol, a picture that connotes an idea or concept. Usually these concepts cannot be expressed in another language because of the cultural experience required to understand the deeper meaning of the characters. Literal translations can thus be misleading. The Chinese language communicates

ABOVE *The peony is a symbol of good fortune, particularly in love and romance.*

through pictures, and symbolism is deeply ingrained in the Chinese way of life, in their culture, and in their philosophies.

This is apparent in Chinese art, architecture, poetry, literature, and craftsmanship. Every word and picture is believed to have subtle energies, meanings, and purpose. This means that all objects placed in a space can stimulate both the Chi of the environment as well as the human Chi of residents at a subconscious, and thus deeper, level.

Symbols do not necessarily have to be physical. Symbols of good and bad fortune can be anything that has the power to stimulate the energies of the space or residence. Sounds, smells, and colors all contribute to the power of symbols. These represent frequencies associated with

aspirations, ideas, and moods. Symbolism also relates to Yin and Yang dimensions of energy. Thus songs, fragrances, and colors that invoke Yang energy often bring laughter and good fortune to dwellings. Too many Yang symbols, however, can cause problems, just as Yin symbols can cause moodiness.

Thus the energy of places can be manipulated to suggest and create happy, sad, exciting, soothing, arousing, or any kinds of mood depending on the balance of Yin and Yang energy. Feelings, moods, and dispositions can therefore be manipulated through the placement of symbolic representations, which in turn can have more of a Yang or a Yin concentration.

THE GODS OF WEALTH

RIGHT *Tsai Shen Yen, one of the gods of wealth according to Chinese tradition.*

The Chinese have different versions of the Choy San, or God of Wealth. All of these wealth deities are believed to bring extremely auspicious money luck and prosperity into the household. These gods are rarely worshiped in a religious sense but they are regarded with some reverence and there are those who "pray" to the gods directly for money. The spiritual connotations associated with these deities relate mainly to Taoist rituals. I have discovered that displaying them in the home is usually sufficient for drawing on their power to attract money luck.

The most popular God of Wealth is Tsai Shen Yen, who is believed to be the deified spirit of a sage of the twelfth century B.C.E., Pi Kan. In certain parts of China and among certain dialect groups he is worshiped on the twentieth day of the seventh moon, mostly by very poor people and gamblers all wanting some wealth luck. He is often featured sitting on a tiger and his heart is said to have seven orifices. Sometimes he is shown seated holding an ingot in his left hand and a golden scepter of authority in his right hand. According to an old text, this spiritual deity is associated with the wealth tree. These trees have branches that are strings of cash, and fruits that are ingots of gold, all of which can be obtained simply by shaking the tree.

Another extremely popular God of Wealth is the powerful Kuan Kung, also known as Kuan Ti, the God of War and Literature. Kuan Kung was actually a war-hero general of the Three Kingdoms period, recognized for brave deeds and meritorious service. He was deified in the sixteenth century. Kuan Kung is the patron saint of both the police and the triads, the tutelary deity of all money-making enterprises, and a powerful protector of people such as politicians, leaders, and business tycoons.

If you want to display the gods of wealth in your house, place them on a high table or shelf preferably facing the front door. If you have an altar it is not a good idea to place these deities on the same level as your Buddhas.

Another image of wealth is that of the fish which, to the Chinese, conjures up the word "yu," which also sounds like the word for abundance.

BELOW *Kuan Kung is regarded as a particularly powerful deity, looking after the interests of many important people.*

For this reason fish have always been associated with abundance. So, when we see plenty of fish we see abundance; this is something that is rooted in the culture of the Chinese. Thus fish fill a space with feelings of abundance that are strengthened by generations of memory.

An aquarium of happy, swimming fish usually represents precious Yang energy which brings good fortune. This is why keeping goldfish is so popular with the Chinese. When placed in the living or dining room, fish create feelings of abundance.

But place an aquarium in a bedroom, where Yin energy should predominate, and you will create an imbalance, which could lead to loss and the possibility of a robbery.

BELOW *Happy, healthy fish swimming in a pond or an aquarium help enhance conditions for prosperity.*

CHAPTER FIVE: SYMBOLIC FENG SHUI

THE SYMBOLISM OF THE HOUSE

RIGHT *According to Feng Shui, the house is the embodiment of the person who dwells within it – if the arrangement of the house is not harmonious and contains blockages then the well-being of its occupant is affected.*

In Feng Shui, the house actually symbolizes the person. The door is the mouth, the rooms on either side of the main door are the lungs, the center is the heart, the back door is the anus, the roof is the head, and the windows are the eyes and ears. The house should be symmetrical, like the human body.

When the house is awkwardly shaped, or if something is missing, it affects our well-being. If it sits on precarious or unstable land, the people inside are likely to feel unstable. If we open the door every day and there is a wall or tree directly in front of it, we are constantly confronting an obstruction. This symbolizes blockage and it causes energies to stagnate, inducing blockages and obstructions in our life. To use a metaphor, it is hard to breathe when something is blocking your mouth. When the house is dirty with blocked drains and layers of grime, the body feels uncomfortable and in need of a wash. When there is insufficient sunlight, the body suffers, just as when there is too much sunlight the body also suffers. Balance and harmony are extremely important.

Meanwhile even inanimate objects, such as pictures, paintings, jewelry, sculpture, and so forth, possess Chi, or energy. There are symbols that invoke various kinds of meanings to our subconscious mind and thus affect the energy quality of places and spaces. Feng Shui acknowledges the influence of symbolic associations on the psychological and physical well-being of people that occupy any

ABOVE *Good Feng Shui will stimulate the Chi in your living environment, helping to improve your prosperity.*

space. Consequently in Feng Shui it is vital to surround ourselves with images or symbols that "empower" our minds, bodies, and homes with positive growth energies.

We have also seen that the shapes, color, vegetation, and direction of a mountain are symbolic of different types of energy. For instance, if we have green, round mountains behind us, this offers protection and positive earth energies. However, we cannot obtain any kind of benevolent protection from mountains that are predominantly sharp or rocky.

Everything in the living space around us has symbolic meaning and Feng Shui is the art of creating an environment rich with auspicious symbolism that elicits prosperity within every dimension of our life. Once we become aware of our environment and its effects, we can empower and energize it with suitable symbols.

Used correctly, Symbolic Feng Shui becomes a reinforcement that takes us into an upward cycle of progress and growth. The more energy we put into creating such an auspicious environment the more it benefits us. Therefore in Feng Shui everything around us and in our living space should be carefully selected and placed. Color, location, number, shape, size, type, and so forth can all take on a special meaning and will affect us in a particular way.

The goal is to make as many things as possible promote your well-being. No matter which way you turn, which room you go into, positive images and stimuli are always activating mental and human Chi. These induce positive thoughts that in turn help you to realize personal goals and desires.

THE MOST AUSPICIOUS CHI LIN

The dragon horse, or the Chinese unicorn, is a fabulous creature of good omen. It is the symbol of longevity, richness, enchantment, illustrious offspring, enormous riches, and great spiritual wisdom. The dragon horse is reputed to be so special a creature that many legends associated with the birth of Confucius and other wise men feature omens associated with it. Some say that Confucius' mother became pregnant by stepping onto the footsteps of the dragon horse soon after she returned from the mountains where she had undertaken a year-long religious retreat. A dragon horse is said to have emerged from the Yellow River and appeared to Fu Hsi, the first legendary emperor, bearing on its back a mystical map from which Fu developed many wonderful methods for improving harvests and using water to bring great wealth. In Buddhist texts and ancient art, the dragon horse is shown carrying the texts on wisdom. In China, the Chi Lin (also Gi Lin) is regarded as one of the four great mythical creatures said to be endowed with mystical powers and signifying great good fortune wherever they appear.

The auspicious attributes of the Chi Lin make it a perennial favorite with artists and artisans who, over the centuries, have perfected this image using various media. Chinese homes are fond of displaying Chi Lin because he represents great good fortune. This use of good fortune symbols associated with mythical creatures and with special wealth deities is due to the belief that human beings lack the purity of karma to "see" these wonderful beings or creatures. As a result, man has to resort to making physical images of them in order to create their "presence" in the home. Because the creatures are so powerful, even just displaying their manmade image is believed to create auspicious luck wherever they happened to be positioned.

The main attribute of the dragon horse is its perfect benevolence to all. Endowed with great compassion, its presence in the home will instantly reduce all bad luck arising from poor astrological birth times. It is always displayed alone, and never in pairs. It should not be confused with the protective Fu dogs. In recent times, specially designed and crafted dragon horses standing elegantly amid a field of coins and gold ingots have come on to the market. These symbols are used to simulate the dragon horse's magical presence very effectively.

Place the dragon horse in your living room in the north to enhance your career, in the east to improve your health, and in the southeast to attract wealth. You can also display a small image of it on your office table to attract good fortune. The dragon horse is an excellent gift for anyone who is starting a new job or project.

BELOW *The Chi Lin is one of the most potent images of good luck in Chinese mythology, and such images are found in many homes.*

CHAPTER FIVE: SYMBOLIC FENG SHUI

ALL THE SYMBOLS OF GOOD FORTUNE

It is impossible to list all the symbols of good fortune but included in this chapter are some of the more popular representations which can be obtained with little difficulty and placed in the home.

The main symbols that can be activated within the home are:
- Symbols of wealth and success. These symbols include Chinese coins; the sailing ship; the wealth vase; the three-legged toad; the dragon fish, or arrowana; the goldfish; lucky gold calligraphy; the pot of gold; the auspicious red bat.

ABOVE *The wealth vase is a popular symbol of prosperity in Chinese homes, often containing lucky red packets. It should be crystal or ceramic.*

- Symbols of longevity. The most popular longevity symbols are the red-topped crane; the everlasting pine tree; the peach of immortality; the deer; Sau, God of Longevity; the bamboo; and the cicada.
- Symbols of love, romance, and conjugal bliss. Empowering love energy benefits from the peony flower; mandarin ducks; the double-happiness sign.

In addition to the above three major categories of good fortune symbols there are:
- The four celestial creatures of good fortune, which are the dragon, the phoenix, the unicorn, and the turtle.
- Eight auspicious or precious objects. The mystic knot; the conch; the canopy or parasol; the vase; the wheel; the double fish; the lotus; the banner of victory.
- Auspicious fruits and flower symbols. These include oranges;

ABOVE *The lotus flower is very lucky image to have in the home, and is an attractive symbol of good fortune.*

lime plants; pomegranates; tomatoes; the plum. Flowers such as the chrysanthemum, the peony, the orchid, and the plum blossom are all suitable.
- Symbols of protection, which include the Fu dog; the tiger; the eagle; the fan; and various types of Taoist charms and amulets.

BELOW *A pair of mandarin ducks positioned in the home is auspicious for romantic love and happy marriage.*

THE AUSPICIOUS FISH IN FENG SHUI

The Chinese word for fish, "yu," means "abundance and affluence." The goldfish symbolizes wealth: "gold," as in goldfish, in abundance ("yu"). This meaning is thus "Year after year, may you live in affluence." The double fish is also one of the eight precious symbols of great good fortune. Feng Shui recommends placing fish tanks to symbolize good fortune especially when filled with the lucky goldfish, the arrowana (dragon fish) or the colorful koi or Japanese carp. It is also believed that a tank of black fish (i.e. black goldfish) can be placed in an inauspicious or afflicted corner of a building to help ward off the bad Chi caused by poison arrows.

The best location for a fish tank in the house is in the living room, along the north wall or along the east or southeast walls. Fish tanks should not be placed in the south unless for specific purposes such as overcoming bad flying stars in the south. For the most auspicious results, observe the following guidelines:

🐟 Keep a single arrowana. Buy the best you can afford.

🐟 Keep nine goldfish, at least one of which should be black.

🐟 Keep plenty of koi: these are very sociable fish and they love company.

🐟 Keep fish in a pair to symbolize romance and love. Goldfish are best.

BELOW Place a single arrowana, or dragon fish, in your fish tank to help attract wealth and success into your life.

ABOVE Goldfish symbolize wealth. The optimum number to keep is nine, including one black fish.

In addition, remember that:

🐟 Fish motifs hung off rooftops help to encourage good luck for the coming year.

🐟 It is auspicious to eat raw carp called "Yee-Sang," during the seventh day of the Chinese New Year.

🐟 Aquariums should not be placed in the bedroom or in the kitchen.

🐟 Aquariums should be rectangular or round. Fish are also excellent if kept in large ceramic decorative urns.

CHAPTER FIVE: SYMBOLIC FENG SHUI

THE CURRENT PERIOD OF SEVEN: 1984 through 2003

ABOVE *Seven golden elephants located in the west part of the house are extremely auspicious in the current period of 1984–2003.*

In Feng Shui, this period is considered to be the period of seven when anything placed in numbers of seven create powerful energy patterns. When placed in the west the potency increases because seven is also the number of the west. Thus, during this period anything hung or displayed in the west part of the home or living room which symbolizes the number seven and the element gold will be auspicious. Examples of such symbols of good fortune – dragons, phoenixes, horses, elephants, and so forth – in the color of gold to imitate the metal element will be very lucky when they are placed in the west part of the home. Make sure, of course, that there are seven of each of the good fortune symbols.

RIGHT *The phoenix is one of the celestial creatures of good fortune – seven of these beautiful creatures will bring great fortune, particularly if colored gold.*

THE SIGNIFICANCE OF NUMBERS

Next, it is also useful to note the other numbers which are lucky, irrespective of the period. These significantly lucky numbers are 1, 6, 7, and 8. Thus, when you display anything for good luck, one way of doing it is to keep them in these lucky numbers.

Examples of items displayed for good luck would be:

 A painting with six dragon fish would be perfect for the northwest corner of a room.

 A single tortoise in the north. One is the number of the north and keeping a tortoise here would symbolize various types of good fortune, including longevity, protection, support, staying power, and wealth luck.

 Six coins hung in the northwest to simulate the luck of the northwest, which benefits the father of the family. Empowering this corner of the home is always a good thing since the northwest also signifies the luck of patronage from important people. It also brings excellent networking luck.

 Seven crystal balls in the west, which brings enormous good fortune to the family and especially to the next generation. The crystal balls represent the earth element that produces gold hidden in its depths. The circular shape is excellent for inducing the luck of the metal element. Additionally, crystal balls also symbolize smooth, unobstructed movement for the family.

 Eight bright lights in the northeast. Lights always signify good fortune and the northeast is one of the best corners of the home in which to have lights. This simulates the luck of knowledge for residents so that stupidity or carelessness does not cause misfortune. Light is also excellent for bringing good fortune in education to the younger generation of the family. Eight is the number of the northeast and is thus particularly suitable for this corner of the house or room. In addition, the number eight is always considered lucky anytime and anywhere so that placing the number eight on motor cars, addresses, and telephone numbers is said to symbolize good fortune.

Finally, in addition to the above lucky numbers there is also the ultimate lucky number, which is nine. This number represents the direction south, and it is also representative of the fullness of heaven and earth. Remember that nine of everything, ranging from the number of goldfish to keep to the number of coins that are tied to your receipt book, always brings good fortune.

BELOW *A single tortoise or turtle in the north is generally auspicious.*

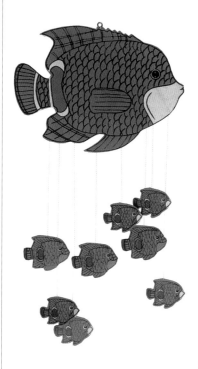

ABOVE *If it is not possible to have live fish, a mobile can be as effective, but make sure there are nine fish.*

ABOVE *Hang six coins in the northwest to elicit luck from influential people.*

CHAPTER FIVE: SYMBOLIC FENG SHUI

ENERGIZING GOOD FORTUNE SYMBOLS

RIGHT *The interior of your home can be adjusted to take advantage of auspicious elements. Note the position of chandelier, spotlights, plants – and goldfish pond! Note also the feeling of space which simulates the auspicious Bright Hall inside the house.*

When you have decided which of the good fortune symbols you wish to invite into your home, you should first look for a suitable corner to display the object without it being too obvious. Good fortune symbols should blend in with the décor of the home and, most importantly, they need to be energized. They must also be washed clean of any stagnant energy which might be hanging onto them. This latter consideration becomes a factor when you bring home an antique, which may have stood for many years in someone else's home, or had many owners.

The best way of "purifying" the energy of an antique object is to have it thoroughly cleaned and, before bringing it into the home, to rub it with sea salt after which it should again be wiped clean. If it won't be spoiled by water, soak it in a salt bath for a period of seven days and seven nights.

Meanwhile, you should also give thought to empowering the object that you are bringing into your home. These are different ways of energizing different objects but the best and simplest method is to tie a red thread to the object. The red color symbolically awakens the energy field around the object,

thereby enabling it to interact harmoniously with the Chi in the living space. If you do not have suitable red thread, you can also stick auspicious red paper onto the bottom of the object.

Placement according to the five elements

The final consideration is to work out the corner in which you are going to place the object. Finding

RIGHT *Soak crystals in a bowl of salt water to wash off any stagnant Chi.*

THE FUNDAMENTALS OF FENG SHUI

the best place for any decorative object or painting brought into the home in order to benefit the Feng Shui of the house can sometimes be a tricky proposition.

You must remember never to place large objects in a way that transforms them into poison arrows. Thus, for instance, do not place a large statue in the middle of the path of vision of the main front door. This creates a blockage inside the house. Similarly, do not hang so-called fortune windchimes all over the place either.

The best way of deciding on the suitable placement of good fortune objects is to apply the theory of the five elements, or Wuxing theory. Using the Later Heaven arrangement of the trigrams on the Pa Kua as a guide, find out which element is dominant in each compass direction. This enables you to identify the dominant Chi, or energy, of each corner of the home or individual room. You then look at your object or ask yourself which

element is symbolized by it. You can determine this by referring to the color or the shape of the object itself or the medium in which it is made. For example, gold elephants are best placed in the west or northwest, while water features are suit the north, the east, or the southeast.

Applying the five elements enables you to empower and strengthen the different corners of your home. It does not matter what each of the corners represents because, in the overall scheme of things, we all want our lives to be complete. Thus, when we energize every corner of our home, it causes every aspect of our life to manifest good fortune and abundance. Use the table below to

identify the appropriate objects for each of the eight corners of the home, based on compass readings.

BELOW *The use of the color red in objects is auspicious, such as the ribbon on this dragon and the red plant pot in the room shown opposite.*

ENERGIZERS

COMPASS CORNER	ELEMENT	NUMBER	ENERGIZE WITH... (suggestions only)
North	Water	1	Aquariums, ponds, blue, wealth vase, gold, windchimes, fish...
South	Fire	9	Lights, plants, red, horse, phoenix, lotus, peonies...
East	Wood	3	Plants, fruits, flowers, dragon
West	Metal	7	Windchimes, ingots, cranes
Northwest	Metal	6	Deities, peach, bells, bowls
Southwest	Earth	2	Double happiness, ducks, peonies, lights, crystals
Northeast	Earth	8	Crystals, lights, urns, bowls
Southeast	Wood	4	Three-legged toad, sailing ship, bats

CHAPTER FIVE: SYMBOLIC FENG SHUI

SYMBOLS OF PROSPERITY, SUCCESS, AND WEALTH

Chinese coins

In recent years many people have discovered the benefits of sticking Chinese coins onto invoice books and file folders to enhance business luck. Authentic Chinese coins from Imperial China are round with a square hole. This symbolizes the unity of heaven and earth. The Yang side is the side with four characters, while the Yin side has two characters. Tie three of these coins together with red thread and stick them Yang side up onto your files, cashboxes, and on doorknobs and cash registers. Also, keep three coins inside your purse or pocket book to ensure good money luck.

If you want to create the money energy of these coins you can also tie ten coins together to simulate the ten emperor coins. This symbolizes the wealth of ten emperors. If you are a businessman or businesswoman, hang these coins on the wall near to where you sit, since this will create auspicious business luck.

ABOVE *Chinese coins, held together with red ribbon, are used to improve good fortune in business and finance.*

The sailing ship

This is my personal favorite wealth symbol. Go out and search for a model sailing ship. The best kinds are the old galleons, which were used as merchant ships bringing home treasure in the old days, particularly silks and gold. Such ships will most likely be made of wood. Fill their decks with pretend gold, or the real stuff if you are rich enough. The sailing ship bringing gold will bring even greater wealth.

When you place the ship laden with gold in your home or office you must make very sure that it is pointing inward. If the ship faces outward it means that your wealth is being carried away. Do not place the ship too high up on a ledge.

LEFT *A model ship symbolically brings home gold from foreign parts to increase the wealth in your home, but make sure it points inward, into your home.*

The best place for it is the coffee table of the living room, so it is near the main door, but not pointing at it. The idea is to simulate a harbor (your home) where the ship has brought you much gold.

Do not get warships that have cannons on their decks. Warships symbolize death rather than wealth, and warships with cannons merely bring poison arrows into the home.

The wealth vase

Wealth vases can be made from almost any kind of ceramic or crystal (earth element) container. You can also use metallic vases (often from India) but these are not as efficient as the earth element vases. This is because in the cycle of

BELOW *A crystal wealth vase, containing symbols of prosperity such as red packets, and semiprecious stones.*

ABOVE *A gold three-legged toad is an important and widely available symbol of prosperity.*

the five elements earth produces gold. The size of your wealth vase depends entirely on your imagination. I have seen people use very small containers with great success. Likewise, I have also seen people use very large containers with equal success.

The best shapes are those with a large opening which narrows into a neck and then broadens out again; this hourglass shape allows money (or wealth) to go in but does not let it out as easily. The broad base symbolizes lots of storage space for the wealth. Place three coins tied with red thread inside the vase, and then fill the vase with semiprecious stones, rice, or colored beads. The best fillers are seven types of semi-precious stones. Choose from quartz, malachite, lapis lazuli, crystal, rose quartz, tiger's eye, turquoise, pearls, coral, amethysts, citrines, and topaz. These are not very expensive if you get the tumbled polished varieties, but if you do not want these stones you may also use uncooked rice grains. Whatever you use, fill the vase to the brim. Then if you can, add some soil from a rich man's house to borrow some of his energy — other than asking his permission, you need not know him personally.

Place the wealth vase inside a cupboard away from public display.

The three-legged toad

The Taiwanese Feng Shui industry has produced some stunning representations of this three-legged toad, which I popularized some years ago. These toads can be made from any material and the best ones are those made to look like gold, with eyes of semi-precious stones. Do not buy toads made of wood, pewter, or silver. Those made to look like gold have the correct symbolism. They do not need to be too large. As long as they look like a real toad they will bring great prosperity luck.

The toad is usually sitting on a bed of coins and imitation gold ingots and inside its mouth is a coin which is symbolically being offered to you. Do not place the toad directly in front of the main door. Instead, place it diagonally to the door about waist high. The toad has two front legs and a tail, which is seen as the third leg. Do not get toads that have a Pa Kua on their backs unless you are already rich and need such a toad to symbolize protection. If you want the toad to attract wealth Chi, you must make sure there is no Pa Kua on its back.

ABOVE *Arrowana fish bring great wealth luck.*

The dragon fish, or arrowana

The popular dragon fish has found itself in increasing demand in recent years as more people discover the wonderful benefits of keeping this excellent wealth energizer in the home. In Singapore they are being bred in captivity and prize specimens are being sold for quite a lot of money.

If you are thinking of keeping this fish, do not feed it with live bait. (I did so many years ago: it creates bad karma to cause the death of live fish food and I am sorry I did it.) Instead, feed them with frozen shrimp.

It is best to keep just one dragon fish, and you must make certain the tank is large enough. Select a dragon fish with a pointed tail. Those with round tails are not the real thing. Keep the fish in your living room on the east, southeast, or north wall.

The goldfish

Goldfish are just as lucky as the arrowana and they bring as much good Chi. Keep nine goldfish in the north, east, or southeast corner of your living room. Of the nine, keep at least one black goldfish. Do not overfeed them. If they are kept in a pond in the garden, make sure you have a cover to protect them from birds and marauding cats. If any of your goldfish die, do not panic; there are no negative connotations. Simply replace the dead fish. If you keep the goldfish in the north corner, adding a few fast-swimming guppies will also help to energize your career luck.

The red bat

Few people realize just how lucky the red bat is in the Chinese pantheon of good fortune symbols. If a colony of bats decides to roost in your home it is said to bring enormous good luck; if they descend on your business, you must not shoo them away either. If you cannot have the real thing, however, many Chinese ceramics depict these very lucky creatures. Displaying them in the house is considered to be very auspicious.

ABOVE *Goldfish are an important source of good fortune Chi, and are relaxing to watch in a pond or an aquarium.*

ABOVE *Bats are very lucky symbols, especially if real bats inhabit your home, but an ornament like this with an auspicious red bat is the next best thing.*

SEE ALSO
❖ Feng Shui Tips for Entrepreneurs. *pp.277–83*

CHAPTER FIVE: SYMBOLIC FENG SHUI

SYMBOLS OF LONGEVITY AND HEALTH

ABOVE *The crane has been a powerful symbol of longevity and good fortune in China for centuries. The most auspicious location for a crane is the west corner of your garden.*

The crane

After the phoenix, the crane is the most popular bird symbol of good fortune. In many old Chinese legends, the crane often features prominently, and it is a creature endowed with many mythical attributes. It is reputed to be the immortal patriarch of birds. There are said to be four types of crane – the black, the yellow, the white and the blue – of which the black is the most potent longevity symbol. These birds are said to live to an age of 600 years.

Cranes are reputed to be most auspicious for the departed souls when placed on the top of coffins, since they are said to be able to carry the soul to paradise most efficiently. The crane is probably the most popular symbol of longevity and it is generally depicted under a pine tree, which is also a symbol of old age. In ancient China, a white crane was used to symbolize a court official of the rank of fourth level.

I highly recommend having this bird in your home to symbolize good health and freedom from illness for all members of the family. Place the crane in your garden, preferably in the west corner.

The pine tree

Because it is evergreen, the Chinese look on the pine tree as a symbol of longevity. The pine is also a symbol of lasting friendship, signifying the presence of friends who stand by

you even in adversity. Pine trees are also excellent protectors against wandering spirits who might enter the home to disturb residents. Those with gardens should have at least one pine in the garden. There are pine trees in China that are said to be 1,000 years old.

The peach

This is sometimes referred to as the fairy fruit because it is the symbol of immortality. It is also the emblem of marriage. It is believed that the peach tree of the gods grows in the western paradise of Hsi Wang Mu, and this tree is said to blossom once every 3,000 years and to yield the fruit of eternal life. The wood of the peach tree is said to be extra-potent when used as a

ABOVE *The hardy pine tree symbolizes long life and also offers protection against harmful spirits.*

special amulet to protect the wearer against illness and disease.

The peach fruit is considered to be most auspicious to have around during a marriage. It is also believed that parents can safeguard their daughters' future marital happiness by serving peaches each spring. This is tantamount to activating marriage luck for the daughters.

ABOVE *The deer's longevity is said to stem from its ability to seek out the fungus of immortality.*

The deer

Once again, because the deer is said to live to a very old age, it is another symbol of long life. It is said that the deer is the only animal which has the ability to search out the fungus of immortality.

Sau – God of Longevity

Perhaps the most popular emblem of longevity is the God of

BELOW *For a long and healthy marriage, eating peaches is considered very beneficial.*

LEFT *The god Sau will protect those in the home from illness and accidents, and help prolong life.*

Longevity himself. Known as Sau, he is often pictured as emerging from a peach, or in the company of his other two associate gods, the star gods of happiness and wealth, Fuk and Luk. Displaying the three of these gods together is a most auspicious combination.

Sau is always pictured smiling, gentle, and kind-looking. He has high forehead, sometimes carries a staff and sits on a deer, and is often surrounded by other symbols representing longevity.

A painting of the God of Longevity makes an excellent birthday gift to present to an elderly family patriarch. In fact, keeping images of the God of Longevity in the home is believed to be one of the best ways of creating good health luck for all the residents, including helping to guard against fatal diseases and tragic accidents.

Bamboo

This is another symbol of longevity, probably because of its durability and the fact that it is evergreen, flourishing throughout the cold

winter months. The bamboo is also regarded as a most auspicious plant and its stems have many Feng Shui uses. Fashioned into windchimes and flutes, the bamboo is believed to have the power to dissolve the Shar Chi, or killing energy, associated with sharp edges and corners. Hung by itself and energized by a red thread, the bamboo stem is also excellent for nullifying the effects of overhead beams and other threatening sharp edges.

Furniture made from bamboo is believed to be most auspicious and signifies good fortune which can be sustained. If you are already successful, having at least one set of bamboo furniture in the home placed in the east or southeast will assure you of continued good fortune. There are many varieties of bamboo in China and it is said that each of these bamboo varieties represents variations of life aspirations.

Cicada

This is believed to be a most powerful symbol of immortality. The cicada also represents the ability to make a great comeback. When your luck has been very bad and you desperately need it to turn around, the best symbol to display in your home is the cicada. In the old days cicadas made of jade were often buried with the dead in the belief that this would afford them great wealth in the afterlife. The

cicada is also an emblem of happiness and eternal youth.

Young people about to embark on a career will benefit from the placement of the cicada in their office. Try to get a cicada carved in a semiprecious stone.

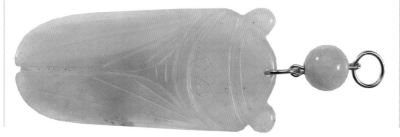

ABOVE *Bamboo not only symbolizes longevity, it also promotes good Feng Shui. Windchimes and furniture made from bamboo help to neutralize harmful energy.*

LEFT *An image of a cicada, especially a jade one, can transform bad luck into good and ensure well-being and longevity.*

...YMBOLS OF ROMANCE AND MARRIAGE

The peony

The peony is the king of flowers and signifies conjugal love. If you have young daughters of marriageable age in the family, displaying a painting of the peony will assure them of loving husbands who will look after them. Thus the peony signifies good marriage luck, especially when hung in the southwest corner of the home.

The peony should not be hung or displayed in the bedroom of an older married couple as this generates the Chi of young love. The risk is that the husband could well develop a roving eye as a result of such placing.

Mandarin ducks

Displaying a pair of mandarin ducks is also emblematic of young love and romance; furthermore, it denotes love that has a happy ending, unlike butterflies which symbolize love which has a sad ending. The mandarin duck has always symbolized young married love. Do not keep one or three mandarin ducks. Always keep a pair and place them in the corner that signifies marriage and love, which is the southwest. You can also keep them in your bedroom.

Double happiness sign

This is the symbol that is almost always associated with marriage. The double happiness symbol is said to signify marriages that are happy, fruitful, and long-lasting, hence it signifies happiness

multiplied many times over. If you are a newly wed couple incorporate this sign into your bedroom furniture, and certainly wear wedding rings that incorporate the double happiness sign in their design.

ADDITIONAL SYMBOLS OF GOOD FORTUNE

The four celestial creatures of good fortune

All the four celestial creatures of good fortune – the dragon, phoenix, turtle and tiger – will bring auspicious luck into the home when their images are displayed there.

Of the four, the dragon is the ultimate symbol of good fortune. A single dragon carrying a pearl, two dragons fighting over a pearl, or nine dragons displayed on a screen – any of these signifies good fortune. The dragon is best placed in the east side of the home, but can be placed anywhere and will still bring good fortune. Do not keep it in the bedroom: this will be too Yang and cause you sleepless nights. The dragon is also an excellent symbol for your business but you should make sure that it is shown looking fat and prosperous.

The phoenix is a symbol of auspicious opportunities. Placed in the south of the home the phoenix brings loads of opportunities for making money and for starting out on distinguished careers. If you do

ABOVE *The tortoise is a symbol of long life as well as an excellent all-round symbol of good fortune.*

not have the phoenix any winged creature with fine plumage can take its place. The tortoise is the ultimate symbol of good fortune; it signifies

so many positive things that its presence in the home brings nothing but good fortune and protection against misfortunes.

The tortoise is a creature of great longevity and thus symbolizes this in Feng Shui. Its hard shell also signifies protection against adversity, illness, and people with bad intentions toward you. If a tortoise should find its way into your home, welcome it and feed it… it signifies wealth about to come to your family.

The unicorn is a symbol of protection, similar to Fu dogs, and both are a great substitute for the tiger. Remember that of all the animals the tiger is to be feared the most. Indeed, during every tiger year many rich tycoons see their businesses collapse and many natural disasters occur. Fu dogs or unicorns also afford protection but they are not as fierce as the tiger.

ABOVE *The celestial dragon holding a pearl is the most powerful symbol of good fortune.*

LEFT *The dragon tortoise with baby brings eight types of luck, but especially wealth.*

RIGHT *The dragon phoenix vase symbolizes marital happiness.*

RIGHT *The dragon horse brings fame, honor, wealth, and success to the home.*

WATER FENG SHUI FOR WEALTH

*T*he correct Feng Shui flow and occurrence of water often spells extreme good fortune that manifests as wealth and prosperity. Water is another word for wealth! Thus good water brings money and bad water takes money away. Water is also one of the two components of Feng Shui, the other being wind. When water is placed in harmony with the winds, therefore, great good fortune comes about.

Water Feng Shui is a Compass Formula method which reveals the methods of analyzing water flows. The formula differentiates between big water (natural bodies of water) and small water (manmade water flows). Both types of water have the potential to bring enormous prosperity to anyone applying Water Feng Shui techniques. This addresses the way the water flows pass the main door, the way it turns near the vicinity of the home, and the way it exits, or goes out of sight. There are auspicious and inauspicious orientations of water. And there are methods of orientating water flow such that it simulates the awesomely auspicious water dragon ... for those keen on reviving their money luck go deep into this chapter to discover the flow of water that may be just the one for your home!

LEFT *Water has the capacity to bring enormous prosperity to anyone practicing Water Feng Shui, whether it be at home in a domestic environment or at work in a corporate environment.*

CHAPTER SIX: WATER FENG SHUI FOR WEALTH

AUSPICIOUS AND INAUSPICIOUS WATER

RIGHT *Water (Feng) and wind (Shui) are the two main components of Feng Shui. The flow of water on earth was also linked with the flow of invisible Chi currents in the atmosphere.*

ABOVE *Water features outside homes or work buildings can bring beneficial Chi energy, if laid out according to Feng Shui principles.*

The harmonious flow of water in the vicinity of any home or building is traditionally regarded as an auspicious feature. Most Feng Shui masters advise that the presence of water always spells enormous prosperity and brings opportunities for business growth, and when oriented correctly water in all its manifestations attracts good fortune to the home. This is because the flow of water is believed to mirror the flow of the invisible Chi currents that swirl around the earth.

According to ancient texts on the subject, however, the Chi created by water can either bring great wealth or it can cause all the wealth of the family to drain away. Thus, while water has the potential to attract great wealth luck, if not correctly oriented it can also take away your luck.

BELOW *Carefully designed and placed water features have great potential for attracting good luck to the home.*

THE DOS AND DON'TS OF WATER IN FENG SHUI

For water to be auspicious, it should always be slow - moving and clean. Rivers that meander gently past in full view of the main door are said to be excellent. From a Feng Shui point of view, therefore, rivers that meander evenly across flat land are more auspicious than those that run fast, perhaps descending into rapids and waterfalls. According to Form School Feng Shui, the river that "embraces the house like a jade belt" is said to be the most auspicious manifestation of water.

This kind of configuration is said to bring enormous good fortune for the family which will last for at least five generations.

Rivers that flow past one's home should never be straight, nor should they appear to be aimed at one's building since they then become transformed into poison arrows that carry dangerous killing Shar Chi. Water should always "embrace the home" not shoot at the home. Thus, when a river seems to flow directly toward the main door of a house, this is not a good sign.

It is also believed that water should never flow behind the home or building as this signifies missed opportunities. This configuration indicates that, while opportunities for advancement and success may be plentiful, it will be difficult for residents to take advantage of these opportunities. Thus, when a river flows behind a building the Feng Shui is not auspicious.

Another general rule about water is that it must not appear to be flowing away from the home, especially away from the main door of the dwelling. Water flowing away is a sure sign of loss. I know of buildings with elaborate water features, presumably installed with

Feng Shui in mind, but quite oblivious to the fact that the water flows outward instead of inward, resulting in residents of the buildings suffering severe losses.

In corporate terms, there are a number of such examples. The Lippo Building, in the Central district of Hong Kong, saw the financial collapse of several well-known companies it housed, including the Alan Bond Group, the Bank of Credit and Commerce International, and Peregrine Investments, a high-flying merchant bank. The Lippo Building was surrounded by a canal system that was designed so that water flowed outward and away from the

building, with disastrous results.

Thus, the exit direction of water becomes an important factor when considering the general Feng Shui of water. This is also why exit flows are crucial in the design of water dragons in the garden and when implementing the various recommendations on water flows contained in the *Water Dragon Classic*. This is the famous treatise on water which is believed to contain the secrets of auspicious orientations and flows of water for all the twenty-four categories of door directions. This formula is an advanced technique practiced by masters of Water Feng Shui in Taiwan.

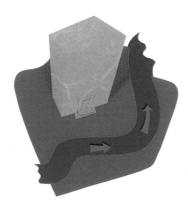
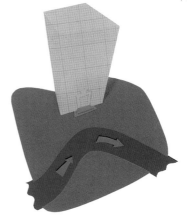

CHAPTER SIX: WATER FENG SHUI FOR WEALTH

BIG WATER AND SMALL WATER

ABOVE *Natural water such as this lake at Hallstat, Austria, can be very auspicious for Chi energy if houses and other buildings are designed to take advantage of it.*

Water Feng Shui differentiates between big water and small water. Big water refers to natural water while small water refers to artificially created water. Both types of water have potency in terms of good or bad Feng Shui. Thus, when property developers create landscaped grounds that include water features, they really should ensure that Feng Shui is considered. It is foolish to assume that all water brings good Feng Shui. When carried out incorrectly, or when the flow is harmful, water simply carries all your money away.

However, while artificially created water is potent, it is nothing compared to the potency of auspicious natural water, whose wealth-bringing potential is vastly superior to artificially created water.

Natural water is part of the natural landscape of the environment. Natural water occurs everywhere – as seas, oceans, rivers, streams, lakes, and waterfalls. These bodies of water occur in thousands of different shapes and sizes, in all kinds of terrain. Water Feng Shui, which taps into the auspicious Chi of natural waters, requires the size, shape, and surrounding attributes of the water to be carefully investigated so that the wealth-bringing Chi of the water flowing by is effectively directed to flow into the house.

It is possible to design houses and buildings to take advantage of natural water by simply following the guidelines given previously. But to be really effective, the best technique is to apply the *Water Dragon Classic* techniques that offer specific recommendations on:

ℓ The way that the water flows past the main door.

ℓ The way that it moves around the compound of the home.

ℓ The way that the water leaves or exits the home.

The instructions given in the *Water Dragon Classic* usually require the house orientation to be changed or altered to "tap" the water flowing past. In the old days the main doors of dwellings were often determined after carefully calculating the orientation of any river or water nearby. Thus, if you have a view of a river it would be advisable to apply at least the main points of the formula to ensure that your home benefits. Remember that even little brooks and streams can be most auspicious.

Artificially created water, like fish ponds, swimming pools, and manmade waterfalls and fountains, can create auspicious features

which work as efficiently as natural water features. Indeed, water features like decorative ponds are becoming increasingly popular in modern gardens and general landscaping in public parks and gardens. These become purveyors of excellent Chi, bringing good fortune to all those who are close enough to benefit.

For those who cannot afford to build expensive water features, applying the water flow guidelines in the *Water Dragon Classic* to humble domestic drains can create an auspicious flow of water. Note that these guidelines apply primarily to houses in the Far East, in countries such as Malaysia, and to drainage systems designed to carry away heavy (usually monsoon) rainwater. It is therefore less appropriate to Western homes. When the flow of such water around the home is correctly oriented, it can be more potent in bringing good luck than merely decorative features such as ponds and waterfalls.

ABOVE *Manmade water features can be just as effective as long as the water Feng Shui guidelines are followed.*

ACTIVATING BIG WATER

The most important guidelines to follow in the activating of big water are those that ensure that:

❦ The orientation of the main house door is auspiciously related to the direction that the big water flows in, either to the left or right.

❦ The water is located in a direction which represents a compatible element to where your main door is located.

Whether the big water is flowing from *left to right* or *right to left* is vital, and this depends on the category of house, which in turn depends on the direction the main door faces. If the big water is not flowing in the correct direction, it is advisable to adjust the direction of the main door. It is not always possible to live beside auspicious natural big water. Residents in urban areas, for example, are hardly likely to be able to tap into a natural waterway unless the town or city has been built around a large lake or has a river flowing through it. It is, therefore, always advisable for residents to tap the good fortune Chi created by any big water around them.

This is especially appropriate for houses or buildings located near rivers. When living near a river or other big water ensure that you face the water. If you cannot get your main door to face the river, it is advisable to demarcate the river outside your house by building a wall to symbolically block out the view of the river.

While a view of the river is important, the direction of its flow is even more significant. Thus the successful tapping of a river's auspicious influences depends on whether it is flowing past the house in the correct direction.

ABOVE *Homes should face the river and the flow of water should be appropriate to the direction faced by the front door.*

WATER FLOWING FROM RIGHT TO LEFT		WATER FLOWING FROM LEFT TO RIGHT	
MOST AUSPICIOUS FOR HOUSES WITH MAIN DOORS DIRECTLY FACING:		MOST AUSPICIOUS FOR HOUSES WITH MAIN DOORS DIRECTLY FACING:	
Ting/Wei	(south to southwest)	Ping/Wu	(south)
Kun/Sen	(southwest)	Ken/Yu	(west)
Sin/Shih	(west to northwest)	Zen/Cher	(north)
Chian/Hai	(northwest)	Chia/Mau	(east)
Kway/Choh	(north to northeast)		
Gen/Yin	(northeast)		
Yi/Shen	(east to southeast)		
Shun/Tze	(southeast)		

The directions given in the two diagrams for water flows in front of the main door are based on the *Water Dragon* formula. These are deemed to be the most auspicious directions for each door category.

If you live near the sea, it is better to live in a condominium (in a part of a bigger building) than a bungalow since this balances out the effect of the huge water symbolized by the sea. Usually, living near the sea can cause the presence of too much water, thereby leading to an imbalance. However, if the house is not too isolated, and specific measures are taken to balance it with other elements that diffuse the effect of a preponderance of water, then the sea brings good luck.

It is also as well to be aware of the size of the waves on the beach opposite your house. If it is very windy with frequent storms, the effect is not considered auspicious unless some kind of symbolic protection can be constructed.

FAR LEFT *The direction that your main door faces will determine whether or not the flow of water is auspicious.*

LEFT *Not every house is oriented correctly toward big water. It may be necessary to build a wall to create symbolic protection.*

SEE ALSO
❖ The Water Location Formula
pp.254–5

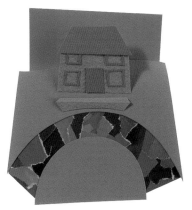

CHAPTER SIX: WATER FENG SHUI FOR WEALTH

ACTIVATING SMALL WATER

ABOVE *An artificially created waterfall is an attractive addition to any garden and may help increase your bank balance too. The best location for a waterfall is in the north corner of your garden, or in the east or southeast.*

RIGHT *This gently bubbling fountain, crafted in a curved bowl, is excellent Feng Shui, and mirrors the positive accumulation of Chi.*

The best way to activate small water for Feng Shui purposes is to align man-made structures such as ponds according to the *Water Dragon* formula, with drains requiring the most careful attention. However, it is also possible to introduce other manmade structures into your garden if you wish, and if you have sufficient space to do so. Three examples of artificially created water structures – waterfalls, fountains and fishponds – not only have the potential to improve your Feng Shui but they also add considerable beauty to a well-planned garden.

Waterfalls are among the most popular manmade examples of small water. A small, artificial waterfall in your garden and in front (but not directly) of your main door is particularly effective in creating auspicious Sheng Chi. Ideally, the waterfall should be located in either the north corner of the garden, or alternatively in the east or southeast.

These are compatible sectors in terms of element relationships. According to Feng Shui guidelines, a beautiful waterfall in full view of the main door brings opportunities for business and career expansion as well as much auspicious money luck. When building a waterfall, build it in relation to the size of your house. A waterfall that is too large will overshadow the house, creating too much Chi energy. Also, when using rocks and boulders for decoration, make certain they do not resemble anything hostile or threatening that could create Shar Chi,

thereby hurting the front door.

Do not place the waterfall directly in front of or facing the main door. This could have the effect of blocking favorable Chi that may be flowing into the house. Waterfalls are best located toward the left-hand side of the main door, from the inside looking out.

Fountains are very popular and equally effective features which can be installed in the garden to enhance your Feng Shui. These come in various designs, with the water bubbling forth in several different ways. In effect, any

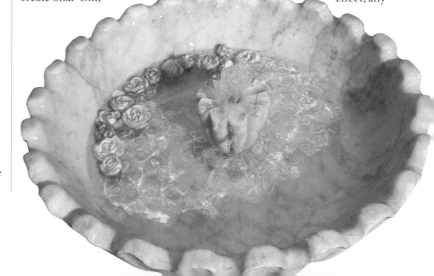

design will do. The best and most effective place to locate a fountain is in the front garden in full view of your main door. However, do make sure you have enough space to install a fountain. To get the maximum benefits from a water fountain, it is best to have at least 20 feet (6m) of space in front of your door. This enhances the Feng Shui of the house considerably. Fountains are best located in a sector of your compound which is symbolized by the water element (i.e. the north) or the wood element (i.e. the east or southeast) as these are compatible sectors. If you are fond of fountains, you can also install miniature fountains in either your home or office.

An example of successful corporate adaptation was undertaken by Prudential Asia in Hong Kong, who correctly installed a fountain at their headquarters in Alexandra House. From day one in 1987 they have never looked back. Prudential Asia is probably one of the most successful nonbank funded investment bankers and asset managers around.

As with waterfalls, a sense of balance is important when creating a fountain. Do not let it be so large as to totally dominate the garden, so that it overwhelms you with too much energy. This does more harm than good. Balance is a fundamental aspect of Feng Shui.

A fishpond is a great favorite with garden enthusiasts. In Malaysia, the keeping of koi, or Japanese carp, is a popular hobby and it makes sense to use the fishpond as a Feng Shui tool. It is probably one of the most effective ways of creating favorable and auspicious Sheng Chi.

The presence of fish is also very propitious since fish are generally regarded as symbols of wealth and good fortune. The Chinese often refer to them when discussing growth and expansion.

ABOVE *The best fishpond location is the north, east, or southeast.*

ABOVE *Keep the design of your fishpond simple and uncomplicated.*

ABOVE *A fishpond in the shape of a figure eight is very auspicious.*

Fishponds need not be elaborate or too large. They should be located in the north, east, or southeast sectors of the garden. The women of the house might also be reminded that ponds, and especially fishponds, must never be located on the right-hand side of the main door (inside looking out). This is because, although they may be auspicious and bring wealth, they also have the potential to bring additional relationships into the

home. When a pond is located on the right of the main door, the men of the family tend to stray or have a wandering eye and, even worse, may leave their wives altogether.

The illustrations on this page are suggestions for fishpond shapes. It is also possible to combine other auspicious symbols like waterfalls and fountains. You may like to keep koi. Make sure the water is deep enough and kept moving.

In general, in terms of Feng Shui there is a negative attitude toward swimming pools. Most Feng Shui experts do not recommend the building of swimming pools in the home unless the house is enormous, with sprawling grounds, and looks more like a country club than an average-sized bungalow. This is because swimming pools tend to overwhelm the house. The large areas of water create an imbalance and, when located in the wrong sector of the garden, with resulting elemental incompatibility, they cause more bad fortune than good. Secondly, swimming pools, especially if they are rectangular, could inadvertently create Shar Chi by their corners. If directed at a door, this could create misfortune.

If you really want to have a pool, make it a modest size, and designed to a round, oval, or kidney shape. If the shape of the pool seems to wrap around the house, this simulates an auspicious configuration of water. If you feel that a smallish pool defeats the object of having a swimming pool, forget the idea and go to a public pool instead.

ABOVE *For the Chinese, eight is a very auspicious number. That makes it a good shape for a fishpond.*

BELOW *Avoid swimming pools with corners, as this will encourage negative Shar Chi — the best design is a modest round, oval, or kidney-shaped pool.*

CHAPTER SIX: WATER FENG SHUI FOR WEALTH

ACTIVATING THE RAINWATER DRAINS OF A HOUSEHOLD

No Water Feng Shui can be complete if the drains of a household or building are not taken into consideration. This refers only to exposed drains, where the flow of water – generally the flow of rainwater – can be seen. Anything that is covered from view can safely be factored out of the equation since these are regarded as being nonexistent.

While drains may seem rather insignificant, their influence over the intangible forces that create good or bad Feng Shui can sometimes be spectacular. Auspicious drainage flows are so effective and so subtle in attracting good Feng Shui luck that anyone interested in the practice of Feng Shui for wealth and money should focus on them as part of the practice. The formula for doing this correctly makes up the bulk of the

Water Dragon formula. In the old days in China when wealthy mandarins of the emperor's court built their water dragons they built elaborate waterways around their courtly homes. Today, using the humble drain instead of building elaborate waterways around the home is similarly effective.

When investigating the potential for activating good water Feng Shui for your house, it is also necessary to determine how the public drains outside your house are located with regard to your land.

Domestic drains in modern houses – especially in the Far East – are normally designed to flow around a house before exiting into a public drain outside. These public drains may be located either in front, at the back, or by the side of your house or land. Their orientation and direction of flow

BELOW *In the old days the homes of prosperous courtiers in China were surrounded by waterways built especially to create good Feng Shui. Today, modern homes can make use of their drainage system to the same effect.*

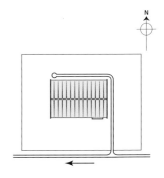

ABOVE *The flow of water in drainage needs to be assessed by examining the floorplan of a house.*

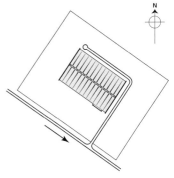

ABOVE *Some fairly simple adjustments can be made to the flow of waste water to promote good Feng Shui.*

also affects your Feng Shui. Sometimes their location can also create difficulties for you in that you may not be able to let your drains flow out in the direction you wish because the public drain is inconveniently located. When investigating whether public drains will bring you good or bad luck, note the direction of the water flow and find out if this corresponds to the good direction based on the orientation of the main door. Remember that water should:

❧ Flow from left to right when the main door faces any one of the cardinal directions.

❧ Flow right to left when facing a secondary direction.

THE FENG SHUI OF WATER

Emperor Xia Yu, founder of the first Chinese dynasty before 4000 B.C.E., was said to have left his footprints all over China trying to harness the big rivers like the Hwang Ho, or Yellow River, and the Yantze Kiang. He was revered as the emperor who succeeded in conquering the waters by understanding their true nature.

"Feng" (wind) and "Shui" (water) are the two components of Feng Shui. Of the two, water was easier to study as it was terrestrial. China was also an agricultural society where the presence of water meant the difference between life and death, between having a good harvest or suffering a famine. Thus, over the centuries water came to symbolize the most important aspect of existence.

Water was also viewed as an unpredictable force which had to be understood and controlled before its huge benefits could be harnessed. Thus over time guidelines developed as to the flow and placement of water that best captured the auspicious Chi of the environment. The *Water Dragon Classic* records five different patterns of water flows, and these reflect the five elements. Illustrated below are the five element waters. Use these sketches to understand any water near your home. If the water flow matches the direction, the water is said to be harmonious and auspicious.

LEFT *In Chinese society, water is not taken for granted, as it often is in the West.*

RULES ABOUT WATER IN RELATION TO YOUR HOME

Avoid buying property with water behind the house. This symbolizes lost opportunity. The best place for a body of water is in front of the house. But note its direction of flow as it passes your main door. Here are some favorable water configurations:

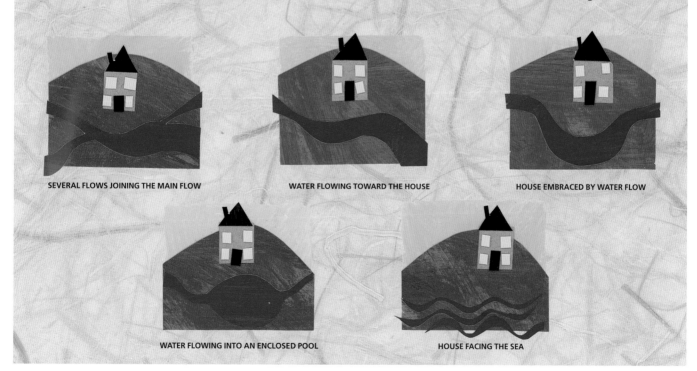

SEVERAL FLOWS JOINING THE MAIN FLOW

WATER FLOWING TOWARD THE HOUSE

HOUSE EMBRACED BY WATER FLOW

WATER FLOWING INTO AN ENCLOSED POOL

HOUSE FACING THE SEA

THE TOOLS OF FENG SHUI

In Feng Shui the tools of the trade center around the Luo Pan – the traditional Master Practitioner's compass which reveals as much or as little as the master wishes to allow the disciple to know. Most authentic Luo Pans contain all the trade secrets of particular masters who usually have the key symbols written on the Luo Pan compass in code. It is because of this that I have always advised amateur practitioners doing their Feng Shui to use an ordinary, Western-style compass. This is because it is so easy to get the orientations using a Western-style compass. From there on readers can then refer to the reference tables in my books to check out the meanings of directions and locations in particular situations. Used correctly, and in conjunction with the eight-sided Pa Kua and the nine-grid Lo Shu magic square, the ordinary compass and its orientations unlocks a huge array of possibilities and permutations in your practice of Feng Shui. The beginner practitioner should invest in a tough and reliable compass to get started.

LEFT *A Feng Shui practitioner studying his Luo Pan.*

CHAPTER SEVEN: THE TOOLS OF FENG SHUI

THE LUO PAN, OR FENG SHUI MASTER'S COMPASS

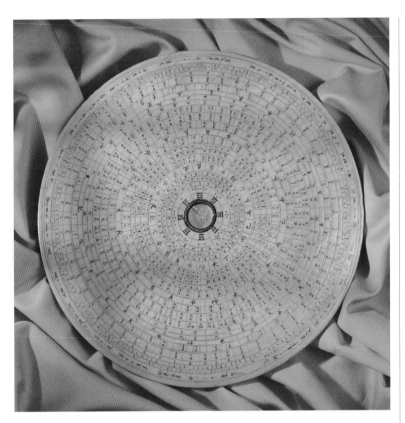

ABOVE *The Feng Shui geomancer's compass, the Luo Pan, comprises intricate rings of Chinese code words and symbols. Feng Shui Masters possess customized versions containing their own secret formulas.*

The Chinese were the first people to develop the Feng Shui compass more than 3,000 years ago. According to popular legend, the Luo Pan was presented to the Yellow Emperor (about the 25th century B.C.E.) by the Goddess of the Nine Heavens to assist him in his heroic battle against the evil wizards clan.

Over the centuries, the Luo Pan has been reformed, redefined, and altered according to new discoveries in land and directional theories by the respective dynasties' Kan Yu experts (today called Feng Shui masters). The Luo Pan has since then become an indispensable tool for the practice of Feng Shui.

For centuries Feng Shui masters have researched, experimented, and studied the meanings encrypted in the various types of Luo Pans. The significance of the encryptions of the Luo Pan are profound and fascinating, especially since every degree and character engraved on the Heaven Dial (the round moveable plate of the Luo Pan) is not only intricately designed, but also contains the secrets of the ancient masters of Feng Shui.

Feng Shui, literally, means wind and water. Many people know that water represents wealth in Feng Shui, but not many know what the wind represents! The wind in Feng Shui represents direction. For Feng

Shui to be effective, the need to study the forces of water and directional influences is of paramount importance. At the same time, the direction, down to a single degree, around the Luo Pan has significant and profound effects on the Feng Shui of a particular location.

The three types of Luo Pan

There are different schools of Feng Shui, and the secrets of these systems are contained in most authentic Luo Pans. In general, however, there are two categories of authentic Chinese Feng Shui: the San Yuan School (Three Cycles System) and the San He School (Three Combination System). Fey Sing (flying stars) or Xuan Kong (time and space) can be classified under the San Yuan School.

Pa-Chai (Eight Mansions Kua formula), Sui-Long (water dragons), San Long (mountain dragons), and environmental Feng Shui are subsets of the San He system of Feng Shui. These are traditional authentic Feng Shui systems. Old masters used different Luo Pans based on the system of Feng Shui that they practiced.

The rings

Depending on which system the Luo Pan is designed for, it can have as few as seven basic rings or up to as many as thirty-six rings!

Every ring contains codes for a specific theory or formula in the application of Feng Shui. Also, different Feng Shui systems have different meanings given to a particular level of a Luo Pan. Once you know the meanings contained in the characters of your Luo Pan, you will be able to accurately measure, locate, calculate, and even predict the natural earth energies, both directional and locational, in a particular area.

In today's modern practice of Feng Shui, two standardized types of Luo Pan are now very popular among practitioners of authentic Chinese Feng Shui. They are the San Yuan Luo Pan and the San Hup Luo Pan. It is very easy to differentiate between the two. The San Yuan Luo Pan has the 64 hexagrams of the *I Ching*. The San Hup Luo Pan has three distinctive rings of the 24 mountains. The third standardized type of Luo Pan is a combination of the San Yuan and San Hup Luo Pan. It is called the Zhung Hup Luo Pan.

Eight-point rule for selecting a Luo Pan

1 Quality of the needle: the needle must be aligned accurately on top of the red line at the bottom of the Heaven Pool (the round compass piece in the middle). The needle must be able to align accurately below the axis cross (the intercrossing nylon strings). Not even a slight deviation of 0.01mm away from the above lines can be tolerated.
2 Heaven Pool's red line: the double dots must be pointing to the "Rat" (direct North 0°) direction while the point should be pointing to the "Horse" (direct South 180°) direction.
3 Accuracy of Axis Cross (the nylon strings): the cross must be able to cross the cardinal axes directly at 0°, 90°, 180°, and 270° of the Heaven Dial. There should not even be a slight deviation, or it renders the Luo Pan totally useless.
4 Quality of the Heaven Dial: every character, trigram, and

number must be printed or carved with great clarity. They must be easy to read. Some words or characters may be blurred in the process of stamping – always double check. The dial should be steady and smooth when turned. It should not be too smooth or too tight.
5 Squareness of the Earth Plate and Spirit Level: the Luo Pan must have the square base. It is used to take measurements by matching it parallel to the wall or door of a house or building. It must come with a spirit level for accuracy of reading.
6 Material quality: what is the Luo Pan made of? Pressure-treated wood, normal wood, or recycled wood? It does make a huge difference. Pressure-treated wood can withstand temperatures of up to 140°C. Recycled wood or normal wood are the cheap renditions found in most Chinese roadside stalls.
7 Measurements and sizes: Luo Pans must come with accurate markings of the exact 360°. Luo Pans come only in standardized sizes. The standard sizes that traditional Feng Shui masters use are the 8¼ inch (19cm) types. The smaller ones such as the 2½ inch (6cm)–4⅛ inch (10cm) types are for convenience. The smaller the Luo Pan gets, the easier it is to make mistakes. Thus it is only when one is very experienced that one should use a small Luo Pan for a professional Feng Shui consultation. Beginners should always start by using a 5⅛ inch (13cm) or a 6⅛ inch (16cm) type. Professional Feng Shui practitioners should always use an 8¼ inch (19cm) Luo Pan.
8 Beauty: if all the above seven points are met, the last criterion is

the beauty test. Some Luo Pans are good but are unattractive. Or they feel rough. When you are looking to buy a Luo Pan, be very choosy. Not only should it be of a high quality, it should also have the right feel (i.e. fabric, smoothness, and look). Your Luo Pan should even look good enough to be used as a decorative Feng Shui energizer. It is not unusual for Feng Shui masters to display their Luo Pans glamorously in their homes. Some have a sense of pride, others have a feeling of peace when they display their Luo Pans. It is also true that many Feng Shui masters today are avid Luo Pan collectors. Many believe that the Luo Pan can ward off evil spirits because it embodies the secret of the *I Ching*, which we all know is the secret of the Feng Shui Ba Gua.

A quality Luo Pan should weigh around 2–3 lbs (1.3–1.5kg). The Heaven Dial (the round plate) should be easily turned around with a firm and steady hand. These days really good Luo Pans are hard to find. Unknowing vendors in the West have been victims of many unscrupulous businessmen in China, selling them cheap and tacky imitations of a real Feng Shui Luo Pan. Be very careful of the Luo Pan that you choose to purchase. Get professional advice before purchasing your Luo Pan.

Please note that the Luo Pan is a tool for professional Feng Shui consultants. You do not need it unless you are planning to become a consultant, in which case when you purchase a Luo Pan do make certain that you also learn to read and understand the Luo Pan.

ABOVE *A Western compass can be used in Feng Shui, but remember that the Chinese place south at the top.*

CHAPTER SEVEN: THE TOOLS OF FENG SHUI

YIN AND YANG PA KUA

The Yin Pa Kua

Shown below is the Yin Pa Kua, which illustrates the placement of the trigrams according to the Early Heaven arrangement. This is also the arrangement of trigrams used in the protective Pa Kua as an antidote to poison arrows. This is the Pa Kua which you hang in front of your door outside your home to counter Shar Chi caused by hostile structures which are hitting the main door. Study the placement of the trigrams carefully for the power of the Yin Pa Kua comes from the arrangement of the trigrams. Many such Pa Kuas presently sold in Chinatowns all over the world and over the Internet have big mistakes in the placement of these trigrams, so do check carefully.

The protective Pa Kua is enlarged on this page and can be traced and made into an antidote to counter a poison arrow which may be sending hostile energies toward

ABOVE *Hang a Yin Pa Kua outside your home to help deflect the killing energy of poison arrows.*

RIGHT *The arrangement of the trigrams is extremely important, here in the Yin Pa Kua, which is often used to protect the main door from exterior poison arrows.*

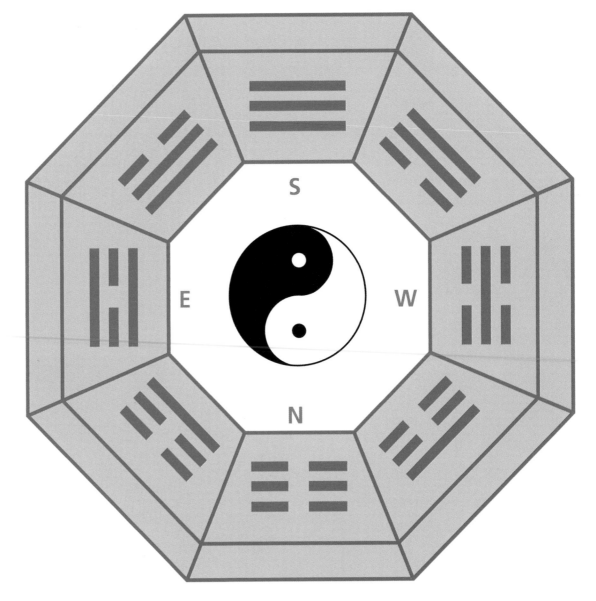

your home. Remember that a Pa Kua must never be hung inside the house but always outside, facing away from the house. Unless this is observed the Pa Kua itself becomes a source of very bad Yin death energy. Note each of the trigrams and where they are placed so that you can recognize a Yin Pa Kua. If you wish to make your own Pa Kua, trace the Pa Kua illustrated onto a board or a piece of wood, then cut out the shape of the Pa Kua. Next, color the background red, then color the trigrams black and place a small round mirror in the center. It does not matter whether the mirror is flat, concave or convex.

The Yin Pa Kua is therefore the Pa Kua used for combating Feng Shui problems caused by hostile structures in the environment outside the home. Remember that this is a symbol of protection. It sends out powerful energies which, if they happen to hit you, will cause you to fall ill or to suffer even greater misfortunes.

Do not use this symbol lightly. Hanging Yin Pa Kuas around your home without understanding their potency is really asking for trouble. They are also not suitable as a Feng Shui cure inside the home. Keep them outside.

The Yang Pa Kua

This is the Pa Kua that should be used for analyzing the Feng Shui of houses and buildings of the living. The trigrams are set out in the Later Heaven arrangement of trigrams. This arrangement differs considerably from that of the Yin Pa Kua. In this Later arrangement the two cardinal trigrams, Chien and Kun, are placed in the northwest and southwest respectively. As such, for purposes of Feng Shui analysis, the northwest is therefore deemed to be the place for the father of the family and the ultimate place of Yang energy (trigram Chien) while the southwest is deemed the place

for the mother of the family, and ultimate Yin energy (Kun). The other six trigrams are placed according to the diagram that is sketched out below.

Each of the eight sides represents one of the eight directions. The eight trigrams placed around this Yang Pa Kua are used in all the Feng Shui formulas, and by all Feng Shui masters to give them clues as to how to energize, activate, and tap the good energies of every corner represented by the eight sides.

This is, therefore, the arrangement used in Yang Feng Shui analysis and the one you should try to become very familiar with. The trigrams placed in each

corner assign the elements and other associations to each of the eight sides and therefore the eight directions of the compass. The more important of these associations are shown in the Pa Kua (below) but there are a host of other corelationships which can be discerned by studying the eight trigrams. These trigrams – Chien, Kun, Chen, Sun, Tui, Ken, Kan, and Li – are fully explained and described in Part 1 under Feng Shui Concepts (*see pages 30–51*). For a fuller understanding of each of the eight trigrams, I highly recommend studying a good translation of the *I Ching*. (*See page 355 for a suitable translation.*)

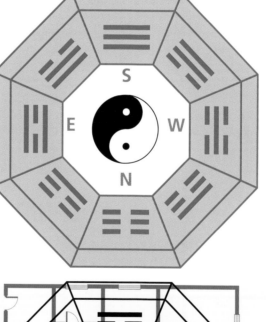

LEFT *A Yin Pa Kua must always be hung outside, facing away from the house. Unless this is observed the Pa Kua itself becomes a source of very bad Yin death energy.*

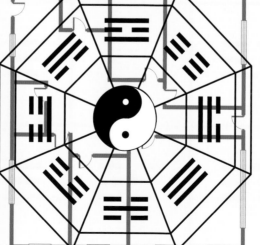

LEFT *To make the Yang Feng Shui analysis, place the Yang Pa Kua over the floorplan of your home.*

CHAPTER SEVEN: THE TOOLS OF FENG SHUI

APPLYING THE TRIGRAMS

In the *Book of Changes*, or *I Ching*, there are additional symbols connected with each of the trigrams as well as extensive commentaries which offer critiques on the character of the lines themselves. For Feng Shui analysis, however, the most significant aspects of the trigrams relate to their directions, their elements, the member of the family indicated, and the basic attributes which each embodies. These should be sufficient for Feng Shui investigation.

Understanding the meanings of the trigrams leads to many useful applications in Feng Shui. The placement of the trigrams around the Pa Kua indicates the sectors in a home suitable for each family member. It also tells us which family member is affected when any sector of the home suffers bad Feng Shui. Examples are missing

corners, or a clash of elements, to name but two. Similarly, the trigrams also tell us which family member is able to benefit from auspicious energies in each different sector of the home.

The analysis can also go deeper if we wish by delving, for instance, into other symbolic representations of the trigrams. Take the example of the trigram Ken, which symbolizes *the mountain* in which all sorts of hidden assets (gold) may be found. This is confirmed by the element of Ken, which is earth, and we know that earth produces metal or gold. Also, the mountain is big, imposing, silent and still, thus indicating a period of waiting and preparation. If you stay in a room located in the northeast, it might be great while you are a student but frustrating if you are looking for promotion or success luck.

When you understand the attributes of the different corners of any home – symbolic element, the family member represented, the colors that energize that corner, as well as the luck aspiration symbolized – you can start to practice trigram therapy in Feng Shui. Trigram therapy is a subtle combination of all the basic concepts of Feng Shui and when you get it right will bring a great deal of auspicious Chi currents, flowing harmoniously, which result in good fortune.

The Lo Shu square and the meaning of numbers

In this diagram, a nine-sector square – called the Lo Shu grid – has been superimposed over the Pa Kua. This represents the next important Feng Shui tool for

RIGHT

Superimposing the Lo Shu square over the Pa Kua adds to possibilities for Feng Shui analysis, and is especially important in assessing the energy locations in the home.

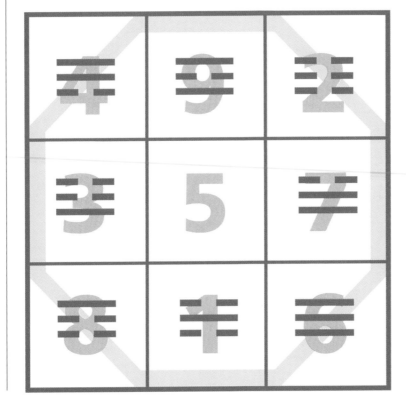

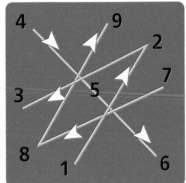

ABOVE *The sequence of numbers on the Lo Shu square forms a pattern which is reminiscent of the Hebrew symbol the Sigil of Saturn. This adds to the magical significance already attributed to the square.*

THE TRIGRAMS AND THEIR ATTRIBUTES

TRIGRAM		NO.	DIRECTION	ELEMENT	COLOR
CHIEN		6	Northwest	Metal	White
LI		9	South	Fire	Red
KAN		1	North	Water	Black
CHEN		3	East	Wood	Green
SUN		4	Southeast	Wood	Green
KUN		2	Southwest	Earth	Ocher
TUI		7	West	Metal	White
KEN		8	Northeast	Earth	Ocher

analysis, which incorporates the impact of numbers for the trigrams. Putting the meanings of the Pa Kua together with the meanings of the numbers of the Lo Shu square allows us to enhance the practice of basic Feng Shui. Thus, every trigram has directions, elements, color, and, now, number affiliations. This is summarized in the table above.

The numbers 1 through 9 shown against the trigrams in the table are, in turn, arranged in a certain magic sequence in the Lo Shu. This is shown in the square left. Feng Shui texts constantly refer to this arrangement of numbers, and their sequence provides clues to the inner meanings of the trigrams. As such, the numbers of

the Lo Shu square have been incorporated into many of the formulas created by Compass School Feng Shui.

The numbers of the Lo Shu square are arranged so that any three numbers added horizontally, vertically, or diagonally come to 15, the number of days it takes for the new moon to become a full moon.

Thus the Lo Shu square features prominently in fortune-telling as well as in Flying Star, the time dimension formula of Feng Shui (see also pages 76–7).

Note the way the numbers move from 1 to 2 to 3 in a movement that forms a symbol that closely resembles the Sigil of Saturn symbol of the Jewish religion. The Lo Shu grid features strongly in

several very potent Compass School Feng Shui formulas. It is said that the secret of the Lo Shu unlocks the meanings of the Pa Kua and that the Lo Shu square and its sequence of numbers are widely used in Taoist "magic" practices.

The numbers on the square become significant when applying the formulas, but they also indicate the numerical energy of the different sectors of the home. For instance, if you plan to keep a tortoise ornament in the home, the designated place of the tortoise is the north and the corresponding number of that sector according to the Lo Shu square is one. Thus you would know that it is auspicious to keep one tortoise, rather than several, in the north.

SEE ALSO
❖ The I Ching pp.34–7
❖ The Trigrams pp.38–9
❖ The Eight Mansions Formula: Pa-Kua Lo-Shu formula pp.72–5

CHAPTER SEVEN: THE TOOLS OF FENG SHUI

THE FENG SHUI RULER: indications of prosperous dimensions

ABOVE *The Feng Shui ruler can be used in many different ways to measure the levels of good fortune in the home.*

There are auspicious and inauspicious dimensions and those who possess a Feng Shui ruler can actually measure their tables, cupboards, windows, and doors and check if the dimensions are auspicious or inauspicious. The Feng Shui ruler or measuring tape has eight cycles of dimensions, four of which are auspicious and four inauspicious. Each cycle measures the equivalent of 17 inches (43cm), and each cycle is categorized into eight segments. The cycle of lucky and unlucky dimensions then repeats itself over and over again to infinity. Once you have familiarized yourself with the Feng Shui ruler you can apply it to almost everything that has a dimension to find the auspicious dimensions. You can use your ruler to measure furniture, doors, and windows, even business cards, envelopes, and notepads. I use mine on everything.

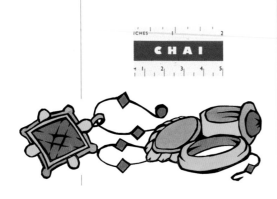

The auspicious dimensions

Chai is between 0 and 2⅛ inches, or 5.4cm. This is the first segment of the cycle and it is further subdivided into four categories of good luck. The first approximate half inch (1cm) brings money luck, the second brings a safe filled with jewels, the third brings together six types of good luck, and the fourth brings abundance.

Yi is between 6⅜ and 8½ inches, or 16.2 and 21.5cm. This is the fourth segment of the cycle. It brings mentor luck, it attracts helpful people into your life. Again, there are four subsections. The first approximate half inch (1cm) means excellent children luck; the second predicts unexpected added income; the third predicts a very successful son; and the fourth offers excellent good fortune.

Kwan is between 8½ and 10⅝ inches, or 21.5 and 27cm. This third set of auspicious dimensions brings power luck. The first subsection denotes ease in passing exams; the second predicts special or speculative luck; the third offers

improved income; the fourth attracts high honors for the family.

Pun is between 14⁶⁄₈ and 17 inches, or 37.5 and 43.2cm. This category of dimensions brings lots of money flowing in if it is in the first subsection. The second spells good examination luck; the third predicts plenty of jewelry; the fourth offers abundant prosperity.

The inauspicious dimensions

Pi is between 2⅛ and 4²⁄₈ inches, or 5.4 and 10.8cm. This category of bad luck generally refers to illness. This dimension also has four subsections which convey other

problems. The first approximate half inch (1cm) carries the warning of money retreating; the second indicates potential legal problems; the third means bad luck, possibly even going to jail. The fourth indicates the death of a spouse.

Li is between 4^2/$_8$ and 6^3/$_8$ inches, or 10.8 and 16.2cm. This category means separation and the first half inch (1 cm) means a store of bad luck, while the second

predicts losing money. The third says meeting with unscrupulous people; the fourth predicts being a victim of theft or burglary.

Chieh is between 10^5/$_8$ and 12^6/$_8$ inches, or 27 and 32.4cm. This category of bad dimensions spells loss. The first approximate half inch (1cm) spells death or departure of some kind; the second foretells that

everything you need will disappear, and you could lose your livelihood; the third warns that you will be chased out of your village in

disgrace; the fourth indicates that you will suffer a forthcoming extremely severe loss of money.

Hai is between 12^6/$_8$ and 14^6/$_8$ inches, or 32.4 and 37.5cm. These dimensions indicate severe bad luck

starting with disasters arriving in the first subsection; death in the second; sickness and ill-health in the third; scandal and quarrels in the fourth.

LEFT *The Feng Shui ruler can be used to calculate auspicious dimensions of almost anything in your home, including furniture, doors, and windows.*

The dimensions can be applied to every item in the home, although the most important objects to measure, from a Feng Shui perspective, are the length, width, and height of doors and windows, beds and tables. Some of the applications are illustrated on the following two pages.

BELOW *The Feng Shui ruler is divided up into eight cycles of dimensions – each one measuring 17 inches (43cm), and each cycle is divided into eight sections.*

THE FENG SHUI RULER

The Feng Shui ruler is widely used in the Far East by Feng Shui enthusiasts. A genuine ruler indicates auspicious and inauspicious measurements for both Yin and Yang dwellings. The upper part indicates the measurements for Yang dwellings (houses of the living) while the lower section indicates the lucky and unlucky measurements for graveyard Feng Shui (Yin dwellings).

The ruler is used to measure the length, breadth, and height of rooms, doors and furniture to determine dimensions and proportions that will encourage good fortune.

The Feng Shui unit of measure is 17 inches, or approximately 43 cm. This Feng Shui unit of measure was derived from the

BELOW The different sections of this ruler have relevance to the measurements of Yang dwellings only.

Characters in red signify auspicious dimensions

Characters in black signify inauspicious dimensions

side of a square, where the length of the diagonal of a square is the square root of the sum of two sides. Western mathematicians called this the "magic square" and the Chinese considered this as "mystical." The Feng Shui unit of measure is divided into eight sections, each corresponding with one of the eight trigrams and each segment representing good or bad luck. The table, right, summarizes the lucky and unlucky dimensions for Yang dwellings. For longer dimensions you simply multiply the "lucky dimensions," thereby using the ruler like a measuring tape.

RIGHT Check each room with your Feng Shui ruler to assess proportions and see whether any can be improved to maximize Feng Shui potential.

LEFT *Constructing a desk with good Feng Shui dimensions will bring you success in your career. Check the height, width, and breadth. You should also adjust the height of your chair, raising it on a platform if necessary to conform with the optimum height of the desk.*

DIMENSIONS INCHES (CM)	LUCK	REMARKS
0–2 (0–5.4)	Good	Prosperity
2–4¼ (5.4–10.8)	Bad	Bad health
4¼–6½ (10.8–16.2)	Bad	Separation
6½–8½ (16. 2–21.5)	Good	Recognition
8½–10½ (21.5–27)	Good	Promotion
10½–12¾ (27–32.4)	Bad	Loss
12¾–14¾ (32.4–37.5)	Bad	Accident
14¾–17 (37.5–43.2)	Good	Happiness

RIGHT *The 17inch (43cm) cycle measurement of the Feng Shui ruler was based on Western mathematicians' "magic square," where the square on the diagonal is the same size as the square on the two sides.*

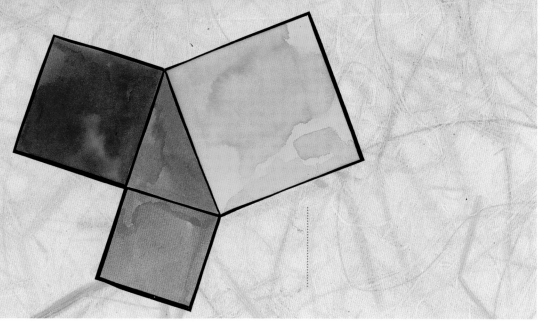

GUIDELINES FOR PRACTICAL APPLICATION

*F*amiliarity with the tools of Feng Shui enables practitioners to understand the deep significance of orientations to many of the more important schools of Feng Shui. Taking correct compass readings and knowing how to superimpose the grids and demarcations over houseplans is a vital part of the analysis. One should never base the analysis of a site location on guesswork, or on visual memory of where the sun rises and sets. Instead, it is really necessary to be quite exact. Demarcation and measurement of floor space within the home must always be meticulously done. The focus in this part of the exercise shifts to the determination of house boundaries, and within these boundaries to the taking of readings. Furthermore, it addresses the problems of diagnosing solutions for irregular shapes, unbalanced layout plans, missing corners, and protruding sectors. How these shape-related problems are treated depends on the diagnosis, which in turn is based on the formulas being used. The kind of luck being energized also has interesting implications. The most important guideline in Feng Shui applications is to stay relaxed and think through diagnostic problems carefully.

LEFT *Follow the guidelines and advice for the practical application of Feng Shui to become familiar with the orientations of your surroundings. With familiarity comes greater awareness as to where to place symbols of good fortune.*

CHAPTER EIGHT: GUIDELINES FOR PRACTICAL APPLICATION

HOW TO READ THE COMPASS

P ractical applications of almost all Feng Shui recommendations require you to take the orientation of your surroundings. Before you can even start to analyze a plot of land or a dwelling place, you should be completely familiar with the orientations of your surroundings. You should know where all the main cardinal directions are and this should be a specific knowledge. The results of any Feng Shui you do will be hopeless if you estimate the directions of the land or dwelling based on your recollection of where the sun rises (which you assume to be east) and sets (which you assume to be west). Estimates are usually wrong by as much as 30° to 40° on the compass.

The first step in practical Feng Shui is to buy yourself a good, reliable compass which will tell you exactly where magnetic north is; from there you can then take your bearings and identify all the other directions. As confirmed in The Tools of Feng Shui (*see pages 110–21*), a Western compass is just as acceptable as the more authentic looking Luo Pan compass. An accurate Western compass will give you your bearings instantly and certainly fits my own requirements.

Something worth noting is that, irrespective of how the directions in this or any other book are labeled as north or south, in reality north, south, east, or west are easily found with a reliable compass. In the practice of Feng Shui all references to compass directions are exactly that – directions as determined by the compass.

Many Feng Shui books, including my own, place south at the top and this differs from Western convention, which always

ABOVE *A compass is essential in Compass Formula Feng Shui calculations.*

ABOVE *A compass need not be the Luo Pan – a Western one will do fine for the amateur practitioner.*

places north at the top. I am simply following Chinese convention. It does not mean that I have changed the directions. In practice, north is north as indicated by the compass and south is south, also as indicated by the compass. Hence, when you are applying a Compass School formula, you must use the compass. Any method of identifying the corners of your house other than with a compass is to follow another school of Feng Shui.

The next step is to study your compass and note that the angles indicated by the compass are expressed as x° bearing from the north, which can therefore be expressed as 0°. It can also be expressed as 360°, the total number of degrees in a full circle. If we take the eight main directions of the compass we can specify the directions in terms of degrees as shown on the chart below.

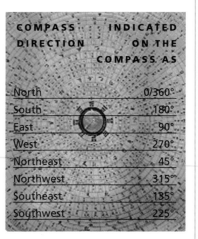

COMPASS DIRECTION	INDICATED ON THE COMPASS AS
North	0/360°
South	180°
East	90°
West	270°
Northeast	45°
Northwest	315°
Southeast	135°
Southwest	225°

Each of the eight directions represents an angle of 45° from the next: 360° divided by eight directions equals 45°.

However, taking directions is quite different from taking locations. The concept of corners and sectors according to the compass will be dealt with a little

later. In the application of Feng Shui formulas, directions of doors are not usually expressed in terms of only these eight main directions.

The next step in taking directions for practical purposes requires you to note that each of the eight main directions is further subdivided into three subsections, so that there are three subsections for every direction. This means that the 360° of the compass are expressed in terms of 24 (3 x 8 = 24) different directions, and the "span of each direction" is now no longer 45° but becomes instead 15° (360 divided by 24 = 15). This is shown in the illustration.

From this illustration you can see that when a direction is said to face, for example, south, there are three subsections of south; you must take the exact degree reading so that you can pinpoint the first, second, or third subsection of south. This sounds rather complicated but it is really quite easy to understand if you think in terms of each direction having three sub-categories of subdirections. When you say your door faces south, you must go deeper and find out if it is the first, second, or third subsection of south. The same applies to the other eight directions.

The final step in taking direction from the compass is to train yourself immediately to equate what you read from the compass with what it means on the ground. Thus, when we say that each compass direction is further subdivided into three sub-directions, how do we visualize this on the ground?

Think of a large pie being cut into slices, each direction representing one large slice

COMPASS SUBSECTIONS

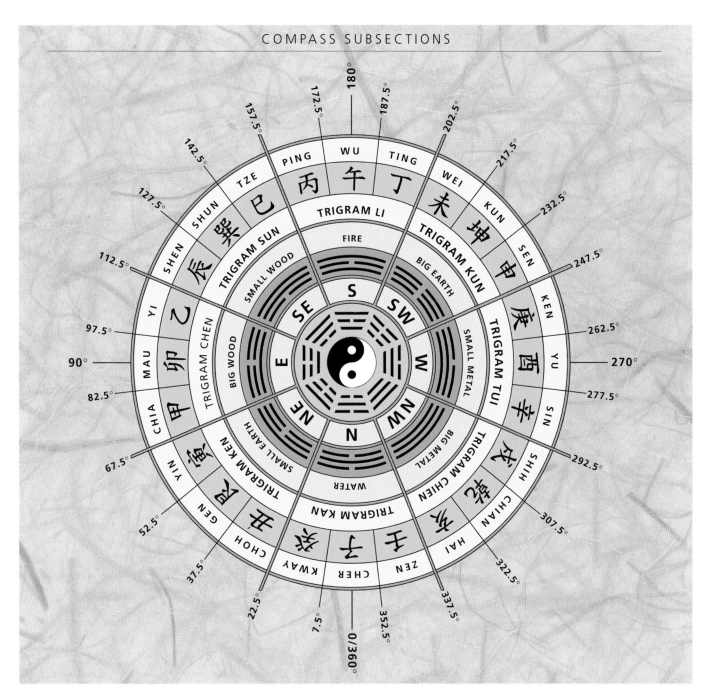

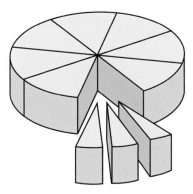

measuring one eighth of the pie. And then think of cutting the slice of the pie further into three smaller slices. Now examine the compass reproduced above.

Note the three subsections of the direction south shown above; they are known as Ping, Wu, and Ting. Like the south, each of the eight directions has three subdirections.

If you think of the compass illustrated above, you will get into the habit of always taking directions

with a more accurate eye. This is because many useful Feng Shui formulas are only as potent as your analysis, as well as the way you implement them.

Once you know exactly what you are looking for from your compass, you should be able to read the compass with no difficulty. The illustration shown here actually corresponds to the first few concentric circles of the geomancer's compass.

LEFT *A pie chart is cut into eight slices representing the main directions of the compass, with one split into the three sub-directions.*

CHAPTER EIGHT: GUIDELINES FOR PRACTICAL APPLICATION

HOW TO TAKE THE COMPASS READINGS

Once you know how your compass works, the next step is to become familiar with taking directions. Here are some pointers before you start.

Where do you stand to take the compass reading? Do you stand near the door, in the center of the room, or in the center of the home? In fact you can take your compass reading from anywhere inside the house; wherever you stand in the room, you will, theoretically, be getting the same reading. The north, south, or any of the directions do not change simply because you take the reading from a different place. Take directions from anywhere inside the room or house that makes you feel comfortable, and which makes analysis easy.

BELOW *Taking compass readings is an art, but with practice you can become proficient and accurate, ensuring that you have the basis for an effective Feng Shui analysis.*

In order to be accurate I always advocate a minimum of three readings, the average of which should be taken in the interests of accuracy. The three readings will vary slightly: this is due to the presence of different types of energy in the atmosphere, which affect the compass. Sometimes the variance can be as high as 10°. Variances should not be a cause for alarm unless they exceed 15°. Such a large variance often indicates that the energy is not harmonizing properly. If you move some of the furniture around or reposition the television or stereo this usually solves the problem. Electronic equipment can send out strong signals that will have an effect on your compass reading.

I have been advised that the best way to take compass readings for Feng Shui purposes is to:
❖ Take one reading from just inside the front door looking out.
❖ Take a second reading from about 3 feet (1m) inside the door.
❖ Take a third reading from about 15 feet (4.5m) inside the home looking out.

When you take these compass readings, place the compass on a flat surface. It is best when the compass comes with a built-in ruler which enables you to position the compass correctly and firmly on the floor or table.

Take the average of the three readings if you want to get a reading of the main door's direction. If you wish you can also take your compass readings when the seasons change. Once again there will be variations in your reading, caused by the natural shifts in the Earth's magnetic fields as the seasons change. However, these variances are not usually very large.

How to demarcate your floor space

The next stage of the practical application of Feng Shui is to decide on the method you wish to use to demarcate your floor space. I have watched Feng Shui masters who are exceedingly fussy about getting the measurements of the premises correct in order to establish very accurate demarcations of compass sectors. I have watched other Feng Shui masters who appeared quite relaxed about this demarcation. Thus your attitude toward accuracy and meticulous attention to detail will reflect who you learn from. My belief is that, since Formula Feng Shui is a very accurate practice, it should follow that demarcations of floor space should also be accurately done. This is to ensure that, when you superimpose the nine-sector Lo Shu square, each of the different sectors is clearly marked out.

There are basically two methods of demarcation that are currently in use by reputable Feng Shui practitioners. One method uses the round compass divided up into eight slices, then superimposed on the floorplan; the other method uses the Lo Shu grid to superimpose the nine-sector grid on the floorplan. As you can see from the illustrations opposite, which show the same house layout with both methods of demarcation, the way in which you mark out the floorplans in your home has a great bearing on the way you apply your Feng Shui principles. Depending on how you mark out the sectors of your house, the application of the five elements for energizing could well be different for the same room.

RIGHT *A room delineated using a compass. Each sector should be marked out* *accurately for the purposes of Feng Shui, but this is not ideal for average home.*

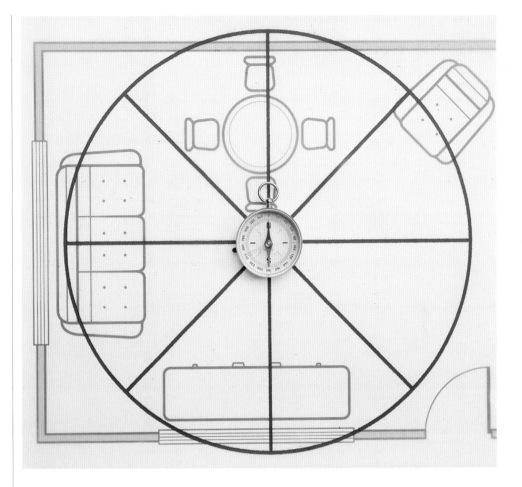

The demarcation of the different rooms in the house varies according to which method you decide to use, the Lo Shu square method or the compass method. I know that the Feng Shui masters in Hong Kong use the compass method to mark out and identify the sectors. In Taiwan, Malaysia, and Singapore, practitioners of Compass Formula Feng Shui prefer to use the Lo Shu grid method. This is also the method that I prefer to use. My rationale for choosing the Lo Shu grid method is based on the fact that the Lo Shu features so strongly in almost all the Feng Shui formulas. In both flying star Feng Shui and in Eight Mansions Feng Shui, the importance of the Lo Shu grid simply cannot be overemphasized. Also, the Lo Shu grid is more representative of the floorplan of a

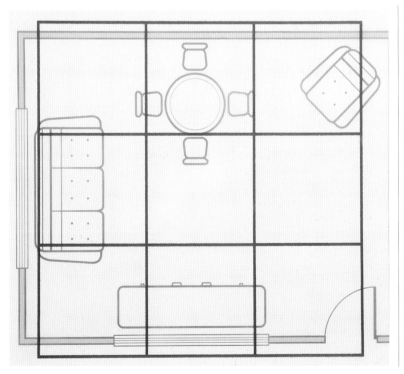

house than the compass. From a practical point of view also, the Lo Shu square (or rectangle) is far easier to work with than the compass circle. I would therefore recommend that you use the Lo Shu grid method.

For those whose homes have multiple levels, the demarcation of each level is undertaken in the same way. Thus, if you want to activate a certain compass sector, you can do it on any level.

LEFT *Many Feng Shui practitioners prefer to use the Lo Shu square to demarcate each* *level, because it is easier to mark off each sector of the room using this method.*

CHAPTER EIGHT: GUIDELINES FOR PRACTICAL APPLICATION

HOW TO DETERMINE YOUR FENG SHUI BOUNDARIES

In addition to demarcating your floor layout plan, you also need to work out the best method of determining the boundaries within which you undertake your Feng Shui reading. While it is very easy to pinpoint the cardinal directions, in reality most houses never directly face any of the cardinal directions. This can create problems. When I am confronted with this kind of problem I "adjust" the Lo Shu square until I can fix the directions as perfectly as possible into the grids. The result is not always absolutely accurate but it does give me a reasonable base from which to undertake my analysis.

Then there are the problems of irregular-shaped house or apartment layouts. In such instances the only way to approach the problem of determining your Feng Shui boundaries is to identify missing corners and extensions of certain corners. If you have really large extensions they can be investigated as being separate from the main house. The general rule of thumb is to treat modular rooms as different grids. Thus, those who have sprawling homes should adopt this approach especially if there is no covered roof or walkway joining the modules together. Garages, for instance, can be considered as extensions if they stick out in the same way as an extension.

When determining the boundaries of a home for Feng Shui analysis, one popular method of interpreting the boundaries is to go with the actual room layout of the home. For instance, if yours is a link or terraced house that is long and narrow, and there is only one room and one corridor along the length of the house, it would seem ridiculous to superimpose a three-grid Lo Shu onto the home. In such an instance, many expert practitioners completely ignore the two outer panels of the grid and use only the center panel to analyze the Feng Shui of the house.

Likewise, when there are only two rooms side by side all the way down a house, the masters "drop" the center panel and use only the side panels to investigate the luck of the house. These issues may seem to be rather advanced Feng Shui practice but they are the same questions that confront any beginner or practitioner.

It is therefore useful to spend some time thinking through the demarcation methods discussed here before you proceed to apply any of the formulas.

ABOVE *A small house like this may need a significantly different approach when using the Lo Shu, and only parts of it may be appropriate for Feng Shui analysis.*

RIGHT *This L-shaped house is split between two Lo Shu grids, one applying to the "main" part of the house, the other to the side extension.*

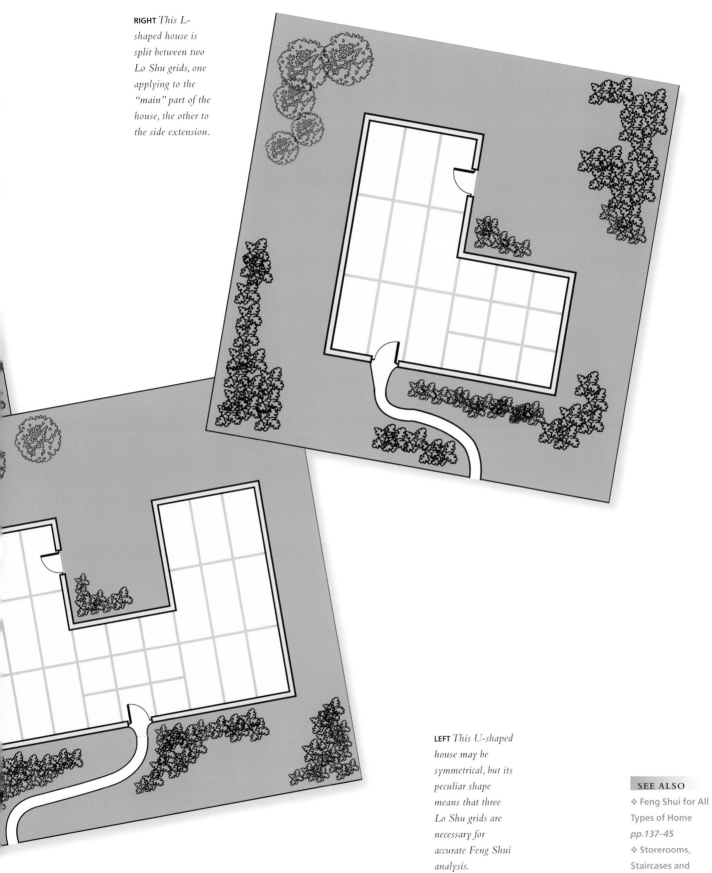

LEFT *This U-shaped house may be symmetrical, but its peculiar shape means that three Lo Shu grids are necessary for accurate Feng Shui analysis.*

SEE ALSO

❖ Feng Shui for All Types of Home *pp.137–45*

❖ Storerooms, Staircases and Garages *pp.188–9*

CHAPTER EIGHT: GUIDELINES FOR PRACTICAL APPLICATION

HOW TO SUPERIMPOSE
THE LO SHU SQUARE

The best way to superimpose the Lo Shu grid is to identify a benchmark direction which ideally should be a cardinal direction. Stand in the center of the home and identify the direction and location of the main door. For purposes of undertaking the drawing of the Lo Shu square, the location is far more important than the direction. This is because, once you have determined the compass location of the main door, it is then easy to draw out the entire Lo Shu square over the floorplan of your house. Then you can fill in the relevant directions and corresponding Pa Kua symbols that are concurrent with each of the corners of the house.

How to identify corners accurately

It is vital to identify each of the corners of the home correctly. This is where the compass reading becomes crucial, but the method you use to measure and draw out the corners is also important. Remember that it is always easier to work with cardinal directions.

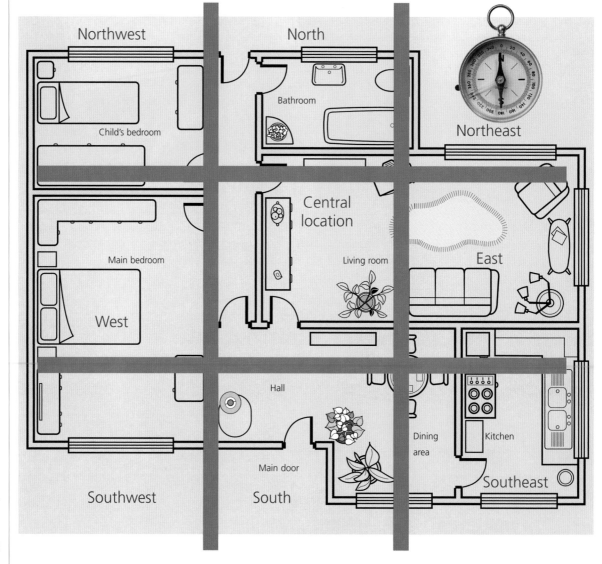

RIGHT *Take the compass reading for the main door first, superimpose the Lo Shu square, and fill in the remaining compass locations.*

HOW TO APPLY THE FORMULAS IN YOUR HOME

There are several different formulas given in this book and these pertain to different parts of your home and to different dimensions of Feng Shui practice. It is not necessary to try to use all the formulas. It is also not possible to get your Feng Shui 100 percent perfect. No one has faultless Feng Shui: there are so many variables that cause things to go wrong. At the same time some of the recommendations are in apparent conflict; no wonder amateurs can sometimes get confused. Attempts to integrate Feng Shui into other New Age practices add to the confusion. My advice is to take the process slowly.

Experiment for yourself and go with what works for you. That was my approach many years ago and continues to be the one I follow today. In the past few years so many "new" Feng Shui methods and techniques have come out that even I feel rather overburdened with the variety and quantity of

techniques now going the rounds. The choice seems to change often.

Study the techniques being offered and ask yourself if it is too much trouble to implement a certain recommendation. If you are like me you will be reluctant to knock down walls and make major renovations. I like the kind of Feng Shui that does not require me to undertake major renovations, preferring always to go with the alternative that offers me the least disruption to normal life.

When you are thinking about the various formulas, select the one that will be easy to implement. Of the three main formula Feng Shui methods that I use, my favorite is the Eight Mansions method of personalized directions and locations. This is also the most potent of the three formulas: it has never failed me, nor has it ever failed any of those I help. If you have to choose one to start with I would go with this one since it is the easiest to practice.

It is also exciting to follow the divinitive aspects of the Flying Star method of Feng Shui. And Water, of course, brings wealth and money. Let your home point the way for you because it is not possible to practice all methods in one home. Be guided by the constraints of your space and, obviously, the size of your budget.

ABOVE *Decide on what you want to achieve with Feng Shui. If your desire is to increase your wealth, you might decide to use the water formulas and incorporate water features in your home.*

LEFT *Your Feng Shui practice may feature the use of energizers in your home – pictures, plants, and crystals – or may concentrate on the balance of Yin and Yang through light and color.*

CHAPTER EIGHT: GUIDELINES FOR PRACTICAL APPLICATION

HOW TO PLACE SYMBOLS OF GOOD FORTUNE

The reason I lay so much emphasis on becoming familiar with the orientations of one's home is because without orientations you simply cannot practice symbolic Feng Shui – the placement of good fortune symbols all around the home. This should be done according to the five element energy patterns in your home.

The placement of good fortune symbols correctly around the home must be the easiest and fastest method of activating good Feng Shui. Those who place these symbols correctly – be they what one irate reader once described witheringly as "tacky three-legged toads and cheap Chinese coins" – will experience noticeable changes in luck after energizing their corners according to the five elements.

Go about practicing the Feng Shui of good luck symbols by first identifying each corner of your home, as well as your living room. Demarcate, for instance, your living room into the nine sector grids of the Lo Shu and then mark out their corresponding directions. In other words, identify the east wall then the west wall, then start to place objects and items in these corners that are harmonious with the element of the corner.

Do not overdo the setting out of crystals, windchimes, and three-legged toads. Usually, the placement of the lucky objects will be symbolic. It is perfectly acceptable, however, to energize every corner. Since every corner represents some kind of good fortune luck, there is nothing wrong with being very greedy and energizing all the corners of the room.

LEFT *Placing Feng Shui symbols of wealth, prosperity, and good luck in every corner of the room will energize them and help to increase the good fortune of the inhabitants.*

QUESTIONS AND ANSWERS

Question: How important is it to fully understand the theory behind Feng Shui and all the meanings covered in this part of the book?

Answer: It is not easy to understand all the meanings on first reading. You can, if you wish, proceed straight to the later chapters for easy Feng Shui tips (*see pages 302–27*) which you can apply immediately. But when you are unsure, or if the graphic illustrated does not exactly fit your situation, then having the theoretical concepts to refer to becomes vital. Thus it is not necessary to instantly understand everything. But do try to take time to think things through when you get confused.

Question: Is the Pa Kua a religious or spiritual symbol?

Answer: I do not regard it as a religious symbol although I do believe there are spiritual connotations attached to the use of the Pa Kua as a protective symbol. I know that Chinese like to have their Pa Kua blessed at the temple before installing it above their front door. I use the Pa Kua only as a last resort. I do not attach any religious or spiritual connotations to it.

Question: What is the significance of the Sigil of Saturn symbol formed by the Lo Shu arrangement of numbers?

Answer: It is a basis for speculating that Feng Shui as a practice is perhaps related to something similar in the Hebrew and other cultures. I believe that the Chinese do not have exclusive knowledge of this environmental practice that promises so much. Other cultures probably have something similar to Feng Shui, but perhaps they are not as well documented or preserved.

Question: Are there any other meanings and associations attached to the trigrams that you have decided not to include in the book?

Answer: Definitely! If you read the *I Ching* carefully and study the multiple meanings of the trigrams and hexagrams, you will discover heaps of information. If you are keen, try to find the Richard Wilhelm translation because it is the most comprehensive. Do not try to study the *I Ching* from a simplified version. It is much too profound a text for frivolous reading.

Question: How important is the Pa Kua in Feng Shui practice?

Answer: The Pa Kua is one of the main analytical tools of Feng Shui. It is also a powerful antidote used to ward off bad luck caused by physical structures that resemble poison arrows hitting your house. When you use the Pa Kua as a defensive tool, you must be fully aware of the guidelines attached to such use. Wrongful placement of the Pa Kua, especially inside the house, can often be the source of major misfortunes. It is important to understand the differences between the two types of Pa Kua.

Question: Why is the Lo Shu arrangement of numbers so important in Feng Shui practice?

Answer: The Lo Shu grid is the basis and foundation of almost all the powerful compass formulas of Feng Shui. The Taoists use the grid as the root of Taoist magical practices. Thus it is important to at least be familiar with the numbers of this grid. In this book I have highlighted two powerful Feng Shui formulas that use the Lo Shu as the basis for calculations. These formulas are the Eight Mansions formula and the Flying Star formulas. I would add that a third area of Feng Shui practice where the Lo Shu is important is the calculation of auspicious and inauspicious days. This is a very advanced area of Feng Shui practice that has not yet been popularized in the West.

Question: Is the compass always used in Feng Shui?

Answer: YES. The compass is fundamental in the practice of authentic Chinese Feng Shui. It is the basis of ALL Feng Shui recommendations. Professional Feng Shui practitioners must know how to read and use a proper Chinese Luo Pan, but for home and amateur use any Western-style compass is adequate. To measure the direction of your main door take compass bearings from just inside the door looking out. Take your bearings of the house orientation from the center of the house. There is no need to change the directions around if you live in the southern hemisphere. If you did you would be practicing wrong Feng Shui.

木火土金水

PART THREE

FENG SHUI IN THE HOME

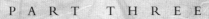

FENG SHUI FOR ALL TYPES OF HOME

Large mansions that have plenty of space to work with usually have better potential to harness good energy. This is because space allows for the free movement of auspicious Chi flows. Such homes are therefore generally easier to work with. It would be ideal, of course, if everyone had perfectly square houses with lots of room that allows for any kind of orientation to be implemented. Then we would be able to design a Feng Shui home. But this is not the way of the real world where irregular shapes, unbalanced layouts, and lack of space are the more common refrain. The master practitioner has an eye for imperfect Feng Shui, which he can then proceed to make perfect! He should be able to create, enhance, or correct the Feng Shui of many types of dwellings. Feng Shui should be able to help all kinds of living space from old bungalows with lots of protruding corners and exposed beams to tiny bachelor apartments that literally have no space for him to work with. This chapter looks at various types of homes, examines different situations, and analyzes the alternative city and country scenarios.

LEFT *This chapter offers a view on how to create, enhance, or correct the Feng Shui of a variety of types of dwelling, from bungalows and cottages to high-rise apartment buildings.*

CHAPTER NINE: FENG SHUI FOR ALL TYPES OF HOME

MANSIONS AND COUNTRY HOUSES

The larger the home, the greater the potential for arranging near perfect configurations of orientations that spell excellent Feng Shui luck. Thus, mansions and country houses that are surrounded by plenty of land have the good fortune to create good flows of Chi in and around the home. Plenty of land also allows for the building of the water dragon, which implies auspicious inflow and discharge of water around the land. It also enables owners and residents to capture or create:

❧ The bright hall effect. This is done by making sure that the main door opens onto an unencumbered field where nothing blocks the flow of Sheng Chi into the home. This bright hall effect brings wealth to the family for many generations. If your house is a mansion, or particularly large, and you have just such a bright hall, make sure the grass is well cared for and ensure you do not place any structure here that impedes the flow of wealth Chi into the home. This is one of the most potent Feng Shui features to capture and the benefits that it

brings make it make it well worth your while having it.

❧ The phoenix hill effect. Having a very subtle, low mound of earth just in front of the main door creates this effect. The mound symbolizes the celestial phoenix which brings excellent career and wealth-creation opportunities. It should be at least about 100 feet (30.5m) from the main door, therefore you need enough land to allow for this.

ABOVE *A mansion erected by a successful businessman. However, the triangular island in front of the house had a very negative effect on the building.*

❧ A pile of gold near your main door. It will be excellent luck to create a pile of medium-sized stones painted to resemble a mountain of gold if your front door faces or is located in the southwest or the northeast.

RIGHT *Those who are fortunate enough to own large mansions with their own grounds can use the surrounding land to their advantage by creating many auspicious Feng Shui features.*

LEFT *A perfect example of a curving path, which will refresh the house with a good flow of Chi.*

BELOW *Wide staircases are better than narrow ones, but should not face the front door.*

A waterfall of gold in your southeast direction. This is a variation of the "pile of gold" idea. If you build a small artificial waterfall in your garden, add a few rocks that have been painted gold and place them in the pond. This signifies that the water is washing gold right up to your doorstep. It is very auspicious to do this.

Probably the most effective thing you can do to improve your Feng Shui is to build water features in your garden in accordance with the *Water Dragon* formula. It is not necessary to live in a very large home in order to do this. As long as you have some land around you, you will be able to simulate a most rewarding water dragon.

Those who live in big houses often have long, straight driveways leading up to their front door. I have seen many such houses and on examining the history of such places I have often uncovered sad stories about the families that inhabited them. Long, straight driveways are the most potent form of poison arrow. They can cause death, serious illness, accidents, and sometimes the complete destruction of a family line altogether. In Feng Shui, there is nothing unluckier than a poison arrow such as this.

It is easy to correct a straight driveway since it is basically a private road which usually belongs to the owner of the house. Owners who have this unfortunate feature on their property are advised to do something about it immediately.

Another common feature of large country houses is the wide, sweeping staircase. This usually brings good luck except when it stops in front of the main front door. Stairs that directly face the front door cause Chi to move too fast, transforming it into killing Chi.

FAR LEFT *At one time, door gods such as these were commonly painted on the main doors of wealthy homes, to preserve the family's fortunes.*

CHAPTER NINE: FENG SHUI FOR ALL TYPES OF HOME

BUNGALOWS AND COTTAGES

RIGHT *Buildings to the left of your home should be higher than the right, symbolizing the auspicious green dragon.*

Almost everything that can be done to enhance the Feng Shui of a mansion or country house can be adapted for small bungalows and cottages. The good news for people who live in bungalows and cottages is that their homes often have fewer problems since, because of their size, these

ABOVE *Clearly defined front and back doors are necessary for bungalows to benefit from positive energy.*

homes are far more manageable. However, for bungalows to have good Feng Shui it is imperative that the house has more depth than breadth. Houses that have depth are able to keep whatever wealth and other assets their owners acquire, while houses lacking depth tend to squander the family wealth. Depth means having at least a minimum of three rooms, i.e. separate compartments, from the main front door to the back door. Generally, having a depth of six rooms is even better although this would suggest a very big house indeed. Other important principles that should be taken note of are:

⚈ Bungalows should have clearly determined front and back doors and a straight line should not run between them. The main front door should be the largest door in the house.

⚈ Regular shaped houses are infinitely superior to irregular shaped houses.

⚈ The land at the rear should always be higher than the front irrespective of compass directions. This signifies the presence of a solid support from behind.

⚈ The land in front of the property should be level with or lower than the front of the house.

⚈ There should not be roads at both the front and back of the house. This is a serious Feng Shui mistake and the only thing to do to rectify it is to plant or grow leafy trees behind the home to provide the back support. When a house is sandwiched between two roads, do not counter the problem by having entrances at both back and front of the home.

⚈ Land on the left should be higher than land on the right. This orientation is taken from the inside looking outward. Land on the left is the dragon, while land on the right

signifies the tiger irrespective of compass direction. Install a very high, bright light on the dragon side if it is lower.

⚈ The house itself should be located in the inner half of the plot of land. When the house is placed too far in front, so that all the land is behind, the effect is the loss of the bright hall, which is a great pity.

⚈ Irregular-shaped land should be corrected with Feng Shui cures. Do this by symbolically "extending out" the missing corner of the land with bright lights near the corner that is deemed to be missing.

⚈ Do not build a high wall or a fence too near to the house. Allow space for the Chi to flow; there should be a gap of at least 8 feet (2.5m) at the minimum. It is also better to be closer to the dragon (left) side than the tiger (right) side of the house. If the dividing wall between you and your neighbor is too close to your cottage, introduce flowering plants to induce good Sheng Chi to flow through and accumulate.

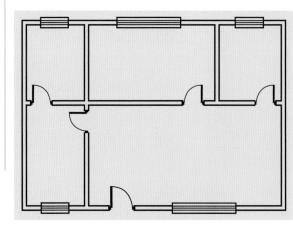

LEFT *It is always preferable to live in a home constructed in a regular shape, even though it may be termed "boxy."*

SEMIDETACHED, TERRACED (OR LINK) HOUSES, AND TOWNHOUSES

For those of you who live in terraced or link houses probably one of the best features you will enjoy will be the depth of the house. Attached townhouses tend to be long and narrow and, while the front may suffer from being too narrow, the depth or length of the house makes up for it. In Feng Shui every house should have a depth equivalent to at least three rooms. Houses that have a depth of six rooms are ideal.

The most common Feng Shui affliction in townhouses, especially those built in the earlier part of this century in Western countries like the UK, is that the staircase often starts directly in front of the main entrance door. This spells bad Feng Shui; if possible, the space between the door and the staircase should

either be decorated with a standing screen, brightened with a beautiful light fitting hung from the ceiling or made less intimidating with some plants strategically placed to create some kind of visual barrier.

People living in terraced or link houses should be careful not to place their beds and work desks against walls that may have a toilet on the other side of the wall. This will have an adverse effect on their sleeping and working direction.

People living in townhouses should be wary of what is placed above the front door. For instance, a toilet located directly above the front door represents a serious affliction that can often be corrected only by relocating the door. If this is not possible, try placing a bright light directly above the front door.

ABOVE *A row of old-fashioned terraced, or link houses. Such homes were usually very deep – excellent Feng Shui.*

LEFT *A staircase directly in front of a main entrance door discourages good Chi. Keep the decor light and bright with plenty of healthy plants.*

BELOW LEFT *The white tiger dwells on the right of the home (when looking outward).*

CHAPTER NINE: FENG SHUI FOR ALL TYPES OF HOME

APARTMENTS AND CONDOMINIUMS

RIGHT *An apartment building situated at mid-level on a hillside will benefit from the supportive energy of the dragon hills behind and the low-lying phoenix hill in front.*

BELOW *Rooftop pools may look glamorous, but represent money flowing out of the building. Water at a high level like this is symbolic of a river about to break its banks.*

Apartment dwellers usually have less control over their Feng Shui than those living in houses. If you want to live in an apartment, the best advice is to choose your apartment very carefully. Use Feng Shui principles to check out the surrounding environment, paying particular attention to the main entrance into the building, and checking also the layout arrangements of the different apartments. Ensure that the entrance into your particular unit is not afflicted in any way by the apartment unit across from you (in the form of poison arrows), or from the unit above you (toilets and kitchens above you could well harm your front door). These problems cause as much harm as an apartment whose main door faces a direction that causes problems for you based on your Kua number.

Large, spacious, and airy apartments are, of course, far preferable to smaller units. Large apartments have fewer tight spots

and are usually better designed. There will be fewer exposed overhead structural beams. Poorly designed, low-cost housing often has this problem. Any heavy overhead concrete beams must be camouflaged in some way, otherwise the residents' health will suffer: the resulting illness will cause a great deal of unhappiness. Penthouses located at the very top of apartment buildings do not necessarily have the best Feng Shui. The advantage of being at the top is that at least you can be certain of not having anything harmful above you. When you are on the lower levels, anything "bad" directly above you is probably repeated as many times as there are levels above you. Thus, the effects of harmful beams, toilets, kitchens, and so forth that lie directly above your dining table or your bed could be invisibly multiplied many times over.

Living on the top floor of a building is excellent when there are other apartment buildings located behind you that are slightly higher, or if there are hills nearby. Apartment buildings that are located against the sides and mid-levels of hillsides are thus excellent.

When you live on the top floor of an apartment building, it is important that you do not have a swimming pool. I know of several very wealthy tycoons who lived in "mansions in the sky." These were located on the top two or three floors of high-rise, luxury apartment buildings. They unwisely installed large indoor swimming pools inside their penthouses and it turned out that all of them ran into severe financial difficulties within six years of moving in. A couple of them even went bankrupt.

Anyone living in condominiums should confine their swimming to pools located within the confines of the condominium areas. It is vital that no swimming pools or artificial fishponds are built inside high-rise apartments. This will bring bad luck to both you and your neighbors.

The dangers of having water on the rooftop are stressed in the *I Ching*. Water is excellent when it does not rise to its zenith. At a high level, water will break its banks and overflow. Water overflowing, especially from a high place, is a symbol of money going out.

It is generally better to live at midlevels and safer, from a Feng Shui point of view, to live in the middle floors. It is not bad luck to live on the ground and lower floors because, according to Feng Shui principles, valleys are usually places of good Feng Shui, places where water flows from all directions. It is

only bad luck to stay on the ground floor when the surrounding roads, railroad tracks and overpasses cause severe imbalance of the energy surrounding the building. Even ground floor apartments can be made most auspicious where the land lying around them is properly landscaped.

Finally, it is important as to whether or not the apartment building is standing on columns, like stilts, with empty spaces at

ground level. The placement of garage and parking facilities on the ground floor leaves an empty space directly beneath the apartment units and this signifies a total lack of foundation and support. It is better not to live in this kind of apartment building. The bad luck is not necessarily severe but it is also difficult to get very good luck either. One way of overcoming this is to live as high up as possible.

ABOVE *This airy top floor apartment gets plenty of light and should have good Feng Shui as it has nothing harmful directly above it.*

CHAPTER NINE: FENG SHUI FOR ALL TYPES OF HOME

STUDIO AND BACHELOR APARTMENTS

BELOW *When choosing wallpaper, do not go for one that incorporates sharp edges in the pattern – it will create Shar Chi.*

These small spaces require special Feng Shui treatment in that the unit itself represents the whole Lo Shu area. Bachelor apartments usually present dilemmas to the Feng Shui practitioner since the bed is in the same room as everything else. I suggest that the sleeping area be somehow demarcated, and clearly marked out. If you use a sofabed or a pull-down bed, treat your apartment as a living area rather than as a sleeping area. But even when you do this it is important to make sure that your bed is positioned in such a way that your sleeping direction is auspicious for you.

One-bedroom apartments are easier to deal with because the sleeping area within the apartment is usually clearly marked out.

Generally speaking, small apartments either have very good

sofabed should be folded back during the day

make sure your sofabed is already positioned in an auspicious sleeping direction

restore the "bedroom" to living room status the next morning.

ABOVE *Even if space is limited in your bachelor apartment, a distinction should be made between the living and sleeping area. Trying to combine the two results is bad Feng Shui.*

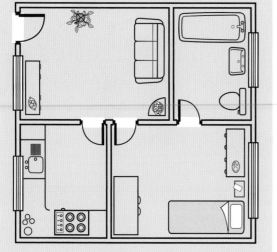

ABOVE *Even in a small apartment, you should aim to make sure that the sleeping area is clearly marked out as separate from the living area.*

or very bad Feng Shui. This is due to the fact that there are only one or two "compartments" and, when the flying stars are calculated, depending on the orientations of the main door, the numbers of a single grid usually apply to the Feng Shui of the apartment. This means that if you have bad luck in your bachelor apartment it might be good idea not to renew your lease when it runs out.

TWO- AND THREE-BEDROOM APARTMENTS

If you live in or plan to live in a medium-sized apartment, in addition to being aware of the features mentioned previously you should also be careful about the way the apartment is laid out. I always recommend that apartment layouts should be as regular as possible and that there should be a large, open area which comprises the living, dining, and foyer areas. This large, empty space is perfect for allowing Feng Shui principles to be put into practice.

How rooms are divided and compartmentalized also has great significance to one's Feng Shui if one is applying Flying Star principles. This is because this method of Feng Shui takes the number of rooms and the way rooms are divided into consideration when analyzing them for lucky and unlucky areas. For this reason, Feng Shui masters who use this method almost always recommend that walls be removed and rooms rearranged.

You will be pleased to know that I seldom recommend changes that require massive renovation of premises, but I do suggest that large, airy spaces are better than a lot of small rooms.

Narrow corridors inside apartments should be well lit and painted in bright, light colors. Small apartments will always have better Feng Shui if they are bright and light because this reduces the excessive of Yin energy from the building. If you have wallpaper, make sure you do not use patterns and designs with sharp edges. These suggest hidden creators of Shar Chi. It is also a good idea to match wallpaper color and designs to the corresponding element of the walls.

BELOW *Small or medium-sized apartments benefit from large, open spaces. Combining living and dining areas enables you to maximize the Feng Shui potential of your home.*

good lighting emphasizes the space

Dining room and living room combined to maximize space

auspicious red flowers

light color scheme

SEE ALSO
❖ The Feng Shui of Bedrooms
pp.160–71
❖ The Feng Shui of Living Rooms
pp.172–81

FENG SHUI FOR INTERIORS

Indoor Feng Shui provides a vast canvas for amateur practitioners to let their creativity flow. There are many dimensions and possibilities to the way you arrange and decorate your interiors. Feng Shui is not a static approach to décor. The key is to go with the flow of Chi. Visualize a current that is slow and meandering, easy and unencumbered. Allow for this gentle movement when you arrange your furniture. Let your indoor traffic curve and turn delicately rather than shoot forward in a straight and hostile manner. Always feel the energy of your rooms. Let it be clean and crisp, light rather than heavy, and vibrant rather than stale. When selecting colors, materials, and fabrics, let harmony of elements prevail and allow for the balance of Yin and Yang. Pay attention to the main door into the house. Let the Yang energy reign supreme at this entrance into your abode. Let the foyer be spacious and allow for some room for Chi to settle and accumulate there. Study well all the things you must guard your main door from, because in protecting your door you will be protecting your Feng Shui.

LEFT *Interior Feng Shui is all about the arrangement of rooms and their layout, their shapes, and the placing of furniture, all of which affect the energy of the home.*

CHAPTER TEN: FENG SHUI FOR INTERIORS

THE FENG SHUI OF HOUSE RENOVATIONS

If you are thinking of making renovations that involve hammering, banging, and knocking down walls you should first take note of the Grand Duke Jupiter. His place of residence changes each year and it is important that you do not disturb him in that corner of your home with the sounds of construction. Upsetting the Grand Duke brings bad luck, so first take note of his location in the year you want to carry out the renovation. To find out the Grand Duke's location each year refer to the table below.

The second thing to do before you undertake any interior decoration is to locate the place of the deadly five yellows. The main guideline on the five yellows is that you must not undertake any renovations where it is located. Thus, if the five yellows is located

GRAND DUKE'S LOCATION

YEAR	LUNAR YEARS			GRAND DUKE JUPITER'S LOCATION
Rat		2008	2020	North
Ox		2009	2021	North to Northeast
Tiger		2010	2022	East to Northeast
Rabbit	1999	2011	2023	East
Dragon	2000	2012	2024	East to Southeast
Snake	2001	2013	2025	South to Southeast
Horse	2002	2014	2026	South
Sheep	2003	2015	2027	South to Southwest
Monkey	2004	2016	2028	West to Southwest
Rooster	2005	2017	2029	West
Dog	2006	2018	2030	West to Northwest
Boar	2007	2019	2031	North to Northwest

YEAR	LOCATION OF THE FIVE YELLOWS
1999	South
2000	North
2001	Southwest
2002	East
2003	Southeast
2004	Center
2005	Northwest
2006	West
2007	Northeast
2008	South

in the kitchen, it is best to postpone the renovation there until the following year, when the five yellows has flown into another grid. In the lunar year 1999 the location of this harmful manifestation of bad energy is the south. This also means that the south is generally afflicted during the year. Use a five-rod windchime to overcome it – especially one with a pagoda design. Note that if you are undertaking massive renovation works on the entire house, the taboos centered around the Grand Duke and the five yellows no longer apply.

THE FRONT OF THE HOUSE

INAUSPICIOUS ENTRANCES

Straight pathways
Corner of another building
A single lamppost
High ground
Main entrance
Land sloping down behind house

AUSPICIOUS ENTRANCES

Winding pathway
Circular driveway
Broad driveway

For the best luck from the front door:
❦ Ensure your main door does not face an intersection or T- or Y-junction passing directly in front of the house.
❦ Check that the door does not face a cemetery, a police station, a funeral home or any building that has a triangular roof pointed at the entrance to your building.
❦ The main door must not face a single tall tree or a single lamppost.

❦ Ensure your house is not at the dead end of a road.

The Feng Shui cure for all of the above problems is to block their negative energies with hedges, plants, and trees or hang a Pa Kua mirror. You can also paint your door a bright red to counter the bad energy.

ABOVE *This home has an auspicious entrance – a broad, winding driveway that does not directly face the house.*

ADDITIONAL GUIDELINES FOR THE FRONT OF THE HOUSE

❦ The house should be on the same level as, or higher than, the road.
❦ The house should not appear to be hemmed in by two taller buildings.
❦ Fencing around the house should be the same height all around.
❦ A fence or brick wall should not be too close to the house.
❦ A brick wall should not appear to make the house into a prison.
❦ The driveway should not face the main door directly.
❦ Do not install barbed wire over the top of the main gate.
❦ The size of the main door should be proportional to the size of the house.
❦ If the main door is a design that is made of two panels, both panels must be of equal size.

bad position: house hemmed in by taller adjacent buildings

CHAPTER TEN: FENG SHUI FOR INTERIORS

THE FLOW OF CHI INSIDE THE HOME

Interior Feng Shui is concerned with the flow of Chi inside the home, the arrangement of rooms, their shapes, the flow of traffic within, and with the way furniture is placed in relation to doors, windows, staircases, and toilets. All of this affects the quality of the energy of the home. Interiors should thus be carefully designed, organized, and arranged, taking into consideration the implications that these will have for the Feng Shui of one's immediate living space.

The Feng Shui of interiors is as important as that of the external environment. It is no good having excellent external Feng Shui if inside the house suffers from stagnant Chi and residents have to endure an unbalanced flow of energy every day. Likewise, it is no good if the energy inside is pernicious and deadly because there are sharp edges all over the place. Similarly, good interior Feng Shui is completely obliterated if the surrounding environment sends killing energy to the home from structures outside. Feng Shui practice is relevant to both the inside and outside of the home, and both must be considered equally.

To begin, get the Feng Shui orientations of your home using the diagram as a guide. Draw the layout plan and then place a layer of transparent paper with a nine-square grid (the Lo Shu) over the layout. Once you have divided the layout of your home into nine squares, you have in fact superimposed the Lo Shu square onto your home. It is important that, when it comes to actual demarcation of sectors (squares), the dimensions should be as accurate as possible. Also, as shown in the diagram, you must include all the covered areas of your house. Parts of the square which fall on areas that are not part of the house indicate missing sectors. The next step is to take readings of compass directions and then identify the different compass sectors of the house (*see pages 126–30*).

RIGHT *By using the Lo Shu grid you can work out how to maximize the flow of Chi from room to room. Here the flow of Chi meanders and is thus lucky.*

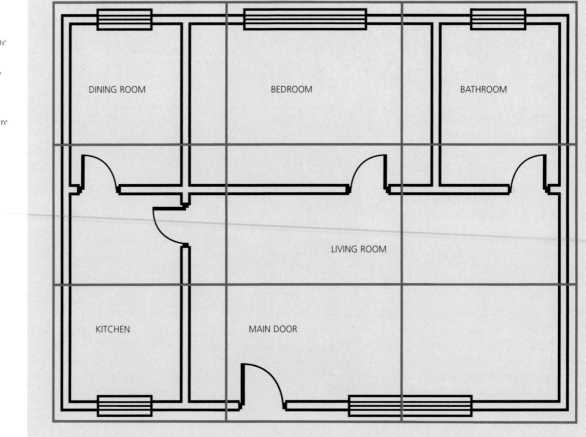

DINING ROOM

BEDROOM

BATHROOM

LIVING ROOM

KITCHEN

MAIN DOOR

THE LAYOUT OF ROOMS

Irrespective of the shape of your house or apartment, the inner half and outer half of the home are determined by the location of the main door. The outer half is the front of the house where you should not locate your private rooms; the inner half is the back part of the house. When designing your layout and allocating rooms, take account of the following general guidelines:

❦ Kitchens and bedrooms should not be located in the outer half of the home if it is a single-level house. If the house has several levels, kitchens should still not be located there, although it is all right for bedrooms to be.

❦ Dining rooms should preferably be located in the center of the home, neither too far to the back nor too near the front, especially to the main door. If you have two dining rooms, the one used for entertaining may be located in the outer half of the home.

Work to allow the traffic flow of your layout meander, as shown in the diagram below.

BELOW *This is not a successful layout: Chi is able to move at too great a speed and strength between the rooms. The long corridor here is the culprit.*

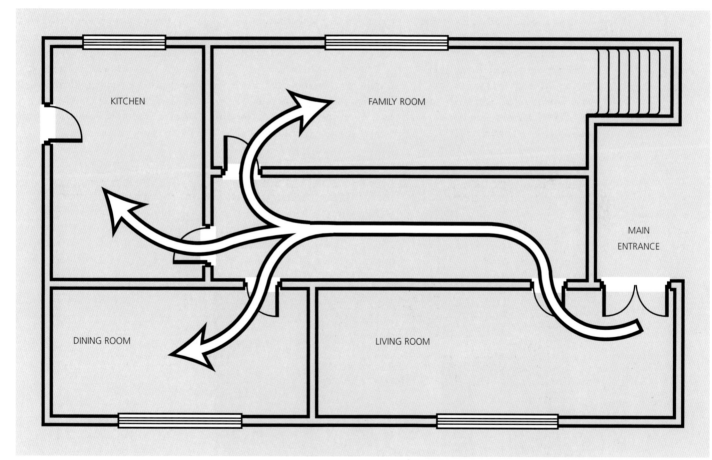

KITCHEN

FAMILY ROOM

MAIN ENTRANCE

DINING ROOM

LIVING ROOM

Auspicious Sheng Chi must always be given a chance to move slowly and gently through the house, and the best way of ensuring this is to design your rooms in a way which allows the flow of traffic through the house to curve. Long corridors and sharp turns are strongly discouraged.

The diagram above shows a layout which incorporates a long corridor, along which several rooms are located. The flow of Chi is much too fast and too strong, and it is not auspicious. There will be lots of quarrels in this home. The problem would have been made worse still if the main door opened straight into the corridor, thus increasing the speed of the Chi. Traditionally, this is a major Feng Shui taboo. The resulting effect is the creation of an invisible but nevertheless lethal poison arrow caused by nothing more than the layout of the rooms and the location of the doors that link these rooms.

SEE ALSO
❖ The Concept of Chi: the Dragon's Cosmic Breath *pp.32–3*
❖ Feng Shui for the Family *pp.192–99*

CHAPTER TEN: FENG SHUI FOR INTERIORS

THE FENG SHUI OF THE MAIN DOOR

The Feng Shui of the main door is the most crucial aspect of your overall Feng Shui. This is regarded as the Kou, the mouth of your home. It is where good or bad luck Chi enters the house. Destroy the Feng Shui of anyone's main door and you destroy his overall Feng Shui luck. Thus, main doors must always be protected against poison arrows, both from outside the house as well as from inside.

There are a great many taboos in the practice of Feng Shui related to the positioning, proportion, dimensions, and characteristics of main doors and it is useful to consider them individually.

Main doors should open inward into a wide space rather than a cramped narrow corridor. Just as it is necessary to have open space inside a bright hall, so it should be relatively spacious outside it. If there is a foyer and it is too tiny, far better to do away with the foyer.

BELOW *The front door represents the heart of your home Feng Shui. A good solid door that opens inward into a wide hallway brings excellent luck. A narrow hallway can be cured by hanging a bright light above the door.*

Cures

🕭 If the door opens outward, change the position of the hinges.

🕭 When the inside foyer space is too small hang a bright light above the door, and keep the light turned on for at least three hours each evening. If the foyer is dark as well as cramped, make sure you leave the light on all day.

🕭 You can also use a mirror to visually enlarge the foyer space, but position it so that it does not directly face the door.

The size of the main door should never be too small or too large but it must be the grandest looking door in the house. This has to do with the crucial factor of balance. The door should not be too large or too small in proportion to the whole house. For apartments use the size and the height of the living room as a guide. A door that is too small is unsuitable because it will not allow good fortune to enter the home. The door should

be at least high enough for the tallest member of the household to walk through without any difficulty, and it should be in proportion to the room. A door that is too large for the room will cause the family to lose their good fortune. This also means ceilings should not be too low. Wealth will be lost and nobody will benefit.

Solid doors are preferable to glass doors. Main doors should always be solid and made of wood or some other strong, durable material. Doors must never be made of clear or opaque glass as this suggests fragility and offers no protection for the home and family. Louver doors are also unsuitable as main doors, although they are acceptable elsewhere.

Be careful of poison arrows inside and outside the main door. Harmful structures from outside are best dealt with by reorientating the door so that the offending edge, sharp angle, or other harmful item no longer hits the door directly. There are many different structures that can harm the main door which are considered in the chapter on poison arrows in the environment (*see pages 317–327*).

The main door can also be harmed by features inside the house and these are shown in the diagrams opposite.

To determine if any of the features indicated as harmful to the main door are actually hurting the door, stand outside and look in. If a feature is directly visible from the entrance just outside the door, your Feng Shui is being negatively affected, and it is advisable either to remove the feature altogether or block it off with a screen or divider of some kind. A row of potted plants is also effective.

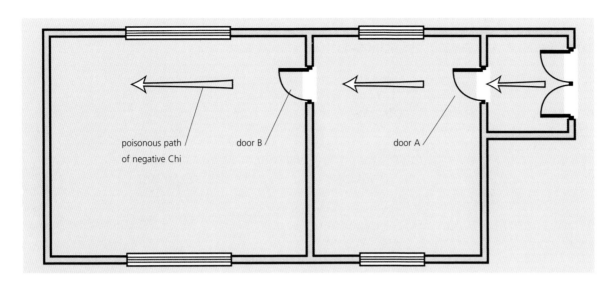

poisonous path of negative Chi

door B

door A

If these features are by the side of the door, they are not harmful.

The main door should not face a toilet itself. If it does, you must make an effort to keep both the lid of the toilet itself, as well as the bathroom door, closed at all times. Next, make arrangements to try and close up the door permanently by creating another door that enters the toilet from another wall. When a toilet faces the main door, it sends severe negative Chi toward all the good energy that enters the home. This feature is a serious problem that should be attended to as soon as possible.

Doors in a straight line are a classic taboo.

When the main door directly faces a second and a third door all in a row, a poisonous path of Chi is created which adversely affects your Feng Shui. The solution is to relocate the inside door marked A in the diagram above. This transforms the straight Chi into curving, and thus auspicious, Chi.

Windows that directly face a door are not a good feature to have in the home. This causes all the good fortune entering the house to flow straight out again. Windows should be placed on walls by the side of the door and never directly opposite the door.

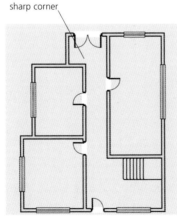

main door

back door

ABOVE *This home has an even shape, a main door larger than the other rooms* *of the house. The layout of the rooms encourages Chi to take a curving path.*

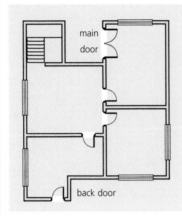

sharp corner

ABOVE *An inauspicious door placement – the front and back door* *form a straight line and there is a sharp corner aimed directly at the main door.*

Good or bad Feng Shui of the main door often depends on the general layout of the house. The two following diagrams show good and bad Feng Shui doors.

A good main door
- The main door is larger than the back door.
- The main door opens into a big spacious living room.

The design of this layout (left) is regular and balanced. The location of the main door is excellent as it forces the Chi to curve and turn from room to room. Both sides of the main door are spacious and comfortable.

A bad main door
- The main door forms a straight line with the back door. This is a major taboo and should be strenuously avoided.
- There is a sharp and deadly corner pointing directly at the front door, marked in the diagram.

Good door placements always open into space. When the entrance is cramped either inside or outside the door, the Feng Shui of home is adversely affected. A cardinal rule is that the main door should never be hit by any configuration, arrangement, or structure that blocks the flow of

ABOVE *Good luck Chi disappears through windows directly in front of the main door – place windows on either side of the the door.*

SEE ALSO
❖ The Front of the House p.149
❖ Create an Auspicious Main Door p.290–1
❖ Entrance Gates p.260

RIGHT *Displaying a good fortune symbol next to your front door will activate propitious Chi energy.*

BELOW *The illustration below is an example of an inauspicious main entrance. Feng Shui antidotes can be used to lessen the harmful effects of negative Chi.*

traffic inward. The diagram below is an example of a very bad door placement. Several adjustments had to be made in order to correct the existing Feng Shui.

You can also enhance the Feng Shui of your main door. Bury three old coins, tied together with red thread, under the ground just inside the main door. If you cannot bury the coins, place them on the floor and cover them with a rug. The concealed coins symbolizes walking on gold each time you go through the door. Several Feng Shui experts have recommended this practice to me, but I believe that it is more superstition than Feng Shui. You can always try it and see if it works for you.

Hang a painting of an auspicious subject near the door to enhance the happy energy of the front door.

Peonies, chrysanthemums, plum blossoms and other good fortune flowers make excellent energizers. I have a beautiful painting of the Sung Dynasty tribute horse hanging next to my main doors on the inside to symbolize plenty of presents coming into my home.

Another excellent feature is the placement of two beautiful good fortune plants (such as the Chinese money plant) on either side of the main door. Again this raises the Yang energy and attracts good fortune Chi into the home. Plants with round, broad leaves are better than plants with long pointed leaves. Plants with thorns are definitely not acceptable.

Be careful what lies above the main door. If the upstairs toilet is inadvertently placed above the main door it completely destroys

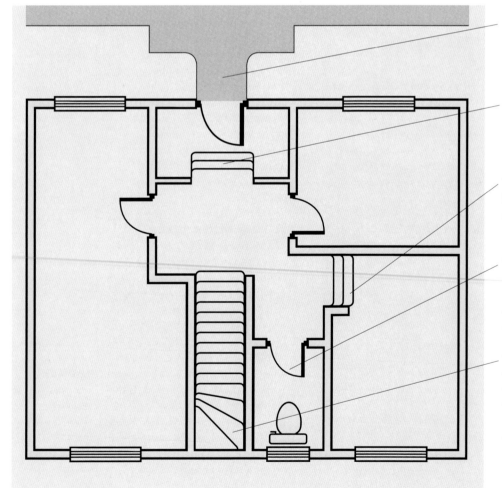

The pathway forms a T-shape and represents a poison arrow aimed at the main entrance. Plants placed on either side of the door will soften the blows of the arrow.

The main door opens to a small foyer, then three steps up into the corridor. This visually reduces the size of the foyer.

The three steps leading down into the basement are also very damaging to the main door.

The toilet door is clearly visible from the entrance. Very near this are three steps leading down to the basement – a screen placed in front of the main entrance can disguise it.

The most damaging feature is this staircase, which directly faces the main door. It goes up for about twelve steps, before turning. This, together with the steps going down to the basement, is the most harmful configuration, which leads to illness and other problems.

the entrance Feng Shui of the home, with often quite serious consequences. Even if it is not directly above the door but only above the entrance foyer, the energies are still not auspicious.

When there are other doors near the vicinity of the main door they create a multitude of effects, some of which can be interpreted as bad luck. We have already noted the ill-effects of a toilet near the main door. In addition, main doors that face doors into bedrooms and kitchens can also cause problems, especially when the two doors are in a straight line.

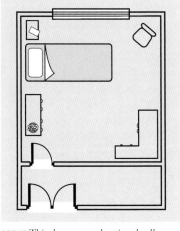

ABOVE *This door arrangement creates unhappy energy by shooting deadly poison arrows directly at the bed.*

In the diagram above, an arrangement like this hurts both the main door as well as the person sleeping in the bed; there will be little chance of success for the individual in such an arrangement. Another effect of this arrangement is that the people in the bedroom will become lazy and indolent. The Feng Shui is certainly not conducive to success.

The solution is either to move the door of the bedroom away from the line of the main door, place a screen between the two doors, or hang a windchime in front of the bedroom door if it happens to be in the west or northwest corners of the home. It is also a good idea to

move the bed so that it lies diagonally to the door.

Finally, make sure that your main door does not face open shelves (which act like knives cutting into the good luck), sinks and stoves (which press down on your good luck), or brooms and mops (which sweep away all the good luck).

Directions for the main door

The *Yang Dwelling Classic* recommends that the best direction for the main door to face is south. This recommendation on orientation was based strictly on landscape Feng Shui considerations, and originated before the advent of Compass School Feng Shui.

The main gate in Beijing's Forbidden City faces south. According to architectural notes, this was to avoid the cold winds from Mongolia, which carried a great deal of yellow dust. In Beijing, many people also avoided placing windows on the north for the same reason. Even today, many Beijing houses do not have windows on the north side.

Certain Feng Shui experts consider the northeast direction as the entrance to hell. They call it the

Devil's Gate, describing it as the direction from which the hungry ghosts enter Earth during the seventh month of each year to wreak havoc on earthly beings. Feng Shui experts consider the southwest (the opposite direction of the northeast) to be the "back door" to hell.

Personally, I have no qualms about locating doors in the northeast. The northeast is represented by the trigram Ken. This trigram stands for the mountain, a location which is said to house hidden gold. It also signifies the youngest son, who is usually regarded as the most precious in the family. The northeast thus symbolizes things that are precious to the family.

ABOVE *Open shelves in front of the main door will have the effect of slicing through and destroying the good energy.*

LEFT *According to Landscape Feng Shui, south is the most auspicious direction for a main door to face. The main gate in Beijing's Forbidden City faces this direction, shielding it from the bad Feng Shui of the northern winds.*

CHAPTER TEN: FENG SHUI FOR INTERIORS

OTHER DOORS: alignments, arrangements, and designs

The next step in interior Feng Shui is to look at other doors inside the home. As with main doors, doors in a straight line are a classic taboo; they transform healthy, auspicious Chi into belligerent Chi because a straight line causes the Chi to move too fast. When doors in a straight line are sandwiched by the front and back doors, expect bad luck. You need to create a barrier or diversion of some kind to force the Chi to slow down and lose some of its sting. For this reason Feng Shui experts strenuously warn against three doors in a straight line. Having taken care of this, there a few other guidelines on doors that are useful to note.

Sliding doors, French-style windows that look like doors, and patio doors should not be aligned in a straight line with the main door. This creates too many mouths in the home, leading to quarrels and disharmony. If you have this sort of arrangement in your home,

LEFT *The main door should be larger or at least the same size as the other doors in your home. A smaller main door will not generate enough luck to fulfill your aspirations.*

keep the secondary doors closed at all times, or hang curtains. Alternatively, you can stop using the secondary sliding doors and turn them into low windows.

Another point to note is that the main door should always be the largest door in the home. It can be the same size as the other doors, but it should never be smaller. If your main door is smaller than another door in the home, try to correct it. This means that your ambitions will be too big for your luck to keep up with. If you want your luck to match your ambitions, ensure that your main door does not let you down. This, of course

also means that all your other doors inside the home should be smaller than the main door.

It is also not a good idea to have too many doors in a long corridor, as illustrated in the picture. Such an arrangement, again, creates too many mouths to feed and general disharmony in the home. Meanwhile, the room at the end of the corridor will suffer from bad luck and the resident here will have ill-health. This is because the room is on the receiving end of the poison arrow that is created by the long, straight corridor itself. If the the doors face each other directly, and are the same size and height, there is nothing wrong with the doors themselves.

Doors inside the home should not be oriented awkwardly. Doors placed close together or toward each other as well as opening outward encourage negative energy since they end up clashing and interfacing. Remember that doors should always open inward. Also, if one door in such an arrangement is larger than another, this causes the residents of the smaller door to be

LEFT *Lush, healthy potted plants will diffuse any negative Chi in your home – but avoid long, pointy leaves.*

RIGHT *Three doors in a line give rise to numerous open "mouths" through which negative Chi can circulate. Keep them closed as much as possible.*

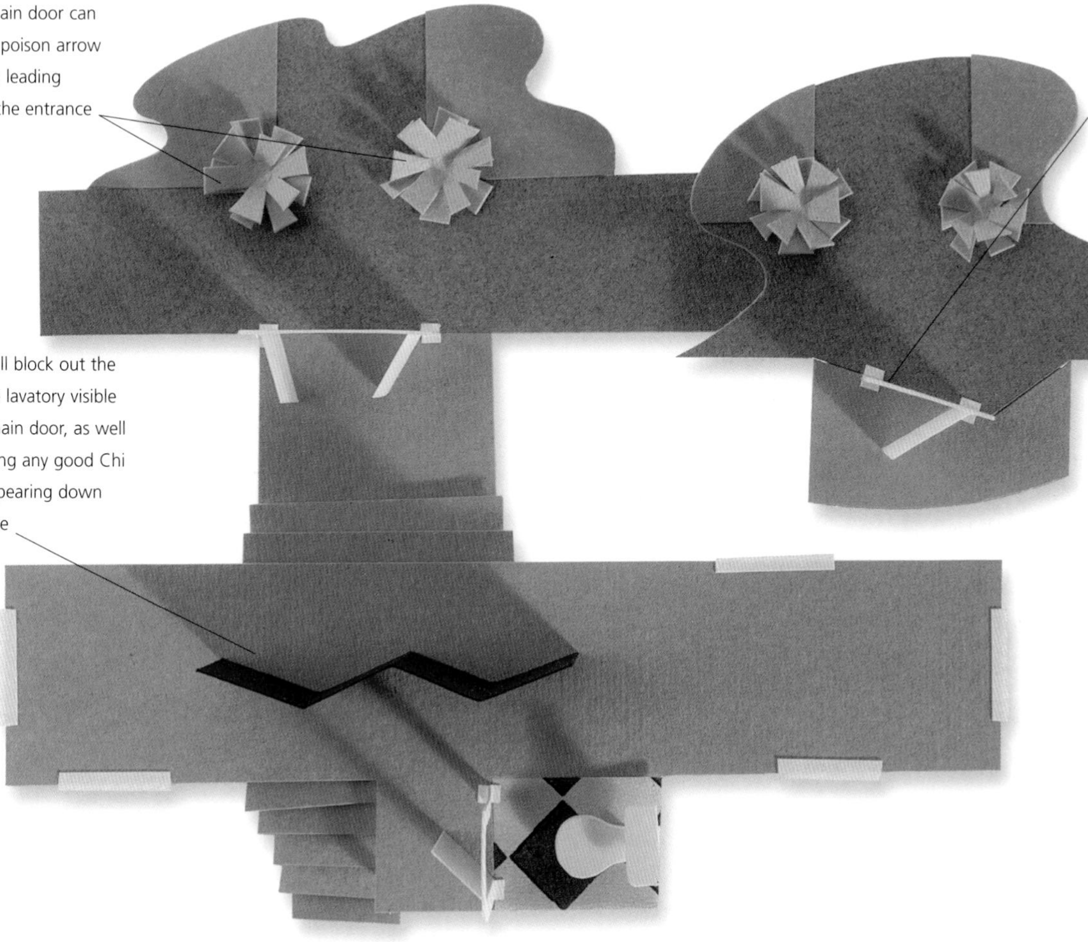

auspicious plants either side of a main door can disarm the poison arrow of the path leading directly to the entrance

if possible, change the direction of the door slightly to slow down the negative Chi before it enters the home

a screen will block out the view of the lavatory visible from the main door, as well as preventing any good Chi from disappearing down the staircase

overshadowed and to suffer from unbalanced Chi. Two doors in line with each other are not a good feature and it is a good idea to place a piece of furniture between them.

The practice of Feng Shui demands an awareness of the subtle energy movements within the living space. With practice this can become second nature. Become aware of the doors in the home, the sort of room each opens into and out of. Also be aware of what is directly facing the door itself, and what the first things are that you see each time you open the door into a room.

In this context, note also everything that is said to harm the main door also harms the other doors within the home, although the harm is usually limited to the occupant of the room which has the affected door. Thus bathrooms, staircases, the sharp edge of corners, and pillars will all cause bad luck and ill-health.

If any of your doors suffer from this sort of Feng Shui problem do not hang a Pa Kua. This has already been mentioned in The Tools of Feng Shui (see pages 111–21), but it is worth emphasizing the point once more. Always hang the Pa Kua outside the house, facing outward. I have come across several cases in Australia and the UK in which practitioners have actually been advising people to hang the Pa Kua inside their homes.

To improve the Feng Shui of your home, place a curtain, a screen, or some plants to soften the effects of the bad Chi. If it is possible to remove the offending structure or object this would be the best solution, but this may not always be possible. Other things not advisable from a Feng Shui perspective are abstract paintings with angular designs, and shelves. Nor should your doors face any of the objects indicated in the illustration above.

If any of your doors is directly facing "hostile objects" remove the items immediately. Garbage cans, crossed swords, or anything that is sharp or pointed create hostile energies that hit the door.

ABOVE *Door arrangements which are causing bad Feng Shui in your home can be improved by the judicious placement of Feng Shui cures.*

SEE ALSO
❖ Using Mirrors to Deflect Bad Energy *p.310*
❖ Good Feng Shui Plants *p.244*

THE CORRECT ALIGNMENT OF DOORS

Doors, and especially main doors, should always open inward in order to allow the beneficial Chi to enter the home and the rooms. The diagrams below illustrate both favorable and unfavorable door openings as well as the correct way of orienting doors.

There are several key points to bear in mind when looking at the arrangement of doors:
🍃 Doors should open inward and not outward from the room.
🍃 Doors should not open "hanging" in the middle of a room.

🍃 Doors should open inward toward the wall of the room.
🍃 Doors inside the home should not be oriented awkwardly.
🍃 The main door should always be larger than or at least the same size as the other doors in the home.

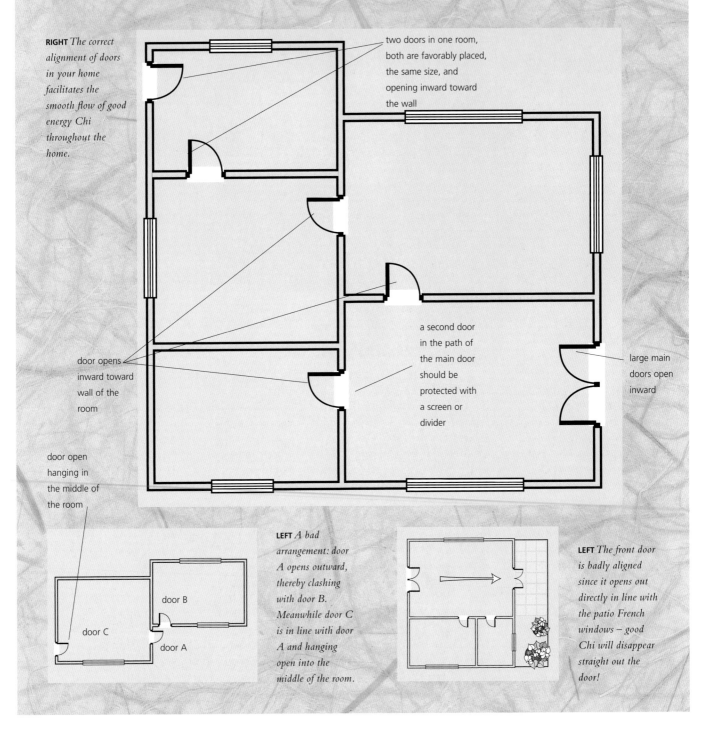

RIGHT *The correct alignment of doors in your home facilitates the smooth flow of good energy Chi throughout the home.*

two doors in one room, both are favorably placed, the same size, and opening inward toward the wall

door opens inward toward wall of the room

a second door in the path of the main door should be protected with a screen or divider

large main doors open inward

door open hanging in the middle of the room

LEFT *A bad arrangement: door A opens outward, thereby clashing with door B. Meanwhile door C is in line with door A and hanging open into the middle of the room.*

door B

door C

door A

LEFT *The front door is badly aligned since it opens out directly in line with the patio French windows — good Chi will disappear straight out the door!*

WINDOWS: good and bad

When investigating the Feng Shui of the windows of your home, first note that the ratio of windows to doors should ideally not exceed three to one. If you have too many windows, the good luck Chi will have no chance to settle and accumulate in the home. It will fly straight out of the window before it has time to do any good.

Also, rooms should always have at least one solid wall and preferably this wall should be the one directly opposite the door, as shown in the diagram. Windows should not directly face the doors.

Windows that have a semicircle above them are acceptable. Such windows, however, often come with an arrow in their design pointing downward. It is better to eliminate the downward-pointing arrow. If you see downward-pointing arrows on any of your grille designs it is a good idea to change the design.

If a window directly faces the edge of a massive building, the building has become a poison arrow threatening the occupant of the room. If this happens to be your bedroom window, you will find it difficult to sleep well, and could also succumb to health problems.

The best way of dealing with bad Feng Shui caused by offensive or harmful views is to block them off with heavy curtains. The definition of a view that causes bad Feng Shui is one that is deemed to represent poison arrows.

Finally, do not allow trees to grow too near to your bedroom windows, especially the windows on the west side of the home. If your child's bedroom window opens directly onto a tree that is too close to the home, the Feng Shui of your child gets blocked. Remember that growing children need plenty of Yang energy, and trees that are too close to the home block off the Yang energy. This can be remedied by trimming the tree. If there are too many trees in close proximity to the house, thin them out or, if at all possible, steel yourself to cut down one or two.

When the whole west wall of your home is overshadowed by trees or covered by vines, the wall is said to be being "strangled" and Yang energy is weak. The west is important for the achievements of your older children; if you want them to benefit from good Feng Shui you must keep all vines and trees here under control.

LEFT *A window that faces the edge of a large building invites poison arrows into the home.*

LEFT *A semicircular shape is auspicious but downward-pointing arrows should be redesigned.*

LEFT *Windows that open out are better than windows that open up and down, such as sash windows.*

RIGHT *The trees next to this home are too close to the windows and the creeping vines "suffocate" the walls – both will restrict the flow of Yang energy.*

THE FENG SHUI OF BEDROOMS

Bedrooms are such an important part of one's life that the Chi should be as conducive as possible to living a happy life. For general Feng Shui luck, particular attention should always focus on the master bedroom since here will be the place where the luck of the patriarch is determined. This governs the financial and material well-being of the family. The matriarch luck is also affected and this means the mental and general happiness of the family. The Feng Shui of the master bedroom is thus very important. Bedroom Feng Shui highlights both the room and the bed placement. Sleeping directions take on vital significance for the luck of the resident. This means both the actual compass direction of sleep as well as the orientation of sleep in relation to the structures, shapes, doors, and windows of the room. Where the feet point and where the head points have Feng Shui implications. Mirrors cause havoc. TV monitors create problems and excessive lighting produces imbalance. Water elements in the bedroom cause loss, and plants are not encouraged either. And bedroom taboos should be carefully noted!

LEFT *It is important to consider the overall effect of the master bedroom upon the entire household. This chapter offers numerous guide-lines to ensure good Feng Shui in the bedroom.*

CHAPTER ELEVEN: THE FENG SHUI OF BEDROOMS

THE MASTER BEDROOM

The Feng Shui of the main bedroom, the one occupied by the father and mother of the household, has an enormous effect on the harmony of the home, on its well-being, and on the finances of the household. There are several aspects of bedroom Feng Shui. Shapes are important, as are positioning of bedroom furniture and decorative objects. The balance of Yin and Yang is also important and good balance of these two cosmic forces is as different for bedrooms as for other rooms. In bedrooms the Yin components, which suggest calmness and quiet, should ideally prevail because the bedroom is a place of rest, recuperation, and relaxation. The layout of your bedroom thus has important Feng Shui implications but this alone does not make for good Feng Shui. Sleeping directions are also vital and suggest the importance of the use of the Compass Feng Shui formulations when deciding on the exact placement of the bed.

There are a number of basic guidelines to be observed:
❂ Firstly, the ideal shape for bedrooms is either rectangular or square. Many bedrooms are L-shaped because of being attached to ensuite bathrooms or dressing rooms, but this is not an auspicious arrangement. My recommendation is to place a divider, as shown opposite, thereby transforming the bedroom into a more regular shape. If your bedroom has an irregular shape, try to regularize it with the use of decorative screens that have good fortune symbols painted on them. Never use mirrors as a Feng Shui cure for the bedroom. Mirrors often do more harm than good in the bedroom.

BELOW Use the Feng Shui bedroom guidelines to help improve the flow of Chi and create balance and harmony in your life.

ABOVE Regulate an inauspicious L-shaped room by using a divider decorated with good fortune symbols. Place such a divider straight, not zig-zagged as shown here.

BELOW An L-shaped bedroom that is corrected with the placement of built-in cupboards.

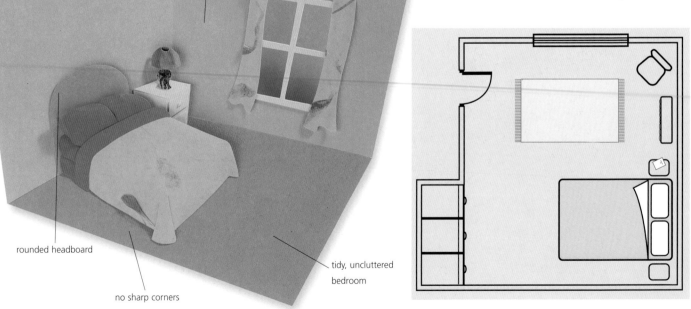

always sleep with a solid wall behind the bed

distance between bed and the window

rounded headboard

no sharp corners

tidy, uncluttered bedroom

FAVORABLE BED PLACEMENTS

The best location for the bed is when it is diagonal to the door, as shown in the first picture, but if this does not tap your best direction, placing the bed as shown in the second picture will also create good Feng Shui.

SOME USEFUL POINTERS
❧ The bed should not be placed directly below an exposed beam.
❧ The bed should be placed against a solid backing, i.e. a wall.
❧ Do not position the bed so that it faces another bedroom door.
❧ Do not put any mirrors (wall or dressing table) opposite the bed.
❧ The bed should not be placed between two doors.
❧ Neither should the bed face a protruding corner.
❧ The headboard must be placed against the wall. It should not "float."
❧ Never move the bed when the wife is pregnant.
❧ A mirror in the bedroom that does not reflect the bed will not cause any damage to the relationship.
❧ Bedrooms should never be located above an empty space, such as a garage or a storeroom. This creates

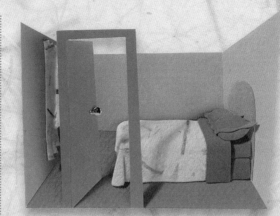

ABOVE *The bed should never face the door. The most auspicious location is diagonal to the door to avoid any direct hits from incoming negative Chi.*

the symbolism of emptiness, with the lack of a base for the sleeping residents. If you sleep above the garage you will be lacking in luck. Success will elude you and plans will not succeed.
❧ Bedrooms should also not be located above the kitchen or dining room. This results in intense bad luck. Sleeping above food that is cooked for the family is very bad, but having the fire below you is equally disastrous. If your bedroom is located in this way, at least ensure that your bed is not directly above the stove.
❧ Another inauspicious feature related to the bedroom's location is the staircase that directly confronts the bedroom door. This is one of the more serious Feng Shui taboos. Attempt to relocate the bedroom door, but if that is difficult, try to place a screen or some sort of divider between the top of the staircase and the bedroom door.

Much of bedroom Feng Shui must focus on the bed itself, and especially the position and orientation of the bed. As well as there being Feng Shui implications in the position of the bed, furniture and objects placed around the bed also affect the Feng Shui of the occupant.

When the bed is inauspiciously placed the marriage and family life of the occupants are usually the first to suffer. Misunderstandings will arise over small, stupid things. Bad bedroom Feng Shui also affects other areas of your life. Your mind becomes unsettled and you will lack concentration. This is because being hit by negative Chi while you sleep means you are being affected for long periods during the day.

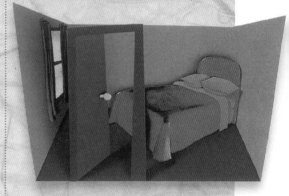

ABOVE *The headboard of this bed is placed against a corner. For good Feng Shui the headboard should be placed against a solid wall for support.*

ABOVE *In this arrangement the bed is not facing the door and a gap has been left between the window and the bed to prevent attack from harmful Chi.*

CHAPTER ELEVEN: THE FENG SHUI OF BEDROOMS

BEDROOM TABOOS

There are many bedroom taboos of which you should be aware. There should be a full length, solid wall behind the bed, providing you with support and a sense of security. This is an important rule, but sometimes you will want to tap a particularly auspicious direction, and then you must weigh up your options. It is not possible to get the Feng Shui of the bed 100 percent correct.

If your bed is immediately underneath a window, support is said to be sorely lacking. If you cannot reposition the bed against a solid wall, close the windows and draw the curtains when you sleep.

Never place the bed between two doors. This arrangement will create harmful killing energy for the sleeping occupant of the bed. Usually the solution for the two doors is either to place a screen strategically or to reposition the bed. But when the bedroom is tiny, the only solution is to keep the doors closed at all times.

The placement of the bed in relation to the door into the bedroom is very important. If the bed is placed directly facing the bedroom door, the effect is usually extreme sickness for the person whose bed it is. This is because a bed placed in this way is in the symbolic death position. If the offending door is the door to an attached bathroom or toilet the effect is even worse. Move the bed so it is diagonal to the door.

Never position the bed with its headboard against a wall which has a toilet on the other side.

Do not sleep in a room directly below a toilet. If your bedroom is located under a bathroom on a higher level it is necessary to ensure that the bed is not directly under

ABOVE *A bedroom door that faces a staircase will activate negative energy.*

ABOVE *Beds placed opposite doorways are in the firing line of bad Chi.*

ABOVE *If your bedroom is located next to the bathroom, make* *sure that the headboard is not positioned against the lavatory wall.*

the toilet. The effect is similar to having water (and in this case dirty water) above your head. Water too close to the bed always spells danger and potential loss. Consequently, the same applies to water tanks. Also avoid placing water features in the bedroom.

Do not have the bed directly under an exposed beam. Such beams are always harmful but in the bedroom they are especially bad. At its mildest a beam directly above

LEFT *A bedroom directly above the garage creates the bad luck of emptiness.*

the bed will cause the occupants to suffer from headaches and ill-health. Beams that cut across the bed can cause marriages to break up or a serious illness which might necessitate an operation. Either move the bed away or create a false ceiling to hide the beam.

Be wary of beds that are in the line of fire from protruding corners. The killing energy caused by these sharp edges is best

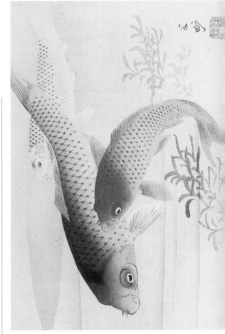

ABOVE *An aquarium or even a painting depicting water in* *the bedroom may give rise to financial hardship or danger.*

deflected in a bedroom by hanging windchimes in each corner. Use windchimes with a pagoda design.

Do not have fancy archways in your bedroom, especially facing the bed. Archways with pointed or triangular tops represent poison arrows inside your bedroom. If you have a similar feature I strongly advise that you get rid of it.

Mirrors in the bedroom are extremely harmful to the marriage or to any relationship. They signify the entrance of a third party to split the couple. This situation can get really bad if the mirror is large and if it directly reflects the bed, either in front of, from the sides or even from above. It is very important to close up these mirrors immediately if you do not want problems with your marriage. If you have a dressing table in your bedroom, try to place it so that the mirror does not reflect the bed; better still, place your dressing table elsewhere. Mirrors placed inside cupboards are not harmful but do discard mirror tiles and other fancy mirrors – they have no place in a bedroom.

Make sure that there is proper Yin and Yang balance in the bedroom. Remember that in the bedroom the attributes of Yin energies should prevail because this is a room for rest and relaxation. Color schemes should be muted. Lighting should be dimmed and there should not be a television in the bedroom. That said, the bedroom should not be so Yin as to completely annihilate Yang energy. Use your common sense and judgment when you take an overview of bedroom Feng Shui. If, for instance, you find yourself feeling lethargic, listless, and lacking in energy, go out and buy a red bedsheet! Introduce soft music but do not go overboard when decorating the bedroom. Remember the bedroom is not the living room. Thus, lamps with shades are better than spotlights, small audio systems are better than elaborate stereos.

You can energize the bedroom for marriage luck, for romance, and to enhance your love relationships. Here are some suggestions.

❧ Diffused soft red or pink lighting is supposed to improve your sex life. Strongly scented candles are also said to have the same effect but this can be dangerous if both partners fall asleep! Candles are excellent for the southwest corner.

❧ Pink, peach, or lilac sheets raise subtle Yang energies that enhance feelings of love and romance.

❧ A pair of mandarin ducks heightens feelings of romance between young couples. Do not keep one or three ducks. One symbolizes loneliness and three signify the presence of a third party.

❧ Other symbols of love, like hearts placed in the southwest corner, are also effective.

❧ Probably the best symbol of conjugal bliss is the double happiness symbol.

❧ For a young couple, the best symbol of a good sex life is a beautiful peony. Do not use this tip if you are a mature married couple since the peony also symbolizes a young and desirable woman. The man might find himself looking for just such a woman.

While bedroom Feng Shui should always observe the taboos relating to orientations, views, structures, and shapes, achieving an auspicious sleeping direction will attract good luck. Always try to sleep with your head pointed toward at least one of your four good personalized directions. Work out your auspicious directions from the chapter on Compass Formula Feng Shui (*see pages 66–79*). In tapping your good direction try not to break any of the bedroom taboos. If both husband and wife have conflicting good directions, go with those that bring good luck to the man.

SOME KEY BEDROOM TABOOS

❧ Mirrors in the bedroom are generally regarded as a very major taboo. Mirrors that reflect the bed will cause the marriage or relationship between the occupants of the bedroom to sour – often because of infidelity and the entry of a third party. Mirrors situated in front of the bed or behind the bed are equally bad. It is strongly recommended that if you have mirrors in your bedroom you should cover them with a curtain or simply remove them altogether.

❧ It is also unfavorable for the bedroom to be directly above a) the kitchen, b) the garage, or c) a toilet. Anyone of these three positions creates the bad luck of emptiness and lack of substance. You must never sleep above anything that is empty or harmful. For exactly the same reason, the door of the bedroom should not face a) a staircase, b) a bathroom door, or c) the kitchen.

❧ Do not place potted plants or an aquarium in a bedroom. You should not even hang a painting depicting water. These indicate harmful Feng Shui. The reason for not placing potted plants is because bedrooms are (Yin) places of rest. Plants are thus regarded as being too Yang for the

LEFT *Beams above your head will shoot deadly poison arrows directly into your sleeping area – this can cause illness or relationship problems.*

bedroom. Water in the bedroom as described causes financial loss or may cause the occupant to be burglarized.

❧ Avoid overhead beams above a study table or above the bed. This creates a heavy burden for the person sitting below, as well as migraines. One remedy is to install a false ceiling. If this is not feasible because the ceiling of the room is already

too low, hang a windchime to dissolve the harmful effect of the beam.

❧ Avoid poison arrows in the form of sharp edges such as open bookshelves, which are like knives pointing at the bed.

❧ The bedroom door must not face the door of another room or the staircase. Avoid having a bed headrest in the shape of a "Chinese coffin."

CHAPTER ELEVEN: THE FENG SHUI OF BEDROOMS

OTHER BEDROOMS

ABOVE *In ancient China, Feng Shui guidelines for the location of family rooms were strictly observed – even concubines in the palaces of the Forbidden City had specified rooms.*

Bedrooms can be designed according to whether they are occupied by growing children or by elderly members of the family. Matching Feng Shui to the bedrooms will help to create the maximum benefit for the occupants. In the palaces of the Forbidden City, the abodes of the young princes differed substantially in design and color from the palaces occupied by the aging concubines of the emperor. Generally, children's bedrooms are better located in the east during their early childhood years, and then moved to the west as they grow up. Older members of the family should preferably be placed on the west side of any home.

These, however, are only general guidelines. Following Compass Feng Shui, the allocation of bedrooms can also be determined according to the personal auspicious directions of individuals and these are worked out according

ABOVE *Each family member has an auspicious compass direction for their bedroom – but the same Feng Shui guidelines apply within each room.*

to date of birth and sex of the child. In addition, you can also allocate bedrooms according to the Pa Kua trigrams placed around the eight directions in the Later Heaven arrangement. According to this arrangement the eight corners that correspond to the eight compass directions also have representative members of the family. The family unit in Feng Shui assumes a patriarch (the father), a matriarch (the first wife), three sons, and three daughters. If you have only one daughter you should match that with the eldest daughter's place; if you have only one son you should likewise match that with the eldest son's place. Children who are formally adopted by the family are counted as children of the family, but children born out of wedlock are not recognized as children of the family. The table below presents the different members of the family and their matching directions.

Generally the main taboos already covered for the main bedroom apply just as much to the other bedrooms of the home, particularly those that address shapes, harmful poison arrows, and structural orientations that cause Feng Shui problems.

Compass direction sector	Suitability
Northwest	Patriarch of the family. Master bedroom
Southwest	Matriarch of the family. Family room
East	Eldest son
West	Youngest daughter
South	Middle daughter
North	Middle son
Southeast	Eldest daughter
Northeast	Youngest son

UNFAVORABLE BED LOCATIONS AND ARRANGEMENTS

Bedroom doors and beds should not face a staircase.

The bed must not placed be underneath an exposed beam.

The toilet door should not be facing the bedroom.

The main front door should not open out into the bedroom.

Bedroom furniture should not be placed pointing to the bed.

The bedroom door should not be facing a stove or oven, or refrigerator.

Do not situate a television set opposite the bed.

Avoid having mirrors on your wardrobe directly facing your bed.

Avoid anything with sharp edges pointing toward the bed.

The best way to sleep is to have your head pointing toward one of your most favorable directions according to the Eight Mansions formula based on your Kua number. However, in doing so you must also make sure you do not arrange your bed in such a way that you are being afflicted in any of the ways illustrated here. In Feng Shui it is essential to take a defensive approach. When faced with a choice, select the option that protects you even if it means not being able to tap the sleeping direction you want.

Some additional examples of structural orientations that cause problems are summarized here. Bedroom doors should not directly face:

- a staircase.

- a freestanding pillar.
- sharp edge.
- a protruding corner.
- a toilet.
- the main front door.
- the back door.
- a stove or oven.
- a refrigerator.
- a sharp object.
- the bed itself.

CHILDREN'S BEDROOMS

ABOVE *War toys should be tidied away in a drawer after use.*

RIGHT *Growing children need the Yang energy of bright, colorful rooms.*

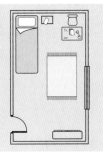

ABOVE AND BELOW *Position your child's desk and bed so that they face the most auspicious direction.*

Because children are always growing and they are usually full of energy, Feng Shui experts recommend that young children's bedrooms should have more Yang than Yin features. This means more light and more noise; rooms should be brighter and generally more lively in terms of color and energy levels. Thus if your child pins up posters of pop stars, plays loud music, has the television or radio blaring through the day – all this spells good Feng Shui. Not only will the children's health and energy levels generally be strong and vigorous but their share of good luck will also simultaneously be enhanced.

Yang components should not be energized to the extent that there is a complete deficiency of Yin energy, i.e. a total absence of quiet, rest, solitude, and dark colors. There must be lightness in the room, but not so much that it overcomes the needs of rest and rejuvenation. Pictures displayed should be friendly rather than hostile. Thus, a lovable dolphin, usually associated with intelligence and happiness, fun and joyousness, symbolizes better Feng Shui than a fierce looking, hostile, and unfriendly alligator.

Symbols of war and fighting – such as tanks, warships, and fighter jets – while they make good toys, will generate a great deal of negative energy in a child's bedroom thereby impeding the flow of the harmonious energy so necessary for a good night's sleep. Keep such toys stored away.

Not many parents realize that the Feng Shui of their child's bedroom, and in particular the placement of the child's bed and desk, can often play havoc with the child's health, his or her performance at school, and with his or her general behavior.

If you want your children to have good Feng Shui, first observe all the rules of bedroom Feng Shui. Next, make certain that the bed location and the child's sleeping direction do not break any of the major guidelines. If the child can sleep with his or her head pointed in the most auspicious personal direction, so much the better.

🐾 Position the desk so that your child can sit facing his or her most auspicious direction. This creates excellent exam luck as well:

🐾 Do not place a desk with a window or a door behind the chair.

🐾 Do not have a tree growing too near to your child's bedroom.

🐾 Do not get hit by a protruding air conditioner or an exposed overhead beam on top of the desk. The Shar Chi creates bad luck.

🐾 Do not get hit by the sharp edge of any cupboard, pillar, or protruding corner nearby.

LEFT *Friendly images on a child's wall generate positive energy.*

STUDENTS' BEDROOMS

Students in college or at boarding school can benefit enormously from Feng Shui. Although their rooms are usually small and might be bachelor apartments, the clever positioning of the bed and the desk alone should take care of two vitally important factors in getting good Feng Shui: the sitting and the sleeping directions. It is not necessary to energize the college room with too many decorative or symbolically lucky objects since these will serve to create imbalance in a small room. Also college students should not try to focus too much on wealth energizers since they have not yet entered the job market. Instead the Feng Shui of students' rooms should be aimed at ensuring that they enjoy good health and that they study, work, and sleep well. With good Feng

Shui their grades will benefit and, when interviewing for scholarships and jobs, good Feng Shui will bring them success in all their endeavors.

In arranging college students' rooms, the student should try to observe basic Feng Shui guidelines, especially when arranging the furniture. Focus on the bed. Make sure you are tapping your Fu Wei direction. This helps you in your studies. Also, when you work, sit facing your Fu Wei direction. Never sleep or work with the door behind you. If you are able to, choose a bedroom that does not have a sink, despite its apparent convenience. Water in the bedroom will cause you to suffer some loss.

Shown here are examples of good and bad bedroom arrangements for students.

Try to observe basic Feng Shui guidelines when arranging the

furniture in a student's bedroom. Focus on the bed (sleeping direction), and the desk (working and studying direction). Never sleep or work with the entrance door behind you.

An inauspicious arrangement

Several things are wrong with this arrangement:
* The door and the window are in a straight line.
* The bed is between the door and the window.
* The desk is between the door and the window.
* The open shelves are sending out knives to the person sitting at the desk. Build some doors to close up the shelves.

Never sit with your back to the door. A rule of thumb is to keep the door within view.

ABOVE *This room bears all the hallmarks of bad Feng Shui.*

---

bed placed in auspicious direction

student's desk is diagonal to door

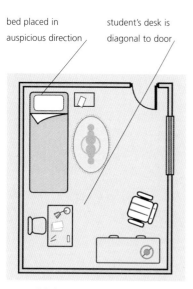

GOOD ARRANGEMENT

ABOVE *The desk in this arrangement is situated away from the door with a solid wall behind for support — never sit with your back to the door.*

---

desk facing door

headboard against solid wall

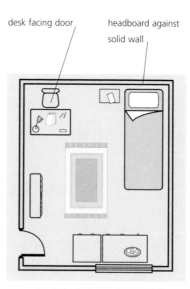

GOOD ARRANGEMENT

ABOVE *Students should aim to place their desk and bed in the most auspicious directions to ensure good health and academic success.*

---

gap between window and bed

no sharp or pointed furniture next to desk

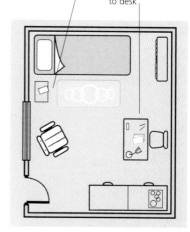

GOOD ARRANGEMENT

ABOVE *Furniture in a student's room should be arranged according to Feng Shui guidelines — avoid poison arrows of sharp edges and open shelving.*

Creating good study luck

There are several methods to create good study and examination luck in your child's bedroom, and these methods are concerned with activating the correct corners of the bedroom. The first method is universally applicable. This involves creating auspicious energy for the northeast corner of the bedroom. The northeast corner is represented by the trigram Ken, which is symbolic of a mountain and is a time of preparation.

The meaning of Ken is that there is a huge store of good things hidden in the mountain; with correct preparation, these good things can be brought out.

The trigram Ken

If there is a toilet in the northeast corner of the child's bedroom, it might be an excellent idea to find him or her another room during the childhood years. Otherwise place a big rock in the attached bathroom symbolically to press down on the bad luck thus created. Alternatively, hang a metallic windchime to exhaust the harmful energy.

Divide the room into nine equal squares in order to find out the exact space which makes up the corner you want.

- Energize the northeast with lights or earth element objects.
- Place a globe on a table in the northeast and then hang a bright Tiffany-style multicolored lamp to energize the corner.
- Hang a lead crystal to catch the light. This is excellent for study and exam success luck.

If you read the chapter on Compass Formula Feng Shui (*see pages 66–79*) you will be able to determine the success directions of your son or daughter based on their date of birth and their sex. Once you know your child's personal success direction you should incorporate it into the Feng Shui of the room. This formula is broad in its scope and usage. In basic Feng Shui, however, all you need do is to ensure that your son or daughter sleeps, works and studies while facing his or her personalized success direction.

It is also possible to energize the personalized success corner by incorporating the theory of the five elements in your practice. Thus, for instance, if the success direction according to the formula is east, you should energize the east corner of the room with wood, which is the element of the east. However, because we are dealing here with the bedroom, it is not advisable to put plants in the east corner of the room. Much better simply to use wooden paneling, wood furniture, or incorporate the color green or brown into the decor of the east corner. My suggestions for energizing the various corners of the bedroom are as follows:

- Energize the east corner with a small porcelain or wood carving of a dragon, or use objects that are made of wood. The same can also be done for the southeast.
- Energize the north with a picture of a turtle or tortoise rather than use the water element. Remember that water in the bedroom causes loss and the possibility of burglary.
- Put up decorative rosettes with different colored ribbons to symbolize success. Use red for south, southwest, and northeast. Use ocher or earth hues for the southwest or northeast, green for the east or southeast, blue for the north, and gold or silver for the west or northwest.

Place all your metallic trophies in the metal corners, i.e. in the west and the northwest. This is particularly beneficial for west group people.

Secret poison arrows

For some months I wondered why my nephew was having such difficulty improving his grades at school. I had given him very specific instructions on how he should sleep, how he should sit while studying and doing his homework, how he should arrange his bedroom, and even which bedroom in the house he should use. I nagged him so much and I am certain that he carried out my instructions to the letter.

And yet, although he seemed to work really hard, he was getting nowhere in terms of tangible achievement; his grades continued to be disappointing. One day, I visited my nephew unexpectedly. The poison arrows I found in his room are worth revealing, and the solutions that I suggested should be followed by readers who want to ensure that the same harmful Chi is not allowed to circulate in their child's work areas.

ABOVE *A mountain in the northeast corner symbolizes the trigram Ken, meaning a hoard of good things to come.*

Bookshelves directly above the desk, or nails, or hooks all represent poison arrows.

My nephew had a bookshelf directly above his desk, with the edge of the shelf directly hitting his forehead. As if that was not bad enough, he had also placed a few nails onto the edge of the shelf (to hang things on, he told me sheepishly); he was not to know that the shelf and the nails represented secret poison arrows. We took down the book shelf immediately, and the nails went with the shelf. My nephew's grades took a quantum leap in improvement after the Feng Shui corrections were made.

RIGHT *Creating an auspicious environment for study means eliminating any secret poison arrows.*

THE FENG SHUI OF THE LIVING ROOM

The living room is the best room to use when energizing to attract all the different types of Feng Shui luck. From activating for success, wealth, and fame to improving relationships and bringing powerful people into the embrace of the family's well-being, there is no better place to work Feng Shui magic than the living room. This is the room that benefits most from Yang energy, and from Feng Shui symbols of good fortune. But the introduction of Feng Shui energizers should be subtle and discreet. Decorative articles with a Feng Shui significance should never shout out loud, since this will almost always be interpreted as being excessive. In addition, balance and harmony should always be the overriding criteria of good Feng Shui. Emphasis on relationship luck is strongly recommended, since the living area is the place where visitors spend the most time. Meanwhile, the dining room is even more important than the living room, since this is where the family's food is enjoyed and displayed. Mirrors and special luck objects should therefore always enhance the area.

LEFT *Feng Shui can activate all kinds of types of luck in the living room, especially relationship, networking, patronage, and mentor luck.*

CHAPTER TWELVE: THE FENG SHUI OF THE LIVING ROOM

ARRANGEMENTS OF FURNITURE

ABOVE *Use a gridded room plan with cutouts of your furniture drawn to scale to help you plan the most auspicious layout of your living room.*

Furniture in the living room usually comprises combinations of sofas and chairs, coffee tables, and perhaps one or more display and side cabinets. Subtle Feng Shui influences can be introduced into the arrangements of this furniture to improve the energy flow within the room, and to create balance and harmony that promotes a feeling of warmth and welcome. This, after all, is where most family entertaining takes place and furniture should be placed so as to enhance good feeling. There are good and bad arrangements: these bring a flow of goodwill from friends, bosses, and colleagues at work, or they create situations were misunderstanding is rife.

I usually advise people first to check the flying star of the living room to see if flying stars are auspicious or if they are positioned in a way that will cause problems. This is an excellent method of investigating the Feng Shui of the living room. Whether or not you know about Flying Star Feng Shui, try to overcome any stars that bring discord and misunderstandings into your relationships. This can be done whether bad stars are present or not. To be on the safe side combat the possibility of flying stars with the presence of "calm and small water." This means having a small ceramic bowl filled with water in the living room, or a small goldfish bowl (with no bubbles or filters so

the water stays calm). Place this against the north, southeast, or east wall. Goldfish are a good choice because, as good fortune fish, they also have a calming effect.

Meanwhile, arrange sofas and chairs in the living room to simulate the best landscape configuration. This instantly creates good Feng Shui. The illustrations on the following few pages suggest furniture layout arrangements that are good Feng Shui and warn against arrangements that create Feng Shui problems.

GOOD LIVING ROOM FENG SHUI

The living room is the area of the house that represents the outer face of the family. This is the room in which the family does most of their entertaining. Unlike the family room, which signifies the inner conditions of the family, the living room affects the family's outside reputation. All relationships with people outside the family and especially influential people are affected by the Feng Shui of the living room. Thus, it is the best place in the house to energize for career, reputation, and success luck.

The living room should have a regular shape – either square or rectangular. Irregular or L-shaped living rooms should ideally be made regular with mirrors that visually extend walls and fill up missing corners. This should especially be done if the missing corner is the vital southwest corner.

BASIC GUIDELINES ON GOOD LIVING ROOM FENG SHUI

- The living room should be regular in shape.
- The living room should be neither the smallest nor the largest room in the home.
- It should be located in the outer half of the home.
- Hang a large family portrait in the living room to symbolically enhance the importance of the family in their dealings with people outside the family.
- It is important that the living room is not higher than the family dining room.
- Mirror walls in the living room should not reflect the main door.
- Block bad energy emanating from protruding corners in the living room with tall plants.
- Keep the living room well lit to ensure lots of Yang energy.
- If you want to energize the home with symbols of good fortune, the living room is the best room for them.
- If you furnish your living room with antique furniture, symbolically "cleanse" the antique furniture of left-over energy from previous owners with incense and sounds from a special "singing bowl" made of seven types of metals.
- Do not place furniture under exposed beams.
- Do not display pictures or ceramics of aggressive or fierce animals.
- Place your lounge furniture in a square or rectangular arrangement, or even a Pa Kua shape arrangement, to be most harmonious.
- Enhance the elements of each corner of the living room by placing element energizers at each corner.

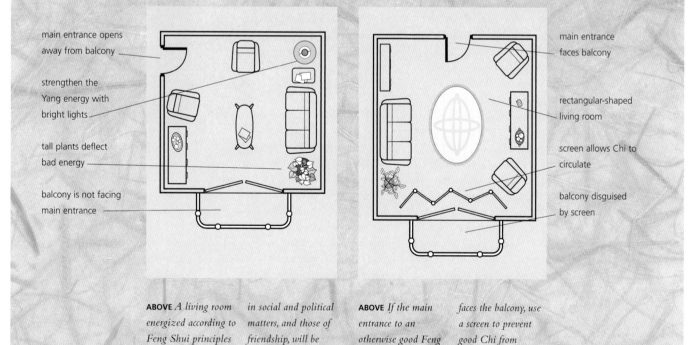

main entrance opens away from balcony

strengthen the Yang energy with bright lights

tall plants deflect bad energy

balcony is not facing main entrance

main entrance faces balcony

rectangular-shaped living room

screen allows Chi to circulate

balcony disguised by screen

ABOVE *A living room energized according to Feng Shui principles will ensure that luck in social and political matters, and those of friendship, will be excellent.*

ABOVE *If the main entrance to an otherwise good Feng Shui living room faces the balcony, use a screen to prevent good Chi from escaping.*

CHAPTER TWELVE: THE FENG SHUI OF THE LIVING ROOM

GOOD FURNITURE ARRANGEMENTS IN THE LIVING ROOM

ABOVE *Arranging your furniture in the shape of the eight-sided Pa Kua energizes all of the eight corners.*

RIGHT *Emulate the supportive black turtle by placing your largest sofa against a solid wall.*

ABOVE *Recreate a Pa Kua shape using your living room furniture.*

❦ Simulating the Pa Kua. This requires the main seating area to be arranged around a circular center table forming the eight-sided Pa Kua shape. This usually results in a fairly square arrangement with side tables making up the diagonal edges. This arrangement is auspicious and allows specific energizing of the eight different locations around the arrangement that make up each of the compass directions. Also, the arrangement will appear balanced and in harmony. There will be a square arrangement outside that complements the round table in the center, thereby simulating the union of heaven and earth. It is thus very auspicious. This arrangement will also work if tables occupy only two of the diagonal sides.

❦ The green dragon white tiger. A large three- or four-seater sofa placed against a solid wall dominates this arrangement. This represents the black tortoise that signifies solid support and creates

protective luck for careers and businesses. If you have this arrangement people doing business with you or those who have authority over you will help rather than hinder you. Next to the sofa on the right, place a single chair to simulate the tiger and on the left side representing the dragon place a two-seater sofa. Directly opposite the main big sofa, place a small footstool. The coffee table placed in the center should be rectangular in shape. This arrangement is most auspicious. Make sure that sofas and easy chairs come with good back support. The sides of the easy chairs should also have arms.

❦ Tapping the solid walls and windows. This is a significant point to factor into your choice of arrangement. It is always good to place your largest sofa or chair against a solid wall. Preferably this wall should be opposite the entrance door into the room. The secondary chairs can have windows behind them unless views are bad, in which case curtains have to be used to shut off the view.

❦ Correct too many doors. When there are more than two doors leading into any room it is advisable to keep some of them closed. In the living room, which is usually near the front door, Chi flows caused by too many doors can become confused and haphazard. Your luck will be equally as haphazard. Correct the problem by using curtains or screens.

❦ Correct too many windows. The ratio of windows to doors should not exceed 3:1. Windows in the living room should follow this ratio; if there are too many windows, curtains and blinds should be used to camouflage their presence. If you do not have any windows in the living room, it is a good idea to simulate them. Any room without a window is missing something. At the same time, windows should be on the walls that are 90° to the wall in which the entrance door is set. When a row of windows directly faces the door it is considered inauspicious since Chi entering the house goes straight out again.

❦ A two-room living room. When two distinct rooms make up the area for entertaining, either because of the presence of a foyer, an annex, or an anteroom, this gives depth to the house and is considered an auspicious feature. A house with interior depth indicates that good fortune will last for a long time and continue through successive generations.

LEFT *Place a large sofa against a solid wall opposite the door.*

LEFT *Too many doors results in unharmonious flows of Chi.*

LEFT *Too many windows allow the good Chi to escape.*

LEFT *A living room with distinct divisions brings good fortune.*

BAD FURNITURE ARRANGEMENTS IN THE LIVING ROOM

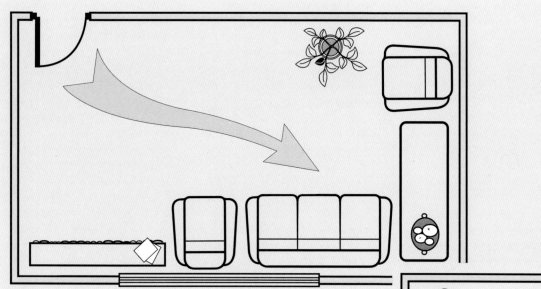

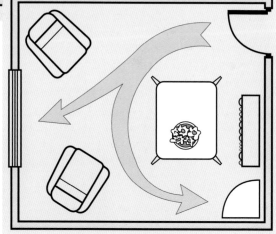

LEFT *As well as creating disharmony, an L-shaped sofa arrangement takes on the shape of an pointed arrow.*

BELOW *A "floating" arrangement, where no thought has been given to the arrangement, is not a firm basis for generating good luck energy.*

🌀 L-shaped arrangements. It is not a good idea to arrange sofas or living room suites into an L-shape. Not only does this form a corner that looks like an arrow, but the L-shape is regarded as generally inauspicious because it is incomplete and unbalanced.

🌀 Disjointed arrangements with no focal point. Furniture that is arranged haphazardly suggests a mind that is disjointed. In terms of luck it also does nothing to attract good fortune. It is always necessary to arrange furniture into a regular shape. Otherwise, Chi flows equally haphazardly through the room.

🌀 Floating arrangements. This is similar to not having any pattern or arrangement. When furniture in the living room "floats," i.e. it is not backed by walls, the luck of the family stands on unstable ground. Friendships and networking will be on shifty ground and friends will not be trustworthy.

🌀 Blocking the flow of Chi. This happens when there are too many pieces of furniture causing the living room to become crowded. Chi flows get blocked and stagnant energy results. This is bad because luck simply cannot flow in to benefit the family.

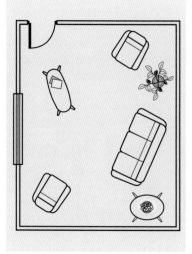

LEFT *Disorganized arrangements lacking a focal point will not encourage a good flow of Chi – reorganize the layout to attract good luck.*

LEFT *The path of good Chi is slowed down and blocked by the cluttered and careless layout.*

SEE ALSO

❖ The Layout of Rooms *p.151*

CHAPTER TWELVE: THE FENG SHUI OF THE LIVING ROOM

THE USE OF MIRRORS IN INTERIOR DÉCOR

Mirrors can seriously enhance the Feng Shui of the living room, especially when they are cleverly placed to reflect beautiful views from outside. This symbolically brings in auspicious Chi and is especially recommended if there is a view of water. Mirrors can also be used to visually extend a particularly auspicious wall or corner. To achieve either of these ends, the best method is to hang a wall mirror, or at least a mirror that is large and imposing enough to make its presence felt.

Wall mirrors are especially auspicious in living rooms and dining rooms since they have the potential to "double" food served on the table. Remember that food always symbolizes abundance and plenty and is thus a wealth energizer. Doubling the food on the table always means doubling your good fortune.

There are some useful guidelines about incorporating mirrors into the interior décor of the rooms in which you entertain and these are summarized below:

℮ Wall mirrors should be large enough to reflect the tallest people in the house. Do not let mirrors cut off heads or feet, since this is obviously very unlucky.

℮ Full-length mirrors are better than small mirror tiles used to make a larger mirrored area. If tiles are too small, they can symbolically cut off the reflection of people. They also tend to distort the reflections of people. If mirror tiles are large enough not to cause this problem, however, they are not only acceptable but very auspicious.

℮ Always make sure that your mirrors are sufficiently thick and of good quality. Bad quality mirrors that develop black spots and distort images cause imbalance and are not auspicious. Change such mirrors immediately.

℮ Mirrors should not reflect the main door because they cause good fortune to be reflected outward. The worst situation is when a large wall mirror directly faces the door so that the door itself is reflected in the mirror. This can cause the father of the household to fall ill (generally with a liver or kidney ailment). Such mirrors also cause bad luck in the family.

℮ Wall mirrors should not directly face a toilet door since this doubles the effects of something that is most inauspicious.

℮ Wall mirrors should not reflect a long staircase that is either going up or going down. This speeds up the flow of Chi, transforming it into malevolent energy.

℮ Mirrors framed with gold-painted designs are very auspicious in a metal room since these suggest an auspicious combination of gold and water. Metal in the cycle of production creates water and water symbolizes gold. Mirrors are believed also to symbolize water.

℮ Mirrors should not face the door into the kitchen and it is especially bad if a stove is reflected in a mirror. I never encourage mirrors in the kitchen. While mirrors in the dining room reflect food, mirrors in the kitchen reflecting the stove are not actually reflecting food being cooked, rather the fire that is cooking the food. Reflecting fire is one of the danger signs of Feng Shui.

℮ Mirrors in the living room should not reflect beams and pillars: in effect, this doubles bad, inauspicious features.

RIGHT *A plentiful food supply is symbolic of wealth. A mirror in the dining room duplicates the effect for increased prosperity luck.*

ENHANCING FENG SHUI FEATURES

Regardless of the dominant element of the living room and the way it has been decorated, certain features always bring good Feng Shui into the living room when they are displayed. Here are four suggestions. See also the chapter on Symbolic Feng Shui (*pages 80–99*) for more ideas on enhancing Feng Shui features.

ℓ One of the best Feng Shui enhancers is the presence of a sailing ship which has been symbolically loaded with gold. Look for fake gold ingots that the Chinese and Taiwanese Feng Shui industry has now started making. They are superb for putting onto the decks of these sailing ships. The choice of the ship is important. You must make sure you do not end up buying a warship with cannons since this will cause you problems. The sailing ships that used to bring back riches and wealth from the colonies, or from traders and merchants, are the best. Ensure that the ship is facing inward rather than outward: this is important because a ship loaded with gold sailing outward is taking away your wealth. When looking for such a ship, select one made of wood with powerful sails that can catch the wind. Place the ship on a coffee table, not too high up. Do not place the ship on a high shelf.

ℓ Another good thing to create is a large, prosperous and abundant-looking wealth vase. Look for a wide-mouthed crystal, ceramic or metal vase. Make sure it is large enough to satisfy you. Place three coins tied with red thread deep inside the vase. Next, fill it with seven types of semiprecious stones, any that take your fancy, large or small. The best and most beautiful are the tumbled stones from South Africa. Choose between amethysts, citrines, quartzes, topazes, tiger's eye, malachite, corals, lapis lazuli, sodalite, cornelians, jade, and so forth. Fill the vase to about halfway, then add a little soil from a rich man's house. Next, fill the vase to the brim with more precious stones and place the vase inside a cupboard, hidden away. This represents the hidden wealth of the household and is very auspicious.

ℓ A third tip for enhancing the living room is to place a three-legged toad near the main front door. I like placing the toad quite low down, perhaps on the second or third shelf of a table. I also like to place the toad indirectly facing the door. Others recommend that it should directly face the door in the daytime and at night it should face inside. I am very relaxed about these different recommendations. Suffice it to say that I have been amazed by how lucky this three-legged toad has been. Such toads are not hard to find now and are being produced from semiprecious stones, copper, brass, and pewter.

ℓ Another good Feng Shui enhancer for the living room is the introduction of a small aquarium of goldfish into the water corner of the room. Choose eight red goldfish and one black one and keep them in a round pot or aquarium. Place water plants inside to act as a natural filter and feed the goldfish yourself regularly. This is a very auspicious feature for your living room because, in addition to symbolizing abundance, it also brings Yang energy. Feeding the fish every day is also very good for your karma. Just make sure you keep the aquarium clean and clear.

LEFT *If you want prosperity and abundance in your household, place a sailing ship loaded with fake gold ingots in your living room – but make sure that it is facing inward, otherwise you wealth is likely to "sail away."*

ABOVE *The three-legged toad is now more widely available and, placed in the right location, can bring enormous wealth luck.*

LEFT *Goldfish are excellent wealth enhancers, and for extra luck make sure there are nine fish including a black one.*

CHAPTER TWELVE: THE FENG SHUI OF THE LIVING ROOM

DISARMING POISON ARROWS

In the living room there are two main types of poison arrows that need to be disarmed. The first type is sharp edges caused by freestanding square pillars and protruding corners. The second is the sharp edges caused by exposed overhead beams. These unlucky features must be dealt with if you want to feel good energy in your living room.

In the living room, the best way to deal with sharp, harmful edges caused by freestanding columns and protruding corners is to use a tall, leafy plant to block off the sharp edges. Creepers are also effective. Remember that live plants will not survive the onslaught of these poison arrows for too long; they, too, get hurt by the sharp edges and you will need to replace them regularly, perhaps every three or four months. One way of overcoming this is to use a fake silk plant. I often use these but I find I even have to change these once a year, because after a while they lose their effectiveness.

Placing mirrors around the entire pillar can also disarm freestanding square pillars, making them disappear and blend in with the rest of the room. The only danger here is that they may blend in so well that you miss them and end up walking into them. Even if you place mirrors around them, do place a small plant next to the pillar where the edge occurs.

Hanging a hollow set of windchimes with five rods or hanging Feng Shui bells from the top of the corner sends good energy that can dissolve the bad Chi emanating from the sharp edges of corners. This cure is particularly effective if the edges are in the east or southeast

corners of the living room. However, they are not as effective for freestanding columns. Windchimes are excellent for enhancing the west and northwest corners but, used as an antidote against harmful structures, they are not effective in these corners. If you hang windchimes in these metal corners, use six- or seven-rod chimes for maximum effect.

Exposed overhead beams are rather tricky to deal with in the living room. The best and easiest method is to arrange furniture in such a way that no one is sitting directly under these beams. If that is hard to do, you might want to round off the sharp edges of the beams and hang windchimes (five rods), thus symbolically softening the weight.

It also helps if you can have a false ceiling that hides the beams. A plaster ceiling is best as long as this does not lower the ceiling too

much. Ideally, ceilings should be at least 9 feet (2.75m) high, since excessively low ceilings cause the Chi to be cramped and stifled.

Another way of coping with exposed overhead beams is to camouflage them with a draped material, or to stick fake (plastic) plants on the edges of the beams. This latter method does work but the result can look rather tacky.

BELOW *The sound of windchimes is soothing and will disperse poison arrows, particularly in the east or southeast corner of the room.*

ABOVE *Trailing a healthy climbing plant around a freestanding column is an attractive and effective way of deflecting the poison arrows.*

SPLIT LEVELS AND FLOOR DESIGNS

Generally, the level of the living room should always be lower than the other main rooms in the home. It should be lower than the bedrooms and definitely lower than, or at least on the same level as, the dining room. The living room is where visitors are introduced and family members are symbolically more important. The dining room symbolizes the rice bowl of the family and, if this is lower than the living room, the effect is deemed to be inauspicious for the family.

Generally, Feng Shui does not encourage split or multiple half-levels. These may seem architecturally aesthetic but they

cause the flow of Chi to be uneven and confused. In fact, families living in houses that have multiple half-levels or mezzanines might find themselves entangled in court cases and facing unwanted problems in their careers and businesses.

When there are such multiple half-levels or different floor levels in the home, the best way to cope with them from a Feng Shui viewpoint is to try to level them with clever interior design. Also, it is vital that all the rooms on the higher levels should be allocated as dining areas for the family. All sunken levels should be for the entertainment areas.

THE DINING ROOM

The dining room is said to be very auspicious when it is placed either in the center grid of the home or when it is located deep inside the home. Homes that are shallow, i.e. where fewer than two rooms make up the depth of the house, are said to be less auspicious than houses with depth. This means having three or more rooms that make up the depth of the house. When there are three rooms, the dining room should be in the center grid; and when there are four, it should be in the inner half of the house. The Feng Shui of the family dining room must auspicious at all times with the suggestion that food is continually available.

Thus, paintings of lush fruits and suggestions of a rich table are more auspicious than any other subject. A very large, decorative mirror to reflect the food on the table is, as we have seen, also a wonderful Feng Shui enhancer.

The dining room is an excellent place for the three star gods – Fuk, Luk, and Sau. In addition, some families also have the big, fat, laughing Buddha in the dining room since this Buddha carries a big bag in which he dumps the family's woes.

The laughing Buddha is very popular with Chinese businessmen, especially those who own or run restaurants. The Buddha's fat belly is said to symbolize abundance. Indeed, to the Chinese, middle-aged men and women are said to be "prosperous" only when they sport a little tummy, or pot belly. This is said to reflect the abundance of good fortune Chi in their bodies.

The act of eating and all food associations symbolize abundance. It is therefore considered inauspicious if food is placed sparingly on the dining room table. The best Chinese table always looks prosperous; the refrigerator is always well stocked; the family rice urn is never allowed to get empty.

LEFT *The laughing Buddha brings happiness into a household. His protruding stomach symbolizes great wealth.*

Dining tables

The best shape for the dining table is round, since this reflects the element of earth. Square and rectangular tables are also auspicious. All the numbers that popularly make up the dining table – 6, 8, and 10 – are auspicious numbers. If you were thinking of having a table for 4, you would best be advised to extend it to 6. Likewise, a table for 10 is better than a table for 12.

On a round table, the "lazy Susan" is an auspicious feature, best placed in the center. This slightly raised, second layer for the food to be placed on and rotated is extremely auspicious, especially if it also has good fortune painted or etched on it. My own "lazy Susan" has two carp etched on glass, signifying the very lucky double fish symbol. Symbols of good fortune and abundance associated with food and plenty are believed to enhance the Feng Shui of dining. Those with rectangular dining tables can, if they wish, have an upraised rectangular deck for the food, also with auspicious symbols painted onto it. Unlike circular ones, however, rectangular food decks cannot rotate.

Dining rooms, and especially dining tables, should not be placed directly below a toilet situated on the floor above, nor should there be anything heavy like a piano or a large cabinet pressing down on the dining area. These are inauspicious: if you can, you should rearrange the position of the dining table. Those living in condominiums will have less control over the placement of the dining table but care can still be taken to control this. It is also not

BELOW *Here is the author's own exquisitely etched glass "Lazy Susan" with a lucky double carp design.*

very auspicious to have a toilet off the dining room; if you have one, I strongly suggest that you keep the toilet door closed at all times. Placing a mirror on the toilet door is a good way of symbolically making the toilet "disappear."

SEE ALSO
❖ The Use of Mirrors in Interior Décor p.178

KITCHENS, BATHROOMS, AND STOREROOMS

In the old days the Feng Shui of the kitchen almost always focused on the stove, and the direction that the mouth of the stove faced was believed to exert tremendous influence over the patriarch's luck, and by extension the luck of the household. Modern stoves are less easy to pin down when it comes to its mouth. I have always assumed the important orientation to be the direction from where the energy cooking the food is coming from. This being the direct translation from the text it does make sense that this particular orientation is vital. Yet the naked fire of the stove is also said to be so powerful, it controls and destroys all the luck of the sector it occupies. Whether or not the luck is good or bad, the kitchen presses down on the luck. Thus it is far better if the kitchen is sited in a sector of bad luck! It is the same with toilets and storerooms. Let them press down on bad luck! The toilet is one room whose location in the house can cause different problems of varying intensity. It is useful to know how to handle these inconvenient problems.

LEFT *Although rooms such as kitchens, toilets, and storerooms may sometimes be considered to be of secondary importance in the overall Feng Shui of a house, they should certainly not be ignored by anyone trying to get the Feng Shui of their house right.*

CHAPTER THIRTEEN: KITCHENS, BATHROOMS, AND STOREROOMS

KITCHEN ARRANGEMENTS AND LAYOUTS

In Feng Shui, the kitchen is the room best suited to "pressing down on bad luck." Thus, kitchens are considered to have excellent Feng Shui placement when they are located in any of the sectors of the house that represent bad luck, either during particular periods or based on personalized directions of good and bad fortune.

Certain sectors of the home are deemed to be unlucky for individuals, based on the application of Compass School formulas. Thus, according to the Eight Mansions formula, which uses the calculation of the Kua numbers, certain sectors of the house are deemed to be unlucky depending on one's date of birth and sex. If your kitchen is located in any one of your unlucky sectors this is a good thing: the kitchen will press down on the bad luck and instead create good luck for you.

Similarly, if the kitchen is in the sector representing the deadly five yellows of Flying Star Feng Shui, it will squash the bad luck that they bring. In 1999, the five yellows were located in the south.

BELOW *Because of its association with the strong energy of the fire element, the presence of the stove or oven in a part of the house that represents bad luck has a beneficial effect.*

The power to press down on bad luck comes from the strong fire element of the kitchen stove. This fire must always be kept under control. Thus the stove should never be energized or strengthened by, for example, the presence of a mirror. This would be dangerous, and could even bring accidents into the residents' lives. The stove is also one of the most significant items of Feng Shui. When auspiciously oriented, the stove can bring enormous good fortune to a family.

This means, therefore, that the power entering the stove should come from the most auspicious direction of the father of the family. The auspicious and inauspicious directions are based on the Kua formula and one of the most potent applications of the formula is to energize the stove by eating food cooked on or in an auspiciously oriented stove. In the old days the mouth of the stove had to face a good direction. Today, however, when almost everything is powered either by gas or by electricity, it is more difficult to work out where the supply is coming from since the pipes or cables are usually hidden away. The Chinese and most Asians use the rice cooker as the easiest way to tap into the favorable directions of their Kua number.

Kitchen arrangements that have good Feng Shui always take the orientation of the stove, oven, or rice cooker into account. The stove must not be placed either next to, or directly opposite, the refrigerator or the sink. This is because of the incompatibility of the water and fire elements. Water puts out fire. Placing a table between the stove and the sink is one way of dealing with this confrontation of two hostile elements.

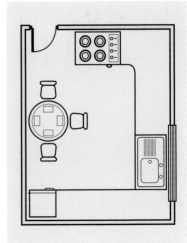

ABOVE *When planning an auspicious kitchen layout, make sure the refrigerator, sink, and oven are evenly spaced for Yin and Yang balance.*

Other important guidelines on kitchen placements are:
- Kitchens should be nearer the back door than the front.
- The kitchen should never be located in the middle of the home.
- The kitchen, and especially the stove, should not be in the northwest. This is described as "fire at heaven's gate" and is said to be most inauspicious. The bad luck manifests itself as danger to the house and breadwinner. A kitchen in the northwest can cause the head of the household to lose his job, fall out of favor at work, or lose money in an important contract. This should be corrected by changing the position of the stove. It is also useful to point out that the northwest location should always be "protected," or should have good Feng Shui, since an auspicious northwest benefits the paternal figure and thus the household.
- The stove should not directly face a toilet. This affects the food being cooked, resulting in bad luck for the family. Keep the bathroom door closed at all times. Another way of correcting this situation is to paint the bathroom door red.

THE FENG SHUI OF KITCHENS

The kitchen signifies two opposing factors in Feng Shui. On the one hand, because it is the place where food is cooked, it represents the manifestation of the family's well-being and wealth. On the other hand, because of the daily use of fire in cooking, the kitchen is also said to have the potency to "press down" on the luck of the corner it occupies. Thus, if it occupies a corner that is unlucky for you, the kitchen location is said to be excellent for you, and vice versa. In kitchen layout you have to take account of two opposing elements. One is the stove, which represents the fire element, and the other is the sink and the refrigerator, which signify the water element. At a superficial level, fire and water are opposing elements. It is thus necessary to seek a proper balance between them.

Unfavorable kitchen arrangements

Feng Shui experts advise that you should not let the stove face outward toward the main door; it should face inward to keep in the warmth of the fire element.

Favorable kitchen arrangements

The kitchen should have sufficient lighting. It should be airy and spacious. The diagram shows a gap between the sink and the stove. This is good. The sink represents Yin, or the water element, and should not be too close to the stove (minimum at least 2 feet/60cm away) which belongs to the fire element, Yang. If your kitchen leaves you unable to provide this space, simply leave a gap between the two appliances.

The direction of the stove

One of the major points raised in the old books on Feng Shui directions – the formula of Eight Mansions Feng Shui – is the direction of the stove that cooks the food for the family; it is described as being vital to the overall well-being and happiness of the family. It stressed that the "oven mouth" of the stove had to face the most auspicious direction of the father figure or breadwinner. This direction is defined as the source of the energy that cooks the food. It thus must come from an auspicious direction. How to determine the oven mouth poses quite a challenge. Look for the source of the electricity or gas as it enters your stove or oven. The Chinese simply use the rice cooker, as rice is their staple diet.

A general guideline concerning the cooker is that its knobs should not face the main entrance/door since this symbolizes food flowing out of the house. Stoves that have knobs facing the ceiling are considered acceptable.

ABOVE *For a good arrangement, the atmosphere should be light, airy and well lit. A gap of around 2 feet (60cm) should be left between the stove (fire element) and the sink or refrigerator (water element).*

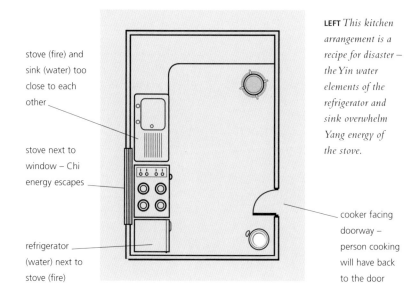

stove (fire) and sink (water) too close to each other

stove next to window – Chi energy escapes

refrigerator (water) next to stove (fire)

LEFT *This kitchen arrangement is a recipe for disaster – the Yin water elements of the refrigerator and sink overwhelm Yang energy of the stove.*

cooker facing doorway – person cooking will have back to the door

GENERAL GUIDELINES ON THE PLACING OF STOVES

- Stoves should not face the main door.
- Stoves should not face the toilet door.
- Stoves should not face any bedroom doors.
- Stoves should not be in the middle of the house.
- Stoves should not be directly under an exposed overhead beam.
- Stoves should not be under a staircase.
- Stoves should not be placed directly under a toilet on the floor above.

Ceilings should ideally have a flat surface and should neither be too high nor too low. Use the Feng Shui ruler to get a dimension between 10 and 12 feet (3 and 3.5m) high. Ceilings that are excessively low cause the Chi to get stifled, while ceilings that are too high mean that the Chi does not benefit the occupant of the room.

RIGHT *The open shelving together with the low, sharp-edged ceiling* *pointing at the bed are sending negative energy toward the sleeping area.*

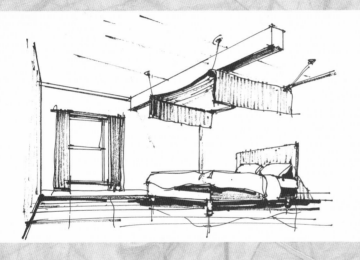

An exposed overhead beam can be cured by concealing it with a plaster ceiling or by creating a canopy over the bed, as with a four-poster bed. The roof of the canopy can be made of cloth and it should stretch over the entire bed.

LEFT *Overhead beams shoot poison arrows straight down to the bed —* *suspending a blanket beneath the beam will help deflect the poison arrows.*

Where the ceiling slopes (as shown in the illustration) it is better to sleep with the head under the higher end of the sloping ceiling. Where the room permits, it is always a good idea to install a false ceiling that evens out the area of the ceiling.

RIGHT *It is extremely inauspicious to work or sleep directly underneath a* *sloping ceiling — reduce the effect by sleeping or working at the higher end.*

BATHROOMS

In the old days in China, many homes did not have toilets or bathing facilities inside. Rich mandarins and important court officials had their toilets brought into and removed from their rooms after use so that human waste was never left in any part of the house. In the poorer homes, toilets were always built a little way from the main house. There were, of course, hygienic reasons for this, but toilets were regarded as bad luck.

In modern homes, toilets and bathrooms are essential. The problem is that toilets will cause Feng Shui uncertainties wherever they are placed. Usually, the more luxurious the toilets and bathrooms, then the greater potential there is for bad luck to befall the residents.

Generally, toilets create bad vibrations in every corner or sector of the house.

❧ In the north they can afflict careers, causing problems with colleagues and bosses. Promotion will prove hard to come by. Overcome this by putting a large stone in the room, or a ceramic, seven-level pagoda. Keep the door closed at all times. Do not use a décor or towels in dominant colors such as blue or black.

ABOVE *A large stone in the north bathroom prevents career success from being compromised.*

❧ In the south they cause negative gossip that will affect the good name of the family. Overcome these problems by placing an urn of water inside the bathroom and keep the room dimly lit.

❧ In the east, they play havoc with the luck of your sons. If you are

LEFT *An urn filled with water guards against malicious gossip in the south.*

childless you will find it hard to conceive a son; if you already have sons they will tend to be rebellious and give you many problems. Hang a five-rod windchime in the bathroom to overcome this affliction. Do not put in plants or flowers since this will only exacerbate matters.

❧ In the west, they cause problems for the children of the household, and also for the health of the residents. This can be corrected by painting the bathroom door bright red. Do not hang a windchime or paint the room white.

ABOVE *A five-rod windchime corrects bad vibrations in the east and southeast.*

❧ In the southwest, they afflict marriage prospects and the relationship between husband and wife. The wife will suffer from an indifferent husband, fatigue, overwork, and ill-health. Put plants and flowers in the room. Do not use crystals or ceramic pots.

❧ In the northeast, they cause children problems at school. A plant in this room reduces its bad effects.

RIGHT *Bathrooms in the northeast sector cause difficulties for children at school – a plant can remedy this.*

❧ In the southeast, they cause financial loss and a slowing-down of income. To overcome this, hang a five-rod windchime or a curved knife in the bathroom.

❧ In the northwest, they hurt the paternal figure and also destroy all the networking and influential luck of the household. Deal with this by installing a bright light.

In addition:

❧ A bathroom above the main door seriously affects the luck of the entire house. All you can do is to change the location of the main door. Avoid buying property with this affliction since it is a difficult problem to correct. Hanging a very bright light in front of the door helps alleviate the bad effects but this is only a temporary solution.

❧ A bathroom directly facing the front door is also a harbinger of severe bad luck. Make sure the door into it does not face any door, stove, bed or dining area.

Since bathrooms cause many problems the best way of dealing with them is to make them as small as possible, so that they never occupy the entire compass sector of any house. This situation offers the lesser of two evils since toilets can either spoil the good luck of one corner or press down on the bad luck of another. My method of ensuring that bathrooms and toilets do not give me too many problems is to keep all of them really small and unobtrusive. They are also shielded from the entrance door so that they are never too obvious.

 *(lotus flowers)*

ABOVE *Flowers and plants are helpful if they are placed in southwest sector bathrooms.*

ABOVE *A bright spotlight in a northwest bathroom protects a family's influential luck.*

ABOVE *Display a curved knife to counteract any financial loss caused by a southeast bathroom.*

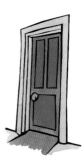

ABOVE *A bathroom door in the west should be painted red to avoid ill health.*

CHAPTER THIRTEEN: KITCHENS, BATHROOMS, AND STOREROOMS

STOREROOMS, STAIRCASES, AND GARAGES

RIGHT *A good location for a storeroom is underneath the stairs – this helps curb bad luck and will not disturb the Chi of the rooms above.*

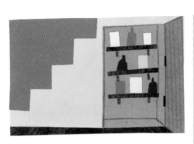

Storerooms, like kitchens, should be located in the bad luck sectors of the home since they are effective in pressing down the bad luck. Storerooms can also be located under staircases and next to bathrooms and toilets, but they should be kept uncluttered.

Ideally, storerooms should not be located directly below important bedrooms, since the occupiers will be sleeping over brooms, mops, and other inauspicious implements.

Garages have the same effect as storerooms. Ideally, they should not be directly under the master bedroom since this suggests that it is above an empty space.

Garages and storerooms that stand alone are not to be regarded as part of the main house when using the Lo Shu square to demarcate the compass sectors of the house. Their impact on the luck of the house is based on the location and direction of the main door. Thus, free-standing garages in the east or southeast will benefit houses with main doors located in the south. In the west or northwest, they benefit main doors in the north. In the southwest or northeast, they benefit main doors in the west or northwest. In the south, they benefit main doors in the southwest or northeast. In the north, they benefit main doors in the east or southeast.

ABOVE *You must include garages and storerooms, if appropriate, when using the Lo Shu grid to demarcate house sectors.*

Staircases are purveyors of Chi inside the house from one level to the next. Generally, straight and steep staircases will cause Chi to move too fast and are not regarded as auspicious. It is better that staircases curve or change direction at each level.

The most auspicious staircases are wide and gracefully curved. These carry auspicious Chi in a gentle, meandering fashion. Their gradual steps have no hollows or openings, ensuring that no energy gets lost as it moves upward into the important bedrooms of the house. When steps do not look completely solid, this means that any money made by the family goes straight out again.

Narrow staircases are never as lucky as wide, broad staircases, but can be enhanced by hanging mirrors and paintings on the walls, thereby also slowing down the flow

ABOVE

The negative Chi caused by narrow stairs is lessened by a landing or curve.

of Chi. If there is a landing or a curve halfway up the steps, the narrowness of the staircase will be compensated for. But long, narrow,

BELOW *A spiral staircase is bad because it acts like a corkscrew, piercing the very heart of your home.*

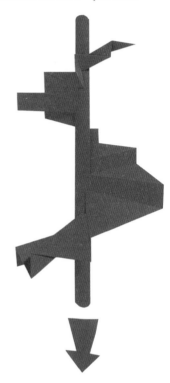

and steep staircases should be avoided and, if possible, corrected.

Staircases should be well lit and landings must have an uplight. Staircases should feel solid. Avoid creaky or badly fitted banisters.

Spiral staircases are to be strongly discouraged since the spiral effect resembles a corkscrew boring into the very heart of the home. If the staircase is carpeted in red the effect is lethal and it will cause severe misfortune.

The top and bottom of staircases should not face a door. If the main door directly faces a staircase, the Chi moves much too fast. This is even worse if the main door faces a staircase that goes both up and down: the door must be relocated, otherwise the Feng Shui of the door is severely affected.

QUESTIONS AND ANSWERS

Question: How important is the Feng Shui of the home compared with the Feng Shui of the workplace?

Answer: No matter how important your work or business may be to you, and irrespective of the number of hours you actually spend at home, much of your Feng Shui luck is determined by the quality of Chi in your home. Even when children live away from home (when they are at boarding school, for example) the Feng Shui of their rooms at home plays a big part in determining the quality of the luck they enjoy. So it is worthwhile investing some time in arranging the Feng Shui of your home so that it is auspicious for every member of the family.

Question: Should we choose bedrooms on the basis of the Eight Mansions formula of auspicious locations or should we choose according to the trigrams arranged around the Pa Kua?

Answer: You will find that because there are different Feng Shui formulas offered in this book there is some overlap and sometimes even contradicting recommendations that force you to make a choice between locations, corners, and directions. When in doubt my advice is to choose the recommendation that is the easiest to implement, or represents the least exposure to harmful poison arrows. In the practice of Feng Shui you will often need to make a decision between two or more alternatives. Use your own judgment to make the choices.

Question: If I discover that my main door is in an inauspicious location but I simply cannot change the door direction, what should I do?

Answer: Try to find another door which you can use as the main door. In doing so you may have to compromise a little; you may have to walk to the back of the house for example, or the new door may be made of glass and is therefore less suitable as the main entrance. But if you find that the alternative door allows you to enter your house through your auspicious direction, and if you find you can escape from severe poison arrows or from your total loss direction, then you should definitely accept the compromise. To change the main door all you need to do is to use the new door frequently and close up the old door.

Question: How important are colors in interior decoration Feng Shui?

Answer: Colors are not terribly important. But they do add to the smooth flow of energy when they are combined correctly, and when they blend in with the elemental energies of the different corners of the home. It is more important to know what colors not to use. Thus avoid bright red in the west and northwest; avoid blacks and blues in the south; avoid white and metallic in the east and southeast; and avoid green in the southwest and northeast. There are many auspicious color combinations: green works well with blue; black works well with white and with green; red works well with yellow; and white works well with blue.

Question: Is there a right way and a wrong way of arranging furniture?

Answer: In Feng Shui interior decoration is less important than room alignments and layout, which control the flow of Chi. Having said that, if you arrange your furniture to facilitate the smooth flow of Chi through the house it adds to the harmony of flow. But remember that if the Feng Shui of your garden or surrounding environment is not taken care of, all the Feng Shui you do for the inside of the home cannot overcome bad Feng Shui from outside.

Question: How bad are the effects of clutter on Feng Shui?

Answer: I have been amazed at how this myth has been perpetuated. Clutter does not bring bad Feng Shui. I can assure you that I have seen perfectly neat houses suffer from the most horrific Feng Shui and I have seen pretty untidy homes enjoy excellent Feng Shui. It is a good idea to spring clean the house once a year to get rid of old tired energy. It is also a good idea to start the New Year with something new. But if you are the the type of person who keeps the home squeaky clean, may I assure you that from a Feng Shui perspective it really does not matter.

Question: How can I use Feng Shui in my small and very cramped studio apartment?

Answer: Use the Kua formula and implement all the recommendations of this Eight Mansions formula technique. When you have used this formula to improve your finances, find yourself an apartment that is less cramped. So focus on sitting and sleeping directions and protect your main door.

木火土金水

PART FOUR

PERSONAL FENG SHUI AND FENG SHUI FOR THE FAMILY

FENG SHUI FOR THE FAMILY

More than wealth, prosperity, and longevity, Feng Shui is most effective for enhancing the overall luck of the family unit. It is especially potent for ensuring harmony between siblings and between the members and generations that make up the immediate family. Feng Shui also takes care of the luck of the extended household if they live together under the same roof. The well-being and luck of the patriarch focuses on the financial well-being of the family, while the good fortune of the matriarch is concentrated on the relationships aspects of the family's well-being. All the children also benefit from specific Feng Shui enhancers, and emphasis is always placed on ensuring that the descendants' luck of the family is accommodated. In the Chinese view of things, this refers to the well-being of the sons of the family. In Feng Shui terms families that lack male heirs are said to lack this category of luck and in the old days this was viewed as a serious shortfall of luck. The inability of principal wives to bear male children was often sufficient reason for the man of the house to bring in secondary wives and concubines. This usually in no way detracted from the importance of the principal wife. While modern attitudes may have changed, Feng Shui continues to be used for creating auspicious descendants' luck for the next generation.

LEFT *Feng Shui knowledge has been passed down through generations, and each member of the family can benefit from Feng Shui techniques.*

CHAPTER FOURTEEN: FENG SHUI FOR THE FAMILY

THE PLACE OF THE FATHER: the northwest

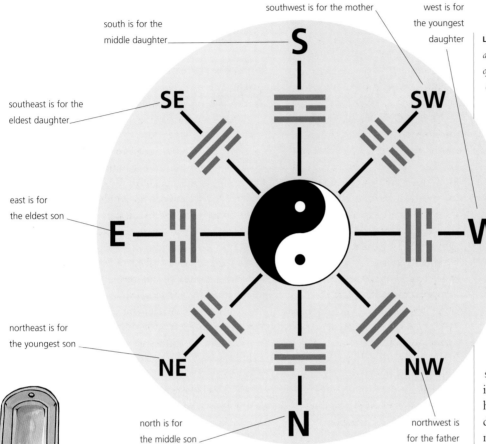

southwest is for the mother

west is for the youngest daughter

south is for the middle daughter

southeast is for the eldest daughter

east is for the eldest son

northeast is for the youngest son

north is for the middle son

northwest is for the father

LEFT *The most auspicious direction of the father or head of the household is the northwest.*

This is of the greatest importance since the entire family is affected by his luck.

ABOVE *If your northwest sector is missing, use a mirror to make the lost corner reappear.*

ABOVE *If the father belongs to the east group the bedroom door should face the north, south, east, or southeast.*

Feng Shui is essentially very family oriented. The eight sides of the Pa Kua represent the essence of the family unit comprising the father, the mother, the three sons, and three daughters. Each family member has a designated direction and this serves as the first guide to indicating the specific location in the home most suited to each member of the family. Following from that analysis, Feng Shui masters usually go on to see whether each of these sectors is afflicted by physical structures in the immediate environment and whether it suits the person, based on the individual's date of birth, and by consulting the Eight Mansions formula. More advanced analysis from there involves numerological analysis of these sectors based on the Flying Star formula, as well as on the indication of the presence of malevolent and killing stars during specific calendar days, months, and years. The whole system of Feng Shui checking can thus be most complex. When you get a Feng Shui consultant in to "feng shui" your home, this is what he or she should do. For a really thorough investigation that will involve a lot of time and real effort, you do need a Feng Shui master.

For beginners, however, I always advise sticking to the basics and focusing on the specific sector indicated on the Pa Kua when they practice their Feng Shui themselves. Remember that simple Feng Shui works just as well as complicated Feng Shui. Using the illustration opposite, you can investigate the relevant corners for different members of the family. The allocation of the sectors according to the family members, based on the Pa Kua and the compass direction, is summarized here. Note that the compass has to be used to demarcate the sectors correctly. Under the system of Chinese Feng Shui, the identification of sectors of the home is based not on the main door but on the compass so that, no matter where you stand, the compass directions stay the same.

The place of the father is signified by the ultimate Yang trigram, Chien, which also means heaven, the leader, and the creative. Three solid lines, firm and unbending, denote Chien. This is the northwest sector of the house. This sector, identified as male and therefore of importance to the whole house, is traced to the arrangement of trigrams under the Later Heaven arrangement. Do not use the Early Heaven arrangement of trigrams to obtain clues for Feng Shui interpretations in and around the home. It is clearly stated in the classical texts that the Later Heaven arrangement of trigrams is to be used for interpreting Feng Shui matters for houses of the living (as opposed to abodes of the dead, or graveyards).

From a Feng Shui perspective if you look after the northwest corner and energize it correctly, the father of the family will have plenty of good fortune. Since he is generally the breadwinner and head of the family, his success benefits the entire family. This makes the northwest of paramount importance. Here are points to note in relation to the northwest:

It is useful to be sure that the northwest sector is not a missing sector. When it is missing the luck of the father suffers, and it is a good idea either to extend (i.e. build and fill in) this sector or hang a mirror on one of the walls to add depth and visually create an illusion that the sector exists. You then energize the reflection as though it were the sector. You can only use this option if the wall that is to be mirrored is in either the living room or the dining room. You cannot do this if the wall is inside any of the bedrooms because mirrors in bedrooms, especially wall mirrors, do a great deal of harm.

You must ensure that neither the kitchen, the stove nor toilets are located in the northwest sector. When the northwest is afflicted in this manner the luck of the husband or father is seriously undermined. The only cure for this is to stop using the toilets and to move the stove away from the northwest. If you cannot move the kitchen, make sure the kitchen is always well lit and bright enough to dilute the strength of the affliction.

If the master bedroom is located in the northwest it benefits the father, and it will be doubly lucky if this also happens to be one of his good directions. This means he should belong to the west group according to the Kua formula of Eight Mansions. If the father belongs to the east group, it is necessary to ensure that the door into the bedroom is facing one of the east group directions (north, south, east, or southeast).

By sleeping in the place of the Chien trigram, the master of the house benefits from superior Yang energy, usually a source of good luck. The only time it does not bring good luck is if the flying star numbers afflict the northwest in some way. However, flying star afflictions usually do not last long and misfortunes caused by these stars are seldom long term.

It is excellent to energize the northwest so as to directly benefit the father or husband of the house. There are several different ways of doing this and it is not necessary to do them all. Usually if you use just one symbol or hang just one decorative object that creates the right kind of Chi, you will successfully energize the sector. This is true of every sector. For the northwest, remember that the element is big metal. The objective is thus to strengthen the element of the sector. Displaying something that symbolizes the big earth element does this, perhaps a mountain, a globe, or a picture that suggests any one of these things. Big earth creates big metal. Precious metals like gold and silver are found in the ground. With the presence of a "mountain" in the northwest, the household benefits from the solid backing and support of the mountain. As suggested in the *I Ching*, the mountain is also the repository of much wealth which manifests itself in the form of precious metals and stones. This, therefore, brings good fortune to the sector. The globe signifies the whole universe and is a powerful symbol of the earth element.

If you prefer to use metal to complement the element of the northwest sector, hang a metal windchime. This should not have any decoration on it, such as a dolphin or a bird, but make sure that it is hollow and that it has six rods. Six is the number of the northwest, and is itself a lucky number, so such a windchime is excellent for the northwest. You can also place a very large singing bowl in the northwest. It is worthwhile considering investing in a large singing bowl. Placed in the northwest and made to "sing" by being hit with a traditional wooden mallet, it will bring exceptional good luck to the father of the family.

The northwest must not be activated with the fire element. It should not have too many lights. It should not be painted red. Rooms in the northwest must be painted either white or earth colors. Do not place water in the northwest unless it is afflicted with bad flying stars. Water exhausts the northwest and thus slows down your good fortune. But if the numbers of the northwest corner are afflicted, water in the corner serves to dissolve some of the bad energy. The general rule, however, is to be on the safe side and not to place either the water or the fire element in the northwest.

Place a very grand-looking chair in the northwest. This symbolizes success, influence, power, and authority for the man of the house. Place a pile of Chinese coins in this corner, or perhaps the three-legged toad. Use all kinds of auspicious enhancers to activate the wealth luck of this corner. The luckier this corner is the more the man of the house will benefit.

If you discover that the northwest is not a good direction for the man of the house based on the Kua formula, it does not mean you cannot activate the corner. Even if the northwest is not a good corner for the father, based on his date of birth, you should still energize the northwest corner of the house since this represents overall good luck for the father. The master bedroom in which he sleeps should not be located in the northwest, nor should any working area of the house occupied by him be situated in the northwest.

ABOVE *Metal is the element of the northwest – a metal six-rod windchime will energize the sector.*

ABOVE *Earth energizes metal – display an object symbolic of earth to enhance the power of the metal element.*

ABOVE *A grand-looking chair placed in the northwest corner is suggestive of power, influence, and success.*

ABOVE *Keep lighting subdued in the northwest, otherwise this will cause an imbalance of Yang energy.*

CHAPTER FOURTEEN: FENG SHUI FOR THE FAMILY

THE PLACE OF THE MOTHER: the southwest

RIGHT *If your bathroom is located in the southwest, this may cause problems for the mother. The auspicious qualities of bamboo stems tied with red ribbon or thread will fend off negative Chi.*

According to Feng Shui, it is as important to look after the mother as it is the father. The place of the mother is the southwest and in many respects it is even more crucial to protect this sector than the northwest. This is because the family is presumed to evolve around the mother. The overall luck of the whole family rests on the quality of the corner of the house that relates to the mother because the trigram Kun represents everything to do with the way the family is regarded by the rest of the world. The southwest also takes care of relationships between parents and children and between siblings. If you want the family to stay together you must therefore protect the southwest. In so doing, you will also be safeguarding the resilience of the marriage and the family unit. Points to note in relation to the southwest include:

❦ Make sure that the southwest corner is not missing and try not to live in houses where this corner is missing. If your house does not have a southwest corner, you should try using mirrors or lights visually and symbolically to "extend" a relevant wall to suggest the restoration of the corner. If you have enough land and the resources to "regularize" the house by actually building in a southwest corner, so much the better. If you cannot do this try the wall mirror cure or

RIGHT *Energize the southwest corner, the ideal location for a mother's bedroom, by hanging up a picture of a mountain.*

ABOVE *If you do not have a southwest corner, try using a mirror to create the illusion of one.*

shine a bright light on the outside part of the southwest corner. Even when the southwest seems to suffer from afflicted or bad flying stars, a missing southwest corner is seldom good in the long run.

❦ Try to ensure that the kitchen and the bathrooms are not located in the southwest corner of the house. Toilets cause illness and problems for the mother; she will lack energy and the marriage may suffer. If the southwest is seriously afflicted, there could also be problems in the marriage. Such problems come in the form, perhaps, of extra-marital relationships, or as serious illness for the wife or

mother of the family. If a toilet in the southwest causes such problems one solution is to place big, hollow bamboo stems in the bathroom. Tie these stems with red thread to activate their essence. The presence of the kitchen in the southwest creates the wood element in the kitchen, and this presses down on the afflicted earth element.

❦ The mother should have her bedroom in the southwest. You could also hang a picture of a mountain in this sector, or of a

ABOVE *Bright lights and a sparkling chandelier will ignite the power of the fire element, which enhances the earth element of the southwest sector.*

mare, since the female horse symbolizes the essence of motherhood. The southwest is of the earth element and fire produces earth. Energizing the fire element would be an excellent way of strengthening the southwest corner. Paint the corner in a fire color (red); keep it well lit, and if possible, hang crystal chandeliers in this corner. Lights in the southwest represent very good Feng Shui because they imply multiple benefits for the occupants.

THE PLACE OF THE SONS: the east

The east is considered to be the best location for all the sons of the family so, if you have one son, place him here. And if you have several sons and your home is large enough you can place all your sons here.

In the palaces of the Forbidden City the young princes – those considered to be potential heirs to the throne – had their quarters in the east wing of the palace, which was energized for them. Even the roofs of their quarters were painted green to simulate the wood element of the east.

Sons are always regarded as the dragons of the family, that is to say they are earthly manifestations of the heavenly dragon. The dragon is also the celestial creature of the east. Thus, placing images of the dragon above the roof in the east sector, or decorating rooms in the east with dragon images, is said to enhance the luck of the descendants of the family.

If a toilet is located in the east, its negative effect is not too harmful but hanging a five-rod windchime in the bathroom should dissolve any bad Chi. If the kitchen is located in the east, this can have a seriously bad impact on the family's descendants' luck (sons rather than daughters.) You can easily correct this by hanging a five-rod metal windchime in the kitchen.

If the east happens to be an inauspicious direction for your son, or sons, based on the Kua formula, it is still a good idea to protect the east sector of the house and to energize its essence. You can also place your son's bedroom in the east but make sure that he sleeps with his head toward one of his auspicious directions rather than toward the east. In other words, you are energizing the location of the east while simultaneously activating his Eight Mansions Kua formula luck.

If you have two or more sons, let the older boys sleep in the east and the younger ones in the other designated sectors of the home.

BELOW *According to Chinese legend, the sons of the family are incarnations of the dragon on earth. Dragon motifs in the sons' auspicious location of the east will ensure that they are blessed with great good fortune. Sons born in dragon years are very much favored.*

The north and the northeast

The other locations in the home suitable for sons are the north and the northeast since these corners represent earth, water and wood. These elements symbolize the essence of family continuity. Without water and earth, wood cannot grow. Wood, as the only element that has life and is capable of growing, represents the continuity of the family name from generation to generation. Wood is the core element of the family.

Place the youngest son sandwiched between the eldest and middle son. The youngest son should be in the northeast between his eldest brother in the east and his second brother in the north. Energize the northeast with earth element objects like crystals and mountains. Energize the north with the tortoise. Never place water in the bedroom, but if the north part of the house does not have a bedroom, a water feature here would be enormously beneficial.

CHAPTER FOURTEEN: FENG SHUI FOR THE FAMILY

THE PLACE OF THE DAUGHTERS:
the south, the southeast, and the west

BELOW *The fortunes of the eldest, middle, and youngest daughters are enhanced by the wood, fire, and metal elements respectively.*

The south, southeast, and west are the three locations in the house suitable for the daughters of the family. In Chinese families, the eldest daughter is considered the most important and she is thus placed in the southeast, which also signifies the precious wood element. The middle daughter is allocated the south and the youngest daughter the west.

The south and west belong to the more decorative of the five elements. South is fire – it brightens the earth with Yang energy – and west is metal or gold. Thus the daughters of the family are its adornments.

Placed in these corners of the home the daughters attract the kind of luck that ultimately benefits the sons of the family as well; for only

with the adornments of minerals and the precious sunlight can the wood take seed and blossom.

Daughters placed in the locations suggested will seriously enhance their well-being and happiness luck. This is not so much the luck of wealth and career success, but rather the enjoyable luck of being recognized, admired, and loved by others.

TABOOS IN THE HOME

Looking after the well-being of the family demands ensuring that certain things are not done in the home that might hurt the next generation. Feng Shui recognizes several taboos in the arrangement of rooms and features in the house that could have a direct negative impact on the children's well-being.

🐾 Never place a water feature directly under the staircase. This will bring bad luck and misfortune to the sons and daughters of the family. If their astrological time of birth is bad it could even lead to early death. So get rid of those elaborately designed waterfalls and fishponds which are placed under the staircase.

🐾 Never place water of any description under any of the children's bedrooms. This is like sleeping on unstable foundations and this will

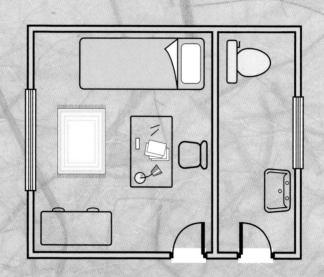

RIGHT *Placing the bed against a lavatory wall is strictly Feng Shui taboo – this can result in ill-health for the children and misfortune for all members of the family.*

affect their development. It can cause illness that may become serious.

🐾 Never place children's bedrooms, especially their beds and their work desks, directly under a toilet or sharing a wall with one. This will seriously affect their concentration,

LEFT *Bad luck will befall the sons and daughters of the house if any type of water feature is placed underneath the staircase.*

their motivation, and their energy. Their schoolwork will suffer. They will become increasingly difficult. Move the desks away and shine a bright light toward the direction of the toilet to dissolve negative energy.

🐾 Never step over any of their school books. Observe this if you want your children to do well at school and in their work. If you step over their books you are creating a negative force field around them.

The bad luck created can be difficult to overcome. Books that have been stepped over can be easily cleansed and purified with aroma or incense sticks.

RIGHT *Stepping over your children's schoolbooks can have negative consequences and affect their academic performance.*

FENG SHUI FOR LOVE AND MARRIAGE

In the language of Feng Shui, love and marriage are synonymous with good family luck and many of the Feng Shui recommendations for energizing this aspiration within home décor tend to overlap. This is because in Feng Shui, love and family usually mean the same thing. There is thus no room for frivolous motivations. Those wishing to energize their homes for marriage luck should be clear that they are ready for a commitment and to start family life. Feng Shui can be very effective in enhancing marriage luck for single people, but while it can bring this about, it does not guarantee a lifelong romance and it certainly cannot necessarily bring about the most romantic of matches. Feng Shui does have the capability of creating what the Chinese refer to as a hei see – or happy occasion – and a marriage falls into this category of luck. For those already married and who need some luck to improve a stale marriage, Feng Shui also offers strong recommendations that are often surprisingly effective. Feng Shui thus holds out the promise of bringing about happiness where loneliness and unhappiness may have prevailed.

LEFT *Feng Shui techniques may help the course of true love to run smoothly.*

CHAPTER FIFTEEN: FENG SHUI FOR LOVE AND MARRIAGE

FENG SHUI FOR LOVE

RIGHT *Feng Shui cannot guarantee to bring you the love of your life, but there are many ways in which it can enhance existing relationships and improve the chances of finding romance.*

Feng Shui can bring personal happiness in the form of excellent love and romance luck, thereby assisting people to achieve fulfillment in their marriage and in romantic relationships. It addresses the universal need for love and offers specific recommendations that allow anyone to tap into auspicious energies that bring romance into their life, improve their love relationships, enhance conjugal bliss between spouses, and even save foundering marriages.

The Chinese view conjugal bliss as the ultimate double happiness event. Satisfaction in the spirit and act of love is considered a significant ingredient for a successful life. To the Chinese, a pleasureable love life adds to health and longevity. In the old days, however, the Chinese did not confine themselves to monogamous marriages. Men often had several wives, and to the young women of those times enjoying auspicious luck in love was synonymous with being the major wife of a successful husband, and becoming the ruling matriarch of a household which included concubines and secondary wives. Thus, being the first wife spelled good fortune for women, and having many wives living harmoniously together spelled good fortune for the men. In a twentieth-century context, this means that Feng Shui must be fine-tuned to ensure that husbands and lovers stay faithful.

In the old days in China, eligible young men and women were brought together by the matchmaker. Good Feng Shui ensured a good match, which was then defined as a match that resulted in the creation of harmonious family luck. This meant happiness for the bride with her in-laws, leading to good treatment for her and her children. A good match was also one that resulted in many strong sons! In the modern context, this also applies. Good marriage luck brings a match that makes everyone happy.

When we speak of activating romance luck using Feng Shui, we are therefore speaking of energizing matrimonial and relationship luck. Feng Shui can be used effectively to enhance matrimonial prospects and bring about conjugal happiness and respect between husband and wife. It cannot promise fidelity within the relationship forever, but it can strengthen the family unit, and by so doing offer harmony and peace within households.

The principle of Yin and Yang, which symbolizes complementary opposing energies, exerts significant influence in the practice of romance Feng Shui. Yin and Yang are primordial forces which represent male and female. To attain the supreme happiness of the whole, Yin and Yang must exist in harmony. Too much Yin or Yang causes an imbalance, which leads to unhappiness and eventually bad luck and misfortune.

Balancing Yin and Yang forces in a relationship between two people therefore suggests that the male and female energies must be in harmony. Thus, for instance, fiery passion must be balanced with coolness; aggression must be countered with receptivity; and strength with weakness. Only then can there be harmony. Where one leads, the other follows: there cannot be two leaders, otherwise the relationship is said to be excessively Yang. Similarly there cannot be two followers, for such a relationship will be excessively Yin. Either situation is unbalanced and thus inauspicious.

Yin and Yang are continually interacting, thereby creating the dynamics of change. When there is good balance between the parties, each alternating between Yin and Yang roles, even as the relationship progresses will there be continuous harmony that leads to good fortune. Achieving this balance between husband and wife and between young couples is what romance Feng Shui is about. And when children of the family reach marriageable age, good romance Feng Shui enhances their chances of finding suitable matches that develop into happy, fruitful marriages or relationships, thereby continuing the whole cycle of life.

Good relationship and marriage Feng Shui is created when the relevant living space benefits from the auspicious breath of the dragon, and when killing energies caused by offensive structures and symbols are completely eliminated or deflected from the living space.

Yin and Yang harmony is woven in with other Feng Shui fundamentals actively to stimulate romance luck. You can jazz up your love life, improve your chances of meeting the right partner, even repair a sagging marriage.

There are different ways to activate good fortune in love; so you should select those that can most easily be applied to your home or to your room, if that better represents your personal living space. Remember that in Feng Shui more is not necessarily better. It is not necessary to use every single method to enhance your luck. Often, using one method correctly is sufficient to change or improve your luck.

LEFT *Passed from generation to generation, the concept of Yin and Yang symbolizes the harmonious relationship between male and female energies.*

CHAPTER FIFTEEN: FENG SHUI FOR LOVE AND MARRIAGE

ENERGIZING THE SOUTHWEST DIRECTION

ABOVE *The trigram Kun, placed in the southwest, is associated with relationship luck.*

The trigram which represents love and relationships is the Yin trigram Kun and, according to the Later Heaven sequence of trigram arrangements, this trigram is placed southwest. This is the corner of any home or room which represents romance, love, and marriage. If this corner has good Feng Shui, the marriage and love aspirations of the members of the household will be positively energized. If this corner has bad Feng Shui, however, bad marriage luck will befall the household, leading to divorce, loneliness, unhappiness, and an almost total absence of marriage opportunities for the unfortunate young sons and daughters of the family.

The trigram Kun

This trigram is made up of three broken Yin lines. Kun is the trigram that symbolizes mother earth. Its inherent meaning is that of the ideal matriarch, the female receptive, the scepter of ultimate Yin energy. Kun symbolizes the person who accepts all the responsibilities of the family, performing the crucial roles of giving birth, raising children, dispensing love and kindness, and keeping the family together, in spite of the hard work involved. Like the earth, the mother grows everything and receives everything back. The earth supports mountains, cradles the oceans, and is always enduring. This is thus a powerful trigram. One of the best representations of this trigram is a mountain. A painting of mountains, hung in the Kun corner, brings beautiful romantic luck.

The element of the southwest corner is earth (symbolized by crystals, stones, boulders, and all

ABOVE *A crystal energizes the earth element in the southwest corner of your home and will bring excellent relationship luck. Raw amethyst is especially favorable for this corner, as are quartz and rose quartz crystal.*

things from the ground). Identifying the relevant element to activate is a vital part of the application. It suggests, for instance, that placing a boulder in the southwest will activate excellent romance and marriage opportunities. It is also useful to note that:

🌀 Earth is produced by fire, so fire is said to be good for earth.

🌀 Earth itself produces metal, so metal is said to exhaust earth.

🌀 Earth is destroyed by wood, so wood is said to be harmful to earth.

🌀 Earth destroys water, so earth is said to overcome water.

These attributes indicate that in order to strengthen the element of the southwest, all objects that symbolize both earth and fire elements can be used, and anything belonging to the wood element should be strenuously avoided. The southwest is also represented by mother earth herself. This suggests that the spirit of the earth energy here is strong and powerful and not easily overcome. Big earth also signifies the presence of gold, or something precious within. Thus, it is beneficial to introduce all five elements into the corner to ensure the fullness of the earth.

Since balance is vital in the practice of Feng Shui, all five elements add subtly to each other. In the case of the Kun corner, subtle attributes of all the five elements can be effectively utilized. The romance luck thus activated will have depth and substance.

Crystals

Some of the best stones to energize the southwest are crystals, especially natural crystals dug from the earth. Raw amethyst, quartz, cornelian, and other natural crystals are harmonious with the southwest sector. Other metals or minerals from the earth are also effective, although the energies created by the display of crystals is enticingly positive. You can also use artificial lead crystals, which may purchased in the form of paperweights, or they may be any of the good fortune symbols fashioned out of crystal. These can be displayed on table tops or shelves.

Faceted crystal beauties are especially potent when combined with lights. Thus, crystal chandeliers attract tremendous good luck. Hung in the southwest corners of rooms, these chandeliers bring marital happiness luck. Chandeliers made with faceted crystal balls are also suitable in other corners of a room. When hung in the center of the home they wrap it with extremely auspicious family luck.

ABOVE *Place some pebbles and cut flowers in a crystal bowl filled with water, then float a candle in the middle – this will help enhance your daughters' marriage prospects.*

This is because the center of any home should represent the area of maximum Chi concentration, since this represents the heart of the residence. The center is also signified by the earth element. At the same time, Feng Shui also warns against siting the kitchen, any storerooms, and toilets in the central part of a home.

Large decorative earthen jars and pots in any rounded shape are excellent for the southwest corners of rooms. Place peacock feathers, artificial silk flowers, or freshly cut flowers inside these jars. On no account display dried or dead flowers or plants, not even decorative driftwood. Dead wood and dried plants signify the failure and death of a relationship.

A globe is symbolic of mother earth. Globes are very effective for stimulating the southwest corners of rooms. Place one on a table top and activate it daily by spinning it. This creates wonderful Yang energy which balances the Yin of the southwest corner particularly well.

A special tip for energizing the southwest corner, and one which is very effective for attracting suitors to any home with daughters of marriageable age, is to place pebbles inside a shallow glass or crystal bowl, fill it with water, float some flowers on the water and place a floating candle in the center. This arrangement brings together a variety of elements and the ritual of lighting the candle daily attracts vital energy to the corner.

The earth element is also activated by using earth tones and hues, therefore colors are important. Thus, curtains in the southwest, quilts, carpets, and wallpaper should contain predominantly earth colors. Be as creative as you like when following the suggestions, they are not exclusive. Some people like to activate this corner with paintings of mountain scenery (these should not show water also). Whatever you use, however, do not overdo it.

The fire element

In the productive cycle of the elements, fire produces earth. This means that fire should be activated in the southwest to energize marriage happiness luck. To the Chinese, red (which is of the fire element) always represents happiness and celebrations. So it follows that in Chinese weddings the bride always wears red.

The southwest sector of the home should always be well lit and, if possible, decorated with crystal fittings. Lights are a potent Feng Shui tool which can be used to manipulate the balance of elements. Always make sure there is a bright light in the southwest corner. Keeping the corner well lit will prevent energy from becoming stale, and favorable Chi created will never get stagnant. Meanwhile this can be supplemented with earth or fire motifs which can be drawn onto the southwest walls of living rooms, or incorporated into wall designs or soft furnishings.

The sun is a powerful symbol of the fire element and, when placed in the southwest, admirably complements the earth element.

The love knot worked in red is extremely effective when used for the southwest corner. The love knot was a great favorite with Chinese ladies of bygone days, when it was used as a symbol of undying love. The knot is constructed so it does not have an end and it appears to go on forever.

Feng Shui for marriage

Marriage is perhaps considered to be more serious than romance and the best way of ensuring good Feng Shui in a marriage is to use the compass Kua formula, based on an individual's sex and date of birth. The Kua number can be calculated using a special formula. Also known as the Eight Mansions, this method of investigating personal marriage and family luck orientations was

given to the author's Feng Shui master by an old Taiwanese Feng Shui grand master. He explained that the family direction can be activated to attract excellent relationship luck within the family, not just between husband and wife but also between parents and children. Couples having problems conceiving children can also use this formula to orientate their sleeping directions, thereby correcting the problem. Most of all, however, the formula is especially useful for ensuring that husbands and wives stay together happily.

ABOVE *Motifs symbolic of the fire element, such as the sun, make excellent energizers for your southwest corner.*

BELOW *It is traditional for Chinese brides to wear red, associated with the fire element, to symbolize joy and celebration. Note also the double happiness knot on the wooden grille.*

CHAPTER FIFTEEN: FENG SHUI FOR LOVE AND MARRIAGE

THE KUA FORMULA

To determine your family/marriage orientation, first determine your Kua number (*see page 72*). Ascertain your Chinese year of birth based on the lunar calendar and use it to get your Kua number. The table below shows your wealth direction and lucky Lo Shu number. Once you know your personal marriage

Your Kua number	Your marriage/ family orientation
One (1)	South for both males and females
Two (2)	Northwest for both males and females
Three (3)	Southwest for both males and females
Four (4)	East for both males and females
Five (5)	Northwest for males, west for females
Six (6)	Southwest for both males and females
Seven (7)	Northwest for both males and females
Eight (8)	West for both males and females
Nine (9)	North for both males and females

direction, there are several ways you can match your individual energies with that of your environment.

Your Kua number offers you your most auspicious direction for ensuring that your personal happiness is safeguarded. It also identifies the luckiest compass location for your love life. The luck referred to here is marriage and family relationship luck. When you activate your personal family direction and location, you will be effectively enhancing your relationship luck.

Try to locate your bedroom in your marriage/family location and try to sleep with your head pointed in your marriage/family direction.

Never sleep with a mirror facing the bed. A television is also

regarded as a mirror as it reflects your image as well. If you have a television in the bedroom, make sure to cover it when it is not in use. A mirror in the bedroom is one of the most harmful Feng Shui features. Mirrors facing the bed suggest quarrels between husband and wife, and even the collapse of a marriage or relationship because of outside influences. If you want a harmonious relationship with your loved one, close cupboard doors with mirrors on them and move your dressing table (with mirror) out of the bedroom.

Never sleep under an exposed overhead beam. The severity of its effects depends on where the beam crosses the bed. If it cuts the bed in half, as well as causing severe headaches the beam also symbolically separates the couple sleeping below it. If the beam is pressing on the heads of the couple, it will cause petty squabbling that will develop into more serious quarrels. If the beam is by the side of the bed, the effect is reduced. If your bed is affected by a beam, move the bed. If this is not possible, try to camouflage it in some way.

Never sleep on a bed placed in front of the bedroom door. Irrespective of your sleeping direction, i.e. whether your head or your feet are pointed toward the door, the position is harmful. One or both of the couple will suffer ill-health. There will be no time for love and health will become a problem. Move the bed out of the way of the door, or place a divider between it and the door.

Never sleep with the sharp edge of a protruding corner pointing at you. This is a common problem. Many bedrooms have these corners, which are as harmful as

free-standing columns. Sharp corners are among the deadliest forms of poison arrows that send out Shar Chi, the killing breath. The solution to this problem is to block off or camouflage the corner. In the living room, plants are ideal for this, but are less suitable for the bedroom. It is better to use some furniture to block the sharp edge.

Make sure your bed is located in an auspicious position according to the principles of Form School Feng Shui before attempting to tap your best personal direction. It is always advisable to start out by first protecting yourself from hidden poison arrows. Next, focus on the placement of the bed in the room.

If you and your partner have different auspicious directions, either sleep in two separate beds or let the direction of the more important partner prevail. Note that the bed is placed diagonally to the door, the best place for the bed from a Feng Shui perspective.

To ensure harmony in the home, bedroom placement is important. Also, check bedrooms are not affected by toilets.

BELOW *For marriage luck, sleep with your head pointing in your marriage direction and the bed in an auspicious position.*

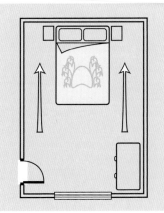

THE EFFECT OF TOILETS

Feng Shui masters of the Eight Mansions Compass School warn that, when the toilet is placed in any one of your auspicious locations, it destroys the specific luck represented by the location. Thus, if the bathroom that is attached to your bedroom is located in your marriage/family corner, the toilet presses down on your marriage luck, causing distress and unhappiness in your marriage or relationship. If the bedroom is occupied by a single person and the toilet is located in either the occupant's family/marriage location or in the southwest (which is regarded as the universal romance corner applicable to everyone), all available marriage opportunities simply dry up.

Toilets are believed to create a great deal of inauspicious energy and the bathroom door should be kept closed when not in use. It is also a good idea to make bathrooms as small as possible. Two other toilet orientations to avoid in respect of the bed and bedroom are:

❀ The bed should not be against a wall which has a toilet on the other side. This blocks the good energy coming through.

❀ The bed should not be placed immediately below a toilet on the upper level, and especially directly below the lavatory. This presses down on the sleeping resident and results in a great deal of misfortune.

THE LOCATION OF TOILETS

The location of the toilet is inauspicious in any sector of the house, since it will flush away good luck wherever it is situated. As far as your marriage or relationship is concerned, the worst location for a bathroom is the southwest, and if your southwest is also your marriage/family direction then this can double the amount of bad luck. Toilets in the west may also affect the marriage luck of your children.

Several measures can be taken to make sure the damaging effects are kept to a minimum:
❀ Always keep the toilet seat closed.
❀ Always keep the bathroom door closed.
❀ Make sure your toilet is small and inconspicuous, large luxurious toilets will exacerbate any problems.
❀ Build a divider or screen between the toilet and the rest of the bathroom to block it from view.

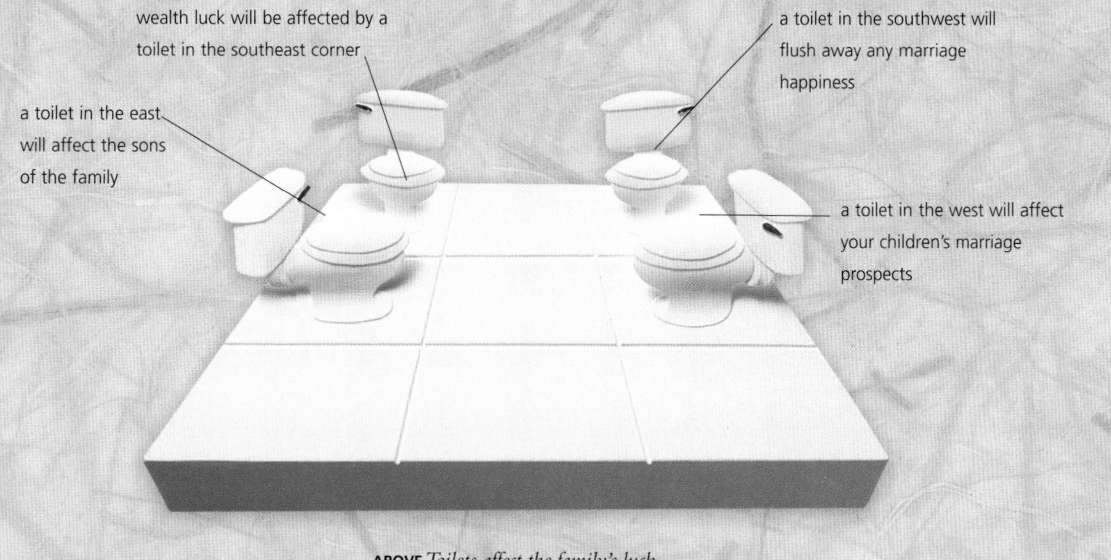

wealth luck will be affected by a toilet in the southeast corner

a toilet in the southwest will flush away any marriage happiness

a toilet in the east will affect the sons of the family

a toilet in the west will affect your children's marriage prospects

ABOVE *Toilets affect the family's luck wherever they are located, but you can take steps to avoid the most inauspicious locations in your home.*

SEE ALSO
❖ Bathrooms p.187
❖ Bedroom Taboos pp.164–5

FENG SHUI FOR HEALTH

I have always been rather reluctant to raise people's hopes on the use of Feng Shui as an alternative remedy for those in search of health cures. In recent months, however, I have received many e-mails and letters from real people who have written to me to share their positive experiences. Many tell me how they have used my Complete Illustrated Guide to Feng Shui to cure themselves with great success, so that I now have greater confidence to push this aspect of Feng Shui practice more strongly. Yes, you can use Feng Shui to try to improve your health and even to cure yourself. One reader in particular, a beautiful lady called Claudia who lives in Johannesburg, wrote to me and later came to see me when I visited South Africa in August 1999. Claudia told me how four years before she had been given three months to live after being diagnosed as having ovarian cancer. She went to a bookstore in search of a book on cancer and bought my book on Feng Shui instead. Using the book, she systematically identified all the "poison arrows" in her home and, one by one, eliminated them. She stopped her chemotherapy treatments and embraced homeopathy instead. Last month her doctor declared her cured. She has also found herself a wonderful man and is to be married at the end of 1999. Claudia has asked me to share her story in the hope that Feng Shui can bring others the same kind of happiness it has brought to her.

LEFT *"The Peach Blossom Spring" by Wen Zhenming. The peach is one of the Chinese symbols of longevity.*

CHAPTER SIXTEEN: FENG SHUI FOR HEALTH

LONGEVITY AND A HEALTHY LIFE

Longevity and a healthy life have always been of prime importance to the Chinese. Hopes for, and expectations of, both have long been a part of their psyche and Chinese tradition is full of doctrines and techniques that address these aspects.

Many legends and folk stories describe the search for immortality. Ancient rulers were reported to have sent emissaries throughout the kingdom in search of the elixir of immortality. The emperor Huang Ti was supposed to have sent three thousand virgin boys and girls into the eastern seas to look for the islands where the peach of immortality grew. Needless to say they were never heard of again, but some believe the Japanese race descended from them. There are also many popular legends associated with the adventures of the Eight Immortals, characters regarded as saints whose faces appear in Chinese homes to symbolize long life for residents.

Through the centuries, however, the search for immortality gave way to more realistic goals, and techniques and practices were developed to extend the life span of people. These techniques drew on the Chinese abstraction of Chi. Chinese sages pronounced that not only was Chi present in the natural environment, it was also the force that defined life itself, so that the physical body was said to be alive because of the presence of Chi. When there was harmony between the environmental and the human Chi, the residents would have a long, happy life.

Further, if this human Chi was strong and vibrant, the health of the physical body would be excellent. When this Chi was blocked, it would cause illness and disease, and when the Chi was extinguished altogether, death would follow.

This approach towards the health of the human body resulted in the development of various sets of movements that exercised both the muscles as well as the five vital internal organs of the body. The organs were compared to the five elements: thus the heart was fire, the lungs were metal, the kidneys were water, the liver was wood, and the spleen was earth. Exercises such as Chi Kung, Tai Chi Chuan, and Taoist revitalization techniques concentrate on creating a harmonious balance of energies in these organs, and these exercises are still practiced to this day.

Many different meditation techniques also developed, focusing on improving circulation and clearing blockages that caused illness. As with the blockage of Chi within the living space, it was also believed that when the body's circulation was obstructed the harmonious flow of Chi within the body would be severely affected, thereby causing ailments and aches.

The Chinese also developed breathing methods that focused on attracting vital energy into the body through its network of meridian points. (Meridians are invisible energy channels in the body.) Energy breathing was seen as a vital part of the healing process and it was considerably enhanced when there was also a harmonious link with the energy, or Chi, permeating the environment.

Feng Shui is thus related to engendering an atmosphere conducive to achieving good health, which always implies living to a ripe old age. Longevity was regarded as a very important component of good fortune. To be able to reap the harvest of a lifetime's work, to live to see sons and daughters marry and gain recognition, to enjoy the pleasures of being grandparents and seeing the family line continue — all are manifestations of longevity good fortune. Thus emblems of longevity, such as the dragon horse, abound in the Chinese gallery of symbols. Gods of longevity, such as Sau, also feature prominently.

BELOW *According to Chinese legend, Emperor Huang Ti sent three thousand virgin girls and boys in search of the peach of immortality.*

YIN AND YANG ENERGIES IN ILLNESS

The inner parts of the body (all the internal organs) are made up of Yin energy

The outer parts of the body comprise Yang energy

LEFT *The health and well-being of mind, body, and spirit relies on the harmonious balance of Yin and Yang energies. An imbalance will manifest itself as illness.*

Classical textbooks on Chinese traditional and herbal medicines usually describe disease and illness in terms of Yin and Yang, and it is diagnosed as being caused either by an excess of Yin or Yang energy.

Too much Yin or Yang, either in the atmosphere or in the food we

BELOW *Chinese herbal remedies, such as tiger balm, are a source of soothing Yin energy which help treat an excess of hostile Yang energy.*

eat, will result in aggressive energies attacking the body. Hostile energies in the environment are described as atmospheric, and when they are in opposition to the energy of the human body there will be a struggle between the opposing energies; illness often results from this struggle. For residents of a space to enjoy good health, the energies of that space must be in harmony with those of the physical bodies occupying that space.

Hostile Yang energy

Wind is a hostile Yang energy. It is regarded as the major cause of many different types of illnesses including the common cold. Thus, Chinese often attribute a whole host of ailments to wind and they treat these ailments by rubbing what is known as wind oil (such as

tiger balm) around the body's upper orifices (nose and navel).

Wind water is a more severe form of hostile Yang energy. This occurs when wind has not been properly treated and has succeeded in penetrating the body. It is a dangerous situation because the hostile Yang energy will by then have reached the inner parts of the body (the internal organs) which represent the Yin energy of the body. The symptoms of this affliction and the illnesses that result will require expert treatment by herbal or other medicines requiring the services of a sin seh, or doctor. Note that:
- The outer parts of the body comprise Yang energy.
- The inner parts of the body (all the internal organs) are made up of Yin energy.

Hostile Yang energy results from an excess of Yang energies, either within the body through the intake of too much Yang food, or in the environment because of unbalanced Feng Shui. It is most common during the hot summer months, when a combination of heat and dampness often plays havoc with the vital balance of Yin and Yang in the atmosphere.

Harmful Yin energy occurs during winter months. Cold is most harmful to Yang energy which circulates superficially around the body. Thus, when Yin cold attacks the body the first to be hit is the Yang energy. If the Yin energy defeats the Yang energy, the pores of the body get blocked and body heat cannot escape, and accumulates within the body.

Yin and Yang in the Chinese diagnosis of illness and disease, however, also distinguish between Yin summer heat and Yang summer

SEE ALSO
❖ The Concept of Balance: Yin and Yang *pp.46–7*

RIGHT *The Pa Kua of Feng Shui with Yin and Yang at the center can help you pinpoint the best locations for good health luck.*

heat, and also between Yin winter cold and Yang winter cold. The differences are subtle, and truly to explain these nuances of diagnosis requires an entire book. For our purposes it is sufficient to note them, and to repeat that Yin and Yang balance needs to be maintained in order to create an atmosphere that is relatively free of illnesses.

Using the Pa Kua

Activating the luck of longevity and good physical health starts with an understanding of the Pa Kua which, with its concentrated circles of definitions around its edges, is a reference tool for analysis. There is

deep meaning in each of the symbols that occupy every one of the eight sides of the Pa Kua. In addition, every corner of this eight-sided emblem is designated by a trigram, and each trigram offers an abundance of meanings for Feng Shui interpretation.

The east direction

The trigram which represents good health is the growth trigram Chen and, according to the Later Heaven sequences of trigram arrangements, this is placed in the east. This is the corner of any home or room which represents good health for the family. If this corner

has good Feng Shui, family members, especially the father, will enjoy excellent health and live to a ripe old age. If this corner has bad Feng Shui, however, all kinds of illness will befall the family. Unless his astrological readings strongly indicate otherwise, the father of the family will not enjoy a long life.

Feng Shui for good health thus starts with an examination of the east sector of the room or home, and in particular the meaning of the trigram Chen.

This trigram has two Yin lines above a single unbroken Yang line. Chen signifies spring, the season of growth. In the language of the *I Ching*, Chen stands for the arousing, characterized by great claps of thunder in the spring sky, animals waking from hibernation, life-giving rain falling. Chen suggests laughter and happiness. The trigram has great strength and energy and because it represents growth and energy it represents life itself. Activating the corner that houses this trigram attracts healthy growth energies. The direction is east, and the element is big wood suggestive of trees rather than bushes, a deep green rather than light green, and large wooden structures (pieces of furniture) rather than small wooden objects (decorative items).

The best method of energizing the east, thereby energizing the luck of good health, is to apply the rationale of the five elements. According to the classical texts, all things in the universe, tangible or intangible, belong to one of five elements. These five elements – fire, wood, water, metal, and earth – are said to interact with each other in productive and destructive cycles. Analyzing the elements in Feng Shui requires an understanding of how the cycles work, and how they may be applied in a practical way.

The wood element

The element of the east corner is wood (symbolized mainly by plants). Identifying the relevant element to activate is a vital part of the application. It suggests that placing, for instance, a healthy plant in the east will activate excellent health luck for residents. From the cycles above, you can see other attributes of the wood element:
- Wood is produced by water, so water is said to be good for wood.
- Wood itself produces fire, so fire is said to exhaust wood.
- Wood is destroyed by metal, so metal is harmful to wood.
- Wood destroys earth, so wood is said to overcome earth.

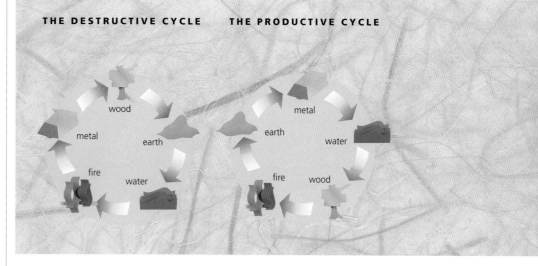

THE DESTRUCTIVE CYCLE   **THE PRODUCTIVE CYCLE**

These attributes suggest that, to strengthen the element of the east, all objects that symbolize both the wood and the water elements can be used. Anything belonging to the metal element should be avoided. East is represented by big wood. This suggests that the intangible forces of wood in this corner are powerful and not easily overcome. Big wood also suggests very strong growth. In addition, wood, being the only element that is alive and capable of reproducing itself, suggests that the Yang energies of its corner, though not immediately evident, are usually strong. The lines of the trigram eloquently suggest this where the unbroken Yang line lies hidden under two Yin lines. Using inanimate objects made out of wood can thus be as effective as setting out potted plants to energize this corner.

Because the east is also the abode of the green dragon, placing a decorative wooden or ceramic dragon would be an auspicious Feng Shui feature in this corner.

Plants

You can stimulate the wood element of the east health corner with healthy plants. Again, try to use fresh flowers or living plants. Artificial flowers are quite effective but never use dead or dried flowers. They suggest stagnant energy.

Try to symbolize happy, healthy springlike plants. Therefore:
- If there is a window in the east corner of the room being activated, place a window box of flowering plants. These will attract healthy Yang energy into the room.
- If you have a garden around your home, try growing a clump of bamboo in the east corner of the garden. Bamboo is one of the most popular symbols of longevity and strength. Any variety will do, but keep it trimmed and shaped.
- If there is an edge caused either by a protruding corner, a square column, or a piece of furniture in the east part of the room being activated, place a plant against that edge. This not only serves to deflect the harmful energies created by the sharp edge, but at the same time it stimulates the vibrancy of the wood element. The plant might, over time, lose its vigor, or die. If that happens replace it with a new plant or perhaps with an artificial silk ficus tree. The killing energies emanating from the corner can sometimes kill live plants.
- You can also place a small plant on a table in the east corner if the room is small. When you are applying Feng Shui always be aware of the need for balance. When you activate an element, do not overdo it: plants, for example, should never overwhelm a room.

ABOVE *In the productive cycle of elements wood, the element of the east (health) sector, is energized by water. In the destructive cycle wood is undermined by metal and in turn overcomes the earth element.*

SEE ALSO
❖ The Concept of Harmony: the Five Elements *pp.40–5*
❖ Good Feng Shui Plants *pp.244–5*

CHAPTER SIXTEEN: FENG SHUI FOR HEALTH

DISPLAYING SYMBOLS OF LONGEVITY

The God of Longevity

Of all the Chinese deities the God of Longevity is one of the most popular. His name is Sau, and he is one of the three-star gods of Fuk Luk Sau so popular with the Chinese. Sau is also often displayed on his own, and not necessarily in the east corner of the room, although this would be a good idea. Sau can also be placed facing the main door, to attract healthy long life into the home. These symbolic deities are rarely worshiped. Their presence in a Chinese home is to create the symbolic energies associated with them.

The God of Longevity is depicted as a smiling old man with a broad forehead. He carries a staff, and is often shown with a deer (another symbol of longevity), and some peaches (fruit of longevity).

It is extremely easy to find Sau in Chinatowns, and if you are visiting China, Hong Kong, or Taiwan, take the opportunity to acquire a statue of this deity. He brings enormous good luck and can be found in ivory (although this cannot be brought into many countries), wood, bronze, or cloisonné, or depicted in hand-painted ceramics. He is also depicted on ceramic jars and in Chinese painting. It is supposed to be extremely appropriate to give the God of Longevity to the father of the family as a birthday present, with all its implications for a long life.

ABOVE *An ivory carving of Sau, the Chinese God of Longevity – an ideal gift for the father of the family.*

The peach, the crane, and the deer

The peach features prominently in all the stories and legends of immortality, and it is believed that the peach tree which bears this fruit stands in the garden of the Queen of the West, Hsi Wang Mu. The Eight Immortals are believed to have found immortality after successfully stealing into the garden and tasting this fruit. The peach tree is also regarded as auspicious, and is often depicted in paintings. It is also a good idea to display peach trees made of inexpensive jade and these can be found quite easily.

The deer is almost always featured with the God of Longevity, although beautiful individual wood carvings are also available. The symbolism of the deer originates from his close association with Sau.

The cranes of longevity have red foreheads. They are almost always depicted in a flock, either flying or standing in water with one leg tucked under their bodies. Cranes are also often drawn with the pine tree, yet another symbol of longevity.

The magical turtle is one of the four celestial animals of Feng Shui cosmology. Together with the green dragon, the white tiger, and the crimson phoenix, the black turtle forms the important quartet that symbolically defines excellent Landscape Feng Shui. Like the other creatures, the turtle is a very important Feng Shui tool. The turtle is also important for its role in bringing the Lo Shu square to the world. Legend describes how the numbers of the square were brought on the back of a turtle that emerged from the Lo River thousands of years ago. The Lo Shu square has unlocked the secrets of the eight-sided Pa Kua symbol.

The turtle symbolizes wonderful aspects of good fortune that make life pleasant, but its most outstanding attribute is as a symbol of longevity. The turtle also symbolizes support. His direction is actually the north and his element is water. This makes his presence in the east sector, the corner which represents good health, extremely compatible. Place a turtle in the east if you want to benefit from the wonderful good health energies his presence brings into the home.

Since turtles are not easy to come by, it is just as acceptable to put tortoises or terrapins in the east corner. Terrapins are ideal but, if the weather where you live is not conducive to keeping them, get a fake tortoise. Remember that the symbol is important. Feng Shui places great emphasis on symbolism: therefore, even a painting or a print will be effective.

ABOVE *Another symbol of longevity, the crane is often depicted standing with one leg tucked underneath its body.*

ABOVE *The presence of a turtle in the eastern sector of your home promises long life and good fortune.*

There is a legend about a family trapped in a cave with a tortoise after a landslide. By emulating the tortoise's minimalist movements – it extended and retracted its head from its shell, and occasionally stuck out its tongue to catch a drop of water from the ceiling of the cave – the family survived for 800 years.

THE CELESTIAL ANIMAL HEALTH EXERCISES

Feng Shui orientations in the home can be supplemented by simple health exercises developed by the Shaolin and Tai Chi masters to allow the human body to create Chi. Anyone can use these exercises to maintain a balanced physical and emotional state, but if there is a specific problem affecting an internal organ, select an exercise according to the five elements theory.

The relaxed dragon

The relaxed dragon exercise helps overcome anger, anxiety, and hostility. Hold the pose as long as you can and repeat several times.
* Stand still with feet apart, shoulder width.
* Take a few deep breaths and visualize yourself as a dragon.
* Bend your knees very slightly, keep your spine very straight, pull your tailbone in.
* Let your arms hang loosely by your sides, palms facing inward. Breathe normally.
* Relax your mouth, and let your tongue touch the top of the palate.

Stand like this for as long as you can. The recommended time is half an hour each morning. Your palms will tingle slightly, and after about ten minutes you will feel the Chi moving up your hands. With time and practice the Chi will move down into the tan tien, in the navel area, where it is believed all human Chi is stored.

The breathing dragon

This exercise is the second stage of the dragon exercise. It is also excellent for firing ambition, but in a nonstressful way.
* Stand still, facing east, and think of the dragon.

* Bend your knees slightly and hold your navel with both hands, spine straight, tailbone in.
* Left hand on the stomach, right palm covering the left hand.
* Breathe in through your nostrils and feel the breath going into the stomach. Very slowly!
* Feel the stomach expand like a drum or balloon.
* When you have breathed as far as you can, bend forward 15°–25°. Breathe out at the same speed as you breathe in, until your stomach feels hollow.
* Straighten. This is one cycle of breath. Do nine cycles!

The flying phoenix

This exercise fights depression and cheers the soul; be aware of the Chi moving even as you do it.
* Stand still, keeping the spine straight, tailbone in.
* Feet apart, same width as shoulders, your knees slightly bent. Imagine yourself as a phoenix.
* Extend your arms horizontally as if spreading your wings ready.
* Keep your arms flexed straight. Then gently bring your palms upright, like wing tips.

* Keep your palms facing outward, absorbing the Chi.
* Let your tongue rest gently at the top of your mouth. Hold this pose for as long as you can.

You will feel your palms tingling; this is the Chi slowly gathering energy before moving inward and filling you with a sense of well-being. Hold this pose for about 15 minutes every morning.

The happy phoenix

The happy phoenix exercise is believed to be so good for the health that those who do it faithfully each morning will live for years.
* Stand straight, left leg half a step in front. Feet shoulder-width apart. Knees slightly bent, spine straight, tailbone in.
* Extend both arms straight in front, palms down. Bend from the waist, keeping the spine straight forward and down, slowly, to about 20°, spine still straight. At the same time as you bend forward, let your arms swings back as if you are about to dive.
* Look down as you bend forward, then straighten up. Repeat this movement nine times.

THE CRANE EXERCISE

The red-combed crane is a popular symbol of longevity and the ancients believed the crane's unique pose gave it its special ability to survive all kinds of diets. They believed the pose stimulated its stomach and internal organs, thereby strengthening the digestive, respiratory and circulatory systems. So the exercise involves standing on one leg.

* Stand with the feet together, toes and heels touching.
* Place the sole of one foot on the opposite calf, then slowly work it up to the inner thigh.
* Raise both hands above your head, inhaling as you do so.
* Join your hands and hold this position for as long as you can.

CHAPTER SIXTEEN: FENG SHUI FOR HEALTH

HEAVENLY HEALTH DIRECTIONS

RIGHT *Encourage good health luck for your family by making sure that everyone sits facing their good health direction at mealtimes.*

Your heavenly health direction can be determined through your Kua number. This is based on the Kua formula of the Eight Mansions school of Feng Shui which suggests that everyone's personal health direction and location can be activated to attract excellent health luck. This means sleeping and sitting in a direction that allows the person to capture his or her *Tien Yi*, literally translated as the doctor from heaven or heavenly doctor direction. Capturing this direction implies enjoying a state of physical and mental fitness. This formula is ideal for people who are constantly tired and lethargic and it will also help anyone suffering or recovering from illness. Bear in mind that Feng Shui is focused on prevention than cure.

Your Kua	Your health orientation
One (1)	East for both males and females
Two (2)	West for both males and females
Three (3)	North for both males and females
Four (4)	South for both males and females
Five (5)	West for males and northwest for females
Six (6)	Northeast for both males and females
Seven (7)	Southwest for both males and females
Eight (8)	Northwest for both males and females
Nine (9)	Southeast for both males and females

Once you have worked out your Kua formula (*see page 206*) you can check out your heavenly doctor direction on the table above.

There are several ways you can use your personalized heavenly doctor direction to ensure good health. Your Kua number offers you your most auspicious direction for ensuring that your physical and mental fitness can be safeguarded. It also identifies your luckiest compass location to ensure you do not fall ill easily, or succumb to annoying bugs. The luck referred to here is best activated for every member of your family according to each person's most suitable direction and location, as indicated in the table.

The bedroom

Perhaps the best way of capturing good health through the use of this method is to try to match bedrooms according to the health location and to try to sleep with your head pointed in the health direction. If your direction is east, for instance, east is where your bedroom should be located, and that is the corner in which your bed should be placed in the room.

Dining and eating

Armed with the Kua formula, you can begin seriously to activate good personal health directions for every member of the family. This is done by arranging family seating orientation around the dining room table. Always sit down to a meal with every member of the family facing their good health directions. Keep a pocket compass handy (not as difficult as it sounds)!

Feng Shui practice becomes most effective with personalized directions and for this reason Feng Shui masters guard their formulas with great care, usually passing them on only to their favorite disciples (my Feng Shui master passed this particular formula to me). While using these directions, however, it is equally imperative to observe important rules that are part of general Form School Feng Shui guidelines. No matter how well you may have orientated your beds, chairs, and other furniture in the home, if in so doing you inadvertently get hit by the pernicious killing breath caused by offensive structures within your immediate vicinity, the killing breath will win out over the good Feng Shui you have created.

SLEEPING FOR GOOD HEALTH

THE LOCATION OF
YOUR BEDROOM

While the Kua formula prescribes the ideal location for your bedroom according to specific compass directions, other factors also have to be taken into account. Thus, irrespective of where the bedroom is actually located in the home, there are certain guidelines which should be observed to safeguard your health. Much of this has to do with ensuring that you are not attacked by Shar Chi, or killing breath, hostile energy that brings illness, bad temper, and depression. Be aware of the following bedroom locations:

❧ Bedrooms located at the end of a long corridor. These cause ill-health. The flow of energy is too strong, especially if the door into the bedroom is placed at the end of the corridor. The situation becomes worse if there is also another door at the other end of the corridor, and if the

bed inside the bedroom is placed with the feet of the sleeping person directly facing the door. Breaking any one of these guidelines attracts health problems for the occupant of the bedroom, and sometimes the energies created can be so strong that the effect can be fatal. The way to deal with such a situation is to change the placement of the bed.

Another way of dealing with this problem is to slant the entrance door to the bedroom.

❧ Bedrooms located in a part of the building that gets no sunlight, or bedrooms without windows. In such cases, the energy of bedrooms is too Yin and lack of sunshine and fresh air also makes the air stale and Chi becomes stagnant. The consequences are most unfortunate, and the bad Chi manifests itself first in illness, but other forms of bad luck soon follow. Such bedrooms should be regularly aired and well lit.

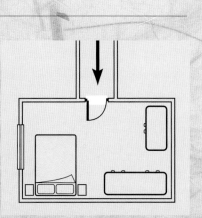

ABOVE *A long corridor gives poisonous Chi the chance to gather momentum – situate the bed away from the door to avoid a direct blow from the deadly Shar Chi.*

❧ Bedrooms located in the basement or ground floor, directly below a toilet, a washing machine, or a stove on the upper floor. These are very unfortunate arrangements since bad harmful Chi gets created daily and presses down on the health of the people sleeping below.

THE PLACEMENT AND
ORIENTATION OF THE BED

Make sure your bed is located auspiciously according to Form School Feng Shui before attempting to tap your best health direction. It is always advisable to start out by first protecting yourself from hidden poison arrows. Take care of any offensive features or structures that

may inadvertently be sending deadly poison arrows toward you as you sleep. These cause headaches, migraines, and other forms of illness. Focus on the placement of the bed inside the room itself.

It is the head of the bed that must be pointed in the health direction you want. If you and your partner have different auspicious directions, sleep

in two separate beds. Note, however, that the bed should be placed diagonally to the door. This is the best placement of the bed from a Feng Shui perspective.

ABOVE *For your health direction to be effective, your bed* *must initially be placed in an auspicious position.*

ABOVE *This may be a lucky health direction, but the bed is pointing* *toward the door – reorient the bed away from the door slightly.*

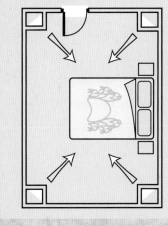

ABOVE *This bed is in the firing line of poison arrows from* *four sharp edges – this can cause serious ill-health.*

CHAPTER SEVENTEEN

FENG SHUI FOR CAREERS LUCK

In all my years of using Feng Shui the area where I have found it to be the most potent, and also to produce the fastest results, has been in enhancing my corporate career. Feng Shui brings amazing upward mobility luck for careers when it is implemented correctly. Indeed, in 1982 when I used Feng Shui to completely redecorate my office at work I was promoted so many times it became embarrassing. I rearranged my furniture and ordered a new desk that was made to Feng Shui dimensions. I then activated my north corner with a painting of a lake (my equivalent of a water feature), energized my south corner with a ridiculously bright red lamp to ensure that my hard work would be recognized, and I even brought in a plant to magnify the income corner of the southeast. My efforts started to bear fruit almost instantly, for in that year I became the Managing Director of a publicly-listed financial conglomerate. My upward mobility did not stop there as soon after I was also offered the plum job of heading a newly-acquired bank in Hong Kong. Having discovered Feng Shui I continued to use it with increasing success, and I am now convinced that career attainment is one of the easiest aspirations to realize through Feng Shui.

LEFT *Give your career a helping hand by using Feng Shui to activate success energies at home and in the office.*

ASCENDING THE DRAGON GATES

RIGHT *In ancient China, scholars who had achieved great academic success were likened to carp swimming against the current to reach the Dragon Gate. Nowadays this can be applied to employees climbing the corporate ladder.*

An old Chinese legend tells of a carp that swam against the current up the Yellow River until it reached the Dragon Gate, or *lung men*. In one mighty leap, it made it to the other side, thereby successfully crossing the Dragon Gate. Other carp who made it were transformed into dragons, while those who did not would forever bear the sign of failure – a large red dot on the forehead. From this legend arose the belief that Dragon Gates symbolized career success. These gates were often adorned with images of carp that had the head of the dragon and the body of a fish to signify its transformation and elevated status; they can often be found in old mansions that once belonged to prominent mandarins. Carp with a red dot on the forehead were similarly deemed to symbolize failure.

In Imperial China, a scholar who passed the Imperial exams to qualify for powerful positions at the emperor's court was compared with the "carp who has ascended the Dragon Gates." Very few made it. Striving to ascend the Dragon Gates – *deng lung men* – represented the beginning of an illustrious career. Families lived in hope that their sons would make it, for success meant the entire family would benefit. This was the route to power, wealth, and great authority. In those days, the merchant class and traders, equivalent to today's entrepreneurs, did not enjoy the status accorded to the learned mandarins who administered the land in the name of the emperor.

Career luck in Feng Shui must thus be seen in this perspective. Career luck does not refer to wealth success, although the attainment of a higher standard of living is implicit in career success. Career luck means getting promoted, attaining elevation in rank, power, authority, and influence in the workplace.

To the mandarins of the old days, each promotion brought them closer to the throne, closer to the center of power. They can be compared with the civil servants of today, the managers of large conglomerates and with tycoons. Some of today's corporate groups are so large that those who own them can indeed be compared with emperors. Managers who enjoy auspicious career luck can make it to the seat of power (i.e. the board) and wield influence and authority in its way as powerful as that exercised by the mandarins of Imperial China.

Career Feng Shui thus brings opportunities for advancement within a bureaucracy. It brings promotion and elevation in rank. Good career Feng Shui protects you against being stabbed in the back, being betrayed, getting fired. It ensures you do not lose out in the cut and thrust of corporate and bureaucratic politics. Career Feng Shui is not about getting rich. It is about becoming powerful and influential. This does not mean prosperity is not included in the good fortune, but power and influence dominate this kind of luck, not money.

This is the Chinese view of career success. Who will benefit most from excellent career Feng Shui? Politicians, civil servants, professionals, managers, in fact anyone who holds a job and is working within an organization where there is a hierarchy.

It is possible to determine the most auspicious directions for one's career based on the Kua formula of the Eight Mansions School. The auspicious career direction of every person is known as the *Fu Wei* direction. Once you know your personal *Fu Wei* direction you can make use of that information in many different ways that greatly enhance your personal Feng Shui. You can use it with equal success in the various rooms of your home as well as in the office. Essentially this means sleeping and sitting in a direction that allows you to capture your *Fu Wei*. Capturing this direction implies embarking on a career path that leads to phenomenal success within your chosen profession. You will feel energized at work and you will actually also start to enjoy working. This formula is ideal for people who are interested in pursuing a career and who have ambitions to climb to the top. It is not for enhancing incomes as much as for personal growth and development, but implicit in good career luck is a significant improvement in both your standard of living and your lifestyle.

LEFT *Using Feng Shui to activate career luck is about achieving success, respect, power, and influence in the workplace – it is not a get-rich-quick scheme.*

THE KUA FORMULA

To determine your career orientation, first determine your Kua number and then check against this table for your career direction and location.

Your Kua number	Your career orientation
One (1) (east group)	North for both males and females
Two (2) (west group)	Southwest for both males and females
Three (3) (east group)	East for both males and females
Four (4) (east group)	Southeast for both males and females
Five (5) (west group)	Southwest for males and northwest for females
Six (6) (west group)	Northwest for both males and females
Seven (7) (west group)	West for both males and females
Eight (8) (west group)	Northeast for both males and females
Nine (9) (east group)	South for both males and females

When you identify the sectors of the home or office, keep their matching elements in mind. The five element theory transcends every school of Feng Shui, irrespective of the method or formula that you are using.

SEE ALSO
❖ The Eight
Mansions Formula:
Pa-Kua Lo-Shu
formula *pp.72–5*

CHAPTER SEVENTEEN: FENG SHUI FOR CAREERS LUCK

MATCHING HUMAN CHI TO ENVIRONMENTAL CHI

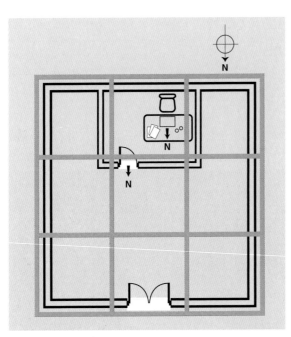

LEFT *If the north is the best direction for your career luck, make sure your desk and, if possible, the entrance to the office are facing this direction – this layout bodes well for career success.*

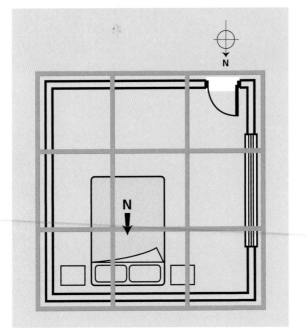

LEFT *Tap your career luck while you sleep by positioning the head of your bed pointing toward your auspicious career direction.*

Once you know your career direction and have demarcated your floor area according to the Lo Shu square, there are several ways you can start to match your individual Chi energies with your environment.

Your Kua number in the table offers you your most auspicious direction to face while you are working. This is for ensuring that you will be more than up to your job or profession. It also identifies the luckiest compass location for

you to site your main doors, your office, your bedroom, and your study to ensure your working luck stays smooth, and that you do not succumb to the stresses and strains of working life. Incorporating this formula into your personal Feng Shui is also a very effective safeguard against losing out in any power struggle with colleagues at the office. People you work for will respect you, while those who report to you will stay loyal.

The luck referred to here is best activated for each individual member of the family according to each person's most suitable direction and location, as indicated in the Kua table.

Perhaps the best way of capturing good career luck through the use of this method is to try to match all your most important doors according to your best career location and to try to work sitting directly facing your career direction. This means locating the important rooms and doors in the sector that are the luckiest for you. It also means that you should place your furniture in such a way that you are working and sleeping according to your luckiest career direction.

If your career direction is north, for instance, your main door, bedroom, or office should be located and oriented in this direction for good career luck. If your office is not located in the north sector of the building, the illustration at the top left–hand side of the page shows some features that will help the career of anyone whose auspicious direction is north.
- The person is sitting facing north as he or she works.
- The entrance door into the office is facing north.

ABOVE *It is possible to restore good career luck to a missing corner in your office by installing a bright light.*

Irregular house and office layout shapes

Offices seldom have regular, square or rectangular shapes, making it difficult in practice to superimpose a nine-sector grid onto floor layouts. More serious is the problem of missing corners. If your career corner is missing, because of the shape of your home or, worse still, your office, your career luck could be seriously undermined. There are ways of getting around this problem, and these are shown here, but correcting the problem merely improves the situation. It does not create the good career luck you would want.

The examples shown on this spread are floor areas that have irregular layouts. The dotted line on the illustration opposite shows how the nine-sector grid is superimposed; by taking directions from the center, it will be possible to see which compass sector(s) are missing.

According to Feng Shui, missing corners mean that the home or the office will be lacking in certain luck aspects. Which types of luck are missing depends on the corresponding compass directions of the missing sectors.

If a missing sector represents your career direction, you can (with reference to the illustrations) partially correct the matter by either:

❧ Installing a light, as shown in the illustration above.
❧ Hang a wall mirror, as shown in the top right-hand illustration.
❧ Building an extension, see right.

What you do depends on your circumstance and whether you have the available space. Having irregular shaped layouts sometimes makes it difficult for you to have your office or desk located in your best corner. If you cannot get the location, tapping the career direction is often good enough. This means that you work facing your best direction. If you cannot tap either the location or direction, try to make sure you work facing at least one of your three other auspicious directions.

The working direction

The working direction is one of the vital determinants of good career luck. Try to work sitting and facing your best personal direction for activating this aspect of your luck. It is a good idea to draw an arrow on your desk to remind you to face this direction when meeting people or when working on a particular project.

ABOVE *Another effective way of improving a missing corner is to hang a large mirror on the relevant wall.*

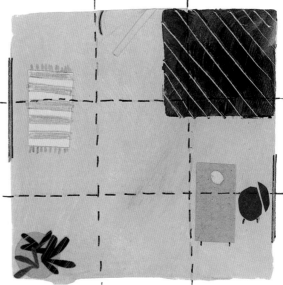

ABOVE *If the missing corner represents your most auspicious career direction, building an extension may help.*

CHAPTER EIGHTEEN

FENG SHUI APPLIED TO TRAVELING AND GOING ABROAD

S afety while traveling abroad can be assured when you actively use Feng Shui rituals just before embarking on your journey. I have included all the methods I know in this short chapter, including some stunning Feng Shui travel advice from my very precious spiritual guru, the venerable Lama Zopa Rinpoche. One day, without much preamble, Rinpoche asked me to write down some words he was translating from a Tibetan text. At first I thought he was giving me a teaching or even an oral transmission… but as I wrote I suddenly became quite excited when I realized that what he was giving me was a translation of antidotes that would ensure safe travel. I recognized the remedies he used as being similar to, or in accordance with, the Five Elements theory or Wuxing. Later Rinpoche explained to me that this was part of a treatise on "combating bad luck from the ten directions." With Rinpoche's permission I have reproduced the remedies here together with the travel mantras that accompany those remedies. Those of you who do a great deal of business travel can use this section to ensure good fortune and safety while on the road.

LEFT *The versatility of Feng Shui is such that it can still be practiced when you are on the move or traveling around the globe.*

CHAPTER EIGHTEEN: FENG SHUI APPLIED TO TRAVELING AND GOING ABROAD

GOOD AND BAD TRAVEL DIRECTIONS

ABOVE *Traveling directly from the UK to Australia is more auspicious for* *a west group person, since they would be traveling from the northwest.*

ABOVE *Traveling from the UK to Australia via the US is also luckier* *for west group people. East group people should try a detour if possible.*

The Pa-Kua, Lo-Shu system of Feng Shui, sometimes referred to as the Eight Mansions theory (and, indeed based on the powerful Eight Mansions formula of Compass School Feng Shui) can be used to assign good and bad directions of travel that are based on the Kua numbers of individuals. Thus, depending on your sex and date of birth, it is possible to determine the directions of travel that are deemed auspicious or inauspicious for you.

This method of Feng Shui can therefore be used to determine the Feng Shui luck of important decisions and moves that involve traveling. These may be an important business trip, a move to a new house or office, a relocation to a new country, or a change of place or abode. The use of Feng Shui for these purposes in a practical sense calls for the practitioner to organize his or her itinerary or move in such a way that the direction of travel is always beneficial.

Travel orientations are determined not on the direction one is traveling in, rather the direction one is traveling from. If you do not observe this, your Feng Shui analysis will be flawed; remember, "wherever you go you should bring good luck with you."

Thus, if you were traveling from the UK to Australia you would be traveling from the northwest, if you flew via Singapore. This direction of travel is deemed to be more auspicious for a west group person than an east group person since the northwest is a west group direction. If you travel to Australia via the United States, you will be flying from the northeast and this, too, is luckier for west group people. Does this mean that all east group people traveling from the UK to Australia will suffer bad luck?

No, it does not. Having arrived in Australia, you should try to stop off for a week or so before traveling on to your final destination. This time make sure that you are

moving from a direction that is good for you. If you are an east group person, travel from one of the east group directions – east, south, southeast, or north. This advice may be difficult to follow if you are only on a short trip but if, for example, you are going to Australia to settle there, it is well worth taking Feng Shui travel advice seriously. This will undoubtedly lead to better fortune.

It is seldom easy to change one's travel route, and it is not always possible to change the direction in which you approach your destination. If, more domestically, you need to travel in the US from Cleveland to Chicago, the route by road or rail is very direct, from east to west. Likewise, if you travel from London to Boston, you travel from the northeast. With such direct routes available, what is the solution?

The answer is to make a detour; even the classical Feng Shui texts advise this. Your detour should allow you to reach your destination from the direction most auspicious to you. This means making unscheduled stops along the way. Thus, if traveling to Boston, you could stop over in New York or Washington before going on to Boston. Before you embark on an important journey look at a map and study the alternatives carefully.

If you are offered what appears to be a very lucrative new assignment or new job that involves relocation, always examine the travel direction; this will give you a first idea as to whether or not the new location will be good for you.

Generally, depending on your Kua number and your country of origin, some continents will be more auspicious for you than others; you will be able to travel directly to certain destinations on these continents from your best direction. Certain export markets tend to be more lucrative and luckier than others for companies looking to export their goods.

This same principle can also be applied when you are moving to a new house or to a new country. Carefully check the direction of travel and make a detour if necessary. Usually, the more permanent the move the more care should be taken to get the travel or relocation orientations correct. Here are the steps to follow:

❧ Plan your route carefully.

❧ Check the Kua numbers of both husband and wife. If the Kua numbers show that the husband and wife belong to different groups, plan to travel separately, with each coming from a different direction. For all children accompanying the parents on the move, as long as they are unmarried their Kua numbers have little significance on the luck of the move. In Chinese interpretations of Feng Shui luck, all unmarried children's luck is determined by the luck of the parents.

❧ If a detour is necessary it is advisable, if practicable, to stay at least six weeks in your stopover point, otherwise the detour will not have much of an effect. This option is best exercised when relocating from one town to another or from one country to another.

❧ When the husband and wife belong to different groups (i.e. east or west groups) it is advisable for the east group partner to travel first. Children should always travel with the mother since the mother's luck most affects the children.

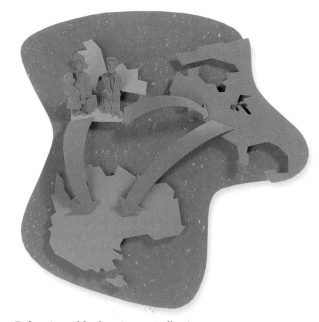

Below is a table showing a small sample of lucky and unlucky directions. Study the table carefully and familiarize yourself thoroughly with the use of these Kua directions. In the application of this method, you will find that, since we are dividing the classifications into the eight directions of the compass, there is room for some leeway in determining the direction of travel since each direction actually occupies 45° of the compass (360° divided by eight directions).

ABOVE *If parents belong to separate travel groups, then the children should travel with the mother, as her luck has more influence on the child's luck.*

LUCKY AND UNLUCKY TRAVEL DIRECTIONS

KUA NUMBER AND GROUP	TRAVEL FROM LONDON TO NEW YORK (from northeast)	TRAVEL FROM AMSTERDAM TO HONG KONG (from northwest)	TRAVEL FROM SYDNEY TO PARIS (from southeast)	TRAVEL FROM BOSTON TO LOS ANGELES (from east)
1 East	Unlucky	Very unlucky	Good for money	Good for health
2 West	Good for money	Good for love	Unlucky	Not good
3 East	Very unlucky	Unlucky	Good for love	Good for study
4 East	Most unlucky	Not good	Good for study	Good for love
5 West	Excellent for men, good for women	Good for health for women, good for love for men	Unlucky for men, most unlucky for women	Not good for men, very unlucky for women
6 West	Good for health	Good for study	Not good	Unlucky
7 West	Good for love	Good for money	Very unlucky	Most unlucky
8 West	Good for study	Good for health	Most unlucky	Very unlucky
9 East	Not good	Most unlucky	Good for health	Good for money

CHAPTER EIGHTEEN: FENG SHUI APPLIED TO TRAVELING AND GOING ABROAD

OVERCOMING BAD FENG SHUI WHEN TRAVELING

RIGHT *It may be impossible to cancel important travel arrangements, but activating special antidotes can prevent or mitigate the effects of bad Feng Shui during travel.*

BELOW *According to Tibetan Feng Shui, dreaming of a fierce animal the night before your journey is a portent of bad travel luck.*

The effects of bad Feng Shui during travel – be it for business or pleasure – usually manifest themselves in illness or loss. Bad Feng Shui incurred during travel is often the result of the following, either individually or as a combination:

🍃 The direction of travel was in conflict with your Kua number. The method of overcoming this conflict, or at least reducing the effect of incorrect orientations, has been dealt with earlier. If it is not possible to make a detour, specific Feng Shui antidotes can overcome the affliction of incorrect travel direction. These measures, however, are only suitable for travel and not for permanent relocation from one house or one country to another.

🍃 You started your travel at an astrologically inauspicious date and time. You cannot, of course, keep checking what is or is not an auspicious date, and more often than not whether it is a good or bad time for one to travel is as much a matter of chance than anything else. There are specific Feng Shui measures to overcome the ill-effects of having inadvertently traveled at an inauspicious time.

🍃 You were unlucky enough to have encountered a bad luck symbol or omen just before embarking on your travels.

To safeguard against the first two problems indicated above, certain antidotes are recommended, based on the theory of Wuxing or the five elements. The method of overcoming bad Feng Shui from the eight directions given to me by my very kind lama, Rinpoche, is excellent for ensuring I am not dogged by bad luck each time I travel. Since I travel a great deal, practicing travel Feng Shui plays a significant part in my life. I have received permission to reproduce Rinpoche's translated text in this book and, as such, it is reproduced as a feature box in this chapter (*see page 231*). I am not sure if this is Tibetan Feng Shui but it was translated from a classical text written by an acknowledged Buddhist master called Nagarjuna. The method used combines the use of the Five Element theory with that of the chanting of holy mantras.

It was the use of Wuxing which suggested to me that this might indeed be part of Tibetan Feng Shui, although it is not described as such in the old texts. (If there are any mistakes in transcribing this translation or in its interpretation, they are entirely my own.)

The Feng Shui method recommended for overcoming travel afflictions depends on the direction of travel and is similar in many respects to the method offered in the Tibetan system. I recommend you use these methods for overcoming bad travel luck only if you have discovered that the direction of travel is not in accordance with your own auspicious directions; if you have inadvertently encountered one or several of the signs that indicate an ill omen (see next section); or if you discover (too late) that you are traveling on a "bad" day but simply cannot change your travel plans.

FENG SHUI METHODS FOR ALL DIRECTIONS

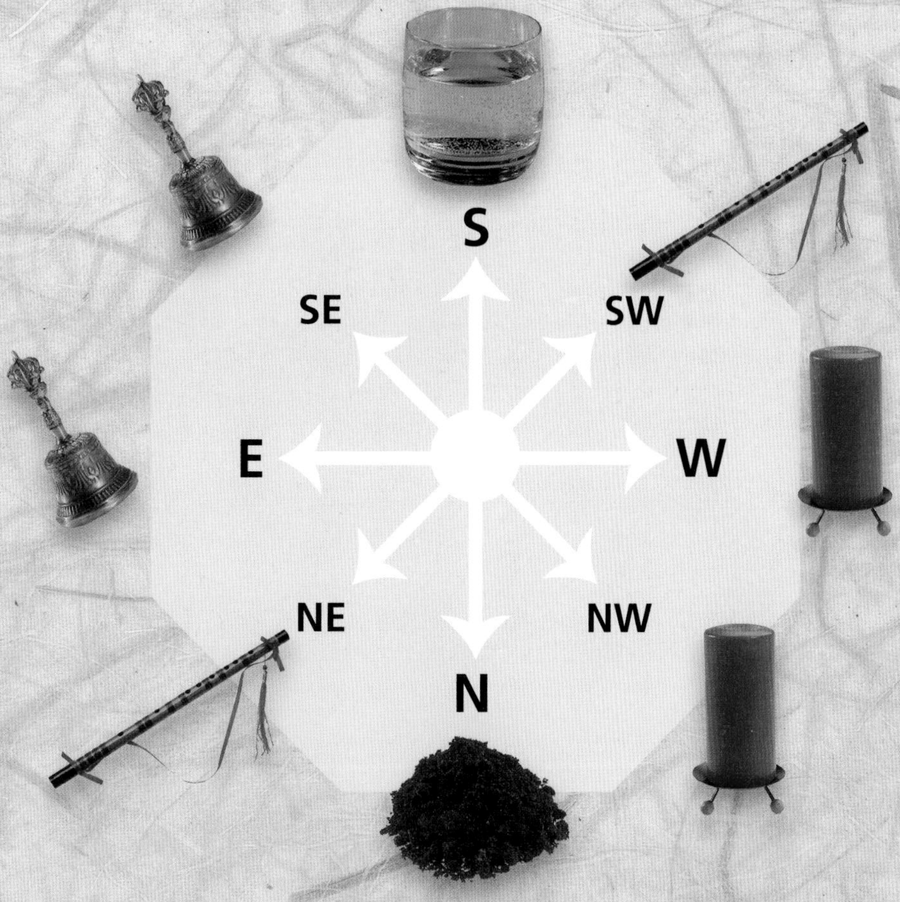

The Feng Shui methods are summarized as follows:

❧ If you are traveling toward the south, drink a large glass of water just before leaving home. Do not drink more than one glass since the symbolism of one is important. Alternatively, you can have a bath and wash your hands and feet before you travel. Washing the feet is important since the feet symbolize your embarking on a journey, and the act of washing is symbolic of cleansing bad Chi.

❧ If you are traveling toward the north, scoop up a mound of earth before you start and throw it in the direction of north. Use paper or a cloth to pick up the earth so that you do not have to wash your hands after doing this. Another method is to point a natural quartz crystal in the direction of north before leaving your house.

❧ If you are traveling toward the east or southeast, ring a bell six or seven times in the direction of east just before you leave. Leave the bell at home. Another method is to symbolically hang a windchime in the east until you return. Remember to take down the windchime when you return from your journey. This method is excellent for families who leave their homes unattended when they are away on vacation, and is also a good way of safeguarding their home. A third method is to use a singing bowl. Strike the bowl with a wooden mallet seven times just before going on your travels.

❧ If you are traveling toward the west or northwest, light a red candle or burn some incense or aroma sticks and point them in the direction of your destination. This will symbolically overcome all the bad Shar Chi that may inadvertently have been created. I like the method of burning aroma sticks because I get the impression of bad energy being instantly purified. This practice is, however, rather esoteric and, for those who wish a less unusual method, lighting a candle is equally effective.

❧ If you are traveling toward the southwest or the northeast, swipe the air three times in the direction of travel with a bamboo stick, preferably one tied with the red thread. This symbolic use of the wood element not only keeps at bay any bad energy that may be encountered in the place of travel, but also safeguards against serious injuries or loss in the event of any accidents or mishaps during travel.

CHAPTER EIGHTEEN: FENG SHUI APPLIED TO TRAVELING AND GOING ABROAD

TIBETAN FENG SHUI

Recognizing signs of imminent travel misfortune

In many Asian cultures, people believe there are specific signs that act as early warning signals against travelling on a certain day or at a certain time. If, for instance, you come across a dog that is either lame or limping, just as you leave for the airport, you would be well advised to postpone your trip. If you cannot, you should definitely allow a few minutes to put into practice one of the Feng Shui antidotes given in previous pages or in the boxed feature on Tibetan Feng Shui. Other warning signs include the following:

🕭 If you have a dream the night before you travel, beware of dreams that feature tigers or other fierce animals. Dreams that feature these animals are clear signals that you will meet up with trouble on your travels. They also signify danger; you should be careful.

🕭 If you cross paths with someone carrying a load on his back it means your travels will create many problems for you. This can mean added responsibility, an extra financial burden, or simply fresh problems that cause you anguish and disturb your mind. Change your time of travel.

🕭 If you meet a funeral procession en route, you should definitely wait another day before setting out. Go home and immediately have a bath. In fact meeting a funeral procession is a sign of pending misfortune and it is often means you may become involved in a court case or lose a loved one. The same results might also occur if you meet up with someone wearing white.

🕭 If during a car journey you have a flat tire or a small accident, try to

have a quick change of clothing before continuing. The accident means that really serious misfortune has been avoided but it is also necessary to change your clothes because this completes the passing of the misfortune.

LEFT *If you see a lame or limping dog before embarking on a journey, be aware that this is an ill omen. If you cannot cancel your trip, use a Feng Shui antidote.*

ABOVE *Meeting someone carrying a load on their back before a journey signifies problems during travel. Reschedule your trip if you can.*

LEFT *Encountering a funeral procession before travel is particularly unlucky – it could mean losing a court case or loved one.*

OVERCOMING MISFORTUNES DURING TRAVEL

ABOVE *Lama Zopa Rinpoche, whose Feng Shui antidotes are invaluable for those wishing to overcome any travel misfortunes.*

A touch of TIBETAN FENG SHUI for overcoming misfortunes during travel and other occasions adapted from a translation by the Venerable Lama Zopa Rinpoche (to read about my precious lama, see his website address on page 355).

The advice offered here comes from the text containing a transmission given by the Buddha Manjushuri to the great Indian pandit Nagarjuna. It was not described as Feng Shui in that text, but I recognize the influence and application of the theory of Wuxing, or the five elements. The destructive cycle is used here to overcome the possibility of misfortunes arising during travel due to what the Buddhists call dependant arising, or due to the ripening of some negative karma which can be averted using these methods, and with these mantras. Misfortunes can also occur when traveling during a bad astrological period.

METHOD ONE

To create protective Feng Shui to safeguard you and your family and to dispel all obstacles while traveling, the advice is to do the following:
If you are traveling east, hold a curved knife and swipe the air in that direction three times. If you are traveling south, fill up a container of water and throw the water in that direction three times. If you are traveling west, burn three pieces of incense and hold them in that direction. And if you are traveling north, take three mounds of earth and throw the earth in that direction.

METHOD TWO

A second method is to hold a curved knife in front of you and then swipe it left to right three times. This helps to avert bad luck from the ten directions. The ten directions are the eight compass directions and the top and bottom. Note that the text warns that if you see a limping dog on your way out, the advice is to cancel the planned journey since this is a sign of grave impending danger. If you cannot cancel the journey, then, in addition to this method, use the first method and recite the relevant mantra given below.

MANTRAS FOR OVERCOMING OBSTACLES DURING TRAVEL

According to Tibetan astrology certain mantras can be recited to control the elements. These are known as *Jung wa ur nen* and are given as follows:
If traveling to the east, place some iron (or metal, e.g. a curved knife) in that direction, then recite
MAMA KARA KARA YEH SO HAR.
If traveling to the south, throw some water in that direction, then recite
MA MA COME COME YEH SO HAR.
If traveling to the west, either light three candles or burn incense sticks, then recite
MAMA RAM RAM YEH SO HAR.
If traveling to the north, place three mounds of earth in that direction, then recite
MAMA SU SU YEH SO HAR.
And then in all four corners – north, south, east, and west – of your home place a small bunch of branches with leaves or some bushy plants and then recite the mantra
MAMA PUTAH PUTAH YEH SO HAR.
In the recitation of the mantras, the advice is to recite one mala (Buddhist prayer beads). If you don't have a mala, recite the mantras 108 times. The advice given here will stop bad luck and enable you to overcome all obstacles encountered during your travels, such as illness, theft, and serious accidents, or simple inconvenience. Please note that starting a journey at the wrong time can cause bad luck, and the mantras are said to overcome such bad luck.

MANTRAS FOR AVERTING BAD LUCK ON OTHER OCCASIONS

There are also mantras which can avert bad luck during the following occasions:

❧ At times of funerals, when the body of the deceased is about to be taken away for burial or cremation. They protect the surviving family members from any bad luck.

❧ During marriage. Chant the relevant mantra as you set out to attend the marriage ceremony. This assures a long and happy marriage.

❧ When starting construction for the building a house.

❧ When starting a new project such as the launching of a new business.

The mantra to recite is
OM AH KANI NI KANI AH GHILA MANDALA MANDA YEH SO HAR.
If you recite this mantra, any astrological mistakes (e.g. due to wrong timing) and their consequences will be overcome, bad things will not happen; rather, auspicious events will occur.

ABOVE *Avoid bad luck by swiping a curved knife three times in the air.*

CHAPTER EIGHTEEN: FENG SHUI APPLIED TO TRAVELING AND GOING ABROAD

ENERGIZING FOR SUCCESSFUL BUSINESS TRAVEL

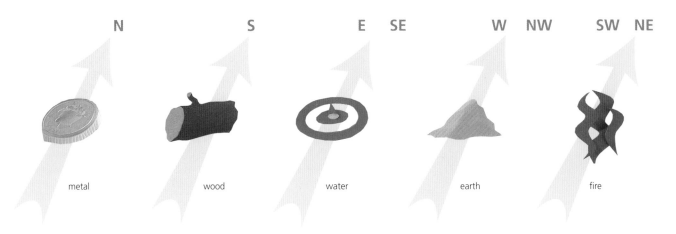

N   S   E   SE   W   NW   SW   NE

metal   wood   water   earth   fire

ABOVE *Traveling north? Energize the metal element.*

ABOVE *Southbound travelers benefit from wood energy.*

ABOVE *Water is best for east and southeast travel.*

ABOVE *Earth protects west and northwest journeys.*

ABOVE *Create fire before northeast or southwest travel.*

Certain practices are said to enhance your chances of business success when you travel. These luck-enhancing rituals are very easy to undertake and depend on the direction in which you are traveling.

If you are traveling toward the north, i.e. if your destination lies north of your starting place, you should ring a metal bell three times in the direction of the north before setting out. If you have a singing bowl, strike the bowl three times and make it sing for you; this will be most auspicious for your travels because the sound of the metal creates the Chi of the metal element, which in turn enhances the element of the north, which is water. Enhancing the elements creates positive Chi to take with you on your travels. This is recommended for those who wish to benefit from business trips.

If you are traveling toward the south, i.e. if your final destination lies to the south of your starting place, energize the element of wood before setting out on your travels. Take a bunch of bamboo tied together with red thread and wave it three times in the direction of the south. This ensures great harmony and excellent luck in relationships on your travels.

If you are traveling toward the east or southeast, i.e. if your final destination lies in either of these two directions, the element to energize will be water, and the best way of doing this is to sprinkle water three times in the direction of your travel. This symbolic strengthening of the water element just before setting out on your journey represents the creation of water energy which will bring you luck when you reach your destination. This is because water enhances the wood element of the east and southeast.

If you are traveling west or northwest, i.e. if your final destination lies in either of these two directions, the element to energize is earth because earth magnifies and supports the metal element of the west and northwest. Do this by sprinkling a handful of earth or sand in the direction of your destination.

If you are traveling southwest or northeast, i.e. if your final destination lies in either of these two earth element directions, to enhance the luck of your travel you would be well advised to create the element of fire before you embark on your journey. Do this by lighting some incense or a candle and holding it up high, and pointing it in the direction in which you will be traveling.

You will now be aware that the method for enhancing travel luck is based exclusively on the five elements – earth, water, fire, wood, and metal. You should energize the element that represents or signifies your destination so that you bring good luck with you. Do not overdo this particular ritual of Feng Shui. Usually it only takes five minutes to create the auspicious Chi flows that activate the power of the untangible forces of the five elements.

LEFT *Strike a singing bowl before your trip to ensure good travel luck.*

QUESTIONS AND ANSWERS

Question: Can Feng Shui really change one's personal luck?

Answer: Most certainly it can. Feng Shui can bring you love, Feng Shui can enhance careers, and Feng Shui can even cure you of serious illnesses. What is so wonderful about Feng Shui is that you do not need to have faith or believe in it for it to be effective. Feng Shui is not a religious practice. As long as you keep an open mind and do not send fierce negative energies towards the manifestation of the kind of luck you wish for, you will find that Feng Shui works quite easily. You have to practice it correctly, of course. As with anything, incorrect practice does not lead to satisfactory results. At the same time you should also be aware that Feng Shui accounts for only one third of your luck. If you do not have the karma or heaven luck to become as rich as Bill Gates, for instance, all the Feng Shui in the world will not bring you the billions for which you crave. But yes, good Feng Shui will make you very comfortable and ensure that your financial situation is better than if you suffered from bad Feng Shui. In the same way Feng Shui can bring you love and even help you find a husband or wife and have a family, but whether the relationship lasts depends as much on your karma as on your own efforts at making it work. There is also a place for mankind luck.

Question: What can I do to improve my love life?

Answer: First, you will have to make sure the southwest corner of your home and room are not afflicted. Next, you should energize this corner with all the symbols of love and marriage, and finally it does help to wear the double happiness ring, since this enhances the Chi of love that surrounds you. You might want to look at my Feng Shui page on jewelry at my website for further information on this and other personal energizers (the website address is http://www.lilliantoojewellery.com). Finally, it also helps if you sleep with your head pointed toward your marriage direction, based on the Kua formula. This activates your personal marriage luck.

Question: How can I improve my popularity?

Answer: The best way to improve your social life and your popularity is to ensure that there are no plants in the southwest corner of your office or living room at home. These create a disharmony of elements in an important corner of the home. Instead enhance this corner with a bright light. Also, do not place anything metallic here as this will exhaust the earth energy of the corner.

Question: How badly does the toilet hurt my health luck?

Answer: Very badly indeed if it is located in a sector of the home which affects your health. According to the trigram arrangements method this is identified as the east sector. If you use a toilet in this part of the home it will have a negative effect on your health. You will succumb easily to bugs, colds, and influenza germs. To overcome this, hang a windchime inside the toilet. Also remember that toilets anywhere in the home bring some kind of bad luck and the way to overcome a particularly troublesome toilet is to place a full-size mirror on the outside of the door. This has the effect of making the toilet "disappear." Another excellent solution is to paint the inside of the toilet door a bright red.

Question: Are all the health exercises necessary to enjoy good health Feng Shui?

Answer: No, but they definitely improve your health since they supplement good flows of Chi around your personal space with excellent and healthy flowing Chi inside your body. The exercises given here are very simple first-level Chi Kung exercises. They are not difficult to do and are extremely potent in making your personal Chi flow evenly and smoothly through your body. If you do them regularly your body will respond and become very healthy.

Question: What is the difference between Tibetan Feng Shui and Chinese Feng Shui?

Answer: I don't really know that much about Tibetan Feng Shui, but from what I have read and have been told it does not appear to be very different. Tibetan Feng Shui uses element fundamentals a great deal. I have reproduced a wonderful section on Tibetan travel Feng Shui, on page 231, that was given to me by my holy guru. This will be especially useful for those of you who need to do a lot of traveling in your work.

木火土金水

PART FIVE

5

FENG SHUI IN THE GARDEN

APPLYING FENG SHUI IN THE GARDEN

Garden Feng Shui puts the spotlight on the natural environment around your home as the landscape plays an important part in determining the quality of energies that surround you. Good auspicious Chi is assured when the plants and flowers in your garden grow strong and lush as this reflects the presence of good growth energy. Healthy growing plants are one of the most potent signs of good environmental Feng Shui. The Feng Shui of your garden can be improved irrespective of its size, design, or type, but your success will depend on how you emphasize the elements and attributes of its location and orientation vis-à-vis the house. The design of your garden should depend as much upon the contours and undulations of its landscape as on its orientation. Check which areas of your garden benefit from the sun and take account of Yin and Yang cosmology and the Five Element theory. Emphasis on these two fundamentals should be applied in equal measure when designing the Feng Shui of a garden. In addition it is necessary to select auspicious plants that are suitable for your own climate. When the Feng Shui of your garden is correct, it creates auspicious good fortune and attracts happy Chi into your home.

LEFT *Feng Shui principles can be successfully applied to the garden using age-old secret formulas to enhance health, wealth, and happiness.*

CHAPTER NINETEEN: APPLYING FENG SHUI IN THE GARDEN

FENG SHUI IN THE GARDEN

Feng Shui can be applied to any garden to energize the landscape and simplify the Chi, thus bringing good fortune or deflecting negative energy.

Gardens in cities or towns are often tiny. Owners have little or no control over elevations and surrounding shapes in the neighborhood. In such circumstances, space must be expanded visually as much as possible with clever use of perspective, patterns, shapes, and colors so that, whatever the orientation, the natural energies of the environment will be enhanced. Where possible, create a meandering pathway to direct auspicious energy in the direction of the house itself.

ABOVE *Use a compass to find out which direction your garden faces.*

BELOW *A small pond, with water trickling into it, enhances the energy of the north.*

Assessing the location of your garden

Apply the Five Element theory to the design of your garden. Determine its compass orientation

with an ordinary compass, standing outside your main door. Do separate readings for the front and back gardens.

Now you can apply the element equivalents to energize the good luck of the garden. The southwest, for example, has big earth as its ruling element; oriental-style gardens with pebbles and stones are therefore best in this sector. You must also check the destructive cycle of elements: in the southeast, for instance, metal is harmful, therefore avoid hanging metallic windchimes or containers here.

A north-facing garden

North is associated with the water element so water features such as a small pond, ideally stocked with carp (koi carp are perfect), or a small turtle or terrapin, will make your garden extremely auspicious especially if they are located at the back of the home. Keeping fish creates Yang energy in the water corner, and a turtle activates the symbolic celestial creature of the north. Do, however, observe the following rules:

- Keep the water constantly moving or aerated. Stagnant water allows dead Chi to accumulate. Fish will energize the water and prevent stagnation.
- Always keep the water clean to prevent harmful Chi being created.
- If any water creature dies, replace it immediately.

Remember that the sound of trickling water attracts Chi, especially when sunlight is allowed to play on the surface of the water. To create movement, use a small

ABOVE *The delicate blossom of ornamental trees counteracts Yang energy in northwest-facing gardens.*

pump or fountain and never keep water in the shade.

If you have room you can dress your water feature with plants, but do not overdo it. Plants should enhance not distract from the main focus, which is the water. If your pond attracts frogs, encourage them: life in the garden represents Yang energy and is excellent Feng Shui.

ABOVE *Cranes are lucky focal points.*

A south-facing garden

South is associated with the fire element and south-facing gardens will be more auspicious if they open out from a dining area rather than from a kitchen. (Kitchens create fire, so an excess of this element will create an imbalance.)

- Because fire provides symbolic warmth, plants will thrive in a south-facing garden.
- A well-lit garden, particularly during winter nights, will enhance the luck of the garden. Lights can be placed at various levels.
- A triangular-shaped garden is most suited to this location. Try to

design your garden around a ceramic garden sculpture of a parrot, a rooster, or a crane (the symbol of longevity and thus doubly auspicious). Better still, have a phoenix – a celestial bird – in this, its most auspicious corner.

A west- or northwest-facing garden

West is associated with the small metal element; northwest with big metal. Round shapes, metal chimes, or bells are suitable for the west; stone or metal sculptures and windchimes for the northwest.

❧ Trees, preferably fruit or ornamental, will counteract the excessive Yang energy created by the strong afternoon sun.

❧ Such gardens should not open out from the kitchen. This will weaken the metal element and deplete any Chi entering the house from the garden.

❧ Create your garden around a small, round sculpture (statues have negative, hostile, or abstract connotations) to enhance the element of the corner. White marble sculptures are particularly auspicious, but must be in proportion with the garden.

❧ Pebbles, stone slabs, or stepping-stones, which represent the earth element, will also enhance this corner, as will three old Chinese

ABOVE *A west or northwest-facing garden benefits from the earth energy generated by pebbles and rocks.*

coins, tied with red thread and placed under one of the stones just in front of your house.

❧ Windchimes attract good luck, especially when tinkling in the breeze. Hang them just outside your main door rather than on a tree: in the destructive cycle of the elements metal destroys wood so avoid this clash of elements.

An east- or southeast-facing garden

East is associated with the big wood element and southeast with small wood. Ornamental trees, bamboo, and flowers are suitable for the east; small leafy plants and flowers are best for the southeast, especially chrysanthemums and orchids.

❧ Try to simulate the auspicious green dragon in your garden design by shaping flowerbeds and selecting plants to represent the flowing shape of the dragon. Alternatively, place a small ceramic dragon to symbolize its presence, or have undulating levels in the garden.

❧ Ornamental trees are associated with both big and small wood, but do not allow the trees to grow so big that they create an imbalance in the garden. Magnolia is most auspicious and peonies equally so.

A northeast-facing garden

Northeast is associated with the small earth element, so designs that incorporate pebble gardens or paths and small rockeries are suitable.

❧ Gardens with oriental themes, herb gardens built around rockeries, and lights are good.

❧ Build brick walls or raised, bricked flowerbeds to simulate the earth element. A low wall represents stability and solidity. Because the earth element is square, square flowerbeds within bricks are great Feng Shui.

A southwest-facing garden

Southwest is associated with the big earth element.

❧ Japanese-style gardens will bring out good fortune Chi.

❧ Large boulders are very auspicious, especially if placed to simulate the crimson phoenix of the south.

❧ Introduce the fire element (such as through lighting) to simulate the Yang energy of fire and strengthen the earth element. The fire element (light) produces the earth element (plants) in the productive cycle of the five elements, creating an ideal balance of elements.

ABOVE *Window boxes and hanging baskets are particularly good for enhancing east- or southeast-facing windows and balconies.*

SEE ALSO
❖ The Concept of Harmony: the five elements pp.40–5

CHAPTER NINETEEN: APPLYING FENG SHUI IN THE GARDEN

GARDEN STYLES AND FEATURES

Feng Shui can be applied to a variety of gardens and garden features with great success.

Windows and balconies

If your windows or balconies face east or southeast, use window boxes or decorative containers to attract good Feng Shui. The plants will energize the wood element and attract a flow of good-fortune Chi energy into your home.

🍃 Plant bright, colorful flowers such as geraniums, snapdragons and dahlias, and gladioli. Do not let white flowers dominate. A variety of foliage plants is also a good idea.

🍃 Artificial flowers are acceptable but must never be dirty, drab, or dusty, giving the appearance of having stagnant energy.

Hanging baskets

Hanging baskets just outside the window are perfect for drawing in energy. They can symbolize an entire garden in miniature.

🍃 Select plants that do not have pointed leaves.

🍃 Ferns, free-flowering plants, and those with long, graceful, trailing stems are best.

Potted trees

Trees in pots – which can be left outside in summer and brought indoors in winter – are excellent Feng Shui energizers for corners. The Chinese love lemon or lime trees, which they believe attract great prosperity luck when in bloom around the lunar New Year.

Trees in pots have a limited ability to grow, and Feng Shui practice is actually against the growth of plants or trees being stunted in any way. Change the compost in your pot if necessary and prune the tree regularly. Health and vibrancy are all-important, since a sickly tree brings bad luck.

Rooftops

If you are planning a rooftop garden, never locate water features such as swimming pools or fishponds there. Water on top of a hill symbolizes great danger: the higher the building (and therefore the garden) the greater the potential for disaster. It is also considered bad Feng Shui to plant trees above ground level.

🍃 Keep rooftop gardens simple. Tiles are better than grass.

🍃 A few curved flowerbeds with shrubs and perennials are ideal.

🍃 Avoid predominantly blue plants, which symbolize the water element. Red tones are good.

Basements

Neglected basement gardens often become the repositories of stagnant Chi, thereby bringing illness and bad luck to residents. Let beneficial Chi flow through by transforming them into well-aired spaces.

🍃 Introduce as much sun as possible into your basement garden. Cut back ivy or creepers that are smothering your walls.

🍃 Attract Yang energy by trimming or cutting down (where permitted) trees that block out the light.

🍃 Install strong, cheerful lighting.

🍃 Plant flowers with bright red and yellow Yang colors and paint walls in equally bright colors to lift oppressive areas.

Walled gardens and courtyards

In many cities and towns gardens tend to get hemmed in by walls or fences of neighboring gardens and buildings. This can stifle the Feng Shui of the garden. Do not neglect or abandon such gardens, therefore, because this results in the accumulation of masses of negative Chi, so that the energy of the garden becomes excessively Yin.

Tight spaces tend to be more prone to unbalanced energy than

BELOW Good Feng Shui in a rooftop garden can be achieved to stunning effect with simple themes.

large open spaces. Courtyard gardens need special attention and detailed planning if they are to be successful. Poor drainage must be corrected since this can lead to damp; dead leaves and other debris should always be cleared away. Plants should not be allowed to die from neglect. Such an accumulation of negative energy has nowhere else to go but into the home.

When designing your courtyard garden, create visual space by using decorating guidelines on perspective, line, and color combinations. Light colors are better than dark and good garden lighting can expand the visual perception of a space wonderfully.

Pay attention to your walls. If you are planting creepers, go for those with small rather than large leaves and make sure they are always well trimmed and do not overwhelm your space. Decorate your walls with trellises, ceramic hangings, or tiled patterns. Climbing plants introduce a vertical element to the garden and, importantly, soften the edges of protruding corners of a wall. Try to select evergreen plants: naked branches and stems on a winter wall are much too Yin.

As to wall materials, ensure that the colors and textures complement the rest of the house and its surrounding structural elements. Also keep an eye on size and proportion, textures and colors. There are

LEFT *Rambling climbers soften stark features and give you the opportunity to garden vertically.*

any number of textured bricks and precast or mottled concrete blocks to choose from. Whatever you ultimately choose, try to ensure that good Feng Shui balance is maintained throughout.

Pergolas

If you plan to erect a pergola, remember that the structure forms a pathway that will lead auspicious Chi from one space to another. In Feng Shui, pergolas are similar to roads or rivers.

To bring Chi into your garden your pergola must be in proportion to the size and shape of your house and garden. In smaller gardens it might be as well not to have a pergola at all. A useful guideline is to try to observe the pergola from above; if it dominates or overwhelms the house it is very inauspicious for the occupants.

Your pergola should curve around the house rather than point toward it. If it is straight and, worse, pointing toward your door the effect is the same as that of a poison arrow bringing killing energy onto your doorstep.

Sculptures

Sculptural features such as statues give off energy that affects the Feng Shui of a garden. Sculptures should be chosen carefully. Some points to note:
℮ Friendly or benign sculptures are better than hostile. Angels or gods give off positive energy.
℮ Avoid sculptures of fierce animals in your garden. These are best placed near the gate of the home to guard it.

In Chinese gardens three celestial animals – the dragon, the phoenix, and the turtle – are great favorites because they are believed to represent abundance, prosperity, and happiness. To enhance your garden with these creatures, place the sculptures of the dragon in the east, the phoenix in the south, and the turtle in the north.

Furniture and patios

Garden furniture in steel, wood, or stone creates Yang energy and effectively extends the living space of the family.
℮ Place metal furniture in the west or northwest.
℮ Wooden furniture should be used in the east or southeast.

℮ Keep stone furniture in the southwest and northeast.

Do not place wooden benches in exposed parts of the garden: rotting wood gives off stale energy which attracts sickness. A metal seat designed around a tree could well end up killing the tree. Keep furniture well maintained; throw away damaged or broken pots and containers. Feng Shui requires everything to be in good working order and generally clean. This encourages good Yang energy to flow abundantly into the garden.

If you have an uncovered outdoor patio be sure that you have an umbrella. As well as providing shelter from the elements, it will also afford symbolic shelter, most important for good Feng Shui.

Try to ensure that pillars are round. Anything square creates poison arrows through sharp edges, but these can be softened with careful planting. Sharp edges also appear in rectangular or square plant containers or flowerbeds. Avoid these too near the house; instead, go for something rounded.

ABOVE *To encourage auspicious Chi it is important for garden furniture to be kept in good condition. A a good quality garden umbrella will provide protection from the harsh elements.*

SEE ALSO
❖ Garden Structures pp.258–265
❖ Good Feng Shui Trees p.246

PLANTS

P lants represent the most positive attributes of the growing wood element – the only element amongst the five that has life. Plants possess intrinsic Yang energies that enhance all the space around them. Plants also manifest the balance of Yin and Yang in the garden, responding to the mix of sunlight and shade, water, and nutrients from the soil. To create a space with good Feng Shui the use of plants is absolutely necessary. If you want good garden Feng Shui you must spend time creating the right mix of plants in your garden, and this mix should take note of orientations, shapes, and colors. There are also auspicious and inauspicious plants and, depending on where you live in the world, it is a good idea to examine the qualities that make a plant auspicious and the characteristics that make a plant inauspicious. Plants which have succulent leaves that resemble money or precious stones are said to be lucky, such as the jade plant. Plants with thorns and prickly branches or with pointed leaves that resemble hostile spears are said to be unlucky. Keep auspicious plants near the home and move prickly plants near to the edges of your garden. This effectively transforms the prickly plants into sentinels guarding your home.

LEFT *The careful choice of auspicious plants and flowers will encourage good Feng Shui in the garden.*

CHAPTER TWENTY: PLANTS

GOOD FENG SHUI PLANTS

ABOVE *The flower of the silver crown; this is a lucky plant to have in your garden since it is symbolic of great wealth.*

If you want to have good Feng Shui it is well worth investing time and energy in making your garden beautiful. Such a garden – planted with an abundance of healthy plants and flowers – is the best indication that a house is indeed enjoying good Feng Shui: it reflects the presence of healthy Yang energy, which is so synonymous with prosperous, happy, and vibrant Chi.

Gardens are equally important because, if they are unkempt and overgrown, they can destroy the existing good Feng Shui of the house. Select plants and flowers wisely according to soil type, sunlight, and the climatic conditions of the garden. Never allow plants to grow wild or unchecked; do not allow weeds to choke flowerbeds and always clear up leaves and other garden debris. All of these things, if left untended, will contribute to overwhelming Yin energy which will swamp the good Chi you want to create. Good Feng Shui can only be created if your plants thrive and are cared for.

The Chinese appreciate every part of the plant – leaves, flowers, and fruit – as well as shape and silhouette. They appreciate the artistry of plants and arrange them in their gardens in curves, in groves, or in groups. They bestow particular cultural attributes on four plants, known as the Four Gentlemen of the Garden. These benevolent men are:

RIGHT *Do not allow the leaves of the money plant to grow too big or it will defeat the object!*

@ The plum, whose blossoms are regarded as pure and superior.
@ The bamboo, which is disciplined and upright.

@ The orchid, which is reclusive and strong in character.
@ The chrysanthemum, which is pure and honest.

Other particular plants are also significant. The peony denotes prosperity and romance, the wisteria is associated with harmony. The magnolia and peony are referred to as immortal and prosperous. The pine, the bamboo, and the plum blossom are symbols of longevity, known as the Three Friends of Old Age.

In Feng Shui certain plants are more auspicious than others. Succulent plants with round full leaves and rich dark leaves are deemed to be the most auspicious and therefore the best. They symbolize money and gold. Such plants include:
@ The jade plant. Probably the best example of an excellent Feng Shui plant, since it attracts money and prosperity. Place it near the front door (inside or out) in a large pot. Do not allow it to grow larger than 3 feet (1m) and, because it is a succulent cactus, try to avoid overwatering.
@ The silver crown. A succulent, leafy good-fortune plant with fan-shaped leaves and a silvery sheen. Do not overwater.

ABOVE *Jade plants attract wealth to their owners.*

@ The money plant. This is a hardy creeper that grows best in well-watered gardens in semishaded areas that are not subject to strong sunlight. It can also be used as an indoor plant. The leaves of the money plant should be small. If they are allowed to grow too big, they tend to become parasitic. They then feed from the tree, become hostile, and therefore inauspicious. In such circumstances your Feng Shui will suffer, so keep a watchful eye on your money plant.

GOOD FENG SHUI FLOWERS

The Chinese regard spring, with its new growth and spirit of optimism, as an auspicious time of year, hence their pleasure in cherry and plum blossom and the symbolism they carry. A great many other flowers symbolize happiness and should, if possible, be grown in your garden if you want to attract good Feng Shui. A small selection is included here.

€ The chrysanthemum. The rich, yellow, round-headed chrysanthemum is particularly highly regarded by the Chinese and the Japanese. Yellow is the most auspicious color in a flower that is associated with fall and a life of ease. Chrysanthemums may be used to equally good effect in the garden or in a window box during the summer.

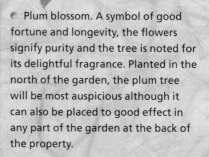

€ Plum blossom. A symbol of good fortune and longevity, the flowers signify purity and the tree is noted for its delightful fragrance. Planted in the north of the garden, the plum tree will be most auspicious although it can also be placed to good effect in any part of the garden at the back of the property.

€ The peony. This is regarded by the Chinese as the king of flowers, a flower of riches and honor, a Yang flower, and the essence of spring. The peony represents feminine beauty and, of the many colors in which it comes, red is regarded as being especially lucky for families with daughters who are looking for a partner. If you buy a peony, plant it in the southwest corner of your garden to attract relationship, marriage, or romance luck in the home.

Other plants which resemble the peony may be used as substitutes although their flowers may not last as long. These include the hibiscus, the gardenia, and the begonia. Begonias are quite easy to cultivate and they are excellent for adding color to the garden. They come in many colors and varieties – the reds, yellows, golds, pinks, and whites are superb Yang colors – but I would advise going for the red, or multicolored varieties that more resemble the peony.

€ The magnolia. The white magnolia especially is a symbol of purity and a single magnolia tree planted in the front garden is said to attract great contentment. Grown in the back garden it is said to symbolize hidden jewels, or the gradual accumulation of great wealth.

€ Narcissus and other bulbs. The Chinese believe that the narcissus symbolizes great good fortune and narcissi are given as auspicious gifts in the New Year. They are relatively easy to grow – but do not choose the dwarf varieties which are not auspicious.

€ The lotus. If you have a water feature, this is the most auspicious plant to have. It is believed to inspire peace and contentment, and to symbolize the opening of opportunities. The lotus blossom is also associated with the Buddha and growing a lotus will engender a growth of spiritual consciousness.

€ The lily. This is regarded as the aristocrat of bulbs. With a wonderful scent and a glorious appearance, in full bloom the lily represents good Feng Shui throughout the year.

CHAPTER TWENTY: PLANTS

GOOD FENG SHUI TREES

Two trees highly regarded by the Chinese and the Japanese are the bamboo and the pine, both of which are ancient symbols of longevity.

❧ **The bamboo.** The bamboo is widely represented in Chinese art, literature, and poetry and is believed to have the power to ward off malign spirits if displayed in the home in the form of, for example, windchimes or flutes. Bamboo acts as a powerful Feng Shui antidote to bad Chi. It also symbolizes durability and endurance (because it flourishes throughout the year), and a bamboo clump on the left-hand side of your home to signify

the dragon is highly auspicious. Planted near the front of the home it attracts auspicious Chi flows.

When planting bamboo, select a type that has been acclimatized to your country or region. Buy a small variety if you have a small garden, or even a decorative bamboo that can be grown in a pot. You should not plant artificially stunted bamboo, or allow a bamboo grove to become overgrown, neither of which is auspicious. Always cut back any dead or old growth.

❧ **The pine tree.** The pine is often planted with the cypress tree because both can survive the harshest of winters; together they symbolize eternal, constant friendship. The pine is also associated with fidelity.

Good fortune fruit trees

Fruit trees are most auspicious. Consider either the peach or the orange tree in your garden.

❧ **The peach tree.** The peach is the fruit of immortality, the fruit that gave eternal life to the Eight Immortals, and the fruit from which Sau Seng Kong, the God of Immortality, is supposed to have emerged. In China it is extremely auspicious to present an elderly member of the family with a basket of peaches or a painting depicting a peach tree, both of which symbolize the promise of eternal life.

❧ **The orange tree.** The symbol of great good fortune, wealth, happiness, and general prosperity, a pair of abundantly fruiting orange trees are regarded as extremely good Feng Shui. Grow a tree within view of your main front door or in view of your back door. Do your best to ensure the orange tree bears fruit in the summer.

ABOVE *The striking golden orange color of oranges is a symbol of abundance and wealth. Keep indoors in winter.*

Bad Feng Shui plants

Feng Shui practice is symbolic and each object in the environment gives off different types of energy that create good or bad Chi. To understand such energies and to find out if they are positive or negative, you should refer to the fundamentals of Feng Shui theory. Certain attributes are analogous with certain shapes and their relationship to each other, and there are symbolic meanings associated with color, size, dimension, and proportion.

A good way of diagnosing the quality of Chi given out by plants and trees is to apply Feng Shui criteria according to the compass equivalents of the Pa Kua Five Element theory. Finding out the Yin and Yang qualities of plants gives an idea of the balance and harmony created in the garden. Remember that as plants grow, their effect changes. Good Feng Shui involves maintaining the garden: trimming, thinning, pruning, replanting, or repotting to ensure energy remains healthy and vibrant.

BELOW *Bamboo is a symbol of longevity; it also has a tendency to run riot in the garden, so be careful where you plant it.*

BAD FENG SHUI PLANTS

Just as certain plants attract good Feng Shui, so there are those that cause problems or have negative connotations and therefore have bad Feng Shui. These plants fall into three categories:

Plants with thorns and pointed, spiky leaves. Keep any plant with thorns well away from the house: the thorns represent poison arrows sending out hostile energy. Cactuses should never be placed near the home, especially large ones better suited to a more arid environment. If needs be, however, you can turn them into guardians of the home, so transforming something hostile into something good. I still prefer not to have them around at all.

Other plants to avoid include mother-in-law's tongue, the agave, the yucca, and anything with stiff, needle-sharp leaves or with sharp spines such as members of the bromeliad family (such as the prickly pineapple).

Stunted plants. Bonsai are beautiful examples of miniaturized trees originally conceived for placing inside the house but unfortunately the symbolic connotations of bonsais are most inauspicious because anything stunted is against the very principles of Feng Shui. Indeed, Sheng Shi, the auspicious breath, translates literally as "the growth" or "growing breath." If you want to have bonsai trees, keep them together away from the house, perhaps in a separate greenhouse. On no account should you keep them near the entrance of your house or near the gate.

Weeping plants. This means trees or plants with downward falling leaves that look sad, such as the weeping willow, the willow myrtle, or the weeping beech. All these are beautiful but their very shape, form, and nature suggest sadness.

Wisteria and other hanging plants have attractive flowers whose

weeping forms are considered attractive and opinions on their suitability are divided. They look wonderful in the spring but their bare branches and stems in winter create a sad Yin effect. Whatever you do, always make sure the flow of Chi is never blocked by stale energy caused by dead leaves or bushes or from creepers growing outside the house.

LEFT *Do not keep cacti, even though they are easy to care for.* *The fierce spines are an obvious source of poison arrows.*

RIGHT *Bonsai trees are often considered quintessentially Eastern, but they actually have bad Feng Shui.*

CHAPTER TWENTY: PLANTS

THE COLOR OF FLOWERS

The colors of flowers play a part in the harmonious balancing of energies and the two most important colors are red and yellow, both of them Yang. That said, the effect of colors should not be overstressed.

Red is particularly auspicious and is the color most frequently used and worn to attract good fortune. You can seldom go wrong with red flowers. Red is best placed in the south where the fire element rules. But red flowers bring good luck wherever they are placed.

Yellow flowers have the same effect but are best placed in the earth corners of the southwest and northeast. Orange, a combination of red and yellow, is an equally strong and beneficial Yang color.

Flowers in red, yellow, or orange will bring happy energy to the garden and to the house itself.

Deep violet and purple are also extremely lucky colors: bluebells in the north corners of gardens and especially in the back garden or behind the house are ideal.

Blues and whites are regarded as cooler Yin colors and are vital for creating Yin–Yang balance in the garden. White should not be allowed to become the focus of attention in the garden: better to balance it with reds, oranges, or yellows. As the color of the metal element, white flowers are best located in the northwest and west parts of the garden. Blue fares well

ABOVE As well as making an attractive feature, hanging   baskets encourage a flow of Chi.

placed in the north, east, and southeast corners of the garden but is less successful in the south corner. Neither blue nor white flowers should be placed in the front part of the garden and should not face the front door or the gate. Keep the front part of the garden for red flowers.

ABOVE The Yin energy of white flowers should be used to balance the Yang energy of more vibrant colors.

BELOW Red peonies create good luck, especially when planted in the south.

RIGHT Bluebells also confer good fortune, and their optimum planting position is in the north.

YIN, YANG, AND CHI

Vigorous, healthy plants with a great deal of foliage, whatever their size, bring plenty of Yang energy into the garden. Large-leafed plants are great Feng Shui energizers when placed next to water, such as a small pond. Climbing vines have good foliage and are effective in the southeast corner of the garden, the location of the small wood element. Plants such as hostas have strong architectural forms and leaves with quilted structures and can be used effectively to counterpoint vines.

The Yin of ferns

Ferns introduce the softening balance of Yin energies to a garden of high-energy Yang flowers and that balance helps to provide an auspicious atmosphere and excellent Feng Shui. The featheriness of ferns tames the sharpest edges in the garden and dissolves any negative energy present. Maidenhair and asparagus ferns are perfect for this.

Hanging baskets

Carefully created with a thoughtful combination of plants and flowers, hanging baskets produce a harmony that permeates the environment by lifting up growth energies and allowing them to flow around them. Plants suitable for hanging baskets include, not least because they offer plenty of color, impatiens, phlox, geranium, and lobelia. There are many more suitable plants to choose from. Choose contrasting leaf shapes to maintain the Yin–Yang balance.

Window boxes

As well as enhancing and softening the façade of any house, window boxes encourage beneficial Chi to come in to the home. Choose any plants you want except, as we have already discussed, prickly or stunted plants. Color combinations are very much up to the individual, but try to construct a color scheme around the vibrant Yang good luck colors red, yellow, and orange. As for the boxes themselves, I recommend terra cotta, which has fewer Feng Shui problems than the more standard wood or metal. Remember to deadhead flowers and to trim off any dried leaves.

Golden leaves and silver stems

For the west and northwest corners of your garden golden leaves or silver-stemmed plants are wonderful energizers that bring the glow of the metal element into metal element corners, thereby activating the existing good luck of the corners. The spiraea, known as the "Gold flame," is an ideal golden foliage plant for such corners. Silver-stemmed bushes are also as effective as far as their Feng Shui is concerned.

The bright hall

Finally, regardless of what you grow in your garden, always keep a small turfed patch directly in front of your front door to create the auspicious and all-important bright hall effect. Keep this patch clear of twigs, leaves, and garden debris. Daffodils create a wonderful splash of refreshing spring color

in the garden and are acceptable because they also represent buried gold; otherwise, however, keep the patch clear. An empty bright hall is an especially effective Feng Shui energizer.

BELOW *Daffodils are ideal energizers for the west and northwest corners of your garden. They symbolize buried gold waiting for the moment to burst out into auspicious and colorful profusion.*

ABOVE *Plants of the* Spiraea *genus, with their beautiful golden leaves, stimulate the the wealth and prosperity energies of the west and northwest corner.*

WATER

The flow of water is always regarded positively in Feng Shui. When your main door faces a moving river or when your house has a view of a body of water, the Chi in the surrounding area is said to be filled with the potential for prosperity. Water is said to bring wealth and wealth luck. Feng Shui offers several techniques for harnessing this type of luck, including ancient formulas for creating artificial waterways that can be built to simulate the auspicious attributes of natural water. Of these formulas the most exciting is the instructions given for building the powerful wealth-bringing water dragon in your garden.

There are also useful guidelines on auspicious water flows that can be applied quite easily. You should endeavor, for instance, to have water apparently flowing towards your home rather than away. Water should always move in a slow meandering fashion and never fast in a straight line. All the main rules that pertain to a good flow of water are contained in the following pages. When you have water flowing corrrectly around your home you will enjoy the Feng Shui that brings wealth luck.

LEFT *The age-old water location formulas are indeed complex, but the successful practice of water Feng Shui can lead to great wealth luck.*

CHAPTER TWENTY-ONE: WATER

THE TWO WATER FORMULAS

BELOW *Use the water formulas to ascertain the most auspicious location of any water features in your garden, paying particular attention to the direction of flow.*

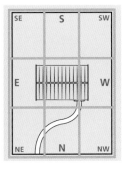

BELOW *The water dragon has the ability to attract financial and other luck to the family.*

Unless you apply the principles of water Feng Shui correctly you will not be able to maximize the Feng Shui potential of your garden. The use of water as an ornamental feature in the garden has long been important to the Chinese and deemed to be a crucial part of Feng Shui, particularly for activating the potential for wealth and prosperity. The north, southeast, and east are excellent locations for water features. Water Feng Shui is extremely accurate if the formulas passed down orally from master to disciple are applied carefully. Only then can we know exactly which location offers the best luck.

Two water Feng Shui formulas are based on the compass. The first addresses the location of a water feature – perhaps in the form of a pond, fountain, a cascade, or even a well – and helps you to discover the most auspicious place to locate that water feature. The second formula is concerned with auspicious flows of water and its exit direction, and is called the Water Dragon formula.

Both formulas describe the auspicious locations for water; they offer recommendations on where water should collect or settle, where the garden should remain dry, how water should move, curve, or meander. If water location and flow are correct, prosperity, health, and happiness will result.

Water Feng Shui is concerned with attracting financial luck and happiness; water represents money and signifies the flow of wealth.

Although building a water dragon feature in your garden will attract money luck, in so doing you will also be activating other auspicious indications of Feng Shui, for good Feng Shui rarely brings wealth alone. When the alignment of energy lines are conducive to auspicious Feng Shui, there are likely to be other benefits as well in terms of longevity and of children who will carry on the family name successfully.

If you decide to construct a water feature in your garden, follow the formulas and methods all the way through. Be as simple as you can in the implementation of recommended directions; in Feng Shui big does not necessarily mean better. Successful Feng Shui has more to do with correct and accurate application. If you commission a Feng Shui consultant, either see that he or she supervises the person building your feature or at least be thoroughly aware yourself of the structure's dimensions and configurations, and work in progress. If you can, build your own water feature to ensure there are no mistakes.

AUSPICIOUS WATER FEATURES

A number of simple water features will bring auspicious Feng Shui to the house and family.

ARTIFICIAL POOLS OR PONDS

These offer great scope for imagination and creativity because you can control their creation from start to finish in terms of measurements and scale. Remember that balance is everything in Feng Shui: ensure that your feature fits naturally into its environment, that it does not dominate. Too much water will turn the element against you.

The Chinese regard waterfalls, fountains, fishponds, or natural cascades of water as auspicious. Any of them can be constructed quite easily, varying from a simple basin, a walled pool, or a hole in the ground to an ornate pool complete with tiles and auspicious statuary. Shape and dimensions of pools are all-important.
* For auspicious Feng Shui the shape of the pool should appear to embrace the house.
* Oval, circular, or rounded pools are always auspicious. Avoid those with edges and sharp corners.
* Water should flow towards the house. Water flowing away from or directly at the home is inauspicious.

ABOVE A small water feature is an important contributor to good Feng Shui in the garden, and has ornamental appeal.

* Ideally your pool should be between 31 and 33 inches (79 and 84cm) deep: this is considered auspicious. Use a Feng Shui ruler to select auspicious dimensions for the width and length of the pool.

Install a pump and filter so that water does not stagnate. Stale and torpid water is anathema to good Feng Shui. Always give thought to the maintenance, cleanliness, and drainage of your pool.

FISHPONDS

A fishpond is considered to be one of the best ways of creating favorable and auspicious Sheng Chi. Keeping fish has excellent symbolic meaning because the fish is regarded as one of the symbols of wealth and success. The Chinese refer to fish when they speak of growth and expansion. If you plan to keep fish, do ensure that you have a proper filter system.

There are a number of fish that are suited to garden ponds: the best is the Japanese koi carp but others include the Chinese carp, or goldfish, and the guppy. Probably the most popular fish in the Far East is the arrowana, known as the Feng Shui fish because it attracts good fortune and prosperity to its owner.

Protect your fish against predators such as cats or birds. Either ensure that your pond is deep enough for fish to be able to hide or cover the pond with protective mesh.

Keeping goldfish or arrowana is believed to be extremely good Feng Shui especially for those in retail businesses, and particularly those in restaurants or catering.

Turtles and terrapins bring great good fortune to the entire household (even turtles in symbolic form) especially when placed in the north. Terrapins can be kept to symbolize the celestial turtle. In countries with cold winters, terrapins will need to be taken inside and kept in an aquarium; they cannot survive the cold outdoors.

ABOVE A rounded pond containing a small fountain energizes good Chi for the owner.

ABOVE Goldfish are an auspicious addition to any pool or pond. Make sure that they are well cared for.

ABOVE A raised garden pool. For any water feature oval or circular shapes have the best Feng Shui.

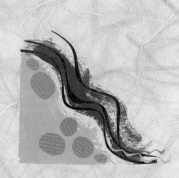

ABOVE A gently cascading waterfall, is a joy, but water must flow toward the home to bring wealth luck.

CHAPTER TWENTY-ONE: WATER

THE WATER LOCATION FORMULA

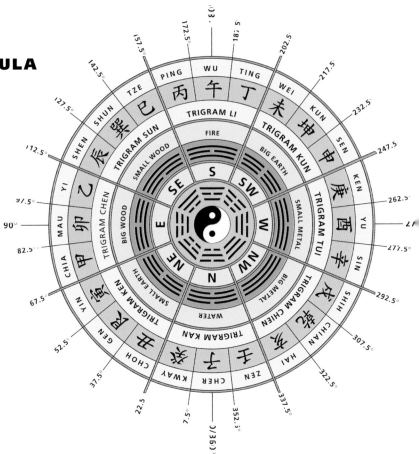

The flow of water in Feng Shui is said to mirror the flow of invisible chi currents that swirl around the Earth, bringing with it great wealth and prosperity. At its most simplistic level, water Feng Shui technology maintains that water flowing toward you or your main door brings you money, while water that is flowing away from your main door takes away all your money.

Under Compass School Feng Shui, the location and direction of the flow of the water takes precedence and the table opposite gives a summary of the water formula. It offers specific directions on the way water should flow past the main door and then the direction it would best flow out of your land. How the water should flow past the main door depends on the direction that the door is facing, looking from the inside out. There are 12 specific categories of door directions (with two further subsections) and each of these has three good fortune directions. These best exit directions relate specifically to the direction of your water course out of the home and land. All other directions result in varying degrees of misfortunes.

To apply the formula, use a good Western-style compass to first ascertain which direction your door faces and then use the table to check its exact subdirection. For example, if your door faces south, but more exactly at 160° from north, then it is facing the Ping direction in category 1. This category door direction requires water to flow past the front door from left to right when standing inside the door looking out.

The next column then shows the best exit flow of water and for category 1 homes it should flow

toward the Sin or Shih direction, meaning that it should flow out at an angle of between 277.5 and 307.5°. The best way to simulate this auspicious flow of water is to build a small water course in that direction. When designing drains to tap the correct exit directions, be as accurate as possible since exiting in the sector next to an auspicious sector can often be the cause of great misfortunes.

The exit directions

By tapping the first exit direction every type of luck may be enhanced for all members of the household. Precious jewels are said to flow unceasingly to the residents and the master or patriarch of the household will enjoy an elevated status in society. Prosperity luck is exceptional and there will be great abundance of money. All the sons and daughters will be intelligent.

If it is not possible to tap this first direction, going for the second

exit direction also brings good fortune. A home that enjoys this exit flow will definitely become a prosperous home and residents of such an abode will benefit from good health.

Selecting which exit direction to use depends entirely on your particular situation and it is sometimes not possible to tap the first or second best directions. In this case, go for the third direction, which is usually said to bring good auspicious luck. However, there are four door categories when the third exit direction brings grave misfortunes and should therefore be avoided.

★ In Door categories 2, 5, and 8, the third water exit directions brings poverty and a breakdown of family fortunes.

★ In Door category 11, the third exit direction brings a mixture of good and bad luck, which ultimately leads to a bad ending for the residents in the home.

A SUMMARY OF THE WATER LOCATION FORMULA

Twelve Door Categories	Direction the door faces	Name of the two subdirections in the category and exact degrees on the compass	Flow of water past main door	Best exit 1st, 2nd, and 3rd
1	South	Ping: 157.5–172.5° Wu: 172.5–187.5°	Left to right	1st: via Sin or Shih 2nd: via Ting or Wei 3rd: via Chia
2	South/Southwest	Ting: 187.5–202.5° Wei: 202.5–217.5°	Right to left	1st: via Shun or Tze 2nd: via Kun 3rd: not available*
3	Southwest	Kun: 217.5–232.5° Sen: 232.5–247.5°	Right to left	1st: via Yi or Shen 2nd: via Ting or Wei 3rd: via Ken or Yu
4	West	Ken: 247.5–262.5° Yu: 262.5–277.5°	Left to right	1st: via Kway or Choh 2nd: via Sin or Shih 3rd: via Ping
5	West/Northwest	Sin: 277.5–292.5° Shih: 292.5–307.5°	Right to left	1st: via Kun or Sen 2nd: via Chen or Hai 3rd: not available*
6	Northwest	Chian: 307.5–322.5° Hai: 322.5–337.5°	Right to left	1st: via Ting or Wei 2nd: via Sin or Shih 3rd: via Zen or Cher
7	North	Zen: 337.5–352.5° Cher: 352.5–7.5°	Left to right	1st: via Yi or Shen 2nd: via Kway or Choh 3rd: via Ken
8	North/Northeast	Kway: 7.5–22.5° Choh: 22.5–37.5°	Right to left	1st: via Chian or Hai 2nd: via Gen or Yin 3rd: not available*
9	Northeast	Gen: 37.5–52.5° Yin: 52.5–67.5°	Right to left	1st: via Sin or Shih 2nd: via Kway or Choh 3rd: via Chia or Mau
10	East	Chia: 67.5–82.5° Mau: 82.5–97.5°	Left to right	1st: via Ting or Wei 2nd: via Yi or Shen 3rd: via Zen
11	East/Southeast	Yi: 97.5–112.5° Shen: 112.5–127.5°	Right to left	1st: via Gen or Yin 2nd: via Shun or Tze 3rd: not available*
12	Southeast	Shun: 127.5–142.5° Tze: 142.5–157.5°	Right to left	1st: via Kway or Choh 2nd: via Yi or Shen 3rd: via Ping or Wu

* see The exit directions, opposite page.

CHAPTER TWENTY-ONE: WATER

OTHER WATER FEATURES

ABOVE *This pond has been greatly enhanced with lush Yang foliage to balance the Yin energy of the water. The miniature waterfalls are ideal for a small garden as they will not overwhelm the home.*

When you are planning a water feature, always consider its size, position, and the direction in which the water flows.

Waterfalls

Waterfalls generate auspicious Sheng Chi, hence their popularity in some people's gardens. There are other points worth noting with regard to waterfalls:

🜨 They should be located in the north, east, or southeast corners of the garden as these are the most compatible element locations.

🜨 Waterfalls create Sheng Chi especially if the water falls toward the house, bringing luck with it, rather than away from the house. Ideally your waterfall should be in full view – but not directly facing or in front – of the main door, bringing with it great business

ABOVE *The sound of gently trickling streams is extremely relaxing, and the movement of the water ensures that Chi does not stagnate. Check that the water flows in a favorable direction.*

opportunities, good career prospects, and financial security.

🜨 Always build your waterfall in relation to the size of the house. Do not allow it to dwarf the house, thus overwhelming it with too much Chi. Remember not to

overwhelm or block the house with too much Chi in constructing your waterfall.

🜨 Ensure that decorative rocks and boulders do not resemble anything threatening, so that they take on the guise of poison arrows.

Fountains

A water fountain will enhance the Feng Shui of your garden especially if it bubbles away merrily, implying the flow of life-giving Chi. Water fountains are best placed in the front of the garden, in full view of the main door. Position it in accordance with the water location formula. In order to enhance the Feng Shui of your house, and to get the most benefit from your water fountain, try to leave a space of at least 20 feet (6m) in front of the main door.

Swimming pools

Swimming pools are not generally recommended in the practice of Feng Shui: unless they are built outside in spacious grounds they tend to overwhelm their surroundings and threaten to create an imbalance of elements. If a swimming pool is sited in an incorrect corner of the garden, then any misfortune or ill-luck that it accrues will be magnified.

If you do decide to install a swimming pool in your garden, make sure that it is an auspicious shape. Rectangular-shaped pools with their sharp corners have the same effect as sharp corners inside the home and cause the harmful Shar Chi, directing poison arrows at the house and its occupants. The best shape for a pool is one with undulating curves without corners – oval, round, or kidney shaped – since this best resembles natural water. (*See also Activating Small Water, pages 106–7.*)

RIGHT *This pool will not cause bad Feng Shui since it does not dominate the garden and the curved shape almost hugs the house like a natural stretch of water.*

ABOVE *Ponds are fairly easy to build yourself. Go for a rounded shape and install a pump to prevent stagnation.*

RIGHT *A bubbling fountain mirrors the life-energy force of Chi. Use the water location formula to decide the best place to position it in your garden.*

GARDEN STRUCTURES

T*he garden structures discussed in this chapter are sculptures, pergolas, pavilions, and other built-up structures that create their own intrinsic energies that can impact either negatively or positively on your Feng Shui. Whether these structures enhance or detract from the Feng Shui of your home depends on what they are, how large they are, and where they are placed in relation to the main door. Generally speaking structures should never block the flow of Chi towards the main door. They must never be too close to the front door or, worse, send poison arrows toward the front door. They should also add to rather than detract from the element energy in the location where they are placed. Thus structures made of metal should never be placed in the north. The theory of the five elements should always be applied when positioning a new piece of sculpture or when installing a new pavilion. Steps, slopes, hedges, fences, walls, rock gardens, and barbecue pits also have an effect on your Feng Shui, which can be good or bad, and these too should be placed in a way that harmonizes with the overall Feng Shui. This section addresses the techniques of determining and achieving this harmony.*

LEFT *Balance, harmony, and proportion are the key words to remember when placing garden structures.*

CHAPTER TWENTY-TWO: GARDEN STRUCTURES

THE FENG SHUI OF GARDEN STRUCTURES

Every structure within the garden – be it sculpture, a wall, gate, or a container – creates its own energy and whether or not this energy is good or bad depends on the way each structure is placed in relation to doors, paths, and the orientation of the house. Feng Shui analysis starts with the structures at the edge of the property, such as a chain-link fence or a pathway. Such structures separate the personal living space from the outside world and can create good or bad Feng Shui.

Remember as ever that balance, harmony, and proportion are relevant to the creation of good energy. Anything sharp, pointed, or hostile will create bad luck Chi.

❦ At all costs avoid poison arrows, anything straight, sharp, angular, or hostile looking.

❦ The structure's size must not overwhelm the garden or house.

Fences and boundary walls

There are some simple guidelines for activating Chi in the garden. Start at the edge of your property and work toward the house.

❦ Your boundary should not be too near the house, especially if it is a wall, because it will cause claustrophobia and prevent good Chi from moving around the house. Solid walls are fine for large estates but, unless they form only one side of the enclosure, are not a good idea close to a house.

❦ The boundary should not be higher than the house. This will cause an imbalance of energies, turning negative Chi inward and bringing bad luck to the residents.

❦ Fences or walls around the house should be of equal height. Anything else causes an imbalance.

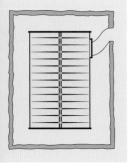

BELOW *The surrounding wall will stifle the Chi because it is much too close to the house.*

ABOVE *Auspicious entrance gates should always open inward,* *be well maintained, and in proportion to the home.*

❦ Be careful of fences or walls with sharp points within their design going either inward or outward, thus creating negative energy. If it points inward, the energy will harm you; if it points outward it will hurt your neighbors. Try to create good Feng Shui by not hurting anyone.

Entrance gates

Not every property requires a main gate; it depends on the scale or nature of the property. From a Feng Shui point of view, however, a clearly demarcated boundary makes it easier to create good Feng Shui.

❦ The size of the gate should be proportional to the house.

❦ Gates should open inward rather than outward.

❦ Gates should be symmetrical.

❦ Gates should be friendly and inviting. Avoid anything hostile with sharp points, such as barbed wire. Classical, more formal designs are better than abstract.

❦ Do not engulf your gate with creepers or vines.

❦ Maintain your gates at all times. Do not allow them to rust.

❦ As a simple guideline, black gates should go in the north, east, and southeast; red in the south, southwest, and northeast; white in the west, northwest, and north.

❦ Gates flanked by pillars are excellent Feng Shui; placing two Chinese lions on each pillar creates further protective energy.

Pavilions

To enjoy good Feng Shui, pavilions – always auspicious features in ancient Chinese gardens – should bind the elements of a garden into an integrated whole and allow good luck Chi to accumulate in the garden. They should have open windows and low walls and, ideally, a view of

RIGHT *Decorative structures must be erected to correspond with the Feng Shui of the main house.*

mountains or water. Paths leading to the pavilion should meander to encourage Chi to enter.

Freestanding structures such as greenhouses, summerhouses, or gazebos affect the Feng Shui of the main house depending on their location in relation to the main door of the house.

☙ Structures in the northwest or west pose no threat as long as they are not directly behind the house.

☙ The west is no threat to a main door in the south sector.

☙ North structures destroy the Feng Shui of a main door in the south sector.

☙ Structures in the southeast or east strengthen the energy of a south main door.

Again, beware of sharp edges on any freestanding structures that will send poison

arrows toward the main door. Gazebos are usually circular and offer good points of focus in the garden. If you want to enjoy the Feng Shui benefits of a gazebo, locate it carefully in accordance with the Five Element theory. The circle represents metal; freestanding structures should always be located in corners whose ruling element complements the element of the main door.

Pathways and stepping stones

Pathways are excellent in a garden because they create a visual flow that encourages Chi to accumulate. It is important to remember that if Chi is to settle and increase the pathway must never be built as a straight line with any sharp angles: this will cause the Chi to rush through the garden and become hostile. Nor should it come straight toward your main door, flooding the house with bad Chi. Instead, ensure your pathway meanders and sweeps in a gentle curve; flowers in a profusion of colors on either side of the path will both enhance the beauty of the garden and create auspicious Yang energy that encourages Chi to settle.

Selecting materials and patterns

In choosing the sort of path you want, remember that harmony is important in the garden. Some materials look harsh, others soft. If your path meanders across a grassy area, ensure that the material you choose suits a lawn and suggests a smooth flow.

Garden paths that are used frequently represent good Feng Shui and are much luckier than those that are seldom used. Therefore, you should design your path so that it is both inviting and comfortable for the people who will be walking on it. Avoid any uneven surfaces or those that are so overdesigned that they lose their practicality. The best paths are probably those laid in brickwork: they are solid, long-lasting, and also look inviting.

Such brickwork can also be laid in a variety of attractive patterns, perhaps herringbone, straight, stretched, or woven, placed either square to the path or diagonal to the path. All of these patterns are acceptable although the actual pattern is of little real relevance to the quality of the Feng Shui – the main concern is the fact that the path should not be straight.

ABOVE *Stepping stones are inviting to tread on, and well-used pathways provide great Feng Shui in the garden.*

SEE ALSO
❖ Pergolas p. 241
❖ Sculptures p.241

CHAPTER TWENTY-TWO: GARDEN STRUCTURES

THE FENG SHUI OF GARDEN STRUCTURES

Patio gardens and terraces

Much of what has already been written in the chapter on applying Feng Shui in the garden (*see pages 240–1, Walled gardens and courtyards*) applies to this section and should be noted accordingly. Small backyards of the houses of city-dwellers will, if neglected, always attract and accumulate Yin energy. Avoid this if you can by creating a patio or terrace garden from such spaces. Feng Shui is most accommodating: no space is too small for it.

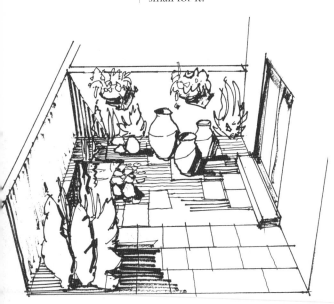

ABOVE *An empty patio or terrace results in too much Yin energy. Bring balance to the area with the stimulating Yang energy of plants. Hanging baskets and potted plants are ideal.*

Try to think of a patio as an inner courtyard, an extension to the house but open to the elements. A small water feature such as a fountain or a pool surrounded by plants will attract Sheng Chi into the home. As we have also seen earlier, decorative features such as small pergolas, trellises and hanging baskets are all good for gardens and can also be introduced into patios, so long as they are in proportion, to auspicious effect. Add interest to the ground plan of your patio by perhaps adding a small paved area with decorative stones. In placing them, always be guided by the elements that are represented by the compass location of your patio garden. For example, the best locations for stones or pebbles are the southwest or northeast, since the ruling element is earth.

Patio gardens are often seen as extensions of the house itself and they often provide excellent Feng Shui by correcting the problem of missing corners in L-shaped or U-shaped houses. If you have a wall that acts as a backdrop to your patio or terrace, try to resist the temptation to swathe it in creepers or vines. Doing this will sap the strength of the wall and have a negative effect on your Feng Shui. Better to introduce hanging baskets or potted plants. If your patio is at the back of the house, you could build a small rockery in simulation of the protective turtle mountain.

A rather nice effect – and one always popular with the Chinese – is the placing of large, empty ceramic pots in patio gardens. Often decorated with symbols of good fortune, their role is to encourage Chi to enter, settle, and accumulate in the area. They are kept empty so that they can capture and store bad Chi.

Sloping gardens

A sloping garden offers creative opportunities for professional garden designers but, from our point of view, offers wonderful opportunities for creative and auspicious Feng Shui. Feng Shui has guidelines for making the most of such a site and they revolve around engaging the tiger/dragon and protective turtle symbolism.

Levels in a sloping garden are an important consideration and such a garden can be broken into a number of levels. In a small garden the choice is naturally limited. In a bigger garden, however, firmer guidelines can be applied. Further away from the house allow the land to slope naturally; closer to the house sloping land should be more formal and contrived, perhaps with artificially created terraces or levels defining high and low ground.

The overall effect of these different levels should always be one of stability: a terrace must appear to be firmly rooted to the ground, and indeed it should be. If you have a retaining wall ensure it is solid and well built so as to afford the stability so essential to your property and to the good Feng Shui of the garden and house. A firm foundation is fundamental to good Feng Shui.

Allow your garden terrace to slope and curve in order to encourage good Feng Shui. Introduce color and variety into your terrace planting. Introducing evergreens between the different

BELOW *Patio gardens must rely on containers for vibrant color and to attract Chi by boosting the wood element.*

levels of the terrace will encourage good-fortune Chi to flow throughout the year, and not simply during the times of year when annuals or perennials thrive.

Grassy banks

A grassy bank is often quite difficult to maintain and can frequently become a bit ragged and neglected. If this is the case, such slopes might be better planted rather than turfed, particularly if they are at the back of the house. The back represents your flank and it must be protected either by higher ground or a clump of trees. Neglect this ground and you neglect the Feng Shui, which will be affected accordingly.

Steps

With regard to closely spaced steps in a garden, there are golden rules which must be observed:
ℓ Curved steps are better than straight steps and they must not be too steep or too narrow.
ℓ Steps must not be visible from the main gate, start directly in front of the main gate or be directly facing the main door.
ℓ Steps must not be directly in line with the back door. Keep garden steps to the side of the house.
ℓ Garden steps should be as wide and spacious as possible and preferably circular.

Rock gardens

For easy maintenance, rock gardens are best placed on level rather than sloping ground. Rocks as decorative items are most suited to the southwest part of the garden, which is the big earth corner.

If, however, you want to plant your rock garden, you can make the slope work for you by bedding rocks into it – so that they resemble a natural outcrop – and creating pathways around the rocks for easy access to plants and shrubs. If you do this, you must ensure that the rocks you select are rounded and not threatening in any way. So close

to your house, they should not resemble anything remotely fierce or hostile. This will attract nothing but bad luck to members of your household: illness and financial loss will almost certainly follow. It is, however, excellent Feng Shui to place good-fortune symbols – a statue of a crane, the symbol of longevity, for example – in the middle of your rock garden.

Barbecues

Inviting friends around for a barbecue continues to be a popular social event all over the world. Any outdoor living space can be enhanced with a bricked barbecue area, but there are rules which must be observed. Make sure that you do not place your barbecue too close to doors or windows: this will discourage beneficial Chi from entering the house.

More important, however, is to ensure that your barbecue is placed in the correct corner of the garden. The south, southwest, and northeast are suitable:

ℓ The south is the fire sector and a barbecue suits the fire element.
ℓ The southwest and northeast are earth corners – remember earth produces fire in the productive cycle of the five elements.

There are also locations you should stringently avoid:
ℓ The west and northwest are metal corners. Fire always destroys metal in the destructive cycle of the five elements.
ℓ The northwest is the sector of the family breadwinner. It is called the gate of heaven since the trigram for this corner is Chien, which represents heaven. A naked flame associated with something like a barbecue in this corner suggests a destructive force rather than positive Yang energy: it symbolically suggests that you are setting light to heaven and burning the fortunes of the household.

If you cannot build your barbecue in a suitable sector, better to do without altogether and use a mobile barbecue which you can store away after use.

BELOW *Shallow steps flanked by containers of pink flowers redolent with Yang energy, combine for good Feng Shui when linking the levels of a favorable sloping garden.*

CHAPTER TWENTY-TWO: GARDEN STRUCTURES

THE FENG SHUI OF GARDEN STRUCTURES

Sculptures and ceramics

Placing ornamental statues and ceramics around the house or garden is popular with many people. This has already been touched upon in the chapter on applying Feng Shui in the garden (*see page 241, Pergolas and Sculptures*), but is worthy of further elaboration.

To the Chinese, such decorative items are always symbolic and there are many symbols that represent the three most important components of happiness to the Chinese psyche: material success, respected descendants, and longevity. Thus the gods of wealth, longevity, and success are especially favored. Chinese symbols of longevity and good health such as the fish, the three-legged frog or toad, the turtle, the crane, and the deer all represent good Feng Shui. The placing of these in the form of

BELOW *The Chinese often use large, decorative containers as garden ornaments with a hidden purpose – they will gobble up bad Chi.*

ceramic ornaments or statues will bring auspicious symbolism into the garden, especially if they are placed in strategic corners such as the west or northwest corners, so that energies created by their presence are subtle rather than overwhelming. There are a number of useful guidelines to follow in the placement of statues and ceramics, but remember that the main rule to follow is not to place statues directly in front of your main door. Leave the area clear so that the Chi can settle in your bright hall before entering the home.

PLACING AUSPICIOUS GARDEN STATUARIES

When placing symbolic statues and ceramics always bear in mind the following Feng Shui guidelines:

🍃 Place symbols of longevity in the west or northwest sector.

🍃 Place symbols of wealth in the east or southeast sector.

🍃 Place symbols of protection in the front part of the garden, facing outward.

🍃 Place symbols of marital happiness – mandarin ducks, for example – in the southwest.

🍃 Place symbols of descendants' luck in the northeast.

LEFT *Traditional Chinese symbols of good fortune should be placed in the location that will enhance their powers. Fish represent wealth and are allied with the east or southeast.*

BELOW *Displaying the Chinese gods Fuk, Luk, and Sau ensures wealth, prosperity, and longevity. Fuk (right) is the god of prosperity. Luk (left) is the god of wealth, recognition, and success. Sau (middle) represents longevity.*

ABOVE *The most beneficial position for a rock garden is in the southwest of the main garden.*

LIGHTING

T*he benefits that lights can bring in garden Feng Shui make them enormously significant. Lights bring precious Yang energy. Lights also represent the fire element, bringing warmth, which in turn brings about the harvest. These two attributes contribute to the harnessing of the wood element. Lights can also be used to correct a large variety of Feng Shui woes. They can be used to fill in corners missing from houses. They can also raise the energies of inadequate or incorrect contour levels in the garden. When the back garden is lower than the front, for instance, placing a light high behind the house serves to raise the Chi energy, thereby correcting a major Feng Shui affliction in the environment. In the same way lights placed on the left side of the garden also enhance the dragon energies of the surrounding environment. Garden lighting is especially important in the south because here the energies of the five elements are synchronized. In the same way light used in the earth corners, the southwest and the northeast, is also most auspicious. In the east and southeast lights become vital during the winter months when wood energies lack the precious warmth of the summer. It is only in the west and northwest of the garden that lighting can be subdued. In general, garden lighting should never be overpowering, or be particularly harsh or bright, as this transforms good energies into bad.*

LEFT *Lighting can be used to great effect to inject vital Yang energy into the garden.*

CHAPTER TWENTY-THREE: LIGHTING

CORRECTING HARMFUL SHAPES AND STRUCTURES

ABOVE *At night, a garden can be completely transformed from its daytime persona by imaginative use of lighting. In Feng Shui, lights can be employed to deaden the impact of harmful structures.*

Cleverly used, exterior lighting is a simple and effective method of attracting and harnessing earth luck, thereby enhancing family and relationship luck.

Feng Shui lighting is an effective solution for houses that are inauspiciously shaped or that have contours which are causing incorrect tiger/dragon placements. Lights are also a striking and useful Feng Shui antidote for missing corners, for correcting inauspicious gradients, and for getting rid of bad energy created by external conditions. A strong spotlight can, for example, disintegrate poison arrows coming from someone else's property.

Three main Feng Shui problems can be corrected successfully with garden lighting:
℮ Inauspicious or irregular house shapes that are causing an excess of Yin energy.
℮ Harmful structures that are located in the vicinity of the house and garden.
℮ A house with inauspicious elevations and contours.

RIGHT *Lamps such as these can be pushed directly into the soil. They are very versatile.*

RIGHT *A perfect light to put over an entrance door to the home, where it will attract good Chi.*

BELOW *If dragon and tiger are in the wrong position, lights on walls and steps can help correct this.*

ABOVE *A good light for a porch ceiling, where it will banish any gloominess causing negative Chi to accumulate.*

RIGHT *Bold, beacon-type lights help repel poison arrows heading toward the house and garden.*

Correcting irregular house shapes

By installing lights you will immediately activate the Yang energy of the fire element. If there are missing corners on your property caused by an irregular shaped house or garden, installing a bright light into that area will introduce Yang energy and stimulate activity and life. Such a light will be potent if it is the same height as the house, but it should in any case be at least 6 feet (2m) high. Install the light so that it illuminates the missing area in the irregular shape and keep it turned on for three hours each night.

Combating poison arrows caused by harmful structures

Bright lights can also be most effective if they are used to combat certain hostile structures, buildings or objects pointing directly at your house. These may be in the form of a straight road, a tree, the pointed roof of another house, or a junction of some kind. If you cannot block them from view, point a bright light at them to simulate the piercing glare of the tiger's eye and thus dissolve bad energy before it reaches your house.

USING LIGHT TO ENHANCE GOOD LUCK AND REDUCE BAD LUCK

Using light to energize good areas of the garden and turn away problems can create substantial improvements in the Feng Shui of your garden.

Energizing the mother earth corner with lights

This is a particularly important part of the garden to energize. In so doing, you will help to ensure that people in the house get along; quarrels and misunderstandings will be reduced; residents' lives will generally be improved. Energize the mother earth corner by placing lights in the southwest part of your garden where they will be at their most auspicious. Garden lights in the south part of the garden enhance the reputation of the family breadwinner and also the household residents.

ABOVE AND BELOW *inauspicious aspects* *Lights address* *of your home.*

Combating a strong tiger side with lights

The west side of the house (on the left of the main door, looking out) is considered to be the tiger side and the tiger becomes a problem if the garden is higher or larger in this area than in others. In such a situation, the tiger is dominating the dragon and has the upper hand. In certain circumstances, when the tiger has the upper hand, it is potentially lethal: it can cause accidents, death or other tragedies to befall members of the family.

To ensure that the tiger remains benevolent and controlled, and that it is protective rather than destructive, place a bright light in the west in order to counteract the worst excesses of the malevolent tiger. A light in the west works effectively because, as a representative of the fire element, it combats the metal element of the western corner: fire destroys metal in the cycle of elements.

If you have stepping stones along the west side of your garden, light them up. A path of lights will keep the tiger under control and afford residents his benefit and protection.

LEFT *Houses built near hospitals suffer from an excess of Yin energy. Lights help to raise levels of Yang energy to balance it out and harmonize the Feng Shui.*

CHAPTER TWENTY-THREE: LIGHTING

HARNESSING THE ELEMENTS AND ACHIEVING FAME

bright spotlights
deflect poison arrows

small lights are fine
in the southwest
corner to attract
earth energy

stepping stones
invite good Chi into
the garden

lights inside a pond
will cause conflicting
fire and water
energies

ABOVE *Lighting in the garden can be used to great effect both to encourage the flow of good Chi and deflect bad energy.*

Lights in a garden can also increase the power of specific elemental forces and attract luck to the house's occupants in the form of fame and recognition.

Lights and water features

If you have stepping stones that lead to a water feature such as a pond, ensure that it is on the north side of your garden. Do not place lights inside the pond: in the cycle of elements, fire and water clash and the result is disharmony.

Likewise, do not light up fountains or similar water features.

You can, however, place lights with water in the southwest of the garden when flying stars are favorable. The southwest is the location of the earth element and lights will both enhance and be favorable to this location.

LEFT *When hostile structures are damaging your house, block them* *out with dense planting or use lights to reflect their evil energies.*

CORRECTING OR BALANCING CONTOURS

Feng Shui says that land behind the house should always be higher than land in front, and that land on the left side of the house (from inside the main door looking out) should be higher than land on the right. This is one of the main tenets of classical Landscape Feng Shui. Sometimes, however, it is not possible to change the lie of the land or correct certain inauspicious contours and in such an instance the use of lights helps enormously. Install lights on a tall pole on the lower land symbolically to raise the energy of the lower level, thereby correcting the imbalance. Remember that bright lights lift energy.

BELOW *A lack of "green dragon hills" to your left can be corrected by installing a tall light.*

RIGHT *A tall bright light will provide protective energy if the front is higher than the back.*

tall spotlight encourages Yang energy

front garden higher than back garden

white tiger hills are too high

bright tall lights simulate the protective green dragon hills

CHAPTER TWENTY-THREE: LIGHTING

LIGHTING IN THE GARDEN

ABOVE *Lighting brings harmony to the dominant tiger (west) side of a garden. The fire element will restore the balance spoiled by an excess of metal energy.*

Lighting up your protective Fu dogs

I have elsewhere recommended the placement of a pair of Fu dogs on top of the entrance gate to your home. This practice is extremely popular in Asia and among people of Chinese origin all over the world. Fu dogs, sometimes mistakenly referred to as Chinese unicorns, are regarded as legendary celestial creatures, like the dragon; the closest approximation today are Pekinese dogs whose faces resemble the Fu.

Fu dog statues come in all sizes and are easily purchased from any Chinese supermarket. If your gate is located in the south sector of your land site, then lighting up the

Fu dog at night would be regarded as an extremely auspicious thing to do because this attracts the luck of recognition and fame. This Feng Shui tip is especially helpful for those in the entertainment business where popularity and celebrity status are vital ingredients to their success. When placing Fu dogs on top of the entrance gateposts it is a good idea to have a spotlight on the ground, shining upward at the Fu dogs. This will ensure that recognition and respect will always be accorded to you and your family whatever your occupation.

RIGHT Lighting up your Fu dogs at night can enhance your family's recognition and fame luck.

ABOVE *If the tiger side of the house (left of the main door, looking outward) has Feng Shui problems, lights in the west help to remedy them.*

A LIGHTED JAPANESE GARDEN IN THE SOUTHWEST

A special landscaped garden in this corner provides excellent Feng Shui. Consciously try to emulate the Japanese garden by using different sizes of smooth stones, ground light, stepping stones, and decorative boulders. Try to have the garden low lying. The combination of lights and stones symbolizes the coming together of the fire and earth elements in the earth corner – fire burns everything to a heap of ashes and this produces earth. This activates the positive, productive cycle of the five elements.

The southwest is the home of the trigram Kun, which represents everything to do with the earth

mother, and highlighting the elements of fire and earth will have enormous energizing effect on your luck. It is also a good idea to tie auspicious red thread around some of the pebbles in the southwest as this activates the stones in that sector of the garden.

RIGHT *Lighting in the southwest corner represents the fire element. Fire will activate the earth element in order to enhance the owners' relationship luck.*

BELOW *Incorporate Japanese techniques into a Western garden by using ground lighting, stepping stones, and smooth boulders or pebbles. This will energize both the earth and fire elements.*

木火土金水

PART SIX

FENG SHUI IN THE BUSINESS WORLD

CHAPTER TWENTY-FOUR

FENG SHUI TIPS FOR ENTREPRENEURS

*I**f** you are building your own business and working toward millionaire status it does not hurt to create good Feng Shui to bring you real business luck. There are many effective ways of harnessing this luck either through symbolic Feng Shui pointers that are easy to apply or through complicated Feng Shui formulas. For those who prefer quick-fix methods, this chapter offers several novel but powerful potent techniques and rituals. These can be implemented instantly to increase your sales immediately and bring in additional income. Feng Shui does not need to be complicated for it to be effective. What is important is to place wealth-bringing energizers correctly. Sailing ships loaded with gold should always sail in and never sail out of your business premises; mirrors should always reflect the cash register and never the door. In both cases one brings in the customers while the other chases the customers away. Pa Kua mirrors should never confront customers as this merely drives them away! Feng Shui is always best approached scientifically and applied with a detached attitude.*

LEFT *Your business can also benefit from Feng Shui – activating the positive energy can create a wealth of opportunities.*

WEALTH ENERGIZING

RIGHT *A crystal wealth vase or bowl is best if it resembles a gourd, a very auspicious symbol. Fill the container with other symbols of wealth and keep it hidden in your home or office.*

Wealth bowl

If you are in business and wish to activate and safeguard your wealth luck, it is excellent Feng Shui to create a "wealth bowl" or a "wealth vase" (or several) to place in your home. If you are greedy you can make two wealth bowls.

Look for a bowl with a wide brim. It can be either a normal bowl shape or, better still, narrow at the neck and then broaden out to resemble a gourd. Such a shape is auspicious because it means that wealth will enter the bowl with ease, but go out with difficulty. This is one symbolic meaning. The other is that the gourd is the traditional container of divine nectar, and therefore auspicious. The bowl can be made of crystal, or ceramic. If it is made of crystal, it should be good quality crystal. Do not use glass or plastic. Your wealth bowl can be as large as you wish.

The next step is to fill the bowl to the brim, so that it is almost overflowing. It should include three essential objects. These are:

❦ When you visit a wealthy person ask for a small plant or some soil. Do not steal it! Place it in a red packet or something similar.

❦ Nine Chinese coins with the square hole in the center, tied with red thread, placed in a red packet.

❦ Real money in any denomination amounting to 988 – perhaps $988 or $9.88, £988 or £9.88. Put the money into a red packet.

Place all three red packets inside the bowl and fill up with some or all of the following:

❦ Semiprecious stones such as jade, amethyst, citrine, tiger's eye, topaz, cornelian, quartz, crystal, malachite, coral, lapis lazuli, or turquoise. Some people recommend having seven types of semi-precious stone to reflect this period's lucky number. I use eight different types of stone in my wealth vase and I am particularly fond of coral and jade, the two stones much favored by oriental women. I also like to have crystals inside my wealth bowl because they are excellent energizers.

❦ Use the eight treasures, i.e. a pair of elephants or the precious horse, the neverending knot, the double fish symbol, the shell, the canopy symbol, the lotus flower, or the vase.

❦ If you prefer you can fill your wealth vase with colored glass or use crystal-like beads. Pearls are also a great favorite.

❦ You can place a small bit of real gold inside your wealth vase, the ultimate symbol of wealth, and for good measure you may want to add some fake gold ingots.

It is not necessary to display the wealth bowl too ostentatiously; in fact the best place is either in the bedroom, or, if it is at the office, hidden away in a cupboard.

You can also place the wealth bowl on your altar to symbolize the offering of something valuable. I have both of my wealth bowls on my altar and an offering to Buddha.

It is a good idea to turn over the contents to refresh the wealth bowl the week before New Year. This brings fresh energy and activates the wealth bowl for the coming year.

A sailing ship loaded with "gold"

This is one of the best methods of successfully increasing your personal wealth, especially if you are an entrepreneurial businessman. In the Far East, the sailing ship has always been a symbol of success in business. In the old days many Chinese entrepreneurs used the sailing ship as their logo since this symbolized the winds bringing more business, more trade, and increased turnover. In fact, next to the dragon, the sailing ship is the most popular symbol used by Chinese businessmen.

To energize your Feng Shui luck for the office, place a model or replica of a sailing ship close to the main door. Make sure that the sailing ship is pointing inward towards the inside of the office. Do not let the sailing ship face outward: this means it is sailing away. Symbolically the ship must be coming in, not going out. The same thing can be done at home. Display a sailing ship near your front door.

A ship with sails that "catch the wind" is considered more auspicious than something like a model of the *Titanic* which, as everyone knows, sank in the Atlantic Ocean. The symbolism of the sails catching the wind and bringing gold to you is most auspicious. Think carefully about

the kind of ship you buy. The next thing to do is to fill the ship with gold. Fake gold ingots, which you can buy for a song, are easily available in Chinese emporiums or flea markets. Stack them up inside the ship. If you cannot find fake gold ingots, place coins and money inside the ship.

The green dragon in your southeast

Those whose wealth luck is important to them should always strive to energize the auspicious good fortune signified by the celestial dragon. Place nine dragons on the east side of your office, business, or home to activate dragon magic. Dragons that come with the symbolic pearl represent wealth. Get hold of these or, alternatively, get a painting with two dragons chasing the pearl. Do not place the dragon/phoenix pairing in the east. Such a pairing is not suitable here; it signifies love rather than wealth.

Differentiate between the five-clawed and the four-clawed dragons. Both kinds of dragon are suitable but it is worth noting that the five-clawed dragons signify the Imperial dynasty and the four-clawed dragons are for commoners. In ancient times, only

emperors were allowed to display the five-clawed dragon.

In terms of numbers of dragons to display, the number nine represents the fullness of heaven. It is also the only independent number and it has the power to magnify and multiply all types of luck – both bad and good. Since the dragon always brings good luck, having nine dragons strongly magnifies this good luck. In the Forbidden City and in Hong Kong on the waterfront a nine-dragon screen is displayed to attract good fortune. Kowloon, the prosperous hinterland of Hong Kong, is the place of the nine dragons.

Businesses that have the dragon as their logos usually enjoy great long-term success. But the dragon, like other good fortune symbols, must be represented correctly. Your dragon should not look hungry; it be fat, healthy, and well fed. Dragons must also never be held captive. They must be able to fly up to the sky, so placing circles around them is not a good idea. Displaying dragons inside locked cabinets will simply cause your projects to fail.

ABOVE *Display the green dragon in the east part of your office or business to elicit great wealth luck – but make sure it looks happy and well nourished.*

LEFT *The sailing ship represents wealth being brought home from foreign parts, and should be symbolically laden with gold and placed facing into the office.*

SEE ALSO

❖ The Concept of Landscape: symbolism of the four celestial creatures *pp. 48–50*
❖ All the Symbols of Good Fortune *p. 88*

Let your southeast wall be lush with green plants

This advice is also appropriate for the entire east part of your home, your office, and your garden. Your plants should overflow into the southeast as well because this is the part of your living and work space that signifies growth in income. The southeast is also the corner of wealth. Both of these sectors are wood sectors in the Five Element principle of Feng Shui. Thus, energizing with lush, healthy plants stimulates this element and attracts wonderful wealth energies into your work and living spaces. Make sure that the plants are well-cared for and trim them regularly so that dried and decaying leaves are never seen, otherwise this will bring your business bad luck.

RIGHT *Plants used to decorate an office are excellent for fostering beneficial Chi energy, but they should be healthy and well-cared for to attract wealth luck.*

A waterfall to bring wealth to your doorstep

Another excellent and serious wealth energizer is a small, man-made waterfall placed within 10 to 15 feet(3–4.5m) of your front door. You can do this in the office, factory, or home, but there are three main things to note:

❦ Make sure that your waterfall is not too large in proportion to the size of your building, your door, and your garden. It is better for it to be too small than too big. Whatever the size of the waterfall, the sound of water should be gentle rather than rushing.

❦ Make sure that the water appears to be flowing toward your entrance and that it is forming a pond in full view of the door. Water that is flowing away signifies money flowing out.

❦ Make sure there is life in the pond, perhaps terrapins or fish. All the better if you put auspicious fish in your pond.

❦ Make sure that the front door is located in the east, southeast, or north sector of the house. If it is located in any of the other sectors this option is not for you unless you have extremely favorable flying stars. If you do not know how to work out and interpret the flying stars, it is best to ensure that your door is in the right sector.

❦ Landscape the waterfall in such a way that there are no hostile

LEFT *All office plants should be well tended to ensure good wealth energy. Remove any dead or yellow leaves – these will create bad luck.*

ABOVE *Wealth luck can be generated by placing a small waterfall near your office; make sure it faces the entrance so the water wealth flows toward you.*

arrangements of rocks pointed at your door. Use nicely rounded rocks with smooth edges.

🌢 Do not place the waterfall directly in front of or to the right of the door. The only place suitable is on the left-hand side of the door. This direction is taken from the inside of the house or building, looking outward.

Bury nine coins in your pathway

This is a wealth Feng Shui tip that was given to me by a Hong Kong Feng Shui master. The idea is either to bury nine coins, or to simulate nine coins in the form of stepping stones leading from the gate to the front entrance of the office or house. This arrangement represents the nine emperor coins, and the combination of round and square shapes in the coins also signifies the unity of heaven and earth. Laying a stepping-stone path like this makes a very auspicious garden feature, which is excellent for improving your wealth.

RIGHT *A path with nine stepping stones leading up to the main door of your office building is regarded as very effective in promoting prosperity.*

Place a "mountain" behind your chair

Everyone engaged in business or in politics should make sure that they have a "mountain" behind their chair in their office. This can be a painting or a picture of a famous mountain. I like Mount Everest, but some masters have told me that this is too fiery a mountain shape. Nevertheless, I still like it. It is purely a personal thing.

It is important to ensure that your picture of a mountain has no water in it, for example, it should not contain any of the streams or waterfalls that appear in so many Chinese paintings. Water behind you signifies lost opportunities and this can create serious bad luck for those in business.

BELOW *Displaying a picture of a mountain behind your office chair will provide you with support during the working day.*

ABOVE *The type of mountain you choose to hang behind you is purely personal. Make sure that there is no water in your mountain picture, since this represents lost business opportunities.*

BELOW *Ayers Rock in Australia is one of the three sacred mountains that represent the earth element. The other two are Mount Kailash in Tibet and Table Mountain in South Africa.*

Place your "bank" behind your chair

A variation of the mountain theme is to place a "bank" behind your chair at work. Try to get a photograph of your bank's head office but make sure that the picture has not been taken with its edges pointing directly outward, this will cause poison arrows to shoot out at you. You want the bank to support you symbolically, not hurt you. This is a very good tip for those running their own businesses.

Stick lucky coins to your order and invoice books

Probably one of the best Feng Shui tips for increasing your sales and turnover in business is to stick three Chinese coins onto all your invoice books and your order books. Do

the same with the important files and cabinets in the office. Remember that all coins have to be energized by tying a red thread or ribbon to the coins. There is no special way to tie up the coins; as long as the coins are tied so that the Yang side (the side with the four Chinese characters) is visible the coins will be auspicious.

Chinese coins with the square holes in the center are best and I personally prefer the old coins to the new ones, but both types are suitable. If you wish you may tie nine coins instead of three coins. Nine is a lucky and auspicious number. Other lucky numbers are six and eight. Seven is lucky for this period but this number becomes very unlucky from the year 2003 onward.

ABOVE *Nine coins will be effective to promote financial success, since nine is a particularly lucky number.*

LEFT *Tying Chinese coins to an invoice or an order book with red ribbon is auspicious, but only if the Yang side of the coins is on top.*

FENG SHUI FOR RETAIL BUSINESSES

Establishing good Feng Shui for shops and retail establishments always begins with finding the right location. The first thing to check is that there are no poison arrows sending killing energy towards the shop entrance. Such energy is like the kiss of death. If you discern something hostile, sharp, or straight pointing directly at your entrance you should try to counter it by using element theory. If your main entrance faces east or southeast — directions of the wood element — then you should use a metal windchime to control the wood energy coming your way. Likewise a poison arrow coming from the north can be controlled with earth implements, while one coming from the south can be destroyed with an urn of water placed strategically by the entrance door. Use the same logic to devise cures for poison arrows coming from other directions. Do not use a Pa Kua as this will also keep customers away. With no bad energy hurting your shop you can then turn your attention to creating good business luck by using several potent and easily installed Feng Shui ideas: use mirrors to double turnover; use activated Chinese coins to create money luck; paste lucky symbols near your cash register and hang good luck bells, bowls, and windchimes.

LEFT *Learn useful Feng Shui tips to enhance your store and attract more customers.*

CHAPTER TWENTY-FIVE: FENG SHUI FOR RETAIL BUSINESSES

TIPS FOR RETAIL BUSINESSES

General advice

Various Feng Shui arrangements can be built into the décor of stores and retail businesses to help achieve higher turnover, ensure harmonious working relationships between staff and employees, and guard against burglary. To start with, selecting the site of a store should be done with care. You need plenty of Yang energy. Busy roads are better for business than quiet roads because there is plenty of Yang energy in busy thoroughfares. Traffic should not be moving excessively fast since this also carries all the luck away.

The location of a store is all-important, so invest as much money in the best location you can afford. Make sure your retail outlet, restaurant, or place of business does not have too small an entrance.

ABOVE *Select a site for your business carefully. A busy street brings plenty of Yang energy to your enterprise.*

Small doors mean small business. Here are some general tips to observe when you are selecting sites for retail outlets.

☯ Look for a building that faces a wide road rather than a narrow road. If your entrance faces an empty space this is excellent since it simulates a bright hall. In a shopping complex, stores that have a large, empty space outside their entrance will always be more successful than those that look out onto narrow corners.

☯ Make sure that your store's entrance is not harmed by the presence of a lamppost, a single tree, the edge of a building opposite, the triangular roof line of a building, or any other poison arrows. If your door directly faces such a structure or object, hang a large convex Pa Kua mirror above your door. Do not hang a Pa Kua

mirror above your door if there is nothing hurting your front door.

☯ Do not rent or buy a retail outlet that lies at the end of long corridor or is located at the end of a cul de sac. Locations such as these are always very inauspicious.

☯ Do not rent or buy a retail outlet that is sandwiched between two larger and higher buildings. Symbolically, your store will be squashed by the adjacent buildings.

☯ Do not rent or buy a store that faces a road where the traffic comes toward you. This is the classic T-junction or intersection and is most inauspicious.

☯ Do not open a retail outlet in a complex that does not have an obvious main entrance. Many shopping malls now have so many entrances that there is no obvious main door. Such places will seldom have good Feng Shui.

BELOW *The location of your store's main door is vital – bad Feng Shui may affect your sales turnover.*

main door faces open space creating the bright hall effect

main door faces T-junction or intersection – this encourages bad Chi

LEFT *Lining your store's walls with mirrors creates a feeling of space and depth, reflecting both the goods and the customers – the creates good Feng Shui for your business.*

BELOW *Mirrors should be full length – cutting the customers in two creates bad luck. The back wall should not reflect the main entrance because this will deflect the good luck Chi.*

BELOW *A mirror on the back wall of your store is auspicious if it is not visible from the entrance, but take care not to reflect staircases or washrooms.*

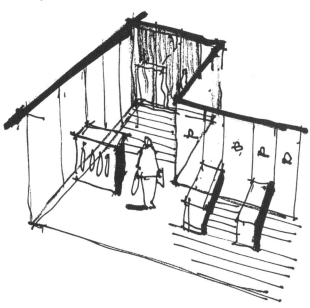

Use mirrors to double your turnover

In almost any kind of retail business, lining the walls with mirrors will expand sales turnover. Place such mirrors on two sides of the showroom so that the entrance does not get reflected. The back wall must not have a mirror, since reflecting the main entrance causes all the luck to flow right through the store and out again. Stores that appear to have depth will have a better chance of success than those that are shallow. Thus, a long, deep store is better than a wide one.

If the back wall cannot be seen from the main entrance, placing a mirror on the innermost back wall should give greater depth and offer more auspicious luck.

When using mirrors in stores, always ensure that the mirror reaches the ground so that customers' legs are not metaphorically cut off; similarly, make sure that mirrors are high enough to reflect the entire image of the tallest customers.

Try not to use small mirror tiles to make up one big mirror. Larger mirror tiles are best. Do not use cheap, thin mirrors that get ruined by damp. Let the mirror reflect the products, the customers, and, most important of all, the cash register. It has the effect of doubling everything. The only things the mirror should not reflect are entrances, washrooms, staircases, and brooms. Mirrors are especially lucky for restaurants, boutiques, jewelry stores, and gift shops.

Energize your cash register with coins and red thread

Another excellent way of energizing is to tie three coins with red thread and then stick them onto your invoice books, order books, and cash registers. If you have a cashbox, you can stick them on that as well.

The enhancing properties of coins are already well known. In the old days, merchant traders would tie coins to almost every container and place them on every piece of furniture.

Putting coins on cash registers is merely an adaptation of this old practice in the modern business environment. If you use a computer for your accounting you might want to consider the image of coins as a screensaver. Actually sticking coins onto your computer will certainly activate good income luck as well.

ABOVE Tie three Chinese coins with red thread or ribbon – the red color activates the auspicious conditions for money luck.

BELOW *Three Chinese coins placed on top of your cashbox will enhance your business's wealth-creating possibilities.*

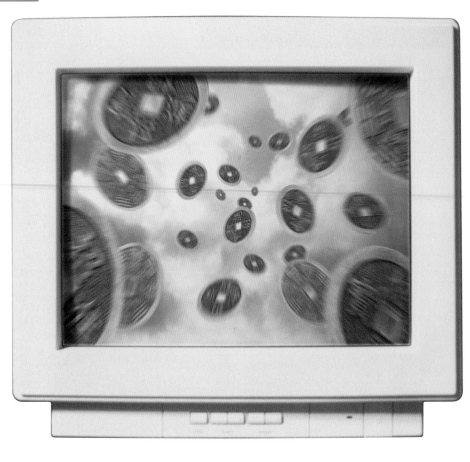

LEFT *To generate wealth luck in your business or at home, try sticking coins onto your computer or using a screensaver that displays coin images.*

Simulate a mountain of gold near your main door

One of the most creative methods of enhancing the luck of a retail outlet is to place a strategic small "mountain of gold" in front of it. This is especially powerful for doors that face either an earth or a metal direction – southwest, northeast, west, or northwest. Select some medium-sized rocks or boulders (about 6–8 inches/15–20cm in size), paint them gold and then build them up into a mound outside your entrance. Do not pile the rocks too high. You are only creating a symbolic mountain: a few rocks or boulders should be enough to activate the symbolism.

ABOVE *A few medium-sized stones painted gold and positioned outside the entrance to your store will increase your good fortune.*

SEE ALSO
❖ Energizing Good Fortune Symbols *p.92–3*
❖ Symbols of Prosperity, Success, and Wealth *pp.94–5*

LEFT *Unobtrusive wealth energizers such as good luck bells, coins tied with red thread, or a small pile of gold rocks will activate wealth luck without affecting the look of the store.*

Hang a good luck bell on your main door

Retail businesses always benefit from hanging a small bell on the handle of the door that is the entrance into the store. This is especially good for entrance doors that face the west and northwest direction. The tinkling of the bell instantly energizes the entrance of the store. It means that whoever enters the store also brings good luck into the shop.

RIGHT *A good luck bell hung on the entrance door will improve the energy of the store if it is positioned so that it rings when the door is opened.*

ABOVE *Use relevant element colors to energize entrance doors.*

ABOVE *Brown brings good luck for south-facing entrance doors.*

ABOVE *White is lucky if the store is west- or northwest-facing.*

ABOVE *The intensity of color does not matter – light blue will be as effective as dark.*

Create an auspicious main door

The main door of the store is the most important Feng Shui feature to take care of. Apart from making certain it is not being "hit" by anything from outside, there are also several things that can be done to enhance its luck.

☙ Use the five elements to bring luck to your door. Energize according to the direction and its corresponding element. Thus, south-facing doors should have fire motifs (triangular shapes, the sun, and lights). North-facing doors benefit from water motifs (wavy).

East and southeast doors benefit from the wood motif (rectangular). West and northwest doors benefit from metal motifs (round and circular shapes). Southwest and northeast doors benefit from earth motifs (square shapes).

☙ Use the Kua formula to determine your best direction for wealth and then try to ensure the main door of your retail outlet faces that particular direction. This assumes that you are running and managing the store yourself. If you are not, you should use the Kua number of the store manager. If the store manager changes regularly

you cannot use the Kua formula. In this case you should depend entirely on Form School Feng Shui for helping your business.

☙ Use a compass to determine which direction your store is facing, then use the five elements to energize it. Thus south-facing doors will benefit from being painted red, brown, or green and if the store directly across the road is also painted in these auspicious colors, it will bring luck to the store. If your main door faces north, the best color for you will be blue, black, or white; again, if the door or color scheme of the

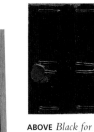

ABOVE *Choose orange for southwest- and northeast-facing doors.*

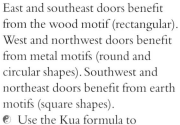

ABOVE *Black for entrances at the north, east, or southeast.*

ABOVE *Attract wealth with a red door to the south, southwest, or northeast.*

ABOVE *Green is the color for the south, east, or southeast.*

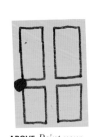

ABOVE *Paint your door yellow for good luck from the west or northwest.*

ABOVE *Blue entrance doors are lucky for north-, east-, or southeast-facing stores.*

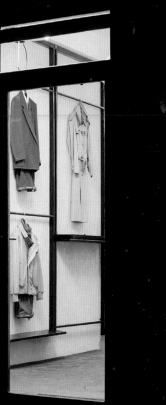

LEFT *A large well-lit front entrance to your store to attract energizing Yang energy – the brighter the entrance, the better for your bank balance!*

store directly across the road from you is painted with any of these colors, it will bring luck to you. If your door faces east or southeast the auspicious colors will be green, blue, or black. If the store faces west or northwest the lucky colors to use will be white, yellow, or metallic. If the door faces southwest or northeast, it will benefit from being painted striking red or yellow.

❦ The bigger your door the better your business. It should not, however, be so big as to appear unbalanced or be difficult for you to manage. Big doors benefit very much from a position that faces a "bright hall" or a wide road.

❦ If there are two or three feeder roads that enter into the main road that passes your main door, your store will be most auspicious. The nearer you are to the junction, intersection, or turn into your road the better, but traffic should be flowing toward your store and not away from it.

❦ If you are planning to erect a canopy at the front of your store it is advisable to use colors that reflect the relevant element of your front door. In any case you must make sure the colors used do not clash with this element.

❦ Keep the front door of your business well lit. When your store front is well lit you are creating good Yang energy, which brings people into your store. Doors that are badly lit repel Yang energy and auspicious Chi. In fact the brighter the front of your store the more business you will do.

BELOW *A bright light placed near the front door of your store creates a vibrant attractive glow, enhancing the conditions for the flow or Chi and therefore attracting customers.*

Place a bright light just inside the store

It is also important for retail businesses to ensure that a bright light is placed in the foyer just inside the store near the front door. This stimulates Yang energy and attracts precious Chi and thus enhances the flow of energy in the store. This is important irrespective of the direction or location of the main door, and would be even more auspicious if there was a previous foyer, no matter how small.

The foyer light should appear to lead the customer's eye into the rest of the store. If the foyer is badly lit then this will result in the auspicious Sheng Chi becoming stagnant resulting in a poor flow of energy – customers will not be attracted to the store. Try to keep the foyer light on at all times, even late at night when the store is closed.

ABOVE *The water element on a north-facing door.*

ABOVE *Yang energy is enhanced with good lighting.*

ABOVE *Canopies must not conflict with the door element.*

ABOVE *Earth element symbols are square-shaped.*

ABOVE *It is lucky if traffic flows toward your entrance door.*

CHAPTER TWENTY-SIX

FENG SHUI FOR CORPORATIONS

Corporations can benefit greatly from good Feng Shui, but only when it is applied correctly using the different powerful formulas that activate long-term luck. Corporate Feng Shui does differ from the Feng Shui that I recommend for residential homes and small businesses. This is because corporations usually have many branches all over the world and the Feng Shui of the head office has to take this into account. I have seen and heard of corporations retaining inexperienced Feng Shui consultants whose knowledge of Feng Shui is inadequate. As a result these corporations suffer the backlash of incorrectly applied Feng Shui theories. My advice to those of you managing big corporations is to use this book to enhance your personal Feng Shui. If you want to improve the Feng Shui of your company and yours is a conglomerate with other offices, then you should look deeper into Flying Star, Eight Mansions, and other formulas. Corporate Feng Shui is a substantial task and even when you use a professional Feng Shui consultant it will take many days to diagnose what needs to be done. This chapter offers some starting points for analyzing the Feng Shui of corporate buildings and high-rise head offices. I have also mentioned corporate signboards and logos, and the importance of the CEO's office. But to get the most out of Feng Shui corporations might wish to seriously consider retaining a genuine Feng Shui master. The difference in performance and profits will more than pay for his fees, however expensive he may appear to be!

LEFT By using Feng Shui techniques major corporations can ensure continued prosperity and abundance.

THE FENG SHUI OF BUILDINGS

ABOVE *Regular, square or rectangular shapes are auspicious, since they are symbolic of the stablizing effect of the earth element.*

RIGHT *Learn to recognize the good and bad Feng Shui implications of your office building.*

Office buildings in the city come in a variety of shapes and designs. Some are more harmful than others and it is important to apply classical Feng Shui guidelines in order to determine the quality of the Feng Shui of one's building. In cities, buildings take the place of hills and mountains, and roads can be treated in the same way as rivers.

The basic guidelines for determining the Feng Shui of buildings are as follows:

❦ Shapes of buildings, viewed from above as well as in elevation, have Feng Shui implications. The best shape for office buildings is rectangular, preferably regular, long, and deep. Rectangular buildings simulate the growth Chi of the wood element. Square buildings are also auspicious. This is the shape of the earth element and it symbolizes being grounded and having a strong foundation. The square is thus reflective of a more conservative kind of luck. Round and Pa Kua shaped buildings are not unlucky but they are not as good as rectangles and squares. Some practitioners prefer the Pa Kua shape because it resembles the Feng Shui symbol, and it is thus easy to arrange interior Feng Shui. I happen to believe that using regular square, rectangular shapes is more efficient.

❦ Irregular shapes, like L-shaped or U-shaped buildings, cause problems through missing corners. If the missing corner is auspicious, based on any of the compass formulas, then the building becomes unlucky. U-shaped buildings are especially unlucky. Buildings that narrow inward in the center or middle floors are extremely unlucky. Always be careful about working for companies that are located in such buildings.

❦ Office buildings should always appear to stand on solid ground. Buildings that stand on columns with open parking lots on the ground and lower floors give the appearance of the building standing on stilts. The empty space at the base of such buildings causes Chi to flow under the buildings rather than into them. Companies with offices in such buildings often tend to suffer from cash-flow problems.

❦ Office buildings should have clearly appointed main entrances. If a building has many entrances, it is not immediately obvious which is the main one. Such buildings seldom enjoy good luck, and Chi flows in and out unevenly. When the entrances are in a straight line or next to each other, Chi also flows out as quickly as it enters. Thus all buildings should have a clearly marked front entrance as well as a spacious front lobby that allows the Sheng Chi to come in, settle and accumulate. Buildings with large, brightly lit foyers enjoy good Feng Shui.

hostile, angular design

clearly marked entrance with fountain

L-shape – unlucky

Chi flows away

U-shaped building – missing corners

Pa Kua and round – good

THE EFFECT OF SURROUNDING BUILDINGS

The elevations and shapes of buildings shown below are examples of buildings that can pose a threat to good Feng Shui. Note the lethal edges of these buildings. If such buildings face your own, it will require Feng Shui protection. Hang a Pa Kua directly to counter the deadly negative energies being shot your way; if that is not strong enough, place a miniature brass cannon outside the main door of your building and aim it at the edge. The buildings illustrated opposite are extremely bad for their surrounding neighbors. The center building resembles a porcupine aiming spikes at everyone around. It also has a roof made of reflective material which reflects blinding rays of sunlight toward its neighbors.

❷ Buildings should beware of harmful cross-shaped façades across the road. Any kind of hostile or angular design can cause killing energy to shoot across to neighboring buildings.

❷ Buildings that cause Feng Shui problems to their neighbors usually eventually suffer from the measures taken by others to protect their own buildings. When Pa Kua mirrors or decorative cannons are used in retaliation, these in turn send out dangerous energies. Feng Shui knowledge is thus useful both for defending your building against hostile structures and also for ensuring it does not hurt your neighbors.

❷ An excellent antidote against hostile neighboring buildings is a large round fountain in front of the entrance into your building. This benefits everyone and brings masses of pleasant and auspicious Sheng Chi into the area.

❷ Low buildings surrounded by other larger, taller ones will have their Feng Shui overshadowed; this can be overcome by shining a bright light at the top of the smaller building.

LEFT *The sharp, angular edges of this building are directing poison arrows at its neighbor.*

LEFT *This structure is particularly hostile due to the spiky nature of the roof construction.*

ABOVE *Another hostile building – neighboring houses should take protective measures, such as hanging a Pa Kua outside their front door in order to deflect the harmful energies.*

clearly displayed logo

building narrows inward with too many entrances – inauspicious

SEE ALSO
❖ Landscape Feng Shui in a Modern Environment *p.64*
❖ The Five Elements of Buildings *p.45*

CHAPTER TWENTY-SIX: FENG SHUI FOR CORPORATIONS

A MAIN ENTRANCE TO THE CORPORATE BUILDING

ABOVE *Use symbolic representations of good luck animals.*

ABOVE *The trigrams Chien or Kun will also activate good fortune Chi.*

ABOVE *Another useful symbol of good luck is the neverending knot.*

ABOVE *Here the Chien trigram presides over the entrance, bringing good fortune.*

Buildings that have grand, solid-looking front entrances will enjoy excellent Feng Shui. There should be only one clear entrance, ideally facing a wide road or an empty space across the road. Buildings that face a park usually benefit from the auspicious "bright hall" effect. It is also more beneficial for the building's Feng Shui if it faces a main thoroughfare. Such buildings benefit from the massive quantities of Sheng Chi and good Yang energy of main roads. Traffic must move on these main roads. Stagnant traffic is like a stagnant river where Chi turns stale and unlucky. Excessively fast traffic is also not good. Traffic should flow slowly, like a lazily winding river. Winding roads are luckier than straight roads.

Steps leading into the building should be ascending rather than descending. Descending steps mean the entrance is below road level and this is inauspicious. Ideally, the main door should be solid and decorated with good fortune symbols, such as the celestial creatures, for example the dragon, or auspicious motifs like the neverending knot, or one of the auspicious trigrams (Chien or Kun).

Main entrances that are made of glass should open into a foyer that is backed by a screen-effect wall decorated with an auspicious painting, symbol, or image. Elevators can then be placed behind this wall. Lobbies should have ceilings that are high enough to give an impression of grandeur. Remember that this is the area where Chi enters; if yours is a corporate head office, the more enticing the area for the Chi to move in and accumulate the luckier the building will be.

Generally, the larger the main entrance into the building, in relation to the overall size of the whole structure, the more auspicious it is. This is particularly applicable when there is a "bright hall" (such as a park or a field) across the road.

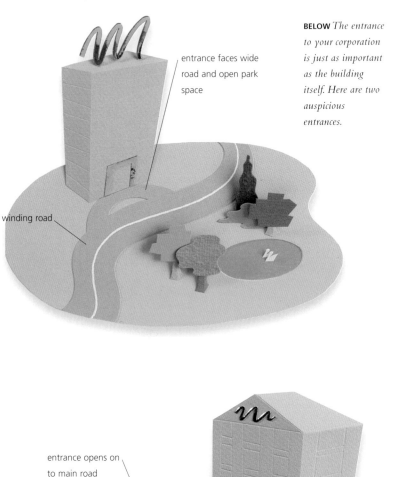

entrance faces wide road and open park space

winding road

BELOW *The entrance to your corporation is just as important as the building itself. Here are two auspicious entrances.*

entrance opens on to main road

sturdy main door

open space

steps lead up to building

THE FENG SHUI OF ROADS AROUND A BUILDING

LEFT *This curving highway resembles a prosperity-bringing river. It will bring great good fortune to those located within a mile of it.*

The number of roads that directly face a building has a serious impact on its Feng Shui. Generally, the T-junction or intersection is deadly because the building directly faces a long, straight road. If the traffic is moving towards the building the Feng Shui is extraordinarily bad because it hits the building with killing energy. Alternatively, if the traffic is moving away from the building it is taking away all the wealth of the building. Thus the T-junction or intersection is particularly to be avoided.

When the building faces a circular interchange like a

ABOVE *Siting your head office opposite a busy T-junction or intersection is likely to adversely affect your wealth luck.*

ABOVE *Roundabouts near your office can be beneficial if the traffic circulates slowly and toward the building.*

roundabout, the Feng Shui depends on how fast the traffic is flowing and whether the roads seem to bring a flow of Chi to the building. Thus, fast-flowing traffic is bad and slow-moving traffic is good. If the traffic seems to flow naturally into the building it brings good fortune. If it seems to be flowing away it is taking wealth away from the building.

When traffic seems to be flowing toward the building, good luck gets magnified when roads feed traffic into the main road passing by your building. This means there is more than one source of wealth for your building.

When analyzing the effect of roads on your office building, think of them as rivers. Feeder roads that enhance the traffic flow of the road passing by your front door always bring greater good fortune, and I have seen large corporate buildings benefit from as many as six feeder roads. This effect often becomes extra lucky when the building sits on land that is just slightly lower than the neighboring elevations. The building has the effect of being located in a valley which catches all the water, and thus all the wealth of the environment.

ABOVE *The energy of a beneficial traffic flow past your building can be increased by feeder roads.*

SEE ALSO
❖ The Significance of Roads *p.65*
❖ Create an auspicious main door *pp. 290–1*

CHAPTER TWENTY-SIX: FENG SHUI FOR CORPORATIONS

HIGHWAYS, OVERPASSES, AND RAILROAD TRACKS

RIGHT *Overpasses and overhead roads create negative energy. However, those living in the condominiums in the block here are too far away to be adversely affected by this elevated highway.*

ABOVE *It is possible to negate the harmful energies of overhead roads by planting trees.*

ABOVE *Railroad tracks can be blocked from sight by trees, but this will not totally obliterate the poison arrows.*

RIGHT *Railroads and railroad tracks "slice" through the Chi with their deadly poison arrows.*

While roads with slow-moving traffic are usually auspicious, buildings fronting fast-moving highways are quite the opposite. Just as Chi tends to dissipate in fast-flowing rivers, so it will also evaporate when traffic is moving excessively fast.

Overpasses and their overhead roads cause deadly Chi to be created for buildings that stand directly beside them. These multi-level roads are like rivers high up the mountain and they symbolize water reaching its zenith, when the danger of overflowing becomes real. This is similar to the effect of "water on mountain," one of the dangerous configurations that the *I Ching* warns against.

Overpasses are also seen as "knives" cutting into the belly of any building that stands next to it. The effect is safe when the overpass seems to embrace the building but deadly if it seems to be aimed at the building. In any case it is best not to work in buildings that are located too near to such roads.

Buildings should not be too close to railroad tracks since these are regarded as poison arrows. Railroad tracks are usually straight and trains often signify poison arrows that have to be avoided.

The best way of overcoming the dangers of these roads and arteries in the environment is to plant trees to block them off visually. If they are too close for you to do that, you should shine a bright light at the part of the building closest to the road and also hang a powerful large Pa Kua mirror aimed in the direction of the road. These cures are, however, wholly inadequate and are at best temporary measures. In the long run it might be best to try and relocate.

PROPITIOUS CORPORATE LOGOS

LEFT AND BELOW *The dragon is a traditional good luck logo but ensure any modern designs you choose do not contain inauspicious symbolism.*

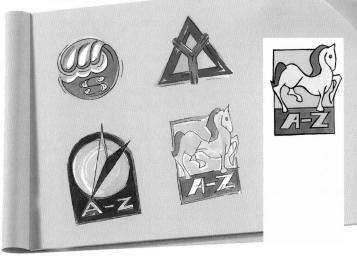

RIGHT *To create excellent corporate Feng Shui, position the company logo on the very top of the office building.*

𝕮orporate Feng Shui would not be complete without a comment on corporate logos, symbols that reflect the company. There are many good fortune symbols that can enhance the Feng Shui of corporations: the dragon is an exceedingly lucky symbol which can be incorporated into logos and brand names.

For modern corporations, however, the traditional dragon might look too oriental and it is perhaps better to design corporate logos according to these guidelines:

⚈ Avoid having logos with too many angular lines or those that resemble arrows or straight lines inadvertently pointing at your company name.

⚈ Avoid abstract designs; these might resemble words or symbols that have negative connotations.

⚈ Avoid designs that are excessively Yin or Yang. This can show up in the use and combination of colors with shapes. For instance, if you combine a triangular shape with the color red and the words are also printed in red, it makes the logo too Yang. If you use a water motif and the words are printed in blue, the logo could be excessively Yin. If possible, maintain a balance.

⚈ Incorporate the Five Element theory into the design of your corporate logo. Choose an element for your logo based on your business or industry. Thus property, mining and real-estate companies would do well to stress the earth element. Electronics companies should highlight the metal element. Plantation companies should use the wood element. Banks and financial institutions should use the water element. Restaurants can use the fire element.

⚈ Make sure you position your corporate name and logo as high up on your building as possible. Do not place your company name and logo at street level if your head office is a tall building.

ABOVE *Water symbols colored blue are too Yin.*

ABOVE *Red triangular shapes are too Yang.*

ABOVE *Abstract logos may contain negative meanings.*

ABOVE *Choose a good fortune symbol for your logo.*

ABOVE *Points and arrow shapes are not auspicious.*

AUSPICIOUS COLOR COMBINATIONS

ABOVE *Silver teamed with deep purple in the office will ensure great prosperity.*

These colors are an auspicious pairing of the water and metal elements.

ABOVE *Black lettering on a white background represents Yin and Yang in harmony as well as an auspicious combination of the water and metal elements.*

The choice of colors and color combinations affects the Feng Shui of a company because all its correspondence and publicity materials will display these colors. Some lucky combinations of colors include:

🌀 Black lettering on a white background. Black and white is an auspicious combination because it reflects the Yin–Yang balance and also signifies the harmony of the elements. Water is black, which stands for money, which derives from metal, itself signified by the color white. Thus, black and white for corporate offices and boardrooms is auspicious.

🌀 Silver on deep purple. This also signifies the balance of Yin and Yang and the harmony of water/metal elements. More than that, however, the combination of these two colors also spells money. This symbolism is particularly powerful in Cantonese-speaking places like Hong Kong: the Cantonese dialect phonetics produce the words "ngan chee," which means money.

🌀 Red and gold is a special color combination that is described as

being very, very bright. Red is the ultimate good luck color and in this case pairing it with gold doubles the significance of "wealth creation." Thus, during the lunar New Year in Chinese communities you will find red and gold are pasted on almost all the symbols of goodwill and good fortune.

🌀 Blue with black or blue with green emphasizes the water element. This combination is most auspicious for businesses that have anything to do with water, e.g. wine producers and bottlers. This color combination is also good for those in the publishing business, which benefits from the wood element.

LEFT *Red and gold are colors that individually symbolize good luck and wealth, so this color combination in the office is doubly auspicious.*

BELOW *Blue with green recreates the water element. This mix will prove lucky for water-related businesses.*

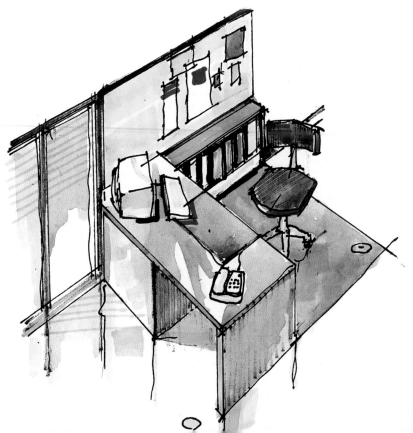

THE PLACE OF THE CEO OR MANAGING DIRECTOR

Probably the most important part of corporate Feng Shui is working out the best Feng Shui for the company CEO or managing director.

Corporate Feng Shui is like home Feng Shui: as long as the head of the family enjoys good Feng Shui, the rest of the family is assumed to benefit. Thus in a company when the CEO enjoys good Feng Shui the whole company benefits.

The CEO's office should be situated deep inside the building. The further inside the office, the more depth the company will have. The power spot in any office is the innermost corner diagonal to the entrance door. If this location also corresponds to the CEO's best direction based on his or her personalized Kua number, the effect will be doubly auspicious. If it does not coincide, make sure that the CEO sits facing his or her Sheng Chi direction inside the office. This ensures that at least the direction the CEO is facing is auspicious even though the direction on which he or she was sitting was not successfully tapped. In addition to this, the CEO's office should also avoid all the standard Feng Shui taboos. These are summarized as:

ॐ Never sit with the back to the door or window.

ॐ Do not sit directly under an exposed overhead beam. Move the desk to another position.

ॐ Do not sit with a pillar or corner edge hitting you. Place a plant to block these out.

ॐ Do not sit against a wall that has a lavatory on the other side. Change the arrangement.

ॐ Do not allow the front part of your desk to get blocked or cluttered with files or paperwork.

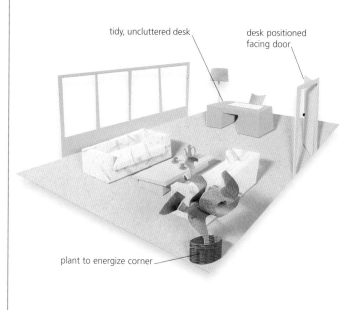

tidy, uncluttered desk

desk positioned facing door

plant to energize corner

ABOVE *Good Feng Shui should start at the top in the managing director's office – then the rest of the corporation will undoubtedly reap the rewards.*

QUESTIONS AND ANSWERS

Question: What are the three most important things for corporations to get right to enjoy good Feng Shui?

Answer: First, to ensure longevity and continuity corporations should operate out of head office buildings which enjoy good Feng Shui. Second, the office of the CEO and the corporate board room should be located in the most auspicious part of the building. And third, the company's corporate logo should be as auspicious as possible. The corporate logo should not be negative or harmful. If it is the corporation suffers acutely in an economic downturn.

Question: Does this mean that badly managed companies with good Feng Shui will still prosper?

Answer: Usually when a corporation enjoys good Feng Shui it will be able to attract efficient and hard-working staff. Decisions made will be good decisions and business judgments will be blessed with good luck.

Question: What about well-managed companies with bad Feng Shui?

Answer: When the company suffers from bad Feng Shui good staff will eventually leave, the company will suffer losses, or be taken over. It will cease to exist. Sometimes the bad Feng Shui pertains only to some of the offices, in which case staff working in the afflicted buildings will get sick and suffer misfortunes.

Question: Should corporations have their Feng Shui updated annually?

Answer: Yes. This takes care of the changing flying stars which address the time dimension of Feng Shui. Since timing plays such an important part in corporate performance I would strongly advise that it does not hurt to supplement standard management resources with Feng Shui expertise.

木火土金水

PART SEVEN

FENG SHUI TIPS FOR ALL ENVIRONMENTS

FENG SHUI CURES AND ANTIDOTES

I can safely say that almost any kind of bad energy can be remedied. Some Feng Shui disasters are easier to cure than others, but antidotes exist for almost every kind of problem. These cures may not wipe out the killing energy completely but they can dissolve a great deal of it, thereby making bad luck easier to bear. There are three theories behind the application of Feng Shui cures: the Five Element theory, which enables bad energy from the ten directions to be effectively countered; the Yin and Yang theory, which enables imbalance to become balanced; and the visual blocking methods, which enable killing energy to become deflected, dissolved, and disintegrated. Over and above these three theories are cures that perform a variety of functions in terms of overcoming bad energy. Such cures are therefore particularly popular with Feng Shui masters. Another popular cure is the windchime, also effective for overcoming many of the unlucky flying stars in the Flying Star method of Feng Shui. A partly esoteric cure for almost all kinds of bad energy derives from the techniques and rituals used for dissolving bad energy. These are the specially created sounds made from bowls and bells, and the aromas made by burning herbs from high mountainous regions.

LEFT Negative energy affects us all, but there is a wealth of Feng Shui cures and antidotes to help soften the blows of any poison arrows.

CHAPTER TWENTY-SEVEN: FENG SHUI CURES AND ANTIDOTES

THE NEED FOR FENG SHUI CURES AND ANTIDOTES

First-time practitioners of Feng Shui often mistakenly believe that Feng Shui has to be perfect to work. In reality, however, there is no such thing as a house with perfect Feng Shui. You will find yourself confronted with tough decisions that involve trade-offs between different Feng Shui schools and the different aspirations of members of the family.

In addition, remember that the environment changes over time, so it is perfectly understandable that good Feng Shui can be transformed into problematic Feng Shui.

In the same way, as time goes by one's Feng Shui luck can change; we are dealing with a dynamic situation that appears to be in a constant state of flux.

To counter the effect of Shar Chi, or killing breath, that may be caused by both tangible and intangible forces, it is vital to be aware of some of the cures that can be used to counter Feng Shui ills. Tangible forces are physical structures that block the free flow of Chi; they can also cause Chi to become hostile and threatening. Incorrect orientations, placement of bedrooms, stoves, and main doors can unleash negative intangible forces. Both tangible and intangible forces can cause loss, illness, and general misfortune.

There are several easy and effective ways of tackling Feng Shui problems. These can either deflect, dissolve, counter, or balance out the presence of negative energy or energy that is excessively Yin or Yang. These antidotes or cures also represent the application of the theory of Wuxing, or five elements, to counter environmental imbalances. Sometimes hostile objects also give out threatening energies that have to be dissolved.

Deciding on the choice of antidotes involves a certain judgment based on experience as well as knowledge of the basic fundamentals of Feng Shui. Contained in this chapter are some of the most effective ways of overcoming negative and inauspicious Feng Shui. Study them carefully and think through the basis of the recommendations. Try to relate what you read here with the fundamentals already covered.

BELOW *In modern towns and cities, it is difficult to avoid buildings and structures that cause bad Feng Shui, so do what you can to alleviate it.*

USING LIGHTS TO LIFT THE CHI

Perhaps one of the most effective ways of dissolving negative energy is to use artificially created bright lights. Apart from being an excellent source of Yang energy, which represents life, bright lights are also deemed excellent for dissolving hostile sharp corners and poison arrows. The energy of bright lights manifests the element of fire which is excellent for destroying any kinds of Shar Chi caused by intangible forces in the metal corners (west and northwest). In the same way, fire is also able to control bad energy in the wood corners of the east and southeast since fire exhausts the wood element. Listed below are some of the Feng Shui afflictions that can be cured by shining a bright light directly at them:

* Lights can dissolve the Shar Chi created by a sharp corner. This can be caused by two walls or the corner of a neighboring building. Either shine the light directly down from the ceiling as a down light positioned directly in front of the corner, or shine the light from the bottom up. Position the light exactly where the corner is created, i.e. where two walls meet, as, for instance, in a protruding corner.

* Lights can also be used to dissolve the hostile energy created by the sharp edges and heaviness of exposed overhead beams. Again, to do this, it is important that the light is positioned to shine directly at the corner of the beam.

* Lights can be very effective in enhancing the energy of tight spaces. It immediately brightens up the stale and stagnant Chi that collects in these places, which may be narrow corridors, forgotten corners, and small foyers.

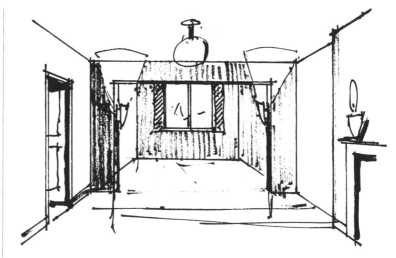

LEFT To counteract the negative effects of overhead beams, use uplighters or spotlights to illuminate them.

* If you have a toilet upstairs placed directly above your main door, installing a very bright light between the door and the toilet will help to overcome the negative Chi being sent downward. In the same way a bright light can be used to deal with lavatories that face and afflict doors in the house.

* A bright light hung directly in front of a staircase is also a good way of overcoming bad Feng Shui caused by stairs that start directly in front of the main door or end at the a bedroom door. To be effective these lights need to be left on for at least three hours every night.

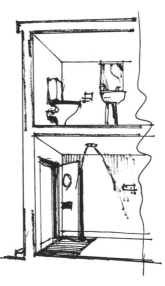

LEFT Cope with a toilet situated above the main door by installing a bright light in the hall directly below it.

BELOW If the first thing you see when you open your front door is the staircase, make sure that there is a bright hallway light to counter it.

RIGHT Chi can stagnate in unused corners: lights can be employed to prevent this.

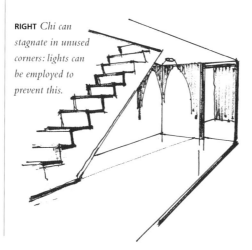

CHAPTER TWENTY-SEVEN: FENG SHUI CURES AND ANTIDOTES

USING SOUNDS TO CREATE YANG ENERGY

ABOVE *The livelier your pets, the better the level of Yang energy in the home. When children interact with pets it will further enhance the energy.*

ABOVE *A birdbath in the garden will stimulate Yang energy, benefiting you and the birds.*

Homes that are left quiet all day, perhaps because their owners are at work, tend to suffer from excessive Yin energy causing residents to become lethargic, tired, and lacking in energy. Thus, homes in which both parents work and children are at school all day will benefit from the creation of sound to break the silence. There are several ways of using sound to enhance the Yang energies of the home. These are summarized as follows:

❀ Keep pets. They represent life. Thus, cats and dogs create lots of Yang energy in the home while everyone is out. Better still if you have more than one dog or cat. Children's rooms will benefit from the presence of hamsters and the backyard will be a much happier environment if it is teeming with life. Try to have birdbaths and fruit trees in the garden to attract birds and squirrels. Grow scented flowers and plants to attract butterflies and bees. These bring Yang energies toward your home.

❀ Keep fish to create Yang energy; fish are also excellent symbols of good fortune. The bubbling water caused by oxygenation and filters

ABOVE *Inviting friends over for a sociable evening will flood your home with currents of positive Chi.*

creates wonderful Yang Chi inside the home. Good fortune fish include the dragon fish (the arrowana), the goldfish, Japanese koi carp, and all the colorful tropical fish that resemble either the goldfish or the carp. Red, gold, and silver are all considered to be good fortune colors while black fish, like the black goldfish, are particularly good at offering intangible protection Chi for the household.

❀ Encourage family members to turn on the television, the radio, or the CD player. Music playing continuously in the home encourages the flow of Chi and does much to counter the buildup of excessively Yin energy.

In my home the television is always on upstairs and downstairs and when my daughter is home music is always playing. As a result, Chi flows happily from room to room.

❀ Encourage friends to drop in and visit: good friendship brings excellent Chi into the home; laughter and happy conversation is excellent. But be careful: just as positive energy brings good Feng Shui, anger and quarreling also create negative energy, becoming Yang energy that gives off negative vibrations. Sometimes excessive anger may be due to bad flying stars and, if you think this is the case, it is a good idea to turn to the section on flying stars to study the natal chart of the home.

❀ Once a month it is a good idea to fill the home with pure sounds – those sounds that are specially created to purify the energy of the home. This can be generated with special bells or with specially made singing bowls. These bowls "sing" beautifully, clear and pure sounds created by the special mix of seven metals that include gold and silver, and send excellent, pure energies into all the rooms in the home. This type of sound is the best. In the old days specially crafted bells and bowls made to secret formulas were often used by Taoist monks (who were also Feng Shui experts) to purify the palace chambers of the emperor and his favorite concubines as well as the imposing homes of wealthy and powerful mandarins.

ABOVE *Bells and metal bowls, known as "singing bowls," resonate, when struck, with beautiful sounds to activate Chi energy.*

BLOCKING, DISSOLVING, AND DEFLECTING WITH SCREENS, WALLS, AND TREES

An important principle of Feng Shui is that, when something in the environment sends powerful poison arrow Chi toward the home, the way to avoid these arrows is to place a structure or barrier to block the straight path of the arrow. If direct blocking is not possible, the next best thing to do is to deflect the path of the arrow. This is based on the principle that negative Chi in the form of a poison arrow travels in a straight line and cannot turn or twist. Thus, as long as you can get out of its way or you can block or deflect it, your door and home can be protected.

Antidotes against poison arrows can be created with screens, trees, and walls – anything, in fact, that can create some kind of physical blockage. To strengthen the countereffect of these blockages, Feng Shui masters often build in the benefits of the five elements.

Thus, trees become powerful blocks when the source of the poison arrow Chi originates from the earth directions of southwest or northeast. This is because wood (as represented by trees) destroys earth in the cycle of control of the five elements. Trees are not as effective when the source of the poison arrow is the west or northwest since wood as an element cannot overcome metal.

Walls that are made of bricks or any kind of gravel, stone, granite, or marble composite are excellent for blocking poison arrows that come from the north. This is because earth destroys water in the cycle of the elements. Walls like these, however, would be less effective in blocking off negative Chi that originates from the east or southeast because they lose out to the wood element of these directions. Barriers made of metal, such as grilles and other metal fences erected to counter the effect of heavy structures that originate from the east or southeast, would, however, be effective.

Other Feng Shui recommendations involve a certain amount of creativity. I have been told that, when you paint your wall in a color that signifies a controlling element, there is additional potency. Thus, a wall painted red would be excellent against negative Chi coming from the west or northwest; a wall painted white would be extremely effective against bad Chi coming from the east or southeast.

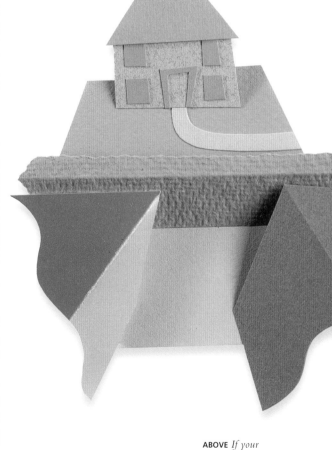

LEFT *Trees will effectively block out harmful energies. Unfortunately they take time to grow!*

ABOVE *If your house is under attack from poison arrows, create a screen to deflect them, for example plant a hedge.*

CHAPTER TWENTY-SEVEN: FENG SHUI CURES AND ANTIDOTES

USING MIRRORS TO DEFLECT BAD ENERGY

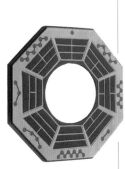

ABOVE *Concave or flat Pa Kua mirrors absorb bad Chi.*

ABOVE *A convex Pa Kua mirror reflects harmful Chi.*

The use of mirrors in Feng Shui brings results that are usually extremely good or immensely bad. Mirrors are powerful Feng Shui tools and for this reason they have to be used with care. When considering mirrors, it is important to be aware of their different uses.

❧ Convex and concave mirrors can be used as defensive reflective tools. Convex mirrors curve outward, sending the reflected bad Chi back to its source. A convex Pa Kua mirror is thus a more aggressive use of a Feng Shui tool than it would be if the mirror were flat or concave. Flat or concave mirrors draw in, absorb, and store the bad Chi until it can be removed. This is a more friendly way of using the Pa Kua. When using concave mirrors it is important to symbolically "purify" the mirror, i.e. wash it in saltwater and cleanse it with an aroma stick regularly. This ensures against the buildup of negative energy inside the mirror. In certain parts of China, where Taoist magic exerts a

LEFT *Use an aroma stick to remove negative energy buildup from concave mirrors.*

great influence over the lives of the people, Taoist Feng Shui monks are known to use mirrors to help them capture "bad" or "naughty spirits," which they then symbolically imprison in pagodas.

❧ In Feng Shui wall mirrors can be used to reflect either good or bad things. In the dining and living rooms mirrors can reflect an auspicious scene of water or a bright hall to good effect into the home. Mirrors, however, can also reflect bad symbols and harmful structures. Thus, when using mirrors it is a good idea to see what the mirror reflects. Inside the home do not allow the wall mirror to reflect the door into a lavatory or into the kitchen. Most of all, never allow the mirror to reflect the door: all this is doing is creating a flow of Chi then chasing it out again the moment it appears. Thus, mirrors facing the main door cause great harm. Over time, the father figure in such a home may fall ill. Mirrors should thus always be placed on walls in such a way that they do not reflect the doors.

❧ Mirrors can also cure the problem of missing corners. This is possible only when the missing corner in question can be "extended outward," into the area of the living room or dining room, since it does more harm than good to have wall mirrors in bedrooms or the kitchen. Mirrors are especially harmful in bedrooms. When the bed is reflected in wall or cupboard mirrors, for example, this can create great discord in marriages and relationships. Using mirrors as an antidote for missing corners is something that must be undertaken with careful thought.

❧ Mirrors can be used as a cure against freestanding square pillars.

LEFT *The poison arrows coming from sharp-edged corners can be cured with mirrors.*

LEFT *Mirrors render any harmful freestanding columns invisible.*

LEFT *The negative energy of a toilet is deflected by attaching a mirror to the door.*

Usually when you wrap a pillar with mirrors, the pillar is made to "symbolically disappear." The problem with this is that the mirror is seldom properly installed on all four sides of the pillar, as a result of which the poison arrows created by the edges of the pillars become even more malevolent. When wrapping mirrors around pillars, do make sure the edges are properly rounded off.

❧ Toilets must never be conspicuous, and mirrors can be used to make lavatory doors disappear. In fact, mirrors can make any door disappear simply because they create a feeling of depth. The door simply vanishes and in its place is the reflected view. If you have a lavatory in a particularly bad corner, e.g. in your southwest or marriage corner, which creates havoc in your love life, the best advice is to cover the door with a large mirror.

USING CRYSTALS AND SUNLIGHT

Crystals play a powerful role in creating harmony and peace at home and at work. If you find that people are quarreling incessantly about very little and you suspect that bad energy is the cause of it, crystals may be the answer to your problem. I suggest you place round crystal balls made of natural quartz crystal in the earth corners of your room, as well as in your home or office. The earth corners are the center, the southeast, and the northeast. When you place six crystal balls in the center of your home you are not only reducing friction and misunderstanding between family members but also creating auspicious and lasting Chi. It does not matter how large or small your crystal is. Crystals can create and store energy. Crystals are great purveyors of both good and bad Chi. When the Chi of the home is positive, crystals magnify this. Unfortunately, they do the same when the Chi is bad.

When you are confident that your Chi is positive and auspicious, you can enhance and magnify this good energy by placing crystals in your home. If anyone at home gets

ABOVE *A quartz crystal ball placed in the earth area of the home alleviates conflict and restores family harmony.*

BELOW *If there is tension between colleagues at work, a crystal ball in the office helps smooth relationships.*

sick, you must wash your crystal balls with saltwater every day until that person recovers. The crystals absorb all the bad energy; like sponges, they soak up all the bad Chi caused by illness, thereby cleansing and purifying the house.

Crystal balls signify smooth sailing for the members of the household, but you should also use your crystals to bring in the Yang energy from outside. Do this by setting your crystal balls for an hour in the bright morning sun so that they catch and soak up its gentle purifying rays. You can also soak the crystal balls in water that has been placed in the sunlight. This action both purifies and energizes the crystal which in turn is magnified for the house.

In Feng Shui the power of crystals comes from their great store of deepest earth energy. Crystals are also considered to be one of the most effective and potent symbols of the earth element. Since Feng Shui is earth luck, by using crystals in your home it is possible to help overcome a great deal of bad energy.

ABOVE *Crystals come in many colors, but all, like this amethyst, counter bad energy.*

ABOVE *A rose quartz crystal is an attractive ornament as well as good for Feng Shui.*

ABOVE *Turquoise is a beautiful color and will enhance earth energy in your home.*

ABOVE *The "smoky" quartz will help your deal with problems caused by bad Chi.*

CHAPTER TWENTY-SEVEN: FENG SHUI CURES AND ANTIDOTES

USING OBJECTS TO CIRCULATE CHI

Using revolving objects

Revolving objects cause Chi to circulate and their use can be an extremely effective way of overcoming Shar Chi that bombards your front door. Any number of factors or poison arrows can cause the killing energy. A revolving object works by dissolving the killing energy and transforming it into harmless energy. Thus, revolving doors are one of the best antidotes against large and damaging poison arrows that often afflict large corporate or public buildings.

If your ceilings at home are too low or there are simply too many corners and plenty of killing energy is created, the best way to deal with it is to install a revolving light. These resemble disco lights and as they revolve they stimulate

ABOVE *Revolving objects, such as fans, increase the movement of Chi around the home.*

LEFT *Installing a revolving door will whisk away poison arrows raining down on a building.*

the Chi to create wonderful, moving Yang energy. I have a colored revolving light that sends out wonderful Yang energy twenty-four hours a day. I never turn off this light and it creates beautiful Yang Chi for every member of my household, a simple but effective cure that dispels all the poison arrows inside the home.

Using boulders and stones

The use of heavy stones and boulders simulates the powerful earth energy of the mountain. This symbolism can be most powerful in overcoming the effect of toilets causing problems in the home. Place a large boulder in the bathroom symbolically to press down on the bad luck created by the toilet. This cure works in all except the southwest or northwest corners. These are earth corners and boulders positioned here merely contribute to strengthening the affliction.

RIGHT *Toilets are a malign influence on the luck of a home.* *A large stone or boulder will help reverse the trend.*

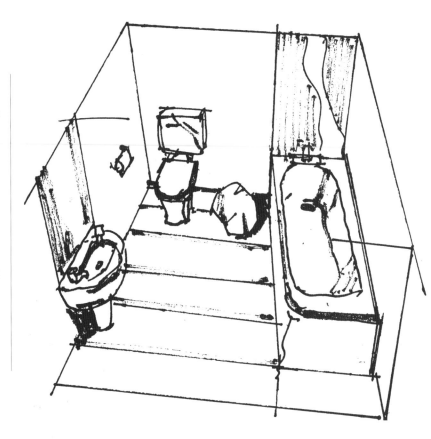

USING SYMBOLS OF PROTECTION

In Feng Shui, symbolic protection is an important part of the practice. Every serious practitioner of Feng Shui will have a number of symbols of protection strategically placed to guard the gate, or the main door (or both) of their house or property.

In China, protective symbols are everywhere – at the entrances to temples, palaces, and major public buildings. The most popular symbols are the powerful Fu dogs which are present in various shapes, sizes, and designs in millions of Chinese homes worldwide.

But, in addition to these Imperial protectors, Feng Shui also recognizes the tiger, the unicorn and various other fierce animals as protectors. There are also what are

ABOVE *Fu dogs, which look more like lions, can be used to symbolically guard the entrance to your home.*

known as door protectors and these are separated into civilian door gods and military door gods. Until the turn of the century, many wealthy Chinese homes in Malaysia and Singapore sported these colorful door gods. These deities would protect residents from harm such as being robbed, cheated, or persecuted in any way. In short, their function was to safeguard the physical well-being of the residents.

More recently, door gods have been replaced by displays of other protective deities. The most popular protective deity is Kuan Kung, originally regarded as the god of war, and patron saint of police and triads alike. Today Kuan Kung is also regarded as the god of wealth.

His image in ceramic or metal or wood, and his fierce countenance, is believed to bring protection to those in business and politics.

People as well as houses also benefited from Feng Shui enhancement and protection. Thus, auspicious symbols and objects were often worn to create good personal luck. In the old days court officials dressed in special robes adorned with auspicious symbols. The emperor himself often wore the dragon image on his robes while the empresses and concubines adorned their bodies with elaborate jewelry fashioned into images of all the good fortune symbols.

The wearing of amulets and protective charms is a very popular and widespread practice. It is regarded by some as the practice of personal Feng Shui. There are safeguards against being robbed while traveling, usually special words stamped onto thin sheets of silver or gold and then rolled and placed in a silver or gold container and worn around the neck.

There are also amulets that protect against sustaining physical injury. These can be written on special colored ricepaper, carefully folded and carried about the person. Many of these amulets are also believed to be able to "cure" specific forms of illness. Thus, those made of rice paper were often burned and drunk with a glass of water, gold or silver amulets were believed to be effective if they were dipped in water, which was subsequently drunk by the sick person.

I am ambivalent about amulets. I have avoided sustaining severe injuries in two nasty accidents, and I am told that my amulets protected me. I have no reason to disbelieve this, but remain unsure whether the wearing of amulets is truly Feng Shui. It could well be Taoist magic!

ABOVE *The dragon horse, or unicorn, is one of the most powerful symbols of protective luck.*

ABOVE *A locket containing words written on ricepaper will ward off the danger of physical harm.*

LEFT *Emperors' robes were often embroidered with dragons to further enhance the power of the dynasty.*

DIFFERENT TYPES OF WINDCHIMES

RIGHT *Windchimes made from hollow rods sound different from solid ones, but are as effective.*

ABOVE *Windchimes blend quite happily into any decorating scheme. You can enjoy their musical effects while they are hard at work fighting off unwelcome energies.*

The windchime is one of the most effective antidotes to sharp edges, protruding corners, overhead beams, and harmfully placed lavatories. When using windchimes to overcome Shar Chi, or killing breath, do use five-rod windchimes since these have the power to press down bad luck. When using windchimes for this purpose both the solid and hollow rods can be used. If there is a pagoda design built into the windchime it becomes even more potent! Remember to differentiate between windchimes that are used as a cure and those used to energize good luck.

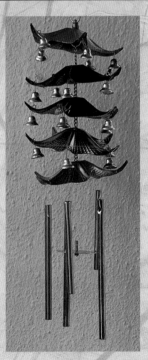

LEFT *The pagoda image included in a windchime is regarded as particularly powerful.*

LEFT *Make sure you have a windchime with five rods for countering harmful Chi.*

PROTECTIVE WRITING AND AMULETS

While it is debatable whether the wearing of amulets and protective writing is part of Feng Shui this is nevertheless a very popular section of the Tong Shu, or Chinese Almanac. In the same way that good fortune symbols are so much a part of Chinese traditional practice so too is the wearing of amulets to "protect" against bad luck, accidents, illness, and succumbing to the shenanigans of wandering spirits.

From the Tong Shu come certain specific writings which are claimed to protect the wearer from a variety of ills. These are written on colored paper, preferably yellow, but sometimes on green or red ricepaper.

ABOVE *The powerfully protective effects of this amulet guard against robbery, loss, and accidents. Some people keep it folded in their wallet to insure against losing cash or income.*

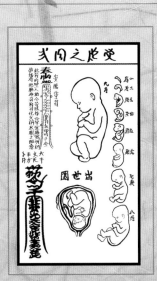

A. This is the writing that is used to protect the house against evil influences that may relish causing problems for the occupants. It must be written out on a piece of red paper and stuck on a wall near the main front door of the house.

B. This calligraphy can be used as protection in any part of the house suspected of being "haunted" by wandering spirits. It can also be placed in corners of the house where the energies feel strange, stagnant or stale – where there are "bad vibes."

C. According to the ancient Almanac, this writing is used to protect pregnant women from being affected by any killing Shar Chi that may be present in the home. The instruction from the Almanac is to copy this charm onto yellow paper, burn it, place the ashes into a glass of cold water, and then drink the water.

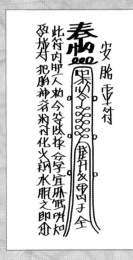

D. This writing is said to cure eye ailments and abdominal pains. Again the instruction is to burn it, and put the ashes in a glass of cold water. The water is then used to bathe the eyes. For abdominal pains, drink the water.

POISON ARROWS IN THE ENVIRONMENT

The Feng Shui of a household is good only for people whose Kua numbers, and thus whose favorable directions, coincide with the orientation of the home. Auspicious Feng Shui occurs only during certain periods according to how the specially calculated Feng Shui stars fly.

The definition of a good Feng Shui house depends on the school of Feng Shui practiced or the method of Feng Shui used. However, it is significant that all the different schools and methods of Feng Shui agree on the one thing – the danger posed by secret poison arrows in the environment. These poison arrows are created by physical structures and features within visual distance of any living space that possesses characteristics that create the Shar Chi, or killing breath. These structures usually have such potent negative power that all schools of Feng Shui recognize their malignant effect on the luck of houses they "hit," and warn against them.

This chapter on poison arrows is fundamental to the correct practice of Feng Shui. It is important to take a defensive approach and to ensure that your home is protected against poison arrows before attempting to energize and create good Feng Shui.

Even when people practicing Feng Shui move on to studying and applying very advanced formulas they must always be aware of the debilitating effects of killing breath caused by poison arrows.

LEFT *Environmental poison arrows present a great challenge to the modern Feng Shui practitioner.*

CHAPTER TWENTY-EIGHT; POISON ARROWS IN THE ENVIRONMENT

SPOTTING HIDDEN SECRET POISON ARROWS

RIGHT *There is no mistaking the poison arrows created by these power plant chimneys, which dwarf nearby houses as well as belching out pollution.*

Poison arrows in the environment are only "hidden" and "secret" if you do not know how to identify them. However, amateur practitioners should have little difficulty once they know what to look out for. There is nothing mysterious about poison arrows. There are a number of guidelines as to what constitutes a poison arrow:

❂ Anything long and straight aimed at a home or building can be classified as a poison arrow. The straighter and longer the "arrow" the more deadly will be its effect on the fortunes of the occupants of the home or building. The most common form of this type of arrow is a long, straight road that joins another road at 90°. Most Chinese are brought up never to live in a house that stands at a T-junction or intersection since the killing Chi which hits at the house will be like "tigers in the night" attacking the residents. The effect is a great deal worse if the main front door is directly facing the road. When the direction of the main front door is moved in a way that deflects the effect of the road, the poison arrow will also be successfully deflected. Another method of dissolving the effect of such a feature is to ensure the level of the house is higher than the road coming straight at it, thus putting the house above the poisonous breath and successfully averting misfortune. A further method is to build a solid high wall (at least 6 feet/2m high) to block out the road. This option is open only to those with enough land since having a high wall too near the house causes another kind of Feng Shui problem. Finally, if all else fails, you might want to consider growing a clump of bushy

trees; these can be very effective in deflecting all the killing breath introduced by the straight road.

❂ Anything that is pointed, sharp, and directly faces the front of the home – and, more especially, is aimed directly at the main front door – is extremely harmful. This can take the form of the sharp edge of a building across the road, the corner of a big building or a large pillar, or a signboard placed in such a way that it seems to be pointing at your entrance. These take on the negative energy of a poison arrow and should be deflected immediately with a mirror. An excellent method of deflecting such a poison arrow is to use a Pa Kua

mirror, the eight-sided Feng Shui symbol with a small, round mirror in the center. Use a Pa Kua with a concave mirror to absorb all the negative energy. I would, however, urge caution when using the Pa Kua. Try to use it only as a last resort: the Pa Kua sends out hostile energy which has the power to combat the killing energy of poison arrows. As such, if you place your Pa Kua high above your doorway to deflect something harmful from across the road, it is advisable to make sure you are not inadvertently hurting a neighbor's house opposite. Hang the Pa Kua above your door facing outward, and never hang it inside the home or

THE FENG SHUI OF ROOFS

POISON ARROWS

Unfavorable

Unfavorable roof shapes are characterized by their:
- Uneven shape.
- Irregular elevation.
- Continuous sloping appearance. This third type is the most inauspicious since it implies that money or wealth is flowing away from the house down the slope, and the occupants are unable to hang onto it.
- Roofs that have blue tiles represent water. Water above a mountain is considered to be a sign of extreme danger and loss. I know of several business tycoons who actually lost their fortunes during a downturn in the economy. All of them either have head offices with blue roofs or they had built a swimming pool in their penthouse suite on the topmost floor of their corporate head office.

Favorable

Favorable roof shapes are regular and even. Their color should be either red, maroon, brown, or gray. Blue and green roofs are definitely not recommended. The best roof designs resemble gentle, undulating slopes that curve upward at the edges. These indicate wealth and prosperity as well as peace and harmony among the residents. It is better not to have a hole in the center of the roof line. Unless the roof opening is an open-air courtyard, a hole in the roof line can be a dangerous feature, so I discourage it.

BELOW *Inspect the roofs in your vicinity to assess whether they are casting any poison arrows toward your property.*

ABOVE *An upward-curving roof brings financial security for the residents.*

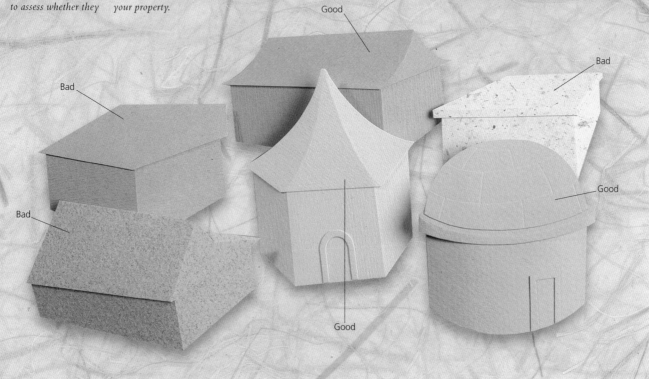

Good / Bad / Bad / Bad / Good / Good

ABOVE *A house facing onto a T-junction or intersection suffers from negative energy aimed directly at the main door.*

neighbor's roof is usually the source of just such a poison arrow. The easiest way of dealing with this problem is to use the Pa Kua mirror, which means sending killing energy back toward your neighbor. A more friendly way of dealing with such a problem is to grow a tree with plenty of foliage and, preferably, big, round leaves. Another effective way of deflecting poison arrows is to hang a five-rod windchime directly above your main door. Use a reasonably large windchime with rods at least 1 foot (30cm) in length. A windchime made of wood (usually bamboo) in this instance will be more powerful than one made of metal.

office because it then turns its great power against occupants. Instead of a Pa Kua you can also use a wall or a clump of trees to dissolve the killing energy of anything sharp pointed in your direction.

❷ Anything that is triangular in shape and peaked is also harmful. This sends killing fire energy your way and can be a powerful force in ruining careers and causing loss of income. The pointed edge of a

❷ Anything that appears to symbolize an obstacle like a big cross is also considered a poison arrow. For this reason it is advisable not to live directly across from a church or any kind of public building that has a large cross as part of its façade, In Hong Kong, there are enormous crosses in the elevation of the Bank of China building and these were believed to have caused Feng Shui problems for the colonial Governor's house since the crosses pointed directly at the old mansion. Sometimes two criss-crossing escalators can also create problems for the building across the road. This was the case in one of the most celebrated Feng Shui "wars" in downtown Kuala Lumpur in Malaysia. The escalators of a building created a big X directly in front of a building across the road, causing sales of the company the building housed to drop dramatically. A Feng Shui master was brought in and he recommended placing an antique cannon aimed directly at the escalators (and therefore at the building across the road). Sales quickly recovered but the business of the occupants of the building with the escalators suffered from bad Feng Shui thereafter.

RIGHT *An innocent-looking signpost pointing in the direction of your house is actually a poison arrow.*

THE USE OF CANNONS IN FENG SHUI

As an antidote to large poison arrows that are hard to deal with, the antique cannon is immensely effective. Antique cannons that have been to war are believed to be extra potent in fighting off the killing energy caused by large, manmade structures. There are also potency differences between "male" and "female" cannons. The shorter, broader female cannons are believed to be more powerful.

Cannons are really the ultimate killing energy symbol. Antique cannons that have tasted blood are quite deadly. If something like that is facing your entrance it will bring losses, illness and severe bad luck. Because of this the cannon as a defensive measure should be used only as a last resort as it will almost certainly bring misfortune to whoever

bears the brunt of its strength. If you find that your house is directly facing a cannon (i.e. if you live near a Department of Defense or near a war museum where cannons traditionally flank the doorway), I suggest the best way of countering the severe killing energy from the cannons is to place another cannon – a male cannon to face a female cannon and vice versa. Anything hostile and overpowering symbolizes not one but a whole army of poison arrows – a

large industrial chimney, an aggressive looking sculpture, a transmission tower or simply a building with fierce edges and sharp pointed façades. Living in the vicinity of such overpowering, man-made structures poses serious Feng Shui problems that are hard to solve. The negative energy is usually too intimidating to be effectively countered. Move away at the first opportunity, but otherwise, the best thing to do is try to change the orientation of your home altogether so that the hostile structure is not directly facing the front of your home. In other words, move the entrance of your home to the opposite side to the hostile structure. This transforms it into a powerful protector. If you cannot do this, find another door to use as the front door.

DRIVEWAYS

The approach to your house can also become a poison arrow if you are not careful. Generally, the approach to the house should be friendly and driveways should always be wide, even, and curved rather than straight and threatening. Driveways that come straight at the house are regarded as poison arrows. They become more harmful if they seem to get narrower as they get nearer the door. This makes them resemble an arrow even more. A driveway parallel to the house is not harmful, nor is it if it is by the side of the house. Feng Shui prescribes circular driveways as being auspicious. If this is not possible, try having a meandering approach.

ABOVE *A geometrically precise driveway leading straight to the house is bad.*

Straight driveways can be effectively softened with clever landscaping that makes use of plants and flowering bushes to break up and camouflage sharp, straight lines.

Driveways should not slope downward, away from the house. This causes Chi to flow outward, thus draining away money and good fortune. Driveways that are either too narrow or too disproportionately wide are also inauspicious. The guideline to follow is to design a driveway that works with the dimensions of the house and does not inadvertently become a poison arrow.

Driveways that are narrower than the main door are inauspicious. A driveway that narrows outward or inward suggests a lack of financial opportunities, and is bad for business and for careers. If you have this sort of driveway either regularize it or place lights at the narrow ends.

BELOW *Curving driveways are the best option.*

CHAPTER TWENTY-EIGHT: POISON ARROWS IN THE ENVIRONMENT

DEALING WITH POISON ARROWS

ABOVE *Children are particularly susceptible to poison arrows, so take whatever steps you can to minimize their effects.*

The most immediate effect of being hurt by poison arrows is usually financial loss or illness. The severity of these misfortunes depends on the individual's astrological chart. Usually young children are the first to succumb to illnesses caused by harmful poison arrows. Thus, if you have only recently moved into a new home and your children seem to take turns getting sick, or when the bug seems to be passing from one occupant of the house to another, look around for secret poison arrows. This is the first line of Feng Shui investigation.

Usually the negative effects of poison arrows outside the home are far more powerful than those found inside the home. They must therefore be addressed as soon as you discover them. At their worst, poison arrows can cause severe illness and even death. A severe and hostile structure can wipe out the fortunes of an entire family.

There are three main methods of dealing with poison arrows:
* Create structures to block and deflect the killing energy.
* Introduce barriers to dissolve the killing energy.
* Place a hostile structure to counter the killing energy.

RIGHT *Tailor your blocking and deflecting methods according to the direction of the poison arrows.*

Blocking and deflecting is best achieved with solid barriers and mirrors. When the poison arrow is visually blocked out of sight its killing energy is deemed to have been effectively deflected. This can be achieved with a wall or a hedge. To make your antidote more powerful, fine tune as follows:
* If the poison arrow is coming at you from the south, build a wall that has water running down it.
* If the poison arrow originates from the north, build a brick wall.
* If the poison arrow is coming from the east or southeast, build a wall with metal grilles. The grilles should be painted gold or chrome to be a more effective counter.
* If the poison arrow is coming from the west or northwest, build a wall and paint it bright red.
* If the poison arrow is coming from the southwest or northeast, plant a thorny hedge.

Dissolving killing energy that is coming toward the house is usually the best antidote. Plant a clump of trees between the poison arrow and the front of the home. The leaves rustling in the breeze dissolve lethal poison arrows, especially those from the southwest or northeast.

A second way of dissolving killing energy is to install a bright, powerful light between the entrance of the home and the poison arrow. This technique works best if the poison arrow is coming from the west or northwest.

A third way is to hang a large metal windchime between the poison arrow and the front of the house. This method is particularly effective if the poison arrow is coming from the east or southeast.

If the threat is from the north, a small mound of rocks in front of the house effectively dissolves the poison arrow; if it originates from the south a water feature with fairly fast-moving water, such as a fountain, would be a good solution.

A more aggressive method of dealing with poison arrows involves the use of mirrors to reflect back the poison arrow so that it hurts the source of the negative energy. A second method is the use of something hostile, like a cannon. Using either a mirror or a cannon suggests fighting back; while this may sometimes be necessary it is always better to counter poison arrows using the first two methods unless there is absolutely no choice.

metal grilles deflect arrows from the east or southeast

deflect poison arrows from the south with a wall that has water running down it

a red wall safeguards the west or northwest

hedges protect the southwest and northeast

a brick wall blocks poison arrows from the north

FIERCE ROOF DESTROYS FENG SHUI OF TAIWAN BANK

On 18 February 1998 the BBC News carried an interesting story about the tragic death of a Taiwanese bank governor who had been aboard an ill-fated China Airlines plane which crashed near Chiang Kai-shek international airport two days earlier. Governor Sheu Yuan-dong and his officials were among 200 passengers on board the China Airlines flight. He was returning from a meeting of regional central bankers that had been held in Bali, Indonesia.

The tragic deaths of the governor and four other top officials of the Taiwanese Central Bank in that plane crash were apparently the latest in a host of calamities to hit the institution. According to a Taiwan newspaper, the *Economic Daily News*, the bank has been plagued by bad luck since it moved to new premises in 1994. The bank's former governor, Liang Kuo-shu, and Chang Pao-hsi, director of the foreign exchange department, had also both died during their tenures at the bank.

Local gossip has it that these calamities were not merely an unfortunate series of coincidental random events. Many attributed the bank's problems to bad Feng Shui.

The paper reported that the bank had long been criticized for its bad Feng Shui design. Construction of the square-shaped, multistorey, concrete building was reportedly hampered by a number of setbacks: bankruptcy of the construction company; a fire on the roof; and a worker being injured when he fell off the building.

According to the report, the front of the Central Bank headquarters directly faces the roof corner of the traditional National Theater hall. This is a Feng Shui taboo. Feng Shui believers say the roof corner of the theater acted as a focus, gathering and directing negative energies directly onto the bank.

Practitioners had recommended a series of improvements to ward off the effects of bad Feng Shui but the paper said these were ignored.

THE KILLING EDGES OF MULTISTOREY BUILDINGS ARE ESPECIALLY DANGEROUS

Possibly one of the hardest poison arrows to combat, and one which creates the most severe negative Feng Shui, is that caused by the sharp edge of a very tall, imposing building; instances of this can be seen in cities where planning approvals have been given with no thought to balance and harmony. Thus, when buildings are constructed next to each other with no Feng Shui input whatsoever, buildings could well find themselves directly facing the edge of another building. This will have a severely dampening effect on the profits of the residents of the building that is being hit. The most effective cure in such a situation is to change the entrance of the building. Otherwise, introduce a revolving door to dissolve the negative energy by slowing it down. In Taiwan, many big office buildings have their edges rounded

RIGHT *Sharp-edged multistorey buildings send out poison arrows to smaller buildings nearby.*

out precisely so as not to hit neighboring buildings. In New York, the grid pattern of city blocks and roads ensures that the chances of buildings being adversely affected by the negative energy generated by edges of surrounding buildings are considerably reduced.

TRIANGULAR ROOF LINES CAUSE DOORS TO BECOME AFFLICTED

One of the most common manifestations of poison arrows afflicting residential homes is the presence of a triangular roof line that directly faces the front door of one's home. This kind of structure particularly hurts a house if it is coming from the west or the northwest, from the east or southeast. The negative fire energy represented by such a feature causes a great deal of misfortune. Use the blocking, deflecting, or dissolving methods to counter this kind of poison arrow.

CHAPTER TWENTY-EIGHT; POISON ARROWS IN THE ENVIRONMENT

TREES, POLES, AND STRUCTURES

Poison arrows do not necessarily appear as imposing structures. They can be created almost anywhere and appear in different forms, such as telephone poles, For Sale signs, mailboxes, and even single trees. The effect of such features is usually a lot less severe than poison arrows caused by large, imposing structures and it is easy to deal with them. Simply place a small Pa Kua mirror to reflect the offending feature and the killing energy will have been effectively negated.

It is unnecessary to go for overkill, but these arrows, though small, do have to be dealt with. Trees become hostile when they present themselves as solid trunks facing your door. A clump of trees is not a problem, only a single tree trunk. Often, hanging a metal

FAR RIGHT Planting an imposing tree with dense foliage, and preferably large, round leaves, wards off negative energies heading for your house.

windchime is sufficient to deal with this problem.

As for telephone poles and other similar obstacles, you can either use a Pa Kua or hang a very bright light outside your front door.

LEFT If you can persuade birds to congregate on the wires of a telephone pole that is overshadowing your house, they will help to dispel its effects! A more conventional solution is to block its energies with a Pa Kua mirror.

CLEVER USE OF TREES

Trees are wonderful friends of good Feng Shui. As trees grow their leaves absorb the poisons that cause air pollution and are thus Nature's way of protecting the environment. When used cleverly, trees bring a great deal of luck to any home. It is thus useful to note some pointers:

🍃 Never grow trees too near to the house or they will overwhelm it with their immense growth energy.
🍃 Never plant a tree directly in front of the main door. It will make it hard for auspicious Chi to enter.
🍃 Always prune trees so that their growth is controlled.

🍃 Always choose your variety of trees carefully so that they stay in balance.
🍃 Grow trees mainly at the back of the house and in the east.

Trees can form a protective barrier between a busy main road and a house.

Trees planted behind a house block out poison arrows.

It is best if trees are grown some way back from the house.

Trees lining both sides of the main entrance ensure Chi can enter the house.

If the house is sited next to a hill, planting a tree will shield it from harm.

Confronting a mountain, wall, or building

If your front door opens onto a high wall or if there is a tall building directly in front of your home, the configuration is very inauspicious, but such a feature is not necessarily a poison arrow. However, the effect is similar to that caused by a poison arrow. The best method of dealing with this unlucky configuration is to re-orientate the house by moving the main door to the back in such a way as to place the wall or building – i.e. the mountain – behind.

If this is not possible, the other alternative is to install very bright lights in front of the house, and keep these lights turned on.

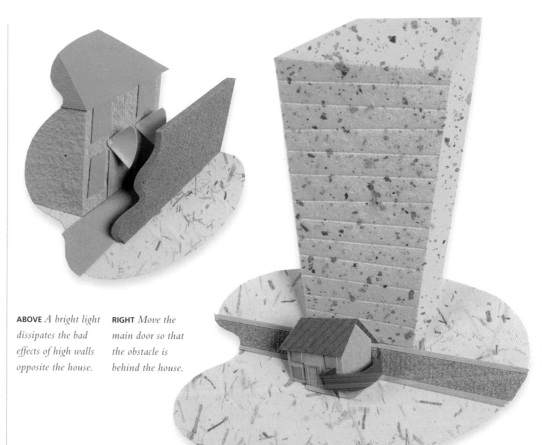

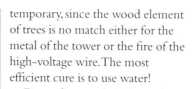

ABOVE *A bright light dissipates the bad effects of high walls opposite the house.*

RIGHT *Move the main door so that the obstacle is behind the house.*

Dangerous structures

There are a number of structures you should be wary of, such as tall electricity transmission towers. Not only do they look physically intimidating, but the high-voltage tension wires associated with these towers emit dangerously strong Chi which can overpower and kill all other energy around them.

Living anywhere near these transmission towers will subject occupants to the danger of serious, even fatal illnesses. All other luck will also be at dangerously low levels. It is hard to combat such powerful energy and it is wiser to move away. If you cannot move away, try building a small pond to negate the fiery energy of the tower; you should definitely paint the outside of your house blue. Another way of overcoming the negative effects of transmission towers is to block them out with big trees. This antidote is at best temporary, since the wood element of trees is no match either for the metal of the tower or the fire of the high-voltage wire. The most efficient cure is to use water!

Depending on their size and design, bridges can also be problematic. Large iron or steel bridges tend to be places of excessively high energy levels that are simply too Yang and too powerful when they are near residential houses. Traffic patterns around these kinds of bridges generate intense movement and high concentrations of energy. Houses located at either end of the bridge will suffer from excessive Yang energy and residents will be unsettled and unbalanced. Situations of conflict will also arise. These locations are suitable for commercial developments such as a shopping center, bus or railroad station, or places of entertainment.

ABOVE *Water tackles problems from the south.*

LEFT *Electricity transmission towers are very harmful structures.*

SEE ALSO
❖ Yin and Yang Feng Shui *p.28–9*
❖ Highways, Overpasses, and Railroad Tracks *p.298*

CHAPTER TWENTY-EIGHT: POISON ARROWS IN THE ENVIRONMENT

YIN BUILDINGS

ABOVE *Spires on places of worship are capable of radiating killing energy, if your main door faces one.*

RIGHT *Churches are sources of great energy, but houses nearby will be overwhelmed by it.*

Places of worship

Places of worship such as temples, churches, and mosques do not send out killing energies and they are not sources of poison arrows. Nevertheless, Feng Shui warns against living too near to such places simply because the energy around them is too strong and any home will be overshadowed. In addition, the energy is usually more Yin than Yang and is thus not very suitable for residential living.

It is also a good idea to avoid living near the spires and crosses of a church since these are structures that can emit killing energy. If your main door faces such a structure either use another side door as the main door or plant a tree between your door and the cross.

Hospitals and prisons

Finally, a major precaution to take in the practice of Form School Feng Shui is to avoid living too close to places where there is a great deal of sickness, death, and unhappiness. Hospitals have great stores of Yin energy. The collective Chi of hospitals tends to generate excessive negative Chi. If you live near a hospital, keep your home well lit and filled with Yang energy. Play music and introduce more red and more bright, vibrant colors into your home.

BELOW *To counteract negative Chi, decide on a decorating scheme that incorporates red and plenty of bright colors.*

LEFT *Inmates' crimes infect prisons and permeate the surrounding environment with negativity – not the best place to live.*

The same advice applies to those who live near police stations and prisons. The negative energy emitted by such places tends to be of a more violent type, perhaps associated with killing and death. Thus you would also want to avoid living nearby if possible.

It is always advisable to do some research before buying your home to make sure that it is not built on land formerly occupied by hospitals, prisons, police stations, or other equally Yin places. Negative Chi tends to cling to such places and it will require the application of strong space clearing and purification methods to make the building habitable, let alone achieve a degree of auspiciousness.

AUTHOR'S CASUARINA TREE CAUSES CHILDLESSNESS FOR NINE YEARS

During the initial years of our marriage we desperately wanted to start a family but my husband and I were to remain childless for nine years. In those days Feng Shui meant very little to me. I was introduced to it by Master Yap Cheng Hai during our weekly kung fu exercise classes with him, but for a long time I did not take him seriously. One day Master Yap came to my house and commented, without being prompted, "No wonder you cannot have a baby . . . look at this tree in front of your main door," and indeed he was right. The beautiful casuarina tree stood tall and imposing not 10 feet (3m) away from our front door. Master Yap continued, "Unless you cut down this tree, not only will you not have a baby, even your marriage will break up!"

The house we lived in did not belong to us, and we certainly could not chop down the tree. Meanwhile our marriage was floundering and eventually we separated. I flew to the States to do my MBA – it was for me a form of escapism. While I was away, my husband supervised the building of our own home (where we still live today). Master Yap had been given a free hand to design our Feng Shui and he designed the house to enhance our descendants' luck. Our bedroom was located in my husband's *Nien Yen* corner and we were sleeping in his Sheng Chi direction (in Feng Shui if you wish to energize anything to do with the family's luck it is the man's direction you must follow).

After I returned from the States we moved into our new home and not six months later I found myself pregnant with Jennifer, our daughter. I did not know it then but that happy event was to be the seed that would eventually convince me to write about the wonders of Feng Shui.

QUESTIONS AND ANSWERS

Question: We have just moved and there are some beautiful trees growing very close to the front of the house. Is this bad Feng Shui?

Answer: Trees provide wonderful Yang energy but they can be harmful if placed too close to the home, since they will overwhelm the occupants. Trees are best planted away from the home where they can exert a protective influence by deflecting negative energies.

Question: We live in a detached house next door to a church, but I've heard that according to Feng Shui principles this is not auspicious. Is this true?

Answer: Yes, the energy emanating from most religious buildings is mostly Yin and will cause an imbalance. Plant a tree between your house and the church to encourage Yang energy.

Question: My bathroom is situated above the front door – is there any way I can improve the negative energy it is sending out?

Answer: Placing a light in your hallway directly beneath the bathroom is the best antidote. Lighting is an excellent source of Yang energy and will help to dispel any bad Chi.

Question: Everyone in our family is out at work during the day, how can I counteract an excess of Yin energy caused by a quiet empty house?

Answer: Playing music encourages the circulation of Chi – you could even leave the radio on while you are out at work to keep it circulating. A bubbling aquarium full of healthy fish will also have the same effect. I would also advise investing in a singing bowl, these beautiful objects create wonderful, pure sounds to cleanse the home and generate Chi energy.

木火土金水

木火土金水

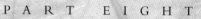

PART EIGHT

FENG SHUI DICTIONARY

A

ALMANAC The Chinese book of auspicious dates. The Tong Shu (also T'ung Shu), or the Chinese Almanac, is one of the oldest books in the world. It originated more than 4,000 years ago and contains the largest number of divination systems ever gathered together in a single volume. The heart of the book is its calendar, which is based on the Chinese Ganzhi, or lunar system, of calculating the days and seasons of the year. The Tong Shu contains auspicious dates for undertaking a variety of daily activities, from selecting the best days for starting a new business to washing and cutting one's hair, to performing harvesting and planting rituals. The Chinese Almanac is one of the most comprehensive and traditional collections of Chinese beliefs and practices in existence. The Tong Shu contains references to Feng Shui practice that are based on flying star calculations of auspicious and inauspicious days for undertaking a variety of domestic and business activities.

ALTAR Let your altar face the door directly. There are basic rules for propitious placing of altars. The Chinese generally believe it is extremely auspicious to have the altar directly facing the front door, so that the minute we walk into our homes we can see the altar. From a Feng Shui point of view, it is also recommended that the altar be placed in the northwest section of the house or living room, since this sector represents the trigram Chien, which in turn symbolizes heaven and heavenly deities. Irrespective of where you place your altar, you should always ensure that your Buddha, Kwan Yin, or any other deity be in an elevated position. The Feng Shui dimension most suitable for altars is at least 60 inches (150cm) high. The altar must always be clean. Keeping lights on continuously, apart from representing auspicious light offerings to the deity, also attracts good Chi energy.

AMULETS A practice popular with the Chinese is the wearing of amulets that are believed to ward off bad luck caused by wandering spirits in the environment. The Chinese believe that young children are particularly vulnerable to these wandering spirits, and many parents obtain special symbols from the temple or use those specially created for them by Taoist priests. It is debatable if this practice can be considered as part of Feng Shui practice. The author herself used to wear protective amulets as a child.

ANTIDOTES Feng Shui antidotes, or cures, are available for almost all Feng Shui problems. Some work better than others and correctly choosing which antidote to use is one of the skills of the Feng Shui master. There are many different antidotes and these are generally summarized as follows. Use:
☯ Bright lights to dissolve bad energy.
☯ Yang energy – lights, sound, and bright colors – to overcome excessive Yin energy.
☯ Windchimes, especially four-rod windchimes, to diffuse bad energy.
☯ The Pa Kua mirror to deflect killing energy.
☯ Bells and singing bowls to purify stagnant space.
☯ Crystals to soften excessive Yang energy.
☯ Colors to correct element imbalance.
☯ Curtains and blinds to deflect bad energy.
☯ The compass to change to more auspicious directions.
☯ Crystals to diffuse excessively strong Yang energy.
☯ Element therapy to correct disharmony.

ANTIQUES Danger of harmful left-over energy. The danger with displaying antiques in the home is that you are unlikely to know the luck of the people who last owned the piece, or the quality of the Chi that still clings to the antique. It may contain very negative energy that could bring bad luck to whoever possesses it. It is particularly risky to keep antique cannons and firearms in the house, because these, especially if they come from clan homes, are likely to have "tasted" blood before.

AQUARIUM A water feature that brings good Feng Shui. It is a good idea to activate the wealth sector of the office (the southeast corner) by introducing a water feature. An aquarium containing lively fish symbolizes growth and activity. You can also activate the southeast corner of your home with an aquarium. However, do not place your aquarium or fishpond on the right-hand side of your front door (standing on the inside looking out) for this may cause husbands to stray or encourage a roving eye.

ARCHWAYS Can be auspicious if they are not overdone. The curved shape of the arch is an auspicious shape because there are no angles to send out harmful poison arrows to the surrounding living space. An archway is more conducive to harmonious Feng Shui than square doorways in the home. Archways also suggest the circular shape that represents the element of gold. They are especially lucky when placed in the northwest and west of the home. They should preferably not be seen in the east and southeast.

ARMCHAIR Formation in Landscape Feng Shui. A vivid way of describing the perfect location for your home is the "armchair formation" of Landscape Feng Shui. This symbolism is part of the Form School. The armchair formation suggests that ideally the home should have higher land at the back (known as the black turtle) to provide support, like the back of an armchair. The left-hand side of the home should be higher, because this is deemed to be the place of the green dragon. The land to the right of your home is the place of the white tiger and should be lower than the dragon. If land on your right is higher than land on your left, the tiger becomes overbearing and dangerous. In front of the home is the red phoenix, which acts as the "footstool." Ideally there should be a small hump just in front of your home.

ARROWANA With its silver scales and sleek, swordlike body, the arrowana has long been used by Chinese businessmen in Malaysia, Singapore, and Thailand to bring good fortune. Also known as the "dragon fish," it is best kept singly or in threes or fives, but never in pairs. When the arrowana is well fed and healthy, it emits a pink or golden glow; it is this glow which is said to bring good fortune. If you wish to keep arrowanas, you should make sure they are well fed and well-looked after. Only strong, vibrant arrowanas have the capacity to bring you great wealth. The aquarium which houses this fish should not be cluttered with water plants or seaweed or have too much sand. A large, bare aquarium will serve to accentuate the beauty and the abundance of the fish. The aquarium is best kept in the north corner since this is the water corner. The aquarium can also be kept in the east or southeast, which are wood corners. This is because water is harmonious with wood. Never keep arrowana in your bedroom.

ARROWS Symbolic of killing energy. Among the most dreaded Feng Shui taboos are secret poison arrows caused by hostile structures in the landscape. *See also* Poison Arrows.

ART There are Feng Shui implications in the art you hang in your home or office and these can cause good or bad Feng Shui without you being aware of it. Indeed, the subject, color, and orientation of paintings all have Feng Shui implications; it is therefore important to consider your paintings seriously when you hang them. The rules for hanging paintings are:
☯ Avoid hanging abstract art in colors that clash with the element of the wall on which you are hanging the painting. Thus, do not hang art depicting metal

objects or those that are painted substantially in white or metallic colors in the wood corners (the east or southeast). In the destructive cycle metal destroys wood; the elements are in disharmony and the painting is creating problems for the wood corner. If you occupy a room in this corner you will suffer from the clash of energies.

❧ If you wish to hang portraits of the monarch, or perhaps the founder of your company, the best wall would be the northwest, since this activates the luck of the trigram Chien. This trigram represents the patriarch, or leader, and hanging a painting of a leader in the northwest creates exceptionally good mentor luck.

❧ The best art to have in the office is landscape art, because Feng Shui is about the landscape. If you can fold landscape into your office in an unobtrusive manner, you will enjoy harmonious Feng Shui. A mountain painting behind your seat symbolizes support. This is one of the best features to create for good Feng Shui in the office.

❧ A painting of water or a stream in front of your desk at work effectively simulates water bringing great good fortune to your office. Paintings of rivers, lakes, and waterfalls are therefore to be hung in front of you and never behind.

❧ Similarly, a painting or a picture of a big, open field in front of you symbolizes the bright hall. This symbolism is enormously lucky, whether real or as a painting, since it suggests a complete and total absence of obstacles. A big, open field suggests that everything will be smooth in your business and in your career.

❧ Make use of the good fortune symbols of Feng Shui by hanging paintings of fruit and flowers that symbolize abundance and auspicious fortunes.

❧ Avoid paintings of wild animals such as lions, tigers, leopards, and eagles inside the home or office. They serve you excellently outside, to protect you and your family, but inside the home they can turn against you and bring ill-fortune, illness, and bad luck.

❧ Avoid so-called character or intellectual art that shows wizened old men or art that records the tragedies of our age. It is far more auspicious to hang paintings of new life and happy occasions. Remember that everything hung on the walls of your home or office affects the Feng Shui of your home or office.

ASTROLOGY Chinese astrology, or fortune-telling, is often confused with the practice of Feng Shui. This is due to the overlap of basic concepts, such as those of Yin and Yang, and the theory of the five elements used in both sciences. Also, many practitioners of the art of divination, especially in Hong Kong, incorporate Feng Shui advice in their recommendations, notably those who use the Four Pillars method of divination. This method is also known as the Paht Chee, or Eight Characters, and is based on the element that is discerned to be "missing" from one's astrological chart. The fortune-teller will advise siting a main door or a sleeping direction that energizes the element that is missing. This method thus uses the Five-Element theory exclusively and is also based on the subjective judgment of the person undertaking the astrological reading. A second method of Chinese astrology is the Purple Star, said to be especially accurate in predicting good and bad periods of one's life. It is the nearest thing to Western astrology but the "stars" it uses in the chart are imaginary stars. Unlike Western astrology, Chinese astrology does not chart the movements of the planets.

AUSPICIOUS FENG SHUI This means enjoying various types of Feng Shui luck. Good fortune in Feng Shui usually refers to eight categories of luck and these include: enjoying wealth, success, and prosperity; having good family life and relationships; enjoying good health and having a long life; enjoying a good love life/marriage; having good descendants' luck, i.e. children who bring honor to the family; enjoying power and the patronage of mentors; having a good education; enjoying a good reputation and becoming famous. Specific Feng Shui measures can be energized to encourage each of these eight different types of good fortune. All the different schools of Feng Shui stress these eight types of mankind aspirations, and if even one of these aspects of good luck is missing, life, and therefore the Feng Shui, is deemed to be incomplete.

B

BAD FENG SHUI The antithesis of good luck. Misfortunes caused by Feng Shui often occur frequently and come so thick and fast that you will not fail to see a pattern developing. Thus, if everyone in the home takes turns getting sick, encountering loss, accidents, and problems at work, you should consider if some structure or alignment may be hurting your home. Almost every kind of negative Feng Shui feature can be diffused to some extent. Certain configurations and arrangements may be harder to deal with than others but all negative arrangements can be ameliorated.

BALANCE Means applying the Yin and Yang concept to Feng Shui. Feng Shui is about balance. This balance is struck between two cosmic forces, Yin and Yang. These two opposing yet complementary energies shape the universe and everything in it. Together, they form a balanced whole known as the Tao – or "the Way" – the eternal principle of heaven and earth in complete harmony. Achieving good Feng Shui has much to do with balancing the concepts of Yin and Yang. One should never forget, when practicing the science of Feng Shui, that balance is everything. Without balance, your Feng Shui will not be auspicious. *See* Yin Energy *and* Yang Energy.

BALCONIES Must be oriented correctly vis-à-vis the entrance. It is not a good feature to have balconies that open in a straight line from the front entrance of the home. This creates an inauspicious flow of energy.

BAMBOO An excellent Feng Shui plant signifying longevity. It is also an extremely useful Feng Shui tool. Bamboo stems can be used in the same way as windchimes, with hollow rods or wooden flutes, to counter the heavy killing breath of an overhead beam. They should be hung in pairs, slanted toward each other at the top, in such a way as to allow the auspicious Chi to rise up to counter the killing breath being emitted from the overhead beam. Because bamboo stems emit no tinkling sound to provide energy, to transform the Chi into friendly and auspicious energy the bamboo stems should be tied together with a piece of red string. The color red will bring out the Yang energy needed. Bamboo stems are also an excellent tool for slowing down Chi. If you have long corridors in your house, the rooms at the end of such corridors suffer from Shar Chi, the killing breath, rushing headlong toward them. This fast-moving Chi can be slowed down using bamboo stems hung in the same way as described above, with a red piece of thread tied between them. These hollow stems encourage the poisonous Chi to rise up through them and in the process turn the Chi into friendly Sheng Chi. The best way to counter a long corridor is to block the room it hits by using a screen or divider of some sort; bamboo stems, flutes, and windchimes can only do so much to help. If these Feng Shui antidotes are, however, much smaller than the corridor itself the best solution is to use both stationary and hanging dividers.

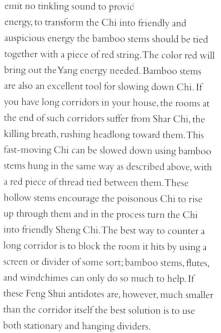

BANKING The business of banking belongs to the water element, and thus the most effective Feng Shui enhancer for a bank is water. Building auspicious water features in the north or the southeast is especially recommended.

BARBECUES Because barbecues represent fire (as do all cooking appliances, stoves, ovens, and so forth), they are best held in the south of the garden, which is ruled by the fire element. This activates the corner that brings recognition and fame luck to the family. It is also the sector of the middle daughter, so holding barbecues here will assist her in her grades and her personal development. If you are not able to locate the barbecue in the south corner of your garden, you should at least ensure it is not placed in the east or southeast, as these sectors are wood sectors. The fire from the barbecue will (symbolically) burn the wood, thus burning away your wealth luck (southeast) and health luck (east).

BASEMENT APARTMENTS These are usually not auspicious. Feng Shui does not recommend living below road level. Basement apartments are therefore not the best units to live in. If you have no choice you can enhance the Chi by installing bright lights at the entrance. This should "raise" the energy, encouraging Chi to flow into the apartment. If the basement apartment opens into a garden at the back, the Feng Shui will be considerably improved.

BATHROOMS Bathrooms are similar to toilets in the way that Feng Shui views them. They are not good to have in the house from a Feng Shui viewpoint. Try to minimize the size and décor of your bathrooms and keep the doors to your bathrooms closed at all times. Bathrooms should never be too large.

BEADED CURTAINS A Feng Shui cure for afflicted doorways. The placement of doors within the home has great Feng Shui significance. You should never have two doors directly facing each other across a corridor. This confrontational positioning will bring about quarrels and misunderstandings between the members of the household, and particularly between the two people whose doors face each other. To soften the negative effect of such a layout, short of changing the placement of the doors completely, hang a beaded curtain across the doorway. This way, the door always appears to be closed. However, if one door faces part of another this has a worse effect. In such a situation, it is advisable to try to place something between the doors, such as a plant, which can act as a divider. Beaded curtains in this instance will not be a suitable solution.

BEAMS Protruding overhead beams cause Feng Shui problems inside the home and office. You can either hang a five-rod windchime or hang two hollow bamboo stems tied with red thread to

overcome the negative Chi. Do not sit directly underneath exposed overhead beams, especially structural beams.

BEDROOMS Important rooms which should always enjoy good Feng Shui. The main thing to remember is that the bedroom is a place of relaxation and rest. The energies that prevail in the bedroom should thus be more Yin than Yang, since a bedroom which is too Yang will cause the occupant to be too active, which may cause difficulties in sleeping. Because of this, many Feng Shui masters warn against activating the bedroom with too many good fortune symbols. Such symbols, which may work well in the other parts of the house, may work against you in the bedroom. Water features are generally auspicious but they do more harm than good in the bedroom. Sleeping with water behind you will cause you to be robbed or to suffer a financial loss. Note that water does not only mean aquariums, fountains, and fish bowls. Paintings of water should also be kept out of the bedroom. It is, however, acceptable to decorate your bedroom in blue, a color of relaxation and calm. Black represents water and this color should not be a prominent feature of your bedroom. The inclusion of mirrors is one of the most common mistakes in modern bedroom interior design. Mirrors are frequently used to create a sense of space. Whether the mirrors are attached to cupboards in the bedroom, or on the ceiling, the reflective edges of mirrors send out Shar Chi onto the sleeping couple. This will cause quarrels and misunderstandings, as well as ill-health. Mirrors also bring a third party into the marriage when they reflect the sleeping couple, causing husbands and/or wives to be unfaithful. Note that anything with a reflective surface, even television sets, which resemble a mirror, should be kept out of the bedroom. If you have mirrors that you cannot take down, cover them with a curtain. Similarly, television sets should be covered with a cloth each night before you go to sleep. Open shelves should be covered up anywhere in the house, not just in the bedroom, where they do most harm. If you have such shelves facing your bed while you sleep each of the shelves will be sending little poison arrows toward you throughout the night. It will only be a matter of time before you fall ill. If you cannot close the open shelves with doors, another solution is to ensure the shelves are lined with books whose spines are set flush with the edge of the shelf, thus getting rid of the shelves. Flowers and plants, especially growing plants, are potent symbols of Yang energy, and are not suitable for the bedroom. If you place plants in a girl's bedroom, this will work against her in the romance stakes. If plants feature in the bedroom of a couple they will quarrel frequently. The only time flowers and plants are justified in the bedroom is when someone is recuperating from an illness and needs Yang energy to recover. Your sleeping direction is a most important consideration if you are to benefit from good Feng Shui. It is therefore vital that your head is pointed in one of your four good directions while sleeping. Check your good and bad directions in the chapter on Compass Formula Feng Shui (*see pages 66–79*). This formula is based on each individual's Kua number. *See* Kua Numbers.

BEDS Sleep in a bed with Feng Shui dimensions. A Feng Shui bed has auspicious dimensions and is decorated with colors that harmonize either with the element of the corner in which the bed is placed, or the element of the year in which you were born. To be safe, it is better to use the element of the corner; this allows the bed to be auspicious for more than one person (i.e. for you and your partner or spouse). Beds with headboards are better as they provide support. Because a bedroom is a place of rest, too much Yang energy is bad and can cause sleepless nights. If you wish to use red, a dark red or maroon is better than a bright, chilly red. Bedspreads are also better in plain colors. Avoid any abstract designs with arrows and triangles: these represent the fire element, which is very bad for the bedroom. It also symbolizes many poison arrows attacking you while you sleep.

BELLS Use tinkling bells to improve turnover in your business. Chinese shopkeepers have long been aware of the efficacy of tinkling bells in attracting customers into their stores. When hung on the door or on a door handle, the ringing of these metal bells creates good Chi each time someone enters the store. This brings in the luck required to make people purchase your products, enhancing your store's turnover. This method is particularly effective for stores selling personal items such as jewelry, clothes, and accessories. The bells can be made of any type of metal. They should be tied with a red ribbon to increase their effectiveness, as this activates their intrinsic Yang energy. The ideal number of bells is six or seven, although most shopkeepers only keep one set of bells. Tiny bells can also be placed inside the store anywhere along the west or northwest wall or high up on the ceiling directly facing the door. This will entice the precious Sheng Chi to enter the store. The bells need not be seen, as long as they work. Their function is a symbolic one and as long as they tinkle a little each time the door is opened they will bring increased luck for the store. In the old days, bells were usually used to announce good news, being symbols of good fortune.

BIRDBATHS Excellent water features suitable for the north, east, and southeast of your garden. Ensure that the water is clean at all times, replacing the water daily if necessary. The more birds you have visiting your birdbath, the better the energy that is created by this water feature.

BIRDS Represent the auspicious phoenix, especially when they are placed in the south part of your home. Thus, keeping sculptures of any kinds of birds in your south-facing garden, or on the south side of your living room, brings luck in the form of opportunity. Live birds in captivity, however, spell bad Feng Shui, captivity being symbolic of retarded growth, and this may well curtail chances of progressing in one's career.

BIRTH DATES These are required in calculating Eight Mansions and Four Pillars Feng Shui. Birth dates are required in the calculation of personalized lucky and unlucky directions. There are two main schools of Feng Shui requiring the date of birth. The first is the Eight Mansions formula, which works out your Kua number. With this number you will be able to refer to a table which details your four auspicious and four inauspicious directions. The second is the Feng Shui method using your Four Pillars. This is the same as the Eight Characters (Paht Chee) method of fortune-telling. This method requires not just the date but also the hour of your birth. In using your birth dates, however, always remember that in using any of the Chinese divinitive sciences you must know your date of birth according to the lunar calendar.

BLACK TURTLES Celestial creatures that bring great good fortune. The black turtle is believed to be one of four celestial creatures that brings good fortune as well as good health and protection. The arrangement of the numbers on the Lo Shu square, one of the most important symbols of analysis in Formula Feng Shui, is said to have originated from the back of a black turtle which swam up from the shores of the Lo River. The arrangement of the numbers one to nine within the square is supposedly based on the markings found on this ancient turtle. Whichever way you add up the numbers, whether diagonally or in a straight line, the numbers always added up to nine. The black turtle is one of the four animals that make up the auspicious "armchair" formation in Landscape Feng Shui (or the Form School method of Feng Shui). The armchair is made up of the green dragon on the left, the white tiger on the right, the black turtle at the back (for support), and the crimson phoenix in front (as a footstool). When a home is built in the middle of these four animals, precious Chi is attracted and created there, leading to much good luck for the occupants of the home. The black turtle is a popular symbol of good fortune for the home. Displayed either as paintings, or figurines, or kept as a pet tortoise or terrapin, the symbolic Feng Shui created is extremely auspicious. These smaller cousins of the turtle are believed to bring the same good fortune as the turtle. If you wish to keep a terrapin or tortoise, keep it in the north sector of the house, but keep only one, since this is the number of the north. Do not worry that your pet will feel lonely without a mate: terrapins are natural loners.

BLUE FLOWERS Good for the north, east, and southeast parts of the garden. Colors are powerful Feng Shui enhancers and playing with colors is a creative way of perfecting the Feng Shui of your garden. Blue flowers symbolize the element of water, thus planting them in the north, southeast, and/or east parts of the garden will activate the luck of these corners. The north sector is for career luck, the southeast is for wealth luck, and the east is for good health.

BLUE ROOFS One of the danger signs in Feng Shui. Try to avoid having a blue roof since this signifies water on the top of your house. Change the tiles if you have to.

BOARDROOMS These can be energized to bring excellent corporate Feng Shui. The best location for the boardroom of a corporation is the place that is diagonal to the entrance, deep inside the office. Boardrooms should not be on the top floor.

BONSAI Though beautiful, bonsai trees are artificially stunted and do not give good Feng Shui. They are particularly harmful to businesses and commercial enterprises since they are the direct opposite of what needs to be energized for growth. If you have a passion for bonsai trees and simply must have them somewhere in your home, avoid placing them in the wood corners (east and southeast) of your house or garden. Placed in the north, they cause the least harm.

BOOK OF CHANGES, or I CHING The major source book of Feng Shui, and probably the main source book of most of China's cultural practices. The seasoned wisdom of thousands of years has gone into the makings of the *I Ching*. Both branches of Chinese philosophy – Confucianism and Taoism – have their common roots in this ancient classic, known also as the *Book of Changes*. The *I Ching* alone, among all the Confucian Classics, escaped the great burning of the books under Emperor Chin Shih Huang Ti in 213 B.C.E. The origins of the *I Ching* go back to mythical antiquity, as a book of divination and as a book of wisdom. All that is great and significant in Chinese cultural history takes inspiration from the *I Ching* – aspects of the many related principles and symbols of the Chinese predictive sciences, its view of the trinity, heaven, earth, and man, the concepts of Yin and Yang, balance and harmony, positive and negative forces, good fortune and misfortune, are all derived from interpretations of the texts and judgments of the *I Ching*'s 64 hexagrams.

BOOKSHELVES These represent knives cutting into you and are bad Feng Shui. If you have exposed bookshelves in your office or study, change them into cupboards by covering them with doors. Unless you do this, the shelves will act as deadly poison arrows, causing you loss and illness.

BOULDERS Signify earth energy and are an excellent Feng Shui remedy. Tied with red string, a boulder is an effective antidote if placed in a bathroom that is in the wrong place in your home.

BOUNDARIES For Feng Shui analysis, boundaries must be accurately measured and taken. Feng Shui is best approached as a method or technique. When using the compass methods it is vital to get measurements and compass readings correct. This enables you to establish the parameters of your space more accurately. Feng Shui works when the space has been accurately demarcated according to directions, locations, and elements.

BREATH OF THE DRAGON The cosmic Chi. *See also* Chi.

BRICK WALLS Feng Shui remedy for blocking out unwanted and inauspicious sights, especially structures that are sending killing breath to the home.

BRIDGES Bridges near your home will be auspicious if they have three, five, or nine bends. They may be straight or curved, beamed, arched, suspended, or floating. They can be pavilion or corridor bridges and can be made of stone or wood, including cane. In China, bridges that are intended to enhance the Feng Shui of gardens are usually built of stone, and the arch formed is usually in the shape of a semicircle.

BRIGHT HALL An excellent Feng Shui situation. One of the most auspicious Feng Shui features a building can have is for the main door to open out onto a park, a football field, or any kind of empty land. This creates what Feng Shui masters describe as the bright hall effect, where auspicious Chi can first collect before entering the home. You should not try to achieve the bright hall effect at all costs. If, say, there is a statue or structure which forms a poison arrow directly facing the front door, it is better to give up trying to create the bright hall effect and the auspicious good fortune that it is supposed to bring than to suffer from the deadly Shar Chi from the poison arrow. Remember always to practice defensive Feng Shui first.

BROOMS Brooms, mops, and cleaning materials should never be left around the home. Keep them hidden away. As well as sweeping away bad luck, they can also sweep away good luck. Brooms are particularly bad fortune if left in the dining room, as they symbolize your rice bowl and livelihood being swept away. Brooms have another use in Feng Shui. They can be an effective tool to ward off burglars and intruders from the house when placed upside down against the wall and facing the front door, but outside the home rather than in. Leave a broom outside only at night; put it away during the day.

BUDDHA STATUES Holy objects must have good Feng Shui. Paintings and statues of Buddhas should be regarded as holy objects. Do not place them below, facing, or near bathrooms. The best place for displaying your antique Buddha statue is the northwest of your entrance hall or living room. *See also* Altar.

BUILDINGS In modern Feng Shui, these simulate mountains. In old days, Form School Feng Shui examined surrounding hills and mountains to determine the quality of the Feng Shui terrain. Today, the practice of Feng Shui has shifted to big cities, where buildings form the landscape and surroundings for homes and offices. Because Feng Shui is symbolic, buildings are now analyzed in the way that surrounding hills used to be.

BULBS Usually considered to be good fortune flowers; they represent hidden gold. These are regarded as lucky flowers and indeed symbolize the blossoming of hidden talents and abilities when they bloom. The Chinese are fond of growing bulbs around the lunar New Year, especially the narcissus, because of their association with the advent of spring.

BUSINESS FENG SHUI This focuses on creating wealth and prosperity luck. In the West business Feng Shui is becoming increasingly important as more career professionals and entrepreneurs recognize the potency and effectiveness of Feng Shui in enhancing turnover and improving bottom lines. Retail businesses can benefit enormously from simple Feng Shui enhancers.

C

CACTUS Cacti and any other types of prickly plants create tiny slivers of poisonous energy which can cause bad luck, illness, and misfortune. They should not be placed in the home and are better outside, where they take on a protective role. Their thorns then counter any Shar Chi heading in your direction. Inside, rather than counter Shar Chi, they create harmful killing breath.

CANNON To be used as a last resort to counter big poison arrows. Cannons are very effective in deflecting killing breath and pointed, hostile objects aimed at your front door. The negative force sent out can be very potent. Antique cannons that have been to war are the most powerful of all.

CAREER LUCK Can be energized with Feng Shui. Good career luck manifests itself in increased opportunities. It does not suggest instant success. When using Feng Shui to activate luck at work be prepared for an increasing workload and responsibilities as well as more opportunities for advancement. Activate the north part of your home, office, or personal space. Since the north is of the water element, a good way to energize this corner is to place an aquarium of energetic fish there, such as guppy. Their vigorous swimming will create the precious Yang energy needed to give your career a boost. Advanced practitioners can use the Feng Shui formula to activate professional career luck. It is also a good idea to make yourself an auspicious work desk whose dimensions have been measured with a Feng Shui ruler.

CASH REGISTER In retail businesses registers can be energized with coins and bamboo. Increase sales by taping three old Chinese coins tied with red thread, Yang side up, onto the side of your cash register. The Yang side has four Chinese words, the Yin side has two. Important files can also be treated in the same way to enhance Feng Shui at work. Alternatively, hang hollow bamboo stems above the cash register, also tied with red thread. The bamboo ensures that you will stay in business for a long time. Let the stems hang perpendicular with their tops tilted slightly toward each other.

CEILINGS Should neither be too low, nor have hostile designs. A ceiling lower than 8 feet (2.5m) suggests you will be weighed down with problems; it should clear the tallest person in the house by at least 4 feet (1.2m). Avoid corner angles or threatening, ornate designs. Beams should be avoided unless they are an integral part of the entire ceiling and especially if they stand alone. Paint your ceiling white or in a bright color, and never black or blue, both of which are very inauspicious.

CHANDELIERS Create excellent Feng Shui if placed just inside or outside the home. They encourage good Chi to enter the house and they work just as well inside or outside the home. They are especially good when placed in the southwest, where the combination of fire (lights) and earth (crystal) brings wonderful romance and love luck to the members of the household. Try to activate the southwest of the whole house with a chandelier, rather than the southwest of a single room. The effect will be more powerful and will benefit the entire family.

CHEN TRIGRAM This trigram symbolizes the dragon, thus a strong Yang line pushes upward below two broken Yin lines, which give way. Chen represents Spring, thunder, growth, and the eldest son, and is placed east on the Pa Kua.

CHI The dragon's cosmic breath and the key to good Feng Shui, it brings good fortune. The concept of Chi is central to the understanding and practice of Feng Shui. Chi is the word used to describe an intrinsic force or energy that is invisible to the eye but can nevertheless be felt and is very potent.

CHI KUNG A form of martial training that allows you to "feel your chi," its slow exercise movements are believed to enable practitioners effectively to move Chi energy within them. Such exercise is believed to help overcome serious illnesses.

 CHIEN TRIGRAM The ultimate Yang trigram that signifies the patriarch. The first trigram in the *I Ching*. Made up of three unbroken lines, Chien is placed in the northwest quadrant of the Yang Pa Kua. Since this trigram symbolizes the patriarch the northwest is said to be the corner of any home that governs the luck of the male paternal.

CHILDLESSNESS Can sometimes be helped using Feng Shui. If you are having problems conceiving, suggest the man changes his sleeping location or direction. Use his Nien Yen direction, which will be based upon his personal Kua number.

CHILDREN The manifestations of good descendants' luck. Children represent the next generation and this is one of the eight aspirations addressed by Feng Shui practice. The west side of the house is the place to energize for ensuring descendants' luck but the children of the house, especially the sons, should sleep in the east part of the house in rooms located in their personal auspicious locations, based on Compass School Formula.

CLOTHES Affect the type of energies you attract. Clothes have a bearing on your luck. Wearing torn clothes is very inauspicious. It attracts poverty energy, which often translates into the most severe kind of ill-fortune. Wearing unflattering clothes has the same effect; as well as making you feel bad about yourself, it depletes your Yang energy and causes you to feel lethargic.

COINS One of the more potent of symbolic Feng Shui tools. They represent wealth and are superb for activating Feng Shui for wealth. Authentic old Chinese coins can be used as Feng Shui coins. The square hole in the middle has Feng Shui meaning. The circle and square together represent heaven and earth. Three coins should be tied together with red string and hung on the inside of your front door to symbolize the money already inside your house. *See also* Cash Register.

COLOR Amplifies the elements. Good color combinations bring good luck. Color therapy in Feng Shui is directly related to the concept of the five elements, each of which stands for a certain color or colors. These are summarized as:
Wood - browns and greens.
Fire - reds, yellows, and orange.
Metal - white, gold, silver, bronze, and chrome.
Earth - ocher and light yellow.
Water - blues, purple, and black.
Each color on its own is neither good nor bad. Combinations of colors cause good and bad luck and this is again based on the destructive and productive cycles of the elements.
Some special combinations that are excellent luck: vermilion with gold; dark rich purple with chrome or silver; black and white.
Good color combinations: two blues one green; two browns one red; two reds one yellow; two yellows one white; two whites one blue.
Unlucky color combinations: two blues one red; two reds one white; two whites one green; two greens one yellow; two yellows one blue.

COLUMNS In the home square, freestanding columns can cause severe Feng Shui problems. Their sharp edges can send out poisonous killing breath, which should be deflected and dissolved by placing plants against the edges. Alternatively, wrap mirrors around the columns. Columns should never be facing the main from door, either inside or outside, where they represent bad Feng Shui. In such a case, the door or the column should be moved.

COMPASS FENG SHUI This technique uses the compass directions to create auspicious Feng Shui. Compass Feng Shui offers several formulas that approach Feng Shui from the perspective of orientations, i.e. compass directions and locations. These formulas are based on the dates of birth of individuals, on sex as well as on the tools of Feng Shui – the Pa Kua and the Lo Shu square. For more details see the chapters on Feng Shui formulas (*pages 66–79 and 100–33*).

COMPUTERS

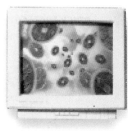

Computers do not cause bad Feng Shui. When placed in the west or northwest they can become energizers in these corners. Use screensavers that bring good fortune. Display images according to the corner where your computer is standing.

CONCEIVING As well as using the husband's Nien Yen direction, also hang a painting of children near the marital bed. Alternatively, place a small representation of the dragon next to the bed to simulate the precious Yang energy needed. *See also* Childlessness.

COOKING Cooking has serious Feng Shui connotations. Feng Shui warns against placing stoves in the northwest of the kitchen. If possible, try to avoid having the kitchen itself in the northwest corner of the house. The northwest corner represents the patriarch, or primary breadwinner of the family; placing the stove or kitchen there is like burning the luck of the patriarch. The northwest is also the corner which represents heaven, the stove in the northwest suggests "fire at heaven's gate," and this is most inauspicious. The northwest is also of the metal element and a stove represents fire, the only element capable of destroying metal.

CORNERS Protruding or missing corners can cause problems. Protruding corners inside the home create vertical sharp edges that send out negative energy thereby creating havoc in households. Nullify this by placing a tall bushy plant against the corner. The second type of protruding corner appears in a room that juts out of a regular-shaped house. Such additions to the layout of the home make it lucky or unlucky, depending on where the main door is located. This applies to the Feng Shui of the entire house and therefore affects anyone living in it.

Location of main door	Lucky location of addition	Unlucky location of addition
North	West and northwest	Southwest and northeast
South	East and southeast	North
East	North	West and northwest
West	Southwest and northeast	South
Southeast	North	West and northwest
Northeast	South	East and southeast
Southwest	South	East and southeast
Northwest	Southwest and northeast	South

Missing corners can be lucky or unlucky for the home in question also depending on the location of the main front door. If the missing corner is unlucky you can try to solve the problem by adding a mirror wall to one side of the missing corner, but only if the mirror is not directly facing anything harmful (see also Mirrors). If it is, shine a bright light into the corner or if possible build an extension. If the missing corner is not hurting the luck of the house you do not need to do anything.

Location of main door	Lucky missing corner, requiring no cure	Harmful missing corner, requiring a cure
North	Southwest and northeast	West and northwest
South	North	East and southeast
East	West and northwest	North
West	South	Southwest and northeast
Southeast	West and northwest	North
Northeast	East and southeast	South
Southwest	East and southeast	South
Northwest	South	Southwest and northeast

To investigate the effect of missing corners on the luck of specific individuals, apply the formulas that investigate an individual's lucky and unlucky directions, either the Eight Mansions or Pa-Kua Lo-Shu formula that uses your Kua number to determine the effect of the directions on your luck, or the Four Pillars method.

CORPORATE LOGOS *See* Logos.

CORRIDORS Long, straight corridors become poison arrows. They symbolize arrows sending Shar Chi throughout the office or home and cause disharmony in human relationships. If your room is badly placed on a corridor, break the flight of a poison arrow by placing plants and windchimes along it, to reduce the negative impact of the arrow.

COSMIC BREATH *See* Chi.

CRANES Birds that are one of the most popular symbols of longevity among the Chinese. They are often seen in Chinese art or are drawn in with Sau, the God of Longevity. Sculptures or other symbolic representations of cranes should be placed in the south or west of your garden.

CRIMSON PHOENIX The celestial creature of the south. The "king of all the feathered creatures of the Universe," the phoenix is said to appear once every thousand years when times are auspicious and a good leader sits on the throne. Phoenixes are said to signify wonderful opportunities for bringing a good name, wealth, and prosperity to the family. Placed in the south the phoenix is represented in Feng Shui by low foothills.

CROSS Directly opposite your house or office, a cross brings bad luck. Crosses are inauspicious signs, whether they appear as church spires or as structural features, because they send Shar Chi toward your house. If you can use a door that does not face a cross as your main door, do so, if not, hang a Pa Kua mirror.

CRYSTALS Excellent Feng Shui energizers, especially when they are placed in the southwest corner. Natural quartz crystal clusters are among the best symbols of mother earth and are extremely effective when used to energize the southwest corner (the big earth corner). The southwest also governs the luck of romance, love, and family happiness. This is applicable irrespective of your particular Kua number. If you energize the southwest corner of your living room, everyone living in the house will benefit. Before displaying the crystal, it should be soaked for seven days and seven nights in salt (sea) water to dispose of any negative energies it may be carrying.

CURTAINS Effective Feng Shui tools, curtains have a dual function in Feng Shui: they can block out excessive sunlight or views of harmful structures in the environment. In Feng Shui what cannot be seen is deemed to have "disappeared." Curtains can be used to enhance the Feng Shui of your living space, whether it be home or the office. Study the colors best suited to each corner of the room according to the compass direction. This comes from the corresponding elements of the directions. For instance, hang a dark blue curtain in the north, the east, or the southeast. Blue is synonymous with water, which is good for these three directions – the north because it belongs to the element of water, the east and southeast because these wood corners will benefit from the water element of the curtain. In the same way, red, yellow, and pink curtains will be excellent in the south, southwest, and northeast; green will be good in the east, southeast, and south; white and metallic colors (gold or silver) are auspicious in the west, northwest, and north; browns will be good in the east and southeast; purples and lilacs will be good in the north, east, and southeast.

CYCLES OF CHI The enhancing, controlling, and weakening cycles. This relates to the five elements and Feng Shui practice requires an appreciation of the interactive cycles of the five elements to understand the cycles of Chi. There are three important cycles to incorporate into Feng Shui analysis. The enhancing or producing cycle explains how one element can help another (or type of Chi) to exhibit its quality and ability. Some masters prefer to describe water as "enhancing" wood. When a tree is watered, it grows. When a fire is fed with wood it burns. In the weakening cycle, wood helps fire to burn and in the process weakens or diminishes itself. Thus within the productive cycle is the seed of weakening energy for one element. The controlling or destroying cycle (some masters prefer the former term) explains how one element can control and suppress another. It does not necessarily destroy the other element since energy, or Chi, cannot really be destroyed. One element can dominate in a particular circumstance over another. Thus a metal knife cuts a piece of wood to transform it. It is controlling the shape of that piece of wood.

D

DESIGN MOTIFS, SHAPES, AND COLORS

All these have Feng Shui connotations. In Feng Shui Art Nouveau is to be preferred to Art Deco simply because the former suggests something more rounded and curved than the latter. However, in the design of motifs and decorations for interior decoration, it is useful to develop different motifs for each of the five elements and then to use them according to the directions symbolized by each element. For example, use the water motif for rooms in the north (water corner) part of the home since such rooms will benefit from having the element there enhanced. Use this table to determine the element motifs most suitable.

Location of rooms	Element motifs/symbols
North, east, and southeast	Water motifs and symbols
South, southwest, and northeast	Fire motifs and symbols
West and northwest	Metal motifs
Southwest and northeast	Earth motifs
East and southeast	Wood motifs

DESKS Can be energized to attract excellent work luck. The desk is an excellent object for Feng Shui energizing. When checking for suitable auspicious dimensions in placing or making a desk, refer to the chapter on the Feng Shui ruler. Energize your desk top with objects that symbolize the five elements. Do this by demarcating on your desk top a Lo Shu grid and then, using a compass, mark out the corresponding compass direction of each of the grids. Energize your desk according to the Lo Shu grid direction in the table. Place the following:

East	A bowl of fresh flowers
Southeast	A small green plant
West	Your telephone
Northwest	Your computer terminal
North	Your cup of coffee
South	A light or something red
Southwest	A lapis globe
Northeast	A crystal paperweight

In addition, check your Kua number and find out your best sitting direction. With the aid of a compass, mark out the direction that you should be facing to bring you good luck. Sit like that as much as possible. Finally, make sure that you have a clear view from your desk, unencumbered by office paraphernalia.

DESTRUCTIVE CYCLES These refer to the negative cycle of the five elements. The theory of Wuxing, or five elements, is a central axis of Feng Shui practice. According to the theory all things in the universe can be categorized as one of the five elements - wood, fire, earth, water, and metal. There is a productive and destructive cycle to these elements.

DINING ROOM In Feng Shui, a most important room. Here, food on the family table can be symbolically doubled with mirrors facing the table. The dining room also benefits the family if it is located in the middle of the home since this signifies the family's presence at the heart of the home. The dining room should always be higher than, or on the same level as, the living room. If you live in a multistorey house, make sure your family dines on the higher level. If you have more than one dining room in your house, make sure the one most regularly used is on a higher level. The dining room should not be next to the bedroom; this creates a lot of unsettling Chi in both rooms. It is also very inauspicious to have a toilet too close to the dining room; if you have this, keep the door closed at all times. Do not let the dining room be located at the end of a long corridor; it is extremely inauspicious for the family to eat in such an unlucky room. To energize the "stomach" of the home further, hang paintings of luscious flowers and ripe, juicy fruits.

DINING TABLE There are four auspicious shapes for dining tables – round, square, rectangular, and the eight-sided Pa Kua shape. Of these, Chinese families prefer the round shape because this symbolizes the smooth procession of everything. The round shape also signifies gold, which means money. Thus round tables are said to symbolize the creation of wealth and prosperity.

DOORS These are especially important in Feng Shui analysis. The size and number of doors as well as the way they are placed in relation to each other in the home have Feng Shui implications. The orientation of the main door is especially important; ensure that it is not being hurt by hostile structures in the outside environment.

DOUBLE HAPPINESS This activates good marriage luck. Displaying the double happiness symbol – the Chinese word for happiness written twice – is excellent and popular Feng Shui.

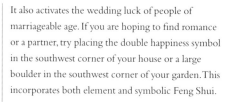

It also activates the wedding luck of people of marriageable age. If you are hoping to find romance or a partner, try placing the double happiness symbol in the southwest corner of your house or a large boulder in the southwest corner of your garden. This incorporates both element and symbolic Feng Shui.

DOUBLING The concept of doubling wealth is part of Feng Shui amplification. Doubling anything makes the outcome more auspicious. Thus a wall mirror should double the food on the dining table. This signifies wealth and is auspicious. The daily income of a restaurant or store should be doubled with a wall mirror that reflects the cash register.

DRAGON The most important symbol both in Feng Shui and in Chinese folklore. The celestial dragon is the ultimate symbol of good fortune in every Chinese divinitive science and is central to the practice of Feng Shui. The direction traditionally associated with the dragon is the east; thus, placing an image of a dragon in the east side of the office or home will bring much good fortune. Gardens can also be activated using the dragon symbol by simulating a dragon on the east side of the house with plants set in a winding flowerbed. However, when using the dragon symbol, there are several taboos which must be noted: never place a dragon inside the bedroom – it is too Yang a symbol in a place of rest; dragons made out of wood, ceramic, or crystal are fine, but avoid dragons made out of gold, cloisonné, or other metals, since the metal element destroys the wood element (the element of the east); sitting at a desk bearing dragon imagery can bring much good luck, but not all people have sufficient Yang energy to sit at such a desk. See also Chi.

DRAINS These can be made effective in creating wealth under the Water Dragon formula. The humble monsoon drain can be harnessed to bring extreme good fortune by applying the Water Dragon formula. (*See the chapter on Water Feng Shui for Wealth, pages 100–9, for further reading.*) The general guidelines about drains are that they should always be kept free flowing; blocked drains signify that all your ventures will meet up with obstacles. Drains should also be cleaned regularly and be flowing past your main door in the correct direction. The rule of thumb for the direction of water flow depends on the orientation of the main front door. This is summarized as follows:

❦ For homes where the main door faces north, south, east, or west, i.e. the cardinal directions (taking the direction from inside the house looking out), drains should flow past the main front door from left to right for the flow to be auspicious.

❦ For homes where the main door faces the secondary directions, i.e. southeast, southwest, northeast, and northwest, the drain should flow from right to left for it to be auspicious.

DRIVEWAYS The Feng Shui of driveways depends on how they approach the home. Long straight driveways that point directly at the main front door in the form of an arrow bring bad Feng Shui. To nullify the bad effect, allow the driveway to curve or meander. A circular driveway is most auspicious since the round shape signifies gold.

E

EARLY HEAVEN ARRANGEMENT Refers to the arrangements of the eight trigrams around what is known as a Yin Pa Kua. This sequence of trigrams is placed on protective Pa Kuas used for deflecting the poisonous breath of harmful sharp structures in the environment.

EARTH The element that most represents Feng Shui at work. Feng Shui is the luck of the earth, and the earth element is an important component in the correct practice of Feng Shui. At the same time the ultimate Yin trigram of Yin, which indicates the essence of the matriarchal energy so important in a home, is Kun, whose element is earth. The center of the home is also said to belong to the earth element. As such it is important that earth Chi should be present in healthy doses for a home to be lucky. Probably the most effective symbol of the earth is the globe. When placed in northeast it assists in harnessing luck for the children. In the southwest and center of the home it magnifies and improves the luck of the family; in the west and northwest it often leads to prosperity.

EAST The place of the dragon and of the wood element. The east signifies the essence of growth energy. The wood element is significant because anything requiring upward thrusting energy will benefit from being in the east. In the old days this was the place reserved for the heirs of the dynasties. Similarly, Feng Shui also advises that sons of the family will benefit from living in rooms that are

located in the east. Since the east is of the wood element it also benefits from a presence of lush green plants and any kind of water feature. Always keep a healthy store of Yang energy in the east and do not allow stagnant energy to collect and accumulate because it is especially harmful.

EAST GROUP This is part of the Eight Mansions Pa-Kua Lo-Shu formula. Based on the Compass School formula, you belong to the east group if your Kua number is 1,3,4, or 9 and the auspicious directions of people in the east group are north, south, east, and southeast.

EAST HOUSE This is defined according to the direction of the main door. An east house is a house that has a main door facing west and northwest. This is part of the Eight Mansions formula of orientation. This particular guideline can create problems of implementation for those who want to arrange the orientation of the main door that needs to face west or northwest but who have to live in a west house.

EDUCATION LUCK A simple way of energizing the luck of education is to activate the earth element of the northeast corner of the bedroom. Place a globe or a cluster of natural crystals to strengthen the earth element of this corner.

EIGHT PRECIOUS OBJECTS Eight treasures believed to be extremely auspicious. Placed together or singly the eight treasures are considered to be extremely auspicious and precious by followers of Buddhism. To attract good fortune to occupants, practitioners of Symbolic Feng Shui usually display the treasures as embroidered fabric screens hung on doors leading into bedrooms and other important rooms. They also portray them as symbols on porcelain or similar pieces of art. Each symbol may also be tied with red thread and worn separately as a lucky charm.

The double fish symbol is believed to ward off evil intentions and is often worn as an amulet. Place it near the entrance of the home to keep away anyone with bad feelings for you; the lotus brings every kind of good fortune. Grown at home it has the potency to turn bad luck into good luck; the conch shell (or any kind of seashell) attracts auspicious travel luck. Place it in your living room. Seashells picked up from

the seashore should be cleaned and soaked in salt water for at least a month before being used. The dharma wheel (or wheel of law) represents the power of the heavenly energy, a painting or representation of this wheel is said to lead to positive spiritual development; the precious vase (or urn) placed near the entrance of houses attracts Chi and encourages it to settle and accumulate. Keep vases empty if placed outside the house but keep them full when inside the house. Fill these vases to the brim with seven varieties of semiprecious stones. If you wish you can transform them into wealth vases and put a small amount of earth taken from a rich man's home; the parasol or umbrella (or canopy) is an excellent symbol of protection. It is believed to ward off burglars when placed near the front part of the home or in the lobby; the mystic knot signifies the neverending cycle of good luck turning into bad luck and into good luck again. Buddhists also see it as the neverending cycle of birth and rebirths. In Feng Shui it is a popular symbol of neverending affection and devotion; the banner of victory symbolizes success in all your endeavors. It is often depicted as a long victory flag similar to those used by ancient Chinese armies. The banner of victory is a particularly auspicious symbol to display if you are in politics, the army, or working in government. It brings an elevation in rank.

EIGHT TRIGRAMS These are the principal symbols of Feng Shui analysis. Placed around the eight sides of the Pa Kua, the eight trigrams are three lined combinations of broken and unbroken lines. The unbroken lines are said to be Yang lines while the broken lines are said to be Yin lines. The eight trigrams are Chien, Kun, Kan, Li, Ken, Chen, Tui, and Sun and they make up the root of the 64 hexagrams that in turn make up the *I Ching*. Understanding the essence and deep significance of these trigrams, as well as the way they are placed around the Pa Kua, unlocks the secrets of the eight-sided Pa Kua symbol.

ELEMENTS (Wuxing) The theory of the five elements. The elements are water, wood, fire, metal, and earth and their interactions make up the theory of Wuxing, which is central to the practice of Feng Shui and to the understanding of Chinese forms of divination and fortune-telling. *See also* Wuxing.

ELEPHANT The symbol of fertility, and good for the luck of sons, the elephant is also the symbol of strength, sagacity, and prudence and is one of the four animals representing power and energy, the other three being the tiger, the leopard, and the lion. The elephant is also one of the seven precious treasures of Buddhism and in Thailand it is regarded as a most precious creature. The Chinese believe that the elephant creates auspicious descendants' Chi. If it is placed inside the home childless couples can be blessed with children; those wishing for sons to carry on the family name are advised to lodge a stone on the back of a precious elephant and display it prominently in the bedroom so as to ensure the birth of a male child.

ELEVATED STRUCTURES These should be examined to see their effect on doors. If such structures as tall buildings or overpasses are placed too close to your main door they are said to cause serious Feng Shui afflictions to both the door and the house. Block off such structures with trees.

EMPTY SPACES *See* Bright Hall.

ENERGY Likened to the dragon's breath, or Chi. Energy is probably the most accurate translation for the word Chi. Another is breath, as in the dragon's cosmic breath. Energy offers the essence of what Chi can do, both positively and negatively.

ENHANCERS Good fortune symbols that, if correctly placed, create good Feng Shui. There are many different symbols of good fortune that can be used to enhance the Feng Shui of corners and rooms. Most Feng Shui techniques also make use of element methodology to enhance the different corners to energize different categories of good fortune.

ENTRANCES These are exceedingly important in Feng Shui, referring to the main entrance into the house, not to the gate. Entrances are where the auspicious Chi enters. If entrances suffer from Feng Shui afflictions the Chi that enters is said to be similarly afflicted. There are also Feng Shui formulas based on sex and dates of birth that offer advice on the kind of orientation that brings the best kinds of luck. If you live in an apartment the entrance into the apartment building is as important as the door into your own apartment. At least one should be oriented in a direction that is auspicious for you. If you live in a house with a garden and you have more than one door into the house, the main door is defined as the one that is most frequently used.

EXTERIOR FENG SHUI Exterior Feng Shui, i.e. the Feng Shui of your surroundings, must not harm your home. Thus garden Feng Shui becomes a significant and important part of Feng Shui practice because the landscape and environment around your home define its Feng Shui. If the exterior Feng Shui is harmful, then anything you do inside the home becomes afflicted. Good Feng Shui therefore begins from the outside.

F

FAME LUCK This can be energized by improving the Feng Shui of the south, which governs the luck of recognition and respect. To energize this luck install bright lights in the south side of the home. If your entrance faces south, certain schools of Feng Shui also suggest this will help you get a good name.

FAMILY FENG SHUI If you wish to enhance the harmony of relationships within the family, the center of the home should be energized. Do this by placing the television room or the dining room in the center of the home, then place a bright light to enhance and magnify the earth mother.

FAMILY PORTRAITS An effective method of creating family closeness is to hang a family portrait in the living or family room. Every member of the family should be included and, to symbolize happiness, each person should be smiling. Arrange the family in a way that creates a shape most suited to the father, or patriarch, of the family. A triangular arrangement is particularly effective when the father is born in a fire or earth year. Make sure that he is at the apex of the triangle. This arrangement creates the element of fire, signifying precious Yang energy. A wavy arrangement is effective if the father is born in a water or wood year. This arrangement creates the water element. It is a Yin shape and is excellent when there is excessive Yang energy in the house, i.e. when there are many sons and no daughters. The father should be in the center and, so as to create the wavy shape that symbolizes water, the heads of others in the picture should be at different levels. The rectangular arrangement suggests the wood element, and is the most common. The heads of everyone in the picture are on the same level. This arrangement also suggests a balanced and regular shape and is suitable if the father was born in a wood or fire year. A square arrangement is similar to the rectangle and is suitable for small families. This shape suggests the earth element and is suitable for everyone, since the earth element also signifies the family. It is especially good if the father was born in a metal year, since earth produces metal in the cycle of elements.

FAMILY ROOM A family room in the center of the house creates harmony. The house will be balanced; the heart of the home is the room in which the family spends time together.

FENG SHUI This translates as wind and water. One of the oldest known disciplines, Feng Shui's relevance to our personal well-being is fast gaining recognition today. This reflects a growing understanding and appreciation of the practice. Feng Shui is the science of arranging the living space through correct orientations and with the creation of harmonious interface between all the objects that make up the environment. Feng Shui brings harmonious Chi, the essential life force, and is beneficial when homes and surrounding land forms are aligned auspiciously. This facilitates well-being, prosperity, health, and longevity. The key to Feng Shui is balance; coordinating time, placement, space, and energy to maximum effect, based on the interplay between people and their universe. However, while the physical world offers rich experiences and the placement of objects within it can alter the flow of energy, self-examination is the most important view of all. We must never forget the importance of also creating mankind luck.

FIRE One of the five elements, symbolized by the direction south. Fire is placed south in the Later Heaven Pa Kua because it is the location of the trigram Li, which stands for fire. To energize the luck of opportunities and the luck of recognition, install a bright light in the south. This not only magnifies fire energy but also brings in the Yang essence so vital for success luck.

FISH Keeping fish is believed to bring good Feng Shui. Fish represent success. If you have an aquarium, it is best displayed near the front entrance or in the living room. The arrowana fish is a particularly auspicious fish to keep. If you cannot keep live fish, the symbol or image of a fish on a vase or in a painting will be good enough. Display these near your front door or living room. *See also* Arrowana.

FISHPONDS These are excellent water features. Fishponds are auspicious not only because of the symbolic meaning of the fish derived from Chinese folk tales but because fish are especially effective when it comes to energizing corners as well. Fishponds are particularly beneficial in the north (water), southeast or east (wood), for they are the element of water and water is compatible with both water and wood (which it nurtures). Keeping fish also creates Yang energy which encourages Chi to circulate, bringing a place to life.

FLOWERBEDS Rectangular or square flowerbeds are better than round ones. The combination of the wood element with the metal element is created when you have round flowerbeds. This is inauspicious. Better to combine wood with wood, i.e. grow your flowers and plants in rectangular flowerbeds. This among other features will determine the Feng Shui of your garden.

FLOWERS Excellent Feng Shui energizers for love and for the benefit of daughters of the house. Fresh flowers are best but once they are past their prime they should be thrown out to prevent harmful Yin energy accumulating. Flowers with thorns are also not good Feng Shui; remove these from roses, for example, before displaying them. Flowers in the bedroom of a healthy person are also not advisable: these will bring too much Yang energy into what is meant to be a place of rest. For those who are sick, however, flowers in a bedroom (as in a hospital room) will give the sick person much needed Yang energy. In Feng Shui fake flowers are as good as real.

They are excellent energizers of fresh Yang energy and are especially effective in the living room. Dried flowers, however, are purveyors of Yin energy and are not recommended in the home. Also avoid preserved or pressed flowers.

FLYING STAR FENG SHUI Flying star Feng Shui is a potent compass formula. It deals with the time dimension of Feng Shui, where the significance of changing forces during the different periods is taken into account. This school of Feng Shui makes use of the intangible influence of numbers, together with the pattern of Lo Shu numbers as they move in a time cycle in the lunar calendar. This formula can tell you the sectors of your home which are auspicious for a certain time period, while warning you against sectors which are inauspicious. You should spend most of your time in rooms that are "lucky" during the period in question, while trying as far as possible to keep the unlucky sectors quiet. For example, if you have an aquarium in the north (which is usually a good sector in which to place an aquarium), and that sector is particularly unlucky for the period in question, it is better to move the aquarium to another sector of the house or another corner of the room. With flying star the prosperity and luck of any residence or commercial building can be investigated and determined. The ruling numbers in each period correspond to the numerical values for each of its ages. For example, in the Lower Period, the ruling numbers are 7, 8, and 9. These numbers come from the Lo Shu grid and their significance relates to the trigrams. They are also associated with the five elements with each having a specific name and distinct connotation. The term "flying star" derives from the stars flying from room to room. Detailed tables have been drawn up showing the different star charts of houses with different door directions that will allow the amateur practitioner to investigate the good and bad luck sectors of any home from one period to the next. These are presented elsewhere in this book in the chapter on Compass Formula Feng Shui (*see pages 66–79*).

FORM SCHOOL A part of the landscape method that looks at shapes and contours in the landscape. Form School Feng Shui is another name for Landscape Feng Shui. This looks at the lie of the land, the shape, elevation, and appearance of structures, the flows of water, the contours of the land, and the terrain. Form School Feng Shui is often regarded as classic Feng Shui, and it is since it directly addresses the luck of orientations and the impact of the winds and waters.

FORMULA FENG SHUI A method that requires accuracy of application. Formula Feng Shui represents a range of different methods that make up the Compass School of Feng Shui. Formula Feng Shui takes the subjectivity out of Feng Shui and it always works when the measurements of dimensions and readings of the compass directions are accurate.

FOUNTAINS Fountains are popular features for energizing water but are more suitable for public places such as parks and shopping malls. They are not suitable for corporate head offices since the direction and flow of water downward can symbolize water flowing toward the building (which is excellent) or away from the building (which is bad).

FOUR CELESTIAL CREATURES The dragon (east), the tiger (west), the phoenix (south), and the turtle (north). The four celestial creatures of Feng Shui each bring a specific aspect of luck to the house they collectively embrace. The dragon brings wealth and prosperity; the turtle brings patronage and support; the phoenix brings opportunity and recognition; the tiger brings protection against the

dark forces. Together, and when oriented correctly vis-à-vis each other, the celestial creatures symbolize perfect Feng Shui.

FOYERS These should be brightly lit to attract good Feng Shui and to raise the Chi. If you do not have a foyer, try to ensure the door opens onto space and that the entrance is not cramped.

FROGS The Chinese regard frogs and toads as creatures that bring auspicious luck. It is believed that a family of frogs living in your backyard can protect you from bad luck. The three-legged frog is particularly auspicious and is usually found with three gold coins in its mouth, signifying the bringing of gold into the house. Place the frog diagonally across the room from the front door, facing inward, not outward, which symbolizes gold going out. Keep frogs out of the kitchen, bathroom, and toilet to avoid bad Chi accumulating, and out of the bedroom.

FRONT DOORS An important focus of Feng Shui analysis. This refers to the main front door, the Feng Shui of which largely determines the Feng Shui of the entire home. It is thus vital to get the Feng Shui of the main door auspicious. *See also* Doors.

FU DOGS Important guard dogs that offer protective Feng Shui. Fu dogs (also known as the Chinese unicorn) are traditionally used by the Chinese to protect against bad luck. Chinese homes are rarely without them. Size is immaterial but they should be in proportion to the size of the house they are guarding. Place them high up on either side of the gate or at table level, and on a stand rather than directly on the floor. Place your Fu dog according to the element of the location. If you are placing it on a gate and the corner where the gate is located is east, placing a pair of metal Fu dogs will be more effective. Gold controls the wood element of the east.

FUK, LUK, SAU The three star gods of health, wealth, and happiness. These are never worshiped, only displayed. They are enormously popular since they symbolize health, wealth, and prosperity, which actually means everything. Few Chinese homes are without these star gods. The best place for them is the dining room in a suitably elevated position. Do not place them lower than the people in the room and do not place them in the bedroom. *See also* Gods of Wealth.

FURNITURE This can be designed to incorporate important Feng Shui guidelines. Feng Shui inspired furniture can be particularly pleasing because it will have few, if any, negative forces. Such furniture should never have any nails driven into it: components should be designed to fit mortise and tenon. The beautiful antique Ming chairs, for instance, are highly prized because nails were never used in making them. Secondly, the chairs are always nicely curved, with no sharp edges or corners. Modern furniture can imitate the concept and essence of this sort of furniture. Sofas should have sizeable back support and armrests. Tables and cupboards should have rounded edges. Bookshelves should have doors to shut out the killing energy of shelves, which resemble blades sending poison arrows into rooms. Avoid metallic furniture, which emits disharmony, and furniture with sharp pointed edges or furniture that is triangular in shape.

G

GANZHI (OR GHANXI) SYSTEM The system upon which Chinese astrology is based. It is packed with cyclic symbols that are associated with the Chinese zodiac animals and the elements. Ganzhi comprises twenty-two symbols grouped into two

sets, ten belonging to the heavenly (or celestial) stems and twelve belonging to the earthly (or terrestrial) branches. The stems refer to the five elements, with a hard (Yang) or soft (Yin) heavenly aspect for each. The elements are earth, water, wood, fire, and metal. They have a productive as well as a destructive cycle. The branches refer to earthly forces and are represented by the twelve animals of the Chinese zodiac - the rat, ox, tiger, rabbit, dragon, snake, goat, horse, monkey, rooster, dog, and boar. The animals control the hour, day, month, and year and represent periods of each. One can be born on a tiger day, in a rat month, at a snake hour, and in an ox year. The combinations express the eight characters which are said to rule one's destiny. Each of the twelve years are further categorized according to the five elements (12 x 5) to produce sixty-year cycles. These cycles repeat themselves. The Chinese believe that the interactions of the twelve earthly branches and the ten heavenly stems rule the entire destiny of man and form the basis of Chinese astrology. In fact, they believe that this interaction controls everything in the universe. Through years of observation, the Chinese have worked out associations between environmental changes and the lunar, seasonal and solar periods in each of the sixty-year cycles. This is the basis of the Chinese Almanac, or Tong Shu, under which auspicious days for undertaking a variety of tasks are identified (e.g. for getting married, for starting a business, or for moving house). *See also* Almanac.

GATES The design and orientation of gates can be used to attract good Chi flows. Gates should ideally have two doors and open inward rather than outward. It is very auspicious to design a gate with the center higher than the sides: this symbolizes the attainment of one's goals. If the center is lower than the sides, it signifies misfortune in your career. Note that your front gate is not your main door; thus, when choosing auspicious directions for your home, you should place greater emphasis on the main door to the house than on the gate leading into the property.

GAZEBOS If correctly built, these can strengthen the Chi of the main door. Gazebos are considered as additions to the garden. Depending on the location of a gazebo, it can enhance or detract from the Feng Shui of the house, especially in relation to its position with the main door and whether it strengthens or weakens its Chi. *See also* Greenhouses.

Location of main door	Good for gazebo/ greenhouse	Bad for gazebo/ greenhouse
East or southeast	North	West or northwest
West or northwest	Southwest or northeast	South
North	West or northwest	Southwest or northeast
South	East or southeast	North
Southwest or northeast	South	Southeast or east

GLOBE A potent representation of the earth element. Especially when made of a semiprecious material like lapis lazuli, quartz, or jasper, a globe is an excellent energizer for education luck when displayed in the northeast corner of a young college student's room.

GOD OF LONGEVITY Sau Seng Kong, the ultimate symbol of longevity. The God of Longevity is an excellent symbol to place in any home and few Chinese do without him: he brings good health and long life. He is always shown carrying a peach and accompanied by the crane and the deer, all of which are also symbols of longevity. He is usually carrying a staff on which hangs the gourd that contains the nectar of the gods. Sau Seng Kong is also recognizable by his deep forehead and domed head, symbolizing his great wisdom. He may be displayed in a painting or as decorations on Chinese ceramics and art objects.

GODS OF WEALTH Special deities placed in the home to generate wealth luck. The Chinese have several deities they regard as the wealth god. One of the most popular is Tsai Shen Yeh, who is often shown sitting on a tiger, to symbolize his control over this animal. In the lunar years of the tiger, displaying the God of Wealth is particularly auspicious. It is not necessary to pray to this deity; simply invite him into your home as a symbolic gesture. One can also hang a knotted cluster of nine Chinese coins tied with red thread, to activate the prosperity attributes of the coins. The best place to display the God of Wealth is on a table between 30 and 33 inches (76 and 84cm) high directly facing the door. Thus, the first thing you see upon entering your home is the wealth god, symbolically greeting the Chi coming into the home, transforming it into healthy prosperous energy that then flows through the rest of the house. If this spot is already occupied by the family altar, place the wealth god diagonally opposite the front door, facing toward it. Do not place your wealth god in the dining room or bedroom. Kwan Kung, usually regarded as a bringer of wealth, is another popular Chinese deity.

GOLDFISH If you keep goldfish (they are lucky), place nine of them in an aquarium or goldfish bowl. Of the nine, eight should be colored and one black. Goldfish are excellent for improving the Feng Shui luck of a home or office and they work best when located in the north, the east, or the southeast of the home. They should never be in the bedroom.

GOOD FORTUNE Good health, good family and prosperity luck. Good fortune luck includes all that one hopes for in life, specifically good health and longevity, wealth and prosperity, good family and descendants' luck, and a good personal reputation. Feng Shui promises all these if you live in harmony with your environment.

GOOD LUCK A specific type of luck in particular areas of your life. Luck is an abstract term and in Feng Shui it refers to the accomplishment or possession of specific categories of good fortune. Feng Shui lists eight types of good luck – wealth, health, family and relationships, children, having a good name, having a good career, having a good education, and having the goodwill of powerful people. Chinese divination readings define luck as different types and grades of luck for each of these eight categories. Money and wealth luck is subdivided into the luck of inheritance, the luck of gambling and speculation, and the luck of business success. In the language of Feng Shui luck thus has many different meanings.

GRASS On an empty patch of land, grass creates the auspicious bright hall when located directly in front of your home.

GRAVE SITES These benefit enormously from the practice of Yin Feng Shui. The correct orientation of grave sites is part of Yin Feng Shui practice, a difficult and extremely potent branch of Feng Shui.

GREEN DRAGON The green dragon of Feng Shui is believed to be the earth dragon. There are nine dragons altogether - the others are wind, sea, water, sky, fire, golden, mountain, and celestial - each

of which is reputedly the creature that controls one aspect of the universal elements. *See also* Dragon.

GREENHOUSES Like gazebos, they can strengthen the Feng Shui of your door. Greenhouses represent additions to the home and these can be good or bad luck depending on the location of the main door. *See also* Gazebos.

H

HANGING OBJECTS Feng Shui cures represented by windchimes, bells, flutes, bamboo stems, etc. Such objects can be hung from beams and ceilings to counter inauspicious Feng Shui features. They should be unobtrusive and be hung as discreetly as possible.

HARMONY In Feng Shui this refers to the harmonious interaction of the elements in the living space. In Feng Shui everything in the universe can be categorized as being one of five elements – wood, fire, water, earth, or metal. For them to be in harmony, elements in each part of the living space should be mutually enhancing rather than mutually destructive. *See also* Elements.

HEALTH LUCK This offers a vigorous, robust, and long life. Using specific parts of the Eight Mansions formula can activate good health luck. One auspicious personalized direction is the health direction. If you use Tien Yi, with your head pointing in the corresponding direction, this can enhance your health and physical well-being. *See* Tien Yi.

HEAVEN LUCK The luck with which you are born and over which you have no control. Heaven luck (or fate) exerts an influence over a person's life. You can improve your heaven luck by harnessing the powers of your earth luck. This is basically the practice of Feng Shui. Mankind luck is created by actions, choices, and behavior - whether or not one leads a virtuous life. Heaven, earth, and mankind luck are collectively referred to as the trinity of luck.

HEDGES Block out bad drain flows and negative sights. Growing a hedge to block out unsightly structures is very effective when these structures are facing you from the southwest and northeast. Hedges can be any height but they should not appear threatening by being too close to the home.

HILLS The natural undulation of the landscape where dragons live and a sure sign of potentially good Feng Shui. The green dragon lives in hills, creating auspicious breath and good energy. Hills should be rolling, with smooth gentle slopes, rather than sharp craggy cliff faces. Where vegetation is lush and green and there is a good balance of sunshine and shade, dragons and tigers are also said to be present. There are five types of hill shape, each one based on the five elements of fire, wood, earth, metal, and water. For Feng Shui analysis it is useful to develop the ability to discern these differences, which offer clues as to their suitability for each individual. Understanding the element connotation of hill shapes, or the shapes of their peaks, also enables practitioners to judge the Feng Shui quality of a range of hills.

HOME The most important place for Feng Shui. Residential Feng Shui affects a person's overall luck. Even when Feng Shui at work may not be very good, if you have a house or a room with good Feng Shui your overall luck will be quite good. Residential Feng Shui is especially important for the well-being of families. In the home the three major features to get right from a Feng Shui perspective are the main door, the bedroom, and the kitchen.

HORSE The animal of the south, it can bring excessive Yang energy. The horse is a symbol of courage, speed, and perseverance and is also one of the treasures of Buddhism. It is auspicious to hang a painting or picture of horses in the south side of the living room because the element of the horse is fire, which coincides with the south direction. Horse figurines placed in the southwest are said to energize luck in social climbing and in the northwest for luck in examinations.

HORSESHOE In Landscape Feng Shui the ideal land formation. A house embraced by three ranges of hills forming a horseshoe and looking out onto flat land is said to have excellent Feng Shui for at least five generations.

HOSTILE STRUCTURES These include buildings, land features, hills, outcrops, overhead roads, overpasses, and other large concrete structures that can send intimidating breath toward your home. *See also* Poison Arrows and study the chapter on Poison Arrows in the Environment (*pages 316–27*).

HOUSE In Feng Shui anywhere that you eat, sleep, and take shelter is defined as your house. No matter how short your stay there, if the Feng Shui of the house is good it will benefit you. On the other hand, bad Feng Shui in such a temporary abode can also cause problems.

HSIA CALENDAR Also known as the Chinese lunar calendar and used in Feng Shui and fortune-telling. All fortune-telling and Feng Shui calculations using an individual's date of birth are based on the Hsia calendar. There are several methods in Feng Shui which require a person's birth details to discover their most auspicious sectors and directions. Fortune-telling methods include the Four Pillars of Destiny, which reveal character, personality, and future destiny. This method incorporate characters from the Chinese Hsia calendar extensively.

I

I CHING, OR THE BOOK OF CHANGES *See* Book of Changes.

ILLNESS This is often the first sign of bad Feng Shui. When occupants living in the same house take turns getting sick, or when children keep falling ill, these are indications that the Feng Shui of the home can be improved. Check to see if there are any poison arrows pointing directly at the home and therefore hurting it, then see if any of the drains around the house or building are blocked. Also make certain that your plumbing and your sewage system are in good order. Sometimes a simple course of action is enough to remove the obstacles that block the flow of Chi and cause bad luck.

INDOOR GARDENS Placed in the correct sector of the home, these bring exceptionally good fortune. If you want an open-air design in your home that calls for indoor gardens and landscaped interiors, make sure that these are located in the east, the southeast, or the south sector of your home. Following this advice allows you to blend harmoniously with the elements that make up your living space. Do not place your indoor garden in the sector which corresponds to the southwest or the northeast. This will cause disruptions in your family life and could also harm the marriage.

INTERIOR FENG SHUI The arrangement of furniture to create auspicious vibrations. This refers to the layout of the home and the allocation of rooms according to Feng Shui guidelines. It also refers to the selection of curtains and carpets and other soft furnishings. The ideal Feng Shui home creates a warm ambience where Yang energy and auspicious Chi flow freely from room to room.

J

JADE BELT This refers to any river and waterway which flows past your main door and seems to be "hugging" your home, bringing good fortune. If you also have hills behind your home this configuration is considered to be excellent Feng Shui. In such a case, enhance the good effect of the water by making certain it flows past your main door in the correct direction. Follow these guidelines:
- If the water is flowing from right to left (from inside the house looking out), your main door should face any of the four secondary directions, i.e. northeast, northwest, southwest, and southeast.
- If the water is flowing from left to right, your main door should be facing one of the cardinal directions, i.e. north, south, east, or west.

JADE PLANT An auspicious shrub that is regarded as the wealth plant. This refers to a variety of plant with succulent dark green leaves, which resemble a piece of precious jade. These plants are especially auspicious placed in the southeast corner or displayed in store windows where they will attract customers into the store.

JAPANESE GARDEN More for meditation than for Feng Shui. The layout and design of Japanese gardens are based more on Zen principles that are excellent for meditation and contemplation than on attracting good fortune Chi. Japanese gardens, however, offer excellent creative ideas on the use of stones and pebbles and these can be incorporated into Feng Shui gardens that have a southwest or northeast facing aspect.

JEWELRY For personalized good fortune luck and protection. People wear jewelry today to attract luck-enhancing Chi and to generate protective physical energies in the same way as our ancestors used to wear amulets and charms. Jewelry adorned with auspicious symbols attracts good fortune. Thus, engagement and wedding rings with the double happiness symbol bring excellent marriage luck. Coin jewelry attracts wealth energy. Genuine jewelry is always better than fake – diamonds are more powerful than crystal, and gold or platinum are better wealth energizers than steel or fake gold.

K

KAN TRIGRAM Placed north, it signifies water and winter. The image is a single strong Yang line sandwiched between and being pressured by two Yin lines. Kan often signifies danger in that it warns that water is a double-edged sword that can go out of control, as when it breaks its banks and overflows. Kan also represents the north sector of any home.

KEN TRIGRAM Placed northeast and signifying the mountain or earth element. Its meaning represents keeping silent. It stands for patience and a time of preparation. To activate the Chi essence of Ken, place an object of the earth element (e.g. crystals, globe, sand, or boulders) in the northeast. This is particularly helpful for students.

KHENG HUA A rare white flower whose blooming signifies exceptional good fortune. This is a variety of succulent cactus, which flowers at midnight. The flower is large and white with yellow stamens. It is both fragrant and beautiful. The kheng hua's very occasional flowering is believed to be a sign that descendants will have career and material success and will rise to prominence.

KILLING BREATH Also known as Shar Chi, this brings grave misfortunes. It is the opposite of the good auspicious Chi. Killing breath creates havoc with your life and your luck and you should endeavor to dissolve, destroy, or deflect killing breath coming your way. *See also* Poison Arrows.

KITCHEN The part of the home with the potential to press down misfortunes. The placement and orientation of the kitchen is extremely important for the Feng Shui of any home. Kitchens (and especially the stove or oven) should never be located in the northwest of the home: this is described as a fire at heaven's gate. The kitchen is best located deep inside the home, closer to the back than the front; it is also better placed on the right of the front door rather than on the left side when you enter the home. If you practice the Compass Formula on Kua numbers, a practical use of the formula is to locate the kitchen in your worst (i.e. your Chueh Ming, or total loss) direction according to your Kua number. Do not site the kitchen in any one of your personalized auspicious sectors since this presses down on your good fortune.

KUA NUMBERS Derived from the Eight Mansions formula for Feng Shui orientations. To determine your personal auspicious and inauspicious directions, first work out your personal Kua numbers. The calculation of this requires your year of birth and your sex. The year of birth must first be converted into the equivalent year according to the lunar calendar; do this by finding out whether you were born before or after the lunar New Year in your year of birth. See the chapter on Compass Formula Feng Shui (*pages 66–79*) for advice on how to work out your Kua number.

KUN TRIGRAM The ultimate Yin trigram, denoting the place of the matriarch or the female maternal. Kun, meaning the receptive, is made up of three broken lines and represents the dark, the yielding, the primal power of Yin. Its image is big earth. It also symbolizes fertility. Placing this trigram in the children corner can help couples to conceive children. Being the ultimate Yin trigram, it can also be used to balance out excessive Yang energy; for example, if the afternoon sun is too strong for the house, displaying a Kun trigram might reduce the inauspicious effects of the sun. Kun is also an important symbol of the earth mother and activating the place of Kun, i.e. the southwest, brings good luck in areas associated with love, social life, family, and relationships with people in general.

L

LAKE An example of big water in front of the house, which brings good luck. The Feng Shui is considered to be very auspicious especially when the waters of the lake are clean, unpolluted, and teeming with life. In such conditions, the lake becomes a source of precious Sheng Chi. To harness fully the good luck of the lake apply the principles of the five elements. Thus, a lake to the north of your front door is better than a lake to the south. This can be engineered by the way you orient your home. Make certain that you have a view of the lake from inside your living room and under no circumstances position your home with the lake behind you.

LAMPS Used to simulate precious Yang energy, lamps are usually excellent Feng Shui when placed almost anywhere. Even in the north corner, which is the place of water, placing a lamp does not spoil the Feng Shui since Yang energy turns water into steam and this creates the symbol of power. Thus you can have lamps all over the home and they will bring good energy. Do not, however, have lamps too bright. Muted, warm lights are always better than harsh white lights. *See also* Lights.

LAND LEVELS The topography and contours of the land and their implications are an important part of Feng Shui investigation into particular sites. Land that is completely flat is generally regarded as

inauspicious and can only be made habitable from a Feng Shui point of view if efforts are made to create variations in height and levels by introducing buildings to attract an auspicious flow of Chi. It is good Feng Shui to live with the mountain behind and therefore supporting one's home. The technique of Feng Shui is to orientate a home in such a way as to capture the maximum good Chi created by the presence of different land levels. *See also* Landscape Feng Shui.

LANDSCAPE FENG SHUI This is based on form, topography, and structure. Landscape Feng Shui is classical Feng Shui. Any practitioner must apply this method to an investigation of the site of any house before introducing other Feng Shui methods. Landscape Feng Shui is also known as Form School and, as the name suggests, it looks at the forms – the structures, shapes, topography, and levels of the land – to investigate the quality of the air and the Chi. The environment is believed to be alive with Chi and whether this is auspicious or not depends largely on the way the winds and waters have shaped the landscape over time. The practice of Feng Shui focuses on the best way to site and orientate the home in any given landscape such that superimposing the imaginary four celestial creatures becomes benign and auspicious rather than hostile or inauspicious. See the chapter on Landscape Feng Shui (*pages 54–65*).

LATER HEAVEN ARRANGEMENT The sequence of trigrams arranged around the Pa Kua and the one used in Feng Shui analysis for the abodes of the living. The Later Heaven arrangement is also known as the "inner world" arrangement where the trigrams are taken out of their groupings in pairs of opposites and instead are shown in a circular temporal progression of their manifestations within the physical earthly realm. What are perceived then are the cycles of the year with four distinct

seasons, the cycles of each day with its day and night and so forth. Under this new arrangement, therefore, the cardinal points and the seasons are more closely related. This arrangement of the trigrams is thus drastically different from the Early Heaven arrangement.

LEAF SHAPES Analyzing the suitability of trees to particular sectors of the garden and the shape of their leaves can determine the luck of plants placed near the home. Thorny and prickly leaves should be discouraged. Round, succulent leaves are considered more auspicious than long knifelike leaves.

LEMON TREE An indicator of good fortune when fully laden with fruit. Placed near the front of the house in the spring this indicates the ripening of good fortune. *See also* Lime Tree.

LI TRIGRAM Placed south it signifies fire. Li, meaning the clinging, is made up of one weak broken line in between two strong unbroken Yang lines. Li is fire, the sun, brightness, lightning, heat, and warmth. Since the south is the corner of the fire element, placing the trigram Li in the south is an effective way of activating the fame luck that the south sector can bring.

LIGHTS Excellent both for energizing good Chi and dissolving bad Chi. Lights are among the most versatile tools in Feng Shui practice. They correct numerous Feng Shui problems not only because they are a source of precious Yang energy but also because lights cause Chi energy to rise. They can solve problems of missing corners, excessively Yin corners, and land levels that are too low. Lights also attract good Sheng Chi, bringing customers to restaurants and good fortune to corporations that keep their front entrances well-lit. Placed in the south they are particularly auspicious and combined with crystals their potency is considerably enhanced.

LILIES Yellow lilies represent vibrant Yang energy and are auspicious. It is far more auspicious to present a bouquet of yellow lilies than one of red thorny roses. White lilies are also a good fortune gift and are excellent for convalescing patients. They bring with them the pure and healing energy of the west.

LIME TREE An auspicious tree to display during the lunar New Year. A lime tree heavy with ripening fruits symbolizes the ripening of good fortune and prosperity. These plants are usually seen at the entrances to the homes of Chinese families during the fifteen days of the lunar New Year. This symbolizes a prosperous start to the New Year. An orange plant will have the same effect. *See also* Orange Tree.

LIONS A pair of lions in front of the gate or main door is an excellent symbol of protection against bad Chi and against people with bad intentions trying to get into your home. The lions need not be enormous, and their size should be proportionate to the size of your door. Lions are an excellent alternative to Fu dogs. *See also* Fu Dogs.

LIVING ROOM The best place in the house for locating Feng Shui enhancing and energizing symbols. The Feng Shui of living rooms and the way furniture is arranged in such rooms takes on significance in the overall Feng Shui of the home. The most auspicious part of the living room is the far end diagonal to its entrance. Placing something significant here, such as a favorite chair, will bring you to the luckiest corner. It is also a good place to display a three-legged frog and a dragon. Living rooms should always be on a lower level than bedrooms and dining rooms.

LO SHU MAGIC SQUARE An important tool of analysis made up of nine sector grids. This square is probably the most important symbol in Compass Formula Feng Shui. The Lo Shu grid was supposedly brought to the attention of the Duke of Chou on the back of a turtle that surfaced in the Lo River. The significance of the grid lies in its arrangement of numbers in a nine sector grid so that the sum of any three numbers in any direction adds up to fifteen, the number of days it takes for the new moon to become a full moon, and because of this co-relation the Lo Shu grid is said to offer clues to the fortunes of people and homes over a time period. Thus Lo Shu analysis very often centers on the time dimensions of Feng Shui. It is therefore the principal tool in the calculation of the flying star method of Formula Feng Shui.

LOGOS Inauspicious logos can bring down a company. A corporate logo should always be designed with its Feng Shui significance in mind. Companies have benefited from auspicious logos, and some have gone under because of very inauspicious ones. For further advice, see the chapter on Feng Shui for Corporations (*pages 292–301*).

LONGEVITY An important Chinese aspiration similar to having good health, longevity is one of the most important components of having good luck. It implies the luck of seeing one's descendants succeed and bringing honor to the family name. It also means a life of good health. In symbolic Feng Shui the emblems of longevity are numerous, and the most important symbol is the God of Longevity, Sau Seng Kong. Other symbols are the pine tree, the bamboo, the peach, the deer, and the the turtle. Displaying any of these symbols in the home is considered to bring excellent luck. *See also* God of Longevity.

LOTUS POND The lotus is a good fortune flower considered a symbol of enlightenment. A lotus pond is always an excellent feature in any garden, and is viewed as being extremely auspicious although not necessarily from a material point of view. Lotus ponds indicate a heightened sense of peace and mind transformation. They encourage spiritual development.

LOTUS SEEDS Signify auspicious offspring luck. The seed of the lotus is an excellent symbol of descendants' luck. Displaying lotus seeds in the home is said to enhance and speed up the arrival of grandchildren. Buddhists value prayer beads made of lotus seeds.

LOVE In the Chinese scheme of things this is used in reference to marriage and family luck. In the language of Feng Shui love is defined as the kind of luck which leads to marriage and for women especially a first marriage. For men, love is related to finding a woman who can take on the role of earth mother, who can bear children and keep house. This is not a very romantic view of love and it is certainly at odds with modern opinion and attitudes . . .

LUCKY NUMBERS Displaying lucky numbers prominently if the number of your house or building happens to be an auspicious one. Auspicious numbers are those that end in 1, 6, 7, 8, and 9, all of which are very lucky, although 8 is particularly popular among the Chinese because phonetically it sounds like "phat," which means "prosperous growth" in Chinese. Nine is considered by most Feng Shui masters to be the premier number because it signifies the fullness of heaven and earth. The numbers 1, 6, and 9 together in any permutation are considered the luckiest combinations. The number 7 is lucky because it represents this period; it will cease being lucky by the year 2003, after which the number 8 becomes the number of the period (years 2003–2023). The number 8 is considered lucky because it represents both current and future prosperity. Most people cannot choose the numbers of their houses, their telephone numbers, or car license plates, but anyone who can should select a number with a lucky combination. An alternative is to play down any unlucky numbers by showing them small, but playing up a good number by showing it prominently. Some numbers are unlucky. The number 4 is considered the death number because phonetically it sounds like "sey," or "die," in Chinese. For many people, however, 4 has brought fabulously good luck! The combination of 2s and 3s together is considered extremely inauspicious: it leads to misunderstandings, quarrels, and other problems. The very worst number of all is 5. In Feng Shui this number brings nothing but problems and difficulties.

LUNAR CALENDAR The Chinese lunar calendar is divided into twelve months of twenty-nine days each. Every two and a half years an extra month is added to adjust the calendar and this extra month is consecutively interposed between the second and the eleventh months of the lunar year. An auspicious day of the lunar calendar is the "first day of spring," generally referred to as the "lap chun." Some years have double lap chuns (considered auspicious years) and some years have no lap chun at all (these years are considered bad luck for births and marriages). In the lunar calendar, the day begins at 11pm, and the twenty-four hours are divided into twelve segments of two hours each, with each one being ruled by one of the twelve animals. For divination purposes one must know the animal symbols that signify one's hour of birth and the animal that signifies one's year of birth. It is just as important to know the elements which rule one's four pillars and in the process understand the meanings of animals, elements, and the Yin–Yang connotations. The difference between good and bad luck lies in how these symbols are combined and Chinese fortune-telling involves interpreting these meanings.

LUO PAN This usually contains secret codes and formulas. The Luo Pan, or the authentic Chinese geomancer's compass, is an elaborately complex instrument comprising up to thirty-six concentric rings drawn around a small magnetic compass. The inner rings around the compass show the eight trigrams and orientations. The rings that follow display the heavenly (or celestial) stems and the earthly (or terrestrial) branches. (These terms are used in the Ganzhi system.) For the layman, use of the Luo Pan can be confusing unless accompanied by deep knowledge of the many permutations between trigrams, stems and branches, and their corollary, the interactions between element and horoscope influences. It is therefore far easier to work from preformulated tables already simplified by the masters and to use a simple Western-style compass. *See also* Almanac and Ganzhi system.

M

MAGNOLIA An exquisite symbol of feminine sweetness and beauty. An especially good flowering shrub to grow in the west side of your home or in a west-oriented garden.

MANDARIN DUCKS Wonderful symbols of conjugal happiness, which should be displayed. A pair of mandarin ducks is said to symbolize a young couple in love. According to symbolic Feng Shui displaying a pair of ducks in the southwest corner attracts the luck of romance and love. Ducks made of wood are not as effective as those made of jasper.

MANKIND LUCK A part of the trinity of luck that you create for yourself. This is the kind of luck in the trinity of luck – *tien*, the luck from heaven; *ti*, the luck from the earth; *ren*, the luck mankind creates for himself. Of the three kinds of luck, both earth luck and mankind luck are within our control. Earth luck is Feng Shui and mankind luck is what we create for ourselves. *See also* Tien Ti Ren.

MARRIAGE Feng Shui is to do with activating the earth elements of the southwest. Just as bad Feng Shui cause havoc in the marriage, good Feng Shui can also create conjugal bliss and family harmony. To energize good fortune in marriage look after the place of the matriarch: this is the place of the Kun trigram - the southwest. The ruling element of this corner is big earth. Thus, objects that simulate or produce this element are said to be particularly good for activating marriage luck. Lights and crystals are thus excellent energizers.

MATTRESSES One big mattress in the conjugal bed is much better than two separate single mattresses. These could cause a rift between husband and wife because they symbolically create a schism between the couple. It is better to have two completely separate beds, or even separate rooms, than to have one bed with two mattresses.

MENTOR LUCK Such assistance from influential people is energized by activating the northwest. The northwest direction is important and takes on great significance because the trigram associated with it is Chien, which symbolizes the leader and blessings

from heaven. Those in need of mentor luck and the support of powerful people should activate the flow of Chi in this part of the home. Hanging a six-rod windchime is one way of doing this because it creates the essence of metal energy.

METAL One of the elements of Feng Shui represented in the west and northwest. Metal is also regarded as gold and the word in Chinese characters is the same. The metal element is made auspicious with the presence of earth since earth produces gold. Thus placing a symbolic earth element object such as a globe in the metal corners of your home brings success and wealth. Metal is destroyed by the fire element. This suggests that installing bright lights, for instance, in the metal corners would be disastrous for the luck of the corner.

MIRROR A major Feng Shui tool to use for business Feng Shui and other purposes. Mirrors are one of the prime Feng Shui tools and have many uses. They can be used to regularize the shape of a room. When there is a missing corner, for example,  installing a wall mirror visually extends the wall outward, thereby filling up the missing corner and restoring the balance of the room. Mirrors can also eliminate freestanding columns in the room. If you have a structural pillar in the middle of the room which you cannot knock down, wrapping it with mirrors in effect makes it "disappear." A column in the middle of the house is especially harmful, since it symbolizes a knife plunged into the heart of the home. If you do not wish to wrap the whole column with mirrors, use plants and creepers instead. Placing a mirror in your dining room symbolizes the doubling of food on the table. Food has always been an important indicator to the Chinese of how well the family is doing, thus an abundance of food is always very good Feng Shui. Similarly, placing a mirror next to the cash register in a retail outlet will double turnover. Mirrors can be used to reflect the Shar Chi, or killing breath, sent toward the front entrance of your home or office by poison arrows. Such poison arrows can also be countered using a Pa Kua or cannon, or by simply reorienting the front door. A mirror is a less hostile way of reacting to someone else's poison arrow hitting at you and should be used if it is enough to dissolve the Shar Chi.

MISFORTUNES Those resulting from bad Feng Shui usually occur continuously. If you feel that a run of ill-luck is down to bad Feng Shui, check on

the regularity of such occurrences. In practicing Feng Shui, be careful not to attribute all the bad or good things that happen to you solely to bad or good Feng Shui.

MONEY LUCK This is created with Symbolic and Water Feng Shui. There are specific measures recommended in Symbolic Feng Shui practice and in the practice of the Water Dragon classic that are specifically focused on the creation of wealth and prosperity luck. Symbols of money are coins and the wealth deities and these can be displayed in the home to attract wealth-creating Chi. Energizing the southeast sector of the home with luscious plants or a water feature is also a popular method of activating money luck.

MONEY PLANT Creepers that symbolize the successful enhancement of income. The money plant is generally found in the tropics. It has yellow and green heart-shaped flowers. The money plant should not be confused with the jade plant. *See also* Jade Plant.

MOON GATE A circular entrance is considered to represent an auspicious balance of Yin and Yang energies and was popular in old times. The round shape suggests the element of gold.

MOTHER EARTH The trigram Kun (made up of three broken lines) which rules the southwest symbolizes "mother earth" (i.e. big earth). It is the ultimate Yin trigram and signifies the female side of all of us. This trigram can be used to enhance relationship luck by doubling it, thus making it into the hexagram Kun (six broken lines), and hanging it in the southwest of the home or room. Another way to use mother earth to energize the southwest (the romance corner) is to display a large globe or map of the world as a representation of mother earth.

MOUNTAIN STAR A divinitive star used in flying star Feng Shui formulas. The mountain star is one of two divinitive "stars" used in this form of analysis. Mountain stars indicate good fortune for any sector they fly into when they carry the numbers 1, 6, or 8 and indicate extremely bad luck when the numbers are either 5 or 2. Flying star Feng Shui is probably one of the most advanced Feng Shui formulas and its interpretation and correct practice require many years of intensive study and experience. The other star used in this method of Feng Shui is the water star and analysis of the flying star chart usually requires that both the mountain and water stars are interpreted and analyzed together. *See also* Flying Star Feng Shui.

MOUNTAINS Mountains in the environment are vital for good Feng Shui. Completely flat land, without undulation or elevated land forms, does not have the presence of the green dragon and is therefore inauspicious. You can symbolize the presence of a mountain in your home or office by hanging a picture of one; the mountain must always be behind you to symbolize solid support, to anchor you, and prevent you from being swept away by misfortune. In Feng Shui analysis, mountain shapes are categorized into five elements and orientations are classified as one of the four celestial creatures. In Feng Shui analysis today, large tall buildings (especially in cities) are considered in the same way as mountains were in ancient times.

MOU TAN FLOWER *See* Peony.

N

NARCISSUS *See* Bulbs.

NATAL CHARTS These offer a Feng Shui reading based on flying star Feng Shui. These are based on special calculations that indicate in some detail the luck of all the eight sectors of any house. The method used is flying star Feng Shui, which divides time into periods and calculates the natal charts of buildings based either on when they were first constructed or on the last time that they were extensively renovated.

NATURAL CONTOURS This refers to hills and mountains in the landscape, particularly those that simulate the dragon and tiger. Landscape Feng Shui looks at the natural land forms and elevations. However, man-made buildings also affect the Feng Shui of a site and are also taken into account.

NIEN YEN The personal direction to activate or energize for good family luck, love, and marriage. This is one of the four auspicious directions allocated to each Kua number in the Eight Mansions formula.

NOISE Noise is generally regarded as a manifestation of, and a way of simulating, intense, loud Yang energy. During the start of spring or at the start of the lunar New Year, people used to create noise by lighting firecrackers, which were believed to scare away any lingering evil spirits from the previous year. Sometimes hanging a fake firecracker in the house signifies the real thing and is supposed to simulate the creation of Yang energy. In Feng Shui, however, merely placing this symbol is deemed sufficient to simulate precious Yang energy.

NORTH Associated with the water element, it is also the place of the tortoise. The north part of your home should be energized with the presence of water. If you cannot place a real water feature, hanging a painting of a water scene is sufficient to keep the energies of the elements in harmony.

NORTHEAST The place of the earth element that also stands for education and scholarship. Displaying objects belonging to this element will keep the element energies in harmony.

NORTHWEST The place of the patriarch signified by the trigram Chien. This is probably the most important corner of any home because of its association with the patriarch, or family breadwinner. Always make certain that the energies of the northwest are kept alive and well. This is the place of big metals so placing earth or metal objects here is an excellent idea. Do not place fire in the form of lamps or lights in this area. Fire destroys metal in the cycle.

NUMBERS The numbers 1 to 9 offer a multitude of good and bad Feng Shui. Numbers have connotations of good and bad luck according to Feng Shui. The general rule is to go with what the number sounds like. Thus, the phonetic sounds of each of the numbers 1 to 9 indicate that 3 and 8 are excellent numbers while the number 4 is to be avoided. Based on flying star analysis the numbers 5 and 2 are the villains while the numbers 1, 6, and 8 are supposed to be excellent. The number 9 is generally considered to be excellent.

O

OFFICE FENG SHUI The same principles apply to Feng Shui at work as they do at home except that in the office the most important consideration is the energizing of wealth and harmony luck to ensure that employees work as comfortably as possible. The directions that benefit everyone will be in accordance with the birth date of the CEO or the most senior person in the office. To ensure the company is protected against downturns in business, the prosperity corner of the office should at all times be kept energized by the presence of a healthy fresh plant placed in the southeast.

OPEN SHELVES These resemble knives, which cut at you and cause untold harm. Their sharp edges send out Shar Chi, killing breath, and with it illness, loss of income, even a dramatic reduction in wealth. Try to block off any poison arrows being sent out by

turning shelves into cupboards with the addition of doors. If you cannot do this, place books or files flush with the edges of the shelves to make them disappear. For shelves with ornaments, round off the sharp edges with sandpaper. Glass shelves are harmful in the north, wooden in the southwest, northeast, and in the middle of the room. Plastic shelves are the least harmful anywhere. *See also* Bedrooms.

ORANGE TREE An orange tree is extremely auspicious and brings the family great wealth luck. This is because the Chinese word for orange, "kum," sounds phonetically like the word for gold. It is considered very lucky to display orange trees in fruit in the home during the lunar New Year, symbolizing a prosperous New Year to come. Because it is particularly good for energizing wealth luck, if you wish to plant an orange tree in the garden, it is best planted in the southeast corner (the wealth corner).

ORCHID An outstanding symbol of strength and bravery. In selecting plants for the garden, if the climate where you live is suitable, the growing of orchids signifies strength and courage as well as a lengthy stay in your career. Orchids are long-lasting flowers that bring good healthy Chi to the home.

ORIENTATIONS These refer to the directions of doors, and sitting and sleeping positions. Orientation is an important aspect of correct Feng Shui practice and it is often necessary to go to some length to take correct measurements and compass directions so that orientations are accurately implemented according to Feng Shui theory. Orientation can also mean the correct siting of the home to take advantage of auspicious features in the environment, such as rivers, lakes, hills, and fields.

P

PA KUA The eight-sided symbol used in the interpretation of good or bad Feng Shui. It corresponds to the four cardinal points of the compass and the four sub-directions and derives its significance from the eight trigrams of the *I Ching*.

PA KUA MIRROR The Yin Pa Kua used for deflecting poison arrows. It is usually painted with a red background to create masses of vital Yang energy, and the trigrams are placed round the Pa Kua in the

Early or First Heaven arrangement. In the center is the mirror that reflects away all the hostile energy coming in its direction.

PARK A park or similar space located in front of your main door represents the auspicious bright hall. The effect is extremely good Feng Shui because Chi is said to be able to settle and accumulate before entering your home. *See also* Bright Hall.

PATHWAYS Winding paths are better Feng Shui than straight pathways. Any path, driveway, and even corridor is less harmful if it is not straight and long. In the garden a winding pathway is best since it causes Chi to meander and this slows it down, allowing it to accumulate.

PATIO A patio is an excellent way of adding a missing corner. Depending on the direction in which the patio is located you can also enhance it with element therapy. Thus, for example, a patio located in the north will benefit enormously from a water feature, while a patio in the south could be made into a barbecue area.

PAVILIONS Structures that can either strengthen or weaken the main door. *See also* Gazebos.

PAVING STONES A winding pathway of paving stones is an excellent feature in the earth corners of your garden.

PEACH The fruit of longevity. Displaying a peach branch in jade in the center of your home will attract longevity luck.

PEACH TREE Many legends surround the peach tree which offers immortality to anyone who eats its fruit. Supposedly growing in the Western paradise, it is said to fruit once every 3,000 years.

PEACOCK The peacock signifies dignity and beauty. For centuries, the attractive colors of the peacock's tail feathers have made them popular emblems of official rank, and fans made out of these feathers are often hung in Chinese homes. The peacock can also be used as a substitute for the red phoenix. *See also* Phoenix.

PEONY The king of flowers and excellent for creating good romance luck. The peony is associated with beautiful and desirable women. The legendary Yang Kuei Fei, reputedly one of the most beautiful women in Chinese history and concubine to the emperor, decorated her bedchamber with peonies all year round. The emperor, who could deny her nothing, had to arrange for these flowers to be sent to her from the south. Parents who want their daughters to marry well should hang a large painting of many peonies in the living room. The more luscious the blooms, the better the fortune. Paintings of peonies, or peonies made of silk, can also be used in the bedroom, but activating the living area is better. If you are already married, hanging a picture of peonies in the bedroom will cause your husband to be more amorous, but perhaps with someone else. Peonies are therefore not good for bringing romance back into the marriage.

PERGOLAS Garden structures that are an excellent solution for missing corners. These bring great variety to a large garden but do check carefully to see if they will add or detract from the Feng Shui of your home. *See also* Gazebos.

PERIOD OF EIGHT The next period, the period of eight (2004–2023), will belong to the third son, the young man we nurtured who now understands the emotive side of his nature and is willing to show us the way. That age will be symbolized by the mountain (Ken). It will be a period when partnerships and ventures, which have stood the test of time, will come to an end or change, with the possibility of new directions surfacing, resulting in a challenge and a shift in policies. In the period of eight obviously the number 8 will be doubly lucky.

PERIOD OF SEVEN We are currently in the period of seven, which began in 1984 and ends in the year 2003. The number 7 is known as the Joyous, or Tui, period, signifying both a mouth and a lake. It suggests bliss, harmony, tranquility, enjoyment, indulgence, mid-fall, and a young girl. Coming after all the responsibilities and ambitious inclinations of the Age of Six, it is also a time of laughter, relaxation, and enjoyment. This time is known in Feng Shui as the "Period of Communications." During this period the number 7 is considered auspicious. But once this period comes to an end the number 7 itself becomes unlucky.

PHOENIX The bird of the south that brings great opportunities. Often depicted in Chinese mythology as the mate of the celestial dragon, the phoenix can be used as a Feng Shui symbol to activate the luck of opportunity. For marriage luck, the phoenix and the dragon together symbolize great conjugal happiness and the Chinese often use the dragon–phoenix symbol at wedding banquets. Place a dragon–phoenix motif in the southwest to activate marriage luck. For career luck, a phoenix on its own symbolizes new opportunities. To activate luck in your job, a picture of the phoenix without the dragon is better because it releases the energy of the phoenix. With the dragon, the phoenix is a Yin creature; without the dragon it becomes a Yang creature, bringing financial success and prosperity. In Landscape Feng Shui, the phoenix is represented by a small mound or slightly elevated land in the south, or at the front of the home. If you do not already have a small mound in front of your main door, you can artificially create one to energize the luck of the sector. As a creature of the south, the phoenix works best when placed in the south sector or corner of the home or office. If you cannot find a suitable phoenix symbol, other birds with fine plumage such as the rooster or peacock are also suitable.

PILLARS Pillars and columns have the potential to cause Feng Shui problems if they are freestanding and face a doorway directly. Square pillars cause more harm than round pillars. Two round pillars flanking a door is good Feng Shui. If pillars are causing problems because their edges are facing you, place a plant against the edge to "hide" the edge.

PINE TREES The pine tree is a hardy symbol of longevity and strength in adversity. It is a good idea to have at least one pine tree in your garden. The leaves of the pine tree are also said to possess excellent qualities for cleansing the home of bad energies. They are thus useful media for space cleaning and purification.

PLANTS Plants always signify good Feng Shui and are suitable enhancers of the wood corners of the home or office. Just as lights suggest the fire element, plants always suggest the growth essence of the wood element. If you grow plants around your home, and especially in the east and southeast, it will greatly

enhance your Feng Shui. Keep plants under control by cutting them back and trimming them regularly. Dying plants should be discarded immediately.

PLUM BLOSSOM Hang a picture of plum blossom to create a happy, long life. With the peony, the lotus and the chrysanthemum the plum makes up the four auspicious flowers. They also collectively represent the four seasons, with the plum signifying winter. The plum is commonly regarded as a symbol of a happy and long life because the flowers appear on the leafless and apparently lifeless branches of the tree until it reaches an extremely advanced age.

POISON ARROWS These are the harmful and hostile structures in the environment that send out killing energy toward your home. Learn to spot them and how to deflect them. Poison arrows have the power to destroy houses with even the best Feng Shui. Always ensure that the front door is not being afflicted by the poisonous breath of an arrow.

POMEGRANATE This symbolizes the luck of many offspring, all behaving in a filial and respectful manner with a successful future ahead of them. The many seeds of the pomegranate make it a symbol of posterity. Many parents advise their young newly-wed second generation to display a painting or sculpture of a pomegranate in their bedroom to create the luck of having many healthy children.

PONDS Water features that are best placed in the north, southeast, and east. Small ponds are extremely auspicious in these directions. Keep the pond well aerated with moving or flowing water. To bring good Chi into the home, keep fish or terrapins in the pond.

PRICKLY PLANTS *See* Cactus.

PRODUCTIVE CYCLE The productive cycle of the five elements creates a harmonious blend of Chi in the living space and this creates good Feng Shui. This cycle indicates that wood produces fire which produces earth which produces metal which produces water which produces wood. Using this cycle to discover the suitability of one element to

another, it is possible to arrange the objects in the living space to conform to the harmony of elements. *See also* Wuxing.

PROTRUDING CORNERS *See* Columns and Pillars.

PURPLE An auspicious color, purple signifies water and is more special than blue. Purple is particularly lucky when combined with chrome and silver.

Q

QUARTZ CRYSTAL Energizers for the southwest used to create romance luck. Natural crystal clusters are excellent emblems of the earth element and are therefore very suitable as energizers for the southwest and the northeast. These two corners are of interest to the younger generation since the southwest represents love and social life and the northeast signifies education luck.

QUIET AREAS The bedroom of the house should be a place of relative peace and quiet, where Yin Chi is to be preferred to too much Yang Chi. However, when the whole house is excessively quiet, luck remains stagnant.

R

REAL ESTATE A business signified by the earth element. Any kind of business involving property and property development will benefit from the energizing of the earth element in its business premises. Crystals, urns, terra cotta pots and decorative stones can be used as good fortune symbols. Work them into the décor of the office or stores and make sure they are placed in the earth sectors, either southwest or northwest.

RECTANGULAR SHAPES These represent the wood element and are most auspicious. The essence of the wood element is that it symbolizes growth. Thus rectangular shapes are also said to signify growth, also making the shape lucky.

RED The most popular and auspicious color, red is the ultimate Yang color. It stands for the trigram Li and represents the fire element. Red strengthens and energizes wherever it appears, particularly in the winter when Yang energy is on the wane. Red is worn on all kinds of happy occasions. When you hang auspicious calligraphy in the home use red as the background color to make the calligraphy come alive. However, red can also cause serious problems

when used in excess. If fire is not kept under control it can burn and destroy, therefore, control it and let it work for you.

RED THREAD Useful for tying onto auspicious symbols to energize Yang energy. Most symbolic objects of good fortune that are displayed benefit from the use of red thread. This signifies infusing the object with precious Yang energy, thereby making it come alive. Thus, when you place coins, boulders, three-legged toads, and other good fortune objects, tie a red thread around them to animate the Yang Chi.

REFRIGERATORS When placing a refrigerator in a kitchen, never put it next to the stove. This will create a clash of elements – water (representing the refrigerator, dishwasher, and sink) and fire (the stove). They should not be placed opposite each other either. Both such arrangements are bad Feng Shui.

RICE URN To the Chinese the rice urn symbolizes the rise and fall of family fortunes. Chinese who follow traditional practices take care to ensure that their rice urn is always well looked after. As the staple food to the Chinese, rice represents the family's livelihood. Wealthy Chinese matriarchs of the old school have been known to bequeath the precious family rice urn to the family of the eldest son. Some families in China continue to use urns that have been in the family for generations. A well-preserved rice urn passed from one generation to another will ensure that a family will remain wealthy even during difficult times. The family rice urn, like the symbolic wealth vase, should be kept tucked away in a storeroom, signifying the family's fortune being safely hidden away. Under the rice there is usually a carefully wrapped red packet containing gold coins to symbolize money. This money is renewed every lunar New Year to ensure continuous good fortune. Usually, if the last year has been a good one, one of the old coins will be kept and new ones added. This preserves the good luck the family has been enjoying for the year to come. The rice urn should be kept closed at all times. Use a strong urn to store your rice.

RIVERS A slow-moving river visible from your home is considered an auspicious Feng Shui feature. Rivers are believed to be purveyors of the good Chi, especially when the water is slow moving, meandering, and clean. Polluted rivers tend to be afflicted with poisonous breath. If your land is near a river orientate your house to face it. Then, depending on the direction the river flows past your front door, let your door face a direction that effectively captures the good Chi of the river. Do this by observing the guideline on water flow extracted from the *Water Dragon Classic*:

🌿 If your door faces one of the cardinal directions – north, south, east, or west – the river should flow past the door from left to right. This direction is taken inside the house looking out as you face the river.

🌿 If your door faces a secondary direction – southeast, southwest, northeast, or northwest – the river should flow past your door from right to left.

ROADS Surrounding roads have good or bad Feng Shui depending on their levels and directions. Roads that seem to hit directly at the home usually result in bad Feng Shui that should be countered with a Pa Kua or a mirror, or simply blocked off from view. Also, one should be wary of living near road junctions or intersections of any sort.

ROCK A rock or a boulder placed in a bathroom can overcome its bad effects. Rocks tied with red thread are an effective antidote for toilets that are located in the north part of the home. Toilets here cause bad luck for career professionals. Rocks can also be used to energize for good luck in the northeast and southwest of the garden. Here a small rock garden stimulates earth energy which brings good family relationships as well as friendships.

ROMANCE This luck can be activated in the bedroom or the southwest corner. Feng Shui advises that by energizing the luck of the female maternal, i.e. the southwest corner, romance and marriage luck are stimulated. This can be done with a variety of symbols, which signify romance, love, and togetherness. A pair of mandarin ducks, the double happiness symbol, and crystal clusters are some of the objects that can be used for this purpose.

ROOFTOPS These should never have water features. If you have a rooftop garden and wish to energize the north corner with a small fish bowl, make sure it is not too large. You must not have a swimming pool on the rooftop, nor should you have a blue roof since symbolically water above a mountain spells danger.

ROOMS Different rooms located in different parts of the home can be allocated according to their orientations. One simple method of allocating rooms for family members is to try and place the patriarch's bedroom in the northwest, and the matriarch's bedroom in the southwest. Young sons should be placed in the east and young daughters in the west. Use the Pa Kua arrangement of trigrams to guide you in the allocation of rooms for the children.

ROUND Because the circular shape denotes the metal element it can also stand for gold. Round shapes are especially suitable in the west, northwest, and north and they can be incorporated into structures and designs used in these corners of the house or garden.

S

SAILING SHIP Filled with false gold, a model sailing ship is one of the more effective Feng Shui energizers and symbols to have in the home. This is especially effective for bringing good business luck.

SCULPTURES Effective Feng Shui enhancers which bring good fortune when placed in the earth corners of the garden. Sculptures made of stone, granite, marble, or in ceramic form are suitable for the southwest and northeast. Metallic sculptures suit the west and northwest. Avoid sculptures with sharp points or angles.

SEASONS Each season has a corresponding element. Winter is of the water element; wood is spring; fire is summer; metal is autumn. Earth is the element for the period in between seasons.

SHADE As important as sunlight, shade adds to the balance of Yin and Yang and is necessary in any environment, a garden or otherwise. However, too much shade in place of sunlight makes for excessive Yin energy.

SHAR CHI Killing energy, or killing breath, caused by poison arrows and an imbalance between Yin and Yang. Shar Chi is the antithesis of Sheng Chi and Feng Shui prescribes various cures to counter it. *See also* Sheng Chi.

SHARP EDGES The sharp edges of corners or buildings create some of the most serious forms of Shar Chi. If the entrance to your house or property is being hit by the sharp edge of a building across the road, try to block it from view. Alternatively, use a Yin Pa Kua mirror to ward off killing energy. *See also* Pa Kua Mirror.

SHENG CHI The dragons cosmic breath which brings energy and growth. If you tap Sheng Chi you are sure to enjoy good health, prosperity, and peace.

SILVER A very auspicious color when combined with purple. In Chinese the word for silver is "ngan." When combined with purple – "chee" – it becomes

"ngan chee," which literally means money. In Feng Shui silver belongs to the metal element and is symbolic of the west and northwest.

SLEEPING POSITIONS Compass School Feng Shui gives each person a Kua number, which then determines an individual's four best and four worst sleeping directions. It is advisable to sleep with your head pointing toward one of your good directions. For further reading, see the chapter on Feng Shui of Bedrooms (*pages 160–71*). *See also* Kua Numbers.

SLOPES AND CONTOURS These have significant Feng Shui connotations. It is always preferable to live on the middle level of a slope than at the top or the bottom, embraced by contours on three sides with the back of the house supported by the slope. At the top of the slope the house is exposed to the elements; at the bottom auspicious Chi will "sink."

SMALL WATER In Feng Shui this generally refers to artificially created water features, such as water in domestic drains and the way it flows, that are not part of the natural landscape.

SOCIAL LIFE Promote your social life by using bright lights to give a boost to the Yang energy in the southwest corner of your garden. This is the place of big earth and it creates great amounts of energy. If you do not have a southwest part of the garden, or if you live in an apartment without a garden, you can install a similarly effective light if you at least have a balcony or terrace in the southwest. Use two lights rather than one: two is the number of the southwest. For those living in small apartments without a terrace, the living room can be energized in the same way by placing a bright lamp in the southwest corner. A red lamp will strengthen the symbolism of Yang energy. The lamp used should be neither too large nor too small and it should be at least 5 feet (1.5m) from the ground, as a standard lamp, a table lamp, or hanging from the ceiling. Note that this does not apply to the bedroom.

SOUTH The place of the phoenix, the summer season. South represents fame and is generally considered one of the happiest directions of the compass. According to the Yang Dwelling Classic, if you site your house with a south-facing orientation it will bring you extremely good Feng Shui. In the south part of your living room keep the corner well lit. Placing something red in this corner is also excellent. *See also* Phoenix.

SOUTHEAST This is the corner to energize if you want to increase your income. Use plants and water to attract income to this corner. Identify the location of this corner with a compass.

SOUTHERN HEMISPHERE North is always north. Countries in the southern hemisphere should definitely not change the compass directions when applying and using Compass School formulas. In recent years some Western writers have attempted to apply Western scientific rationales to Feng Shui to make a case for the compass directions to be flipped when applying Feng Shui in countries south of the equator, such as Australia. They contend that this is

due to winds from the north being "hot" in the southern hemisphere, since the equator lies to the north. From this they conclude that the element for the compass direction north should be fire, not water. Similarly they contend that the element for the south is water not fire. This single change has repercussions on the interpretation of Feng Shui all the way through the formulas and this also affects systems of Chinese astrology and fortune-telling. Authentic Chinese Feng Shui masters reject this line of interpretation. They point to the placement of the trigrams around the Pa Kua as being the arbiter of the element assigned to each of the compass directions. Thus, in the north the trigram placed there according to the Later Heaven sequence is Kan, which stands for water, and hence the north is traditionally associated with water. In the south the trigram is Li, which is symbolic of fire. Thus the element here is said to be fire. The representations of the trigrams give each of the compass directions their different meanings and have nothing to do with the so-called "north winds" blowing into Beijing. This is speculation as to the origins of generalized Feng Shui guidelines based on recommendations given in the *Yang Dwelling Classic*, which advises that the front of the house faces south and the back faces north. Latter-day practitioners, in speculating on the basis for this recommendation, have tried to explain it in terms of wind temperatures. It is important that the compass directions are not turned, making north south and vice versa. This is an absurd interpretation that can give rise to horrific mistakes.

SOUTHWEST The corner of ultimate Yin and good Yin energy, the southwest is a very important direction which benefits the family matriarch. If she is a central force in the home, make sure this direction is not afflicted by the presence of a toilet or a kitchen. An afflicted southwest corner also hurts the marriage prospects of the children.

SPRING The season of the wood element and the time of the year that represents growth and new beginnings; from a Feng Shui perspective it is also a good time to start a new business, launch a new product, or simply start a project or venture in business. The exact date of launching anything, however, should also be done with reference to the Tong Shu. *See also* Almanac.

STATUES Statues of the patriarch should be placed in the northwest while statues of any other members of the family should be aligned according to their auspicious directions. Statues also create excellent Feng Shui if placed in the southwest or northeast.

STEPS Connecting levels of the garden should conform to landscape guidelines, which state that levels being joined by steps must be correct. The levels of the back of the house should be higher than the front and land on the left-hand side must be higher than land on the right-hand side. If your house is located above road level and steps lead up to your front gate this is regarded by some as a most auspicious feature.

STOVE *See* Cooking.

STREAMS Slow moving fresh water represents excellent Feng Shui. If you have such a feature in front of you, try to orientate your home so that the front door is facing the stream and also make sure the flow of the water is correct. Try not to waste this most auspicious Feng Shui.

STUDY If you work from home pay special attention to getting the Feng Shui of your office correct since this will affect your livelihood and your professional reputation. Energize your office with all the relevant good fortune symbols but continue to observe all the taboos and recommendations for office Feng Shui.

SUCCULENTS Any kind of succulent plant or fruit is deemed to be auspicious since it suggests that there is sufficient water to keep it alive and healthy. Succulent cactuses without thorns are excellent in place of jade.

SUN TRIGRAM This trigram is formed by two Yang lines above a single broken Yin line. Known as "the gentle", it is placed southeast on the Pa Kua. It represents the eldest daughter and its element is wood.

SUNLIGHT Sunlight brings pure Yang energy into your home. Wherever possible, windows and doors should be oriented to catch sunlight.

SWIMMING POOLS Must be placed strategically otherwise they cause problems. It is very easy to go very wrong with pools. The guideline is to place them on the left-hand side of the entrance door (inside looking out), otherwise the marriage could end in separation or even divorce. Ideally pools should not be square or rectangular in shape. Instead they should have rounded edges that do not hurt the home. Pools should never overwhelm the house. They should not be so large as to create an imbalance. Remember that too much water is a sign of danger because when water overflows its banks it causes excessively bad luck. It is the same with the presence of natural water. When the body of water is large, it is good to be located a little away from it, so that the Chi wafting toward your home is both balanced and auspicious.

SYMBOLS Feng Shui is full of different symbols that spell good fortune. Learning to place them correctly and in the correct sectors of the home is part of Symbolic Feng Shui.

T

TAI CHI A form of exercise based on the energizing of Chi flows inside the body. The movements are slow but very precise. Though it originated in China, Tai Chi has attracted and benefited millions of practitioners worldwide.

TEN EMPEROR COINS A symbol that represents the wealth of ten reign periods. A very popular feature to hang in the office, placed strategically either behind your chair or on your left side to simulate the dragon, is coins taken from each of the ten emperors' reign periods tied together with red thread. The coins used can either be genuine antique coins from ten different reign periods or copies. In Feng Shui it does not really matter if you use fake coins or real coins, but some people believe that genuine antique coins carry the Chi of their period or origin.

TERRAPINS Placed in the north, these domesticated turtles bring good fortune. It is excellent Feng Shui to keep one or six terrapins in the north sector of the home, be it in the garden or in a courtyard inside the home. If you are able, build a small waterfall which falls into a circular pond with a maximum size of about 3 feet (1m) in diameter. Keep terrapins in this pond, feeding them special food or fresh green leafy vegetables. The terrapins will grow rather large. Keep them as part of your household for they soon learn to recognize you.

They bring great Chi to your home, ensuring a long life for the patriarch, and excellent children who bring honor to the family. They also bring wealth, prosperity, and protection for the home. If you are unable to find terrapins, you can have tortoises instead. They are land creatures and should not be kept in the pond. And if you are unable to build a pond, keeping a ceramic tortoise can symbolize the same kind of energies and is believed to be just as effective, especially if the imagery is accurate.

THORNS Flowers and plants with thorns (such as roses and some cactuses) do not bring good Feng Shui and in fact cause slivers of poison arrows which attack you. Do not place such plants too near you where you work. Over time they will cause problems and difficulties to build up.

THREE FEELING WATER The orientation of water that is good for your house. The *Water Dragon Classic* describes three good feeling water orientations that spell prosperity and success. There are also the seven sentiment waters, which spell bad luck and misfortune. Generally speaking, water is said to be excellent if it comes toward you in a wide form and leaves you in a narrow form, or when it has two or three small branches flowing into the main river that then passes your home. A third auspicious flow of water is when it seems to embrace your home like a jade belt. Water should never seem to flow away from your home in full view of the front door. This always means wealth flowing out. *See also* Jade Belt.

TIEN TI REN Heaven, earth, and mankind, the three types of luck referred to as the trinity of luck. This establishes the perspective of Feng Shui luck which is the luck of the earth. One is born with heaven luck but mankind luck is self-created. These three types of luck account in equal measure for the kind of success and happiness we experience in life. Earth luck and mankind luck are within our control while heaven luck is beyond our control. Many Feng Shui masters believe that, when you have excellent heaven luck and lead a virtuous life, you automatically have good Feng Shui without your even being aware of it. You will get your orientations correct and you will display all the correct symbols of good fortune.

TIEN YI The personalized direction to create good health, also called "doctor from heaven" direction. This is generally regarded as the direction that taps good health. It is a personalized direction that is based on the Eight Mansions Kua formula.

TIGER HILLS The range of hills that lie to the right of your house. According to Form School Feng Shui, land on the right-hand side of your home (the direction taken from inside the home looking out) represents the dragon hills irrespective of the actual compass direction. According to Compass School, however, the west side of your home represents the tiger hills. The author usually uses the Form School method in her own Feng Shui.

TIME DIMENSION Time is an important consideration in Feng Shui philosophy and the cycles of time determine a building's prosperity and well-being. With the interplay between people and their environment, the prosperity of a building, whether it is a business or a home address, will ultimately affect the residents of that structure and the activities within it. Based on Feng Shui principles, time is divided into cycles of 180 years. These cycles have three sixty-year periods each, called upper, middle, and lower. Three ages of twenty years duration are contained in each period, resulting in a total of nine ages for each 180 year cycle.

TOILETS Toilets are always considered to be harmful Feng Shui. Do not decorate the bathroom with expensive fittings, flowers, and fancy adornments. Making it prettier does not enhance it from a Feng Shui point of view. It merely magnifies the bad luck. Bathrooms should be as small as possible, with minimal decoration. The bathroom door should always be kept closed and auspicious objects kept away from it. For example, hanging peonies for love in your romance corner, which happens also to house your toilet, may make you find love, but love that could cause you a lot of heartache.

TORTOISES Like turtles, tortoises are considered by the Chinese to be extremely auspicious. They attract good fortune into the household and protect you from bad luck. Like the turtle, they are associated with the north sector and the number one. If you decide to keep a tortoise in your home, it is better to keep a single tortoise. Since they require minimal care, they are easy to keep. If you are unable to keep a real tortoise, a figurine of a tortoise in the north corner will effectively symbolize the tortoise energy.

TRAFFIC FLOW In cities, roads are now interpreted in the same way as rivers used to be. Thus traffic flows are considered to be similar to river flows. Fast-moving traffic creates Shar Chi while slow-moving traffic creates Sheng Chi and is far more auspicious. Traffic lights and traffic calmers near your office or home are thus excellent since they force the traffic to slow down. However, traffic jams are bad Feng Shui since they signify a blocking of the flow.

TREES These generally represent excellent Feng Shui but it is important that they be trimmed and kept in shape. Broad-leafed trees are effective cures for severe Feng Shui problems. They not only block incoming poison arrows but they also form an effective visual wall which can also double up as back support for any house lacking this vital "black turtle" support. Trees that possess good green foliage are excellent Feng Shui energizers for the east and the southeast corners. Trim them regularly in order that fresh shoots are always discernible. These signify continuous growth and the Chi generated is most auspicious. Avoid palm trees since their long trunks can cause Feng Shui problems. Trees standing in groups do not cause problems but single trees are similar to freestanding columns and emit harmful killing energy.

TRIANGLE This indicates the fire element and is an aggressive symbol that can harm a home when any of its three points are aimed at the entrance of the home. The triangle is often regarded as a protective symbol and is considered excellent when placed in the south because it is the symbol of fire.

TRIGRAMS Made up of three lines each, the trigrams are the root source of the hexagrams of the *I Ching* (the *Book of Changes*) upon which most Chinese divinatory sciences are based. Each trigram has its own special meaning. The predictive power of the *I Ching* is harnessed through the formation of hexagrams, which are usually created or built by tossing three Chinese coins. Each hexagram is made up of two trigrams. As well as making divinations trigram symbols can also be used as Feng Shui enhancers in the home.

TUI TRIGRAM The trigram that spells joyousness. It also describes the young woman who brings happiness. The west is considered the place of the young daughter because this trigram also indicates a lake. If there is a lake to the west of your home it spells the Feng Shui of happiness for your house.

U

UMBRELLA A symbol of shelter that the Chinese believe should never be opened inside the house. The modern umbrella, as opposed to the old-fashioned parasol, is an acceptable variation on the symbol.

UNICORN The Chinese unicorn, also known as the dragon horse, is considered a creature of good omen. It symbolizes longevity, joy, grandeur, illustrious offspring, and wisdom. The unicorn is said to possess qualities of gentleness, goodwill, and benevolence towards all other living creatures. It is an animal of solace and appears only when a particularly benevolent leader sits on the throne, or when a notable sage is born.

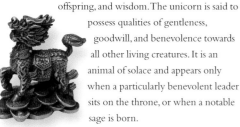

URNS Symbolic receptacles with Feng Shui significance. Placed strategically, urns can bring wonderful good fortune in that they can signify the advent of great wealth. Wealthy Chinese often place a pair of big urns on either side of their entrance door inside the house. The urns have long necks and are kept empty symbolically to signify a vacuum waiting to be filled with wealth. Others prefer the broader based variety which they fill either with rice grains or "pretend gold." Urns filled with semi-precious stones are transformed into wealth urns that symbolize and attract wealth. Urns can be placed either side of your house to absorb noise and to neutralize anything causing you distress.

VASES Can be transformed into wealth receptacles to attract good fortune. *See also* Wealth Vase.

VERANDAS All verandas in the house are considered to be part of the home for the purposes of undertaking Feng Shui analysis. Since no one actually lives or works in these parts of the home, it can be said that the auspicious parts of the veranda are entirely wasted. They are good places, however, to hang windchimes. The enchanting sounds of windchimes in the northwest and west bring excellent Chi into the home.

W

WALLS The walls of your home can be painted in colors that enhance the element of their location or you can hang paintings and display auspicious objects to energize specific types of good fortune. *See also* Color and Art.

WATER This signifies wealth and correct water brings enormous prosperity. Water plays a very big part in Feng Shui recommendations. Although water is also an element of potential danger according to the *I Ching*, and should thus be treated with respect,

it is also the element with the greatest potential for making you rich. For the years up to 2043 water is auspicious when placed in the north, the east, the southeast, and also in the southwest. The north and east are the best locations for water features either in your garden or inside your home. Also read up on the *Water Dragon Classic* and formula.

WATER DRAGON This represents the water formula's best configuration of water flow. There are specific instructions on how to build a Water Dragon in the *Water Dragon Classic*. This is part of the Feng Shui Compass School formula on water flows and water exit directions.

WATER LILIES An excellent substitute for the lotus, the auspicious water lily symbolizes purity. If the fish in your pond or similar water feature are being pestered by birds, planting water lilies will give them protection.

WATERFALLS If you have the land and the budget to do it, building a small waterfall on the north corner of your land is excellent. Make sure that the waterfall is proportional to the size of your house and that the water does not appear to be flowing away from you. Keep the water trapped in front of a window or a door. This symbolizes the luck coming into your home and bringing good fortune. Also make sure the sound of water is soft, rhythmic, and friendly rather than loud. If you are using a pump, opt for the less powerful pump. Remember that slow-moving water is better than fast-moving water.

WAVY LINES A wavy line incorporated into the design motif makes it a water element design suitable for the north, the east, or the southeast of your home or room.

WEALTH LUCK One of eight major types of luck that Feng Shui can generate. Prosperity luck is one of the more obvious and welcome manifestations of correct Feng Shui practice. Simple wealth-enhancing techniques use Symbolic Feng Shui. Thus you can energize for wealth by displaying the three-legged toad or sticking Chinese coins in appropriate places to attract money Chi. It is also possible to energize the southeast with plants or to build a water feature in the north. Probably the most enduring Feng Shui wealth feature is a Water Dragon. Build one if you can.

WEALTH VASE
A personal wealth vase is an excellent way to attract wealth Feng Shui. Your wealth vase can be made of earth or metal elements. Earth element vases could

be porcelain or crystal, while metal element vases are made of copper, brass, silver, or gold. The more precious the material the vase is made of, the more auspicious it will be. The vase can be filled with semiprecious stones such as crystal, malachite, amethyst, citrine, and so on. You can also put your jewelry in the vase. Your wealth vase should be kept hidden away, inside a cupboard in your bedroom, and never facing your front door; this represents your wealth draining away.

WELLS A well is a useful feature to design into the water flow of your house. One of the most important parts of good water flow is to control the exit direction of all the waters of your home. You can do this effectively and efficiently by building a "well," which collects all the water of the home and then allows it to exit in the direction deemed most auspicious for you, based on the *Water Dragon Classic* formula.

WEST If you want to create good descendants' luck in your home to benefit the children (the next generation), energize the metal Chi of the west part of your home. Do this by using white colors, displaying metallic items, and objects such as bells and singing bowls. One of the most effective ways of harnessing the metallic energy of the west is to use an authentic singing bowl to create the clear sound that attracts auspicious Chi. Strike the bowl three times with a special wooden mallet.

WESTERN SUNLIGHT Usually excessively Yang. You should reduce the intensity of the afternoon sun by hanging small faceted crystals that can break up the sunlight into a rainbow of lights. This not only softens the severity of intense Yang energy but also reestablishes the cosmic balance. Creating rainbows inside the home will create happiness for the family.

WHITE TIGER A celestial creature of the west that complements the green dragon. The white tiger is basically a creature that protects the abode. Without the tiger the dragon is said not to be a genuine dragon. The tiger is the wrathful side of Feng Shui. Always keep the tiger under control by ensuring the west does not dominate. For instance, do not allow the west side, or tiger side, of any home to be higher or larger than the east side. Let the dragon remain supreme by using bright lights to keep the tiger under control. Avoid hanging pictures of tigers in your home: few homes can cope with the energy given off by such images.

WINDCHIMES Windchimes are among the most delightful and easiest methods of creating a good feeling in any home. Their tinkling attracts excellent Sheng Chi. Do not hang metal windchimes in the east or southeast: these are wood corners. Instead hang bamboo windchimes in these corners. Metal windchimes should be hung in the west and northwest while ceramic windchimes can be hung in the southwest and northeast. Windchimes energize and correct bad vibes. If you use a windchime to suppress bad luck or to deflect killing energy caused by a poison arrow, hang a hollow five-rod metallic windchime. If possible acquire windchimes that have the design of a pagoda: this is the symbol for trapping killing energy and malignant spirits.

WIND Much of landscape is said to be carved by wind. Avoid places that are excessively windy, such as the top of a mountain or a seashore. When winds become too ferocious, they turn malevolent and carry killing Chi. Protect your home against harsh winds, whether they are warm or cold.

WINDOWS Homes without windows lack openings for the good Feng Shui to flow in, but there should not be too many windows in any home. The ideal ratio of windows to doors is 3:1. Windows that open outward are better than sash windows, but do not worry if you have the latter. Windows should not be placed on walls that are directly facing the entrance door. They are best placed on walls that are on either side of the entrance door. Again, this is the ideal situation and you do not need to worry too much if your

windows go against this guideline. Windows that are directly opposite the entrance allow Chi to fly out the window. Under such circumstances, you will find it difficult to save money.

WOOD One of the five elements but the only one with intrinsic life energy. Thus the wood element signifies growth and is an excellent element to have in all the corners of the home. Life energy signifies Yang energy, which makes for auspicious Feng Shui. The directions that correspond to the wood element are east and southeast and the trigrams are Chen and Sun respectively.

WUXING The Chinese name for the five elements: "Wu" means "five" and "xing" is the shortened form of "five types of Chi dominating at different times." This has been shortened to "elements." Water dominates in winter, wood in spring, fire in summer, and metal in fall. At the intersection between two seasons, the transitional period is dominated by earth. Water, wood, fire, metal, and earth refer to substances whose properties resemble the respective Chi and help us understand the different properties of the five types of Chi. The properties of the five types of Chi are summarized as follows: water – runs downward; there is always danger of overflow. Wood – grows upward; an excellent representation of life and growth. Fire – spreads in all directions; radiant, hot, and able to get out of control. Metal – piercing inward; sharp, pointing, and can be deadly and powerful. Earth – attracts and nourishes; stable, caring, and protective.

Y

YANG DWELLING CLASSIC One of the older texts and classics, said to contain a comprehensive treatise on the practice of Landscape Feng Shui.

YANG ENERGY Intrinsic nature of life energy, brightness, daylight, the sun. This is basically the life half of the Yin–Yang concept. Yang energy is symbolized by activity, by bright light, and by daytime hours. Yang energy is vital for the presence of good Feng Shui in the houses of the living, but it should never be present in such excessive quantities that Yin becomes obliterated completely. When Yin is completely absent, Yang ceases to exist.

YANG PA KUA The Pa Kua is used for analyzing and providing guidelines on how the corners of the compass can be energized to enhance their qualities. The whole of Feng Shui practice takes its cue from this arrangement of the Pa Kua. Those who advise that the directions of the compass be changed for southern hemisphere countries are attempting to rewrite the Pa Kua's sequence of trigrams. It will render all their Feng Shui recommendations wrong and even create harmful results.

YAP CHENG HAI The author's Feng Shui mentor. Yap Cheng Hai comes from an impressive Feng Shui lineage. A Chinese Classics scholar well versed in Chinese heritage and traditions, his expertise spans six decades. He has learned from many other masters (now deceased) and schools of Feng Shui in Hong Kong, Taiwan, and Singapore. He has ventured into Yin Feng Shui, visiting countless Chinese cemeteries

to study ancestral burial sites. The Chinese believe that the orientation of ancestral graves also has an influence on the fortunes of their descendants. The study of authentic Yin Feng Shui is considerably more complex and difficult than Yang Feng Shui. Master Yap is particularly skilled in the practice and interpretations of Parc Chai (Eight Mansions school), San Yuan (flying stars school) and, most renowned of all, the *Water Dragon Classic* (Water Feng Shui). Water Feng Shui's main promise is the serious enhancement of wealth. Master Yap's work and his success in this area of specialization have gained him an international reputation.

YEARLY REFERENCE TABLES Calculated to identify good and bad days. *See also* Almanac.

YIN ENERGY Death energy, silence, darkness, the moon. Yin energy is the diametrical opposite of Yang energy but they do not conflict; rather they complement each other. In other words one follows the other and one gives life to the other. Yin energies are more suitable for houses of death, grave sites, burial grounds, and cemeteries. Yin is darkness and total silence but is also excellent energy for places of rest like the bedroom.

YIN PA KUA The Pa Kua that Feng Shui masters believe possesses "heavenly attributes" and thus is said to invoke the powers of heaven to dissolve, deflect, and fight back against hostile killing breath. This arrangement is reproduced on Pa Kua mirrors that are hung up outside above doors to fight against T-junctions or intersections and triangular roof lines, among other poison arrows. The Yin Pa Kua should never be hung inside the house.

YIN–YANG SYMBOL This eloquently describes the balance of the two opposing yet complementary energies. It shows the ebb and flow of the energy and also signifies that in Yin and Yang there is always a little of the other present. Yin always gives rise to Yang and vice versa and when they are in complete balance the whole of Tao is said to be achieved.

YELLOW Yellow is considered to be as auspicious and as Yang as red. Because yellow used to be the Imperial color and ordinary citizens were not allowed to use it in their clothes or at home, red became the popular favorite and a symbol of good fortune. However, where no such taboo exists you might want to energize the auspiciousness of yellow. Thus bouquets of yellow flowers are said to be very lucky, as are yellow packets of money and yellow curtains and interior décor.

FURTHER READING

Feng Shui

Kwok, Man-Ho and O'Brien, Joanne, *The Elements of Feng Shui*, ELEMENT BOOKS, SHAFTESBURY, 1991

Lo, Raymond, *Feng Shui and Destiny*, TYNRON, 1992

Rosbach, Sarah, *Feng Shui*, RIDER, LONDON, 1984

Too, Lillian, *Creating Abundance with Feng Shui*, RIDER, LONDON, 1999

Too, Lillian, *Feng Shui Good Fortune Symbols*, KONSEP BOOKS, KUALA LUMPUR, 1999

Too, Lillian, *Easy to Use Feng Shui – 168 Ways to Success*, COLLINS & BROWN, LONDON, 1999

Too, Lillian, *The Complete Illustrated Guide to Feng Shui for Gardens*, ELEMENT BOOKS, SHAFTESBURY, 1998

Too, Lillian, *Basic Feng Shui*, KONSEP BOOKS, KUALA LUMPUR, 1997

Too, Lillian, *Feng Shui Essentials*, RIDER, LONDON, 1997

Too, Lillian, *Feng Shui Fundamentals: Careers*
Feng Shui Fundamentals: Children
Feng Shui Fundamentals: Education
Feng Shui Fundamentals: Eight Easy Lessons
Feng Shui Fundamentals: Fame
Feng Shui Fundamentals: Health
Feng Shui Fundamentals: Love
Feng Shui Fundamentals: Networking
Feng Shui Fundamentals: Wealth
ELEMENT BOOKS, SHAFTESBURY, 1997

Too, Lillian, *Lillian Too's Feng Shui Kit*, ELEMENT BOOKS, SHAFTESBURY, 1997

Too, Lillian, *The Complete Illustrated Guide to Feng Shui*, ELEMENT BOOKS, SHAFTESBURY, 1996

Too, Lillian, *Dragon Magic*, KONSEP BOOKS, KUALA LUMPUR, 1996

Too, Lillian, *Chinese Astrology for Romance & Relationships*, KONSEP BOOKS, KUALA LUMPUR, 1996

Too, Lillian, *Water Feng Shui for Wealth*, KONSEP BOOKS, KUALA LUMPUR, 1995

Too, Lillian, *Flying Star Feng Shui*, KONSEP BOOKS, KUALA LUMPUR, 1994, revised 1999

Too, Lillian, *Practical Applications for Feng Shui*, KONSEP BOOKS, KUALA LUMPUR, 1994

Too, Lillian, *Feng Shui*, KONSEP BOOKS, KUALA LUMPUR, 1993

Walters, Derek, *Feng Shui Handbook: A Practical Guide to Chinese Geomancy and Environmental Harmony*, AQUARIAN PRESS, 1991

General

Kwok, Man-Ho and O'Brien, Joanne (ed.), *Chinese Myths and Legends*, ARROW, LONDON, 1990

Wilhelm, Richard (trans.), *The I Ching or Book of Changes*, 3RD EDN, ROUTLEDGE & KEGAN PAUL, NEW YORK, 1968

USEFUL ADDRESSES

Dragon Gate Palace
[for purchase of Feng Shui items]
http://www.dragon-gate.com
Tel: +603-7836252
Fax: +603-7801196

Feng Shui Innovations
1 Taloma Avenue
Lurnea, Sydney
NSW 2170, Australia
website: fengshui-innovations.com.au
Tel: (02) 9826 0002
Fax: (02) 9826 0348

Feng Shui Society of Australia
PO Box 1565, Rozelle, Sydney
NSW 2039, Australia

Helene Weber (Feng Shui consultant based in Paris)
40b Avenue de Suffren
Paris 75015 France
Tel: 33 14783 4066
Fax: 33 156 58 05 89

The Geomancer – The Feng Shui Store
PO Box 250, Woking, Surrey GU21 1YJ, UK
Tel: 44 1483 839898
Fax: 44 1483 488998

Feng Shui Association
31 Woburn Place, Brighton BN1 9GA, UK
Tel/Fax: 44 1273 693844

Feng Shui Company
Ballard House, 37 Norway Street, Greenwich, London, SE10 9DD, UK

Feng Shui Network International
PO Box 2133, London W1A 1RL, UK
Tel: 44 171 935 8935,
Fax: 44 171 935 9295

The Feng Shui Institute of America
PO Box 488, Wabasso, FL 32970,
Tel: 1 407 589 9900 Fax: 1 407 589 1611

Feng Shui Warehouse
PO Box 3005, San Diego, CA 92163,
Tel: 1 800 399 1599 Fax: 1 800 997 9831

Prof Lin Yuni's BHS Yun Lin Temple
Berkeley, California, USA

If you wish to see more on quality authentic Luo Pans, the authoritative site to visit is:
Dragon Gate Palace
http://www.dragon-gate com
Tel: +603-7836252   Fax: +603-7801196
email: luopan@dragon-gate.com

The Venerable Lama Zopa Rinpoche's website:
http://www.LamaZopa.com

Lillian Too's websites:

http://www.lillian-too.com
http://www.worldoffengshui.com
http://www.lilliantoojewellery.com

PICTURE CREDITS

AKG, London: 166l; 210.

Art Directors & Trip: /P. Rauter 230b.

The Bridgeman Art Library, London/New York: /Bibliothèque Nationale, Paris, France 37c; /British Library, London, England 96tl, 220; /British Museum, London, England 282tr; /Fitzwilliam Museum, Cambridge, England 282l; /Freer Library, Philadelphia 164tr; /Private Collection 82t, 108b, 205br, 208–209; /Royal Botanical Gardens, Kew, England 96br; /The Victoria & Albert Museum, London, England 34tr, 84tl.

John-Loup Charmet: 14–15; 30–31.

Goh Seng Chong: 50t; 59b,tr; 80–81; 83; 85tl,tr,b; 87; 92t; 99bl,bcl,bcr,br; 102bl; 112; 138t; 139t,bl; 172–173; 181c,b; 214; 231t,r; 246tr; 254t; 265bl,br; 272br; 281tr; 297t; 304–305; 314bc; 318t.

The Bruce Coleman Collection: /Jane Burton 95tr; /Jules Cowan 242–243; /Gerald S. Cubitt 96tr; /Liz Eddison 262; /M.P.L. Fogden 248br; /Fritz Prenzel 99tc; /Kevin Rushby 246bl; /Kim Taylor 249b.

Corbis Images: 321; /Macduff Everton 21b; /Jack Fields 22t; /Dave G. Houser 28tl.

Dulux Paints: 162–163.

Liz Eddison: 43b; 96c; 106t; 273b; 280t; 281tl; /Gavin Landscaping 272t; /Natural & Oriental Water Gardens 238b, 239b, 250–251, 256t, 258–259.

ET Archive: /British Museum 203; /The Freer Gallery of Art 38, 64t; /RHS Reeves Collection 98tr; /Rockhill Nelson Gallery, Kansas 97tr; /Victoria & Albert Museum 154tr.

The Garden Picture Library: /Linda Barnes 240bl; /Lynne Brotchie 122–123; /Brian Carter 107b, 249t; /Eric Crichton 100–101; /Vaughan Fleming 152b; /Nigel Francis 236–237; /John Glover 239t, 260–261b; /Michael Howes 257l; /Rowan Isaac 240br, 269b; /Lamontage 264–265c; /Joanne Pavia 263; /Gary Rogers 266–267; /J.S. Sira 261tr;

/Ron Sutherland 42b, 47b, 257t, 268tl; /Juliette Wade 257b; /Paul Windsor 244t.

The Image Bank: 16b; /Chinese Tourism Press 33t; /Anthony Edwards 141tr; /John P. Kelly 1426b; /Tom Knibbs 27t, 139br; /Cesar Lucas 142l; /Mahaux Photo 86b; /Pat McConville 182–183; /Andrea Pistolesi 159b; /Kevin Rose 46b; /Gary Russ 145; /Jeff Spielman 312tr; /Dan Sundberg 184bl; /Simon Wilkinson 282–283b.

Images Colour Library: 34tl; 37t; 66–67; 70t; 292–293; /Fotostock 325; /Charles Walker 212.

The Kobal Collection: 21tr.

The Harry Smith Collection: 244b, 327.

South China Morning Post: 20tl.

The Stock Market: 11tr; 32b; 104tl; 119; 141tl; /Richard Berenholtz 309b; /Firefly Productions 318; /Craig Hammell 54–55; /B. Harrington 159b; /Chris Savage 216tr.

Tony Stone Images: 61; 230t; /Theo Allofs 63; /Doug Armand 294l; 297t; /Bruce Ayres 24b, 221; /Christopher Bissell 311bl; /Rob Boudreau 46tr; /Ernest Braun 32t; /Rex Butcher 88tr; /John Callahan 19t; /Laurie Campbell 324; / S. Carter 218–219; /Stewart Cohen 308c; /Connie Coleman 149b; /Cosmo Condina 238tr; /Phillip Condit 270b; /Peter Correz 192–193, 200–201; /Daniel Cox 168br; /P Crowther 218–219; /Chris Ehlers 104br, 136–137; /David Epperson 326tr; /Robert Everts 105tr; /Alain Le Garsmeur 138b; /Margaret Gowan 109t; /Sara Gray 64b; /William S. Helsel 185t; /R. van der Hilst 19b; /Jason Hawkes 43t; /Claire Hayden 41; /John Lamb 47t; /Peter Langone 75br; /Yann Layma 18b; /Mark Lewis 323br; /D.C. Lowe 60; /Laurence Monneret 24tl;/ Pat O'Hara 42t; /Ben Osborne 230c; /Lee Page 284–285; /Greg Pease 228t; /Andre Perlstein 322; /Joseph Pobereskip 316–317; /Ed Pritchard 22b; /Mervyn Rees 228bl; /Jon Riley 18t, 202; /David Schultz 44b; /Pete Seaward 298b; /Mark Segal 26–27b, 276–277; /Hugh Sitton 20tr, 326tl; /Chad Slattery 46tl; /Bob Thomas 98br; /Mark Wagner 224–225; /Randy Wells 103t; /Gary Yeowell 58.

The Wellcome Institute: 16tl.

The Werner Forman Archive: 9t; 26tr; 36; 196bc; 313br.

Elizabeth Whiting Associates: 106b; 141cl; 142r; 144r; 146–147; 149t; 166c; 168tr; 171br; 176cr; 287t; 289t; 291b.

MODEL AND PROP CREDITS

Special thanks go to
Carla Càrrington, R. Chappell, Rukshana Chenoy, Lucianne Lassalle, R. J. Manby-Clarke, Caron Riley, Vincent Riley, Francesca Selkirk, Doug Streeter
for help with photography

With thanks to
Adaptatrap Percussion, Brighton
Bright Ideas, Lewes
Days Gone Bye, Brighton
Dockerills, Brighton
Evolution, Brighton
Graffiti Two, Brighton
Heavenly Realms, Eastbourne
W. D. Hunt, Worthing
Ashley Lawrence Upholstery, Worthing
Elizabeth Simmons (private collection), Lewes
Spellbound and Spirit, Lewes
Tizz's Accessories, Lewes
Welcome Home, Worthing
Winfalcon's Healing Centre, Brighton
for the kind loan of props